*From Congregation Town
to Industrial City*

The American Social Experience

SERIES

General Editor
JAMES KIRBY MARTIN

Editors
PAULA S. FASS, STEVEN H. MINTZ,
CARL PRINCE, JAMES W. REED & PETER N. STEARNS

From Congregation Town
to Industrial City

Culture and Social Change
in a Southern Community

M I C H A E L   S H I R L E Y

NEW YORK UNIVERSITY PRESS
New York and London

NEW YORK UNIVERSITY PRESS
New York and London

Copyright © 1994 by New York University
All rights reserved

Library of Congress Cataloging-in-Publication Data
Shirley, Michael.
From congregation town to industrial city : culture and social
change in a southern community / Michael Shirley.
p.   cm. — (The American social experience)
Includes bibliographical references and index.
ISBN 0-8147-7977-8 (alk. paper)
1. Winston-Salem (N.C.)—History.   2. Winston-Salem (N.C.)—Social
conditions.   I. Title.   II. Series.
F264.W8S48   1994
975.6'67—dc20   93-23446
CIP

New York University Press books are printed on acid-free paper,
and their binding materials are chosen for strength and durability.

Manufactured in the United States of America

10   9   8   7   6   5   4   3   2   1

Contents

Illustrations

Maps

Acknowledgments

This study is greatly indebted to the encouragement and critical comments and suggestions of numerous friends, colleagues, and students. Over the years friends and colleagues read and commented on papers, articles, and drafts of chapters as well as offered important advice in numerous conversations. For this I want to thank Bess Beatty, David Carlton, Paul Cimbala, Steve Hahn, Andrew Hurley, Gail Murray, Bob Korstad, Stephanie McCurry, Bart Shaw, and Ed Shoemaker. Barbara Bellows, Paul Escott, David Goldfield, John Schlotterbeck, Scott Strickland, and Harry Watson offered useful comments on conference papers taken from this manuscript. At Emory University, Dan Carter and James Roark served on my dissertation committee and offered important suggestions for revising the manuscript. Ed Hendricks of Wake Forest University pointed me to local resources in Winston-Salem, while Molly Rawls, curator of the Frank Jones Collection at the Forsyth County Public Library, and Paula Locklair, curator at Old Salem, Incorporated, were very helpful in locating photographs for the manuscript. The staffs at the Moravian Archives in Winston-Salem, the Manuscripts Department of the Duke University Library, the North Carolina Division of Archives and History, and the Southern Historical Collection at the University of North Carolina at Chapel Hill were especially patient and willing to fulfill numerous requests to provide material. At Rhodes College, Ashley Daricek, Sarah Hughes, Ann Sargent, Charles Smith, and Ralene Richards assisted me greatly by the careful attention they paid to their work-study duties in creating samples from the manuscript censuses and tax lists, chasing down references, and editing endnotes and bibliography. Students in my social history and southern history seminars—especially Stuart Chapman, Kay Sessoms, and Susannah Shumate—read portions of the manuscript, debated my arguments, and demanded greater clarity in my ideas. Judith Runyan and Bill Berg carefully advised me on the ins and outs of computers and statistics. Annette Cates patiently filled so many interlibrary loan requests. Angie Bumpus typed and printed numerous revisions of the manuscript. The American Historical Association awarded me a Beveridge Research Grant and the National Endowment for the Humanities provided a Travel to Collections Grant which made possible summer research trips to North Carolina and to the Baker Library at the Harvard Graduate School of Business Administration. Earlier versions of chapters two and three were published as "The Market and Community Culture in Antebellum Salem, North Carolina," *The Journal of the Early Republic* 11 (Summer 1991) and "Yeoman Culture and Millworker Protest in Antebellum Salem, North Carolina," *The Journal of Southern History* 57 (August 1991), and I thank Ralph Gray and John Boles for permission to use portions of these articles here. I must also thank Colin Jones, director of New York University Press, Niko Pfund, editor, Jennifer Hammer, assistant editor, and James Kirby Martin, editor-in-chief of the American Social Experience Series, for their extraordinary patience in waiting for the manuscript and their efforts at making this a better book.

Two people in particular deserve special mention for their contributions. Jonathan Prude originally directed the dissertation at Emory and later took time from his own work to read drafts of articles and chapters, offer thoughtful and important suggestions, and provide unstinting encouragement as I revised the manuscript. Pam Shirley, of course, made the greatest sacrifices as I devoted time and effort to this study. Without her continuing encouragement and support this book would not have been possible.

Introduction

Visitors today to Winston-Salem, North Carolina, can see in the Old Salem restoration village a recreation of the Moravian congregation community and artifacts of congregational life. Old Salem presents a bucolic image of a well-ordered, attractive, even idyllic, village. Walking up Main Street from the village square visitors come to the northern edge of the town and see before them both the smokestacks of the tobacco factories and the office towers of the R. J. Reynolds Tobacco Company and the Wachovia Bank and Trust Company. To their left they see on the opposite hill the brick buildings which originally belonged to the Salem Manufacturing Company, Salem's first textile mill organized in 1836. In this visual sweep of the landscape, in which the new stands in stark contrast to the old, visitors can perceive the parameters of Winston-Salem's history—the Moravian settlement and its textile mill contrasted with the tobacco factories of Winston—and sense the clash of new and old that generated the tensions endemic to social and economic change as the congregation community became the industrial city. It is a compelling story, rich in details describing the textures of life as southerners experienced the changes that occurred in the nineteenth century.

This is a study of the evolution of a southern community as it industrialized during the nineteenth century. Through the nineteenth century profound changes took place in the economic life of Winston-Salem that included transformations in the methods of production, the nature of work, and the structure and composition of the work force. Industrialization took root in the antebellum years as Salem became more deeply engaged with the market that transformed antebellum America. Beginning in the 1830s when the first cotton mill opened, Salem, and later, Winston, moved steadily toward an economy based on manufacturing and trade in a market that extended beyond the surrounding countryside. Over the forty-year period from 1850 to 1890, capital investment in manufacturing reported in the federal censuses rose almost ten times from $271,400 to $2,344,957. The value of manufactured products increased during the same period from $253,871 to $3,269,419. But the most telling statistic concerns the size of manufacturing activities in the community. Throughout the antebellum period most manufacturing activities in Winston and Salem took place in the small shops of local master craftsmen producing for local consumers. In the postwar decades, as the community's entrepreneurs sought their fortunes in the national and international markets, production was undertaken on a larger scale. In 1880 the fourteen tobacco and textile factories, the largest industrial enterprises in Winston and Salem, employed an average of ninety-four workers each. Sixteen other shops, which included those of blacksmiths, wagonmakers, wheelwrights, and cabinetmakers, employed an average of thirteen workers apiece.[1] But, the revolutionary character of industrialization was not in the building of factories and the increased use of machinery, though these developments are significant and cannot be overlooked. Rather, the essence of industrialization was the transformation of economic, social, and political institutions and structures that accompanied changes in the methods of production as well as the emergence of a new mind-set among inhabitants of Winston and Salem that brought new ways of thinking and acting. From this economic transformation new social and political structures and relationships emerged that produced a more differentiated community culture. Indeed, the economic changes that occurred in the North Carolina piedmont during the period redefined the meaning of community in Salem as the Moravian congregation village gave way to the postwar industrial city of Winston-Salem.

The story of community transformation in the nineteenth century has been told by scholars of northern society in several splendid monographs.[2] Though there is a rich scholarship on plantation regions that has dominated the writing of southern social and economic history, areas outside of the cotton belt have received comparatively little attention until quite recently. In the 1980s Steven Hahn and others produced important studies focusing on the economic and social forces that reshaped the countryside as the southern piedmont was consolidated into a market economy, in the process transforming the community cultures of the villages and towns scattered over the southern landscape.[3] However, these studies have focused primarily on either the antebellum or postbellum periods and have not traced the development of economic and social change in southern communities over the course of the nineteenth century. Thus these studies have emphasized discontinuity between the two periods in southern history. Unlike other studies of the nineteenth-century South that have considered communities of planters and yeoman farmers, the subject of this study is a piedmont community of artisans and small farmers united by a single vision of life as members of a religious congregation. The Moravian community at Salem offers an illuminating case of the changes sweeping southern society in the nineteenth century that affected the ways southerners lived in their communities.

William Freehling has recently written, "before and after the mid-1830s in the South, as well as the North, change was omnipresent, varieties abounded, visions multiplied."[4] The agent of this change was the "market revolution" that swept antebellum America, leaving few communities untouched. During the antebellum period the people of Salem found themselves increasingly subject to the impact of economic forces operating beyond the town's boundaries. Greater participation in the market over the course of the nineteenth century unleashed new ways of behavior, leading to the development of a new ethos among the Moravians of Salem.[5] The critical development in the transformation of the congregation community which opened the door to economic development and industrialization was the greater commitment among most Salem shopkeepers to individual freedom, private property rights, and the pursuit of personal economic opportunities free of external restraints. Thus as Salem and its neighboring countryside became enmeshed in the regional and national market economies, the ways people lived, their attitudes and behavior, and their sense of themselves as members of a special community all changed, giving vivid testimony to the power of capitalist transformation.[6] The majority of Moravian shopkeepers in Salem by mid-century embraced a new worldview at odds with the traditional congregational ethos. They transformed the community order of Salem, leaving only the shadow of what was once the congregation of saints.

The transformation of Winston-Salem also reveals the character of industrialization that occurred in the South before 1900. Though most southerners in 1900 were still engaged in agricultural pursuits, and the South remained predominantly an agricultural region, from the 1870s to the end of the century, profound though subtle changes in the character of the southern ethos were expressed in the outlook, institutions, and leadership of the region. In particular, a middle class of businessmen emerged, and prominence and power passed from planters to manufacturers and merchants.[7] This new business class pursued profits and success in the emerging national market economy. These changes altered community life in the piedmont towns of the South where the initial stages of industrialization were well under way by the 1880s. Still bound closely to the region's agricultural economy, southern manufacturing processed the two important staple crops of the region—cotton and tobacco—into products traded in the national and world markets. Southerners, blacks as well as whites, who constituted the region's labor force also maintained strong ties to the agricultural economy, frequently moving from farm to factory and back. These basic facts gave nineteenth-century southern industry a distinctive character. In the postbellum community of Winston-Salem, as individual energies were released in the rebuilding of southern society from the ashes and ruins of a disastrous war, the influx of capital and labor had a transforming effect. New business endeavors were organized and many old businesses expanded, while others were overwhelmed by new market conditions and declined. During the postwar years the railroad connected Winston-Salem to the regional and national economy, opening markets for the town's products as well as making available new sources of raw materials and labor. The expansion of economic activity in Winston-Salem fueled a startling population growth as the community expanded from twelve hundred residents in 1850 to over eleven thousand people in 1890.[8] From the 1820s through the 1880s the people of Salem and the adjacent town of Winston confronted omnipresent change that redefined the meaning and experience of community.

CHAPTER ONE

The Congregational Community
of the Moravians

Winston-Salem's history reaches back to pre-Reformation Europe and the fifteenth-century pietistic movements of Moravia and Bohemia led by the disciples of Czech religious reformer Jan Hus. Hus, who advocated a life of piety which emphasized purity in morals and conduct more than doctrine and consistency, gathered about him devoted followers, the Brethren, who organized the church that became known as the Unitas Fratrum. Rejecting the dogma and rituals of the Catholic church, the Unitas Fratrum, which the Brethren believed to be the oldest Protestant church, seceded from the Church of Rome in 1467 and elected its own ministers. After years of persecution many Brethren went into exile in the seventeenth century, fleeing from Moravia and Bohemia to Poland or Germany. In Germany the Brethren eventually found a protector in Count Nicholas Ludwig von Zinzendorf, an Austrian aristocrat, who offered the Brethren refuge on his estate of Berthelsdorf in Saxony. There, in the summer of 1722, the Brethren, or Moravians as they were coming to be known, created the settlement of Herrnhut and the church was reorganized as the Renewed Unitas Fratrum, with Zinzendorf as its leader. From their settlement at Herrnhut the Moravians of the Renewed Unitas Fratrum then embarked on missionary activities that led to the creation of settlements in Europe, the British Isles, North America, the Caribbean, and Africa.[1]

The Moravians first settled in America in the 1730s in response to English guarantees of religious freedom. After an initial settlement in

Georgia failed due to the unsuitability of the land the Moravians purchased, the Moravians established their first permanent settlement in America in Pennsylvania in 1741 at Bethlehem.[2] The Moravians' urge to colonize did not end with the founding of Bethlehem; they continued to look beyond the countryside around Bethlehem for land that would allow them to live independently and safe from persecution while enabling them to expand their missionary activities. The attention of Moravian leaders turned toward North Carolina and focused on a one hundred thousand-acre tract of land offered for sale by Lord Granville. In North Carolina the Moravians saw a number of benefits: the opportunity to engage in missionary activities among the Indian population there; the provision of property and opportunity for newly arrived Moravians from Europe; and the sale of portions of these lands to settlers tolerant of the Moravians which would generate badly needed revenue for the payment of the Unitas Fratrum's creditors. In August 1752 Moravian bishop August Gottlieb Spangenberg and five associates left Bethlehem and journeyed to Edenton, North Carolina. From Edenton, the Spangenberg party set out for the backcountry in search of a tract of land upon which to build a congregational town.[3] In December, after traversing the colony from the coast to the mountains and enduring illness and hardship, the Spangenberg expedition came upon a broad plateau that divides the Yadkin and Dan river valleys. There they surveyed a tract which Spangenberg designated "Wachovia," named for the family estate of their protector in Saxony, Count Zinzendorf. Considered to be the best land left in North Carolina by 1752, the tract lay on the road to Pennsylvania, about twenty miles south of the Virginia border. Spangenberg's words reveal the attractiveness of the site for the Moravian settlement:

> This tract lies particularly well. It has countless springs, and numerous fine creeks; as many mills as may be desired can be built. There is much beautiful meadow land, and water can be led to other pieces which are not quite so low. There is good pasturage for cattle, and canes growing along the creeks will help out for a couple of winters until the meadows are in shape. There is also much lowland which is suitable for raising corn, etc. There is plenty of upland and gently sloping land which can be used for corn, wheat, etc.

These possibilities inspired Bishop Spangenberg to regard the land as reserved for them by their Lord and where the Moravians could do the work that God had ordained for them.[4] Thus, in August 1753, the Unitas Fratrum purchased from North Carolina's proprietors 98,985 acres of the tract Bishop Spangenberg's party had surveyed the previous fall.[5]

The Moravians did not hesitate to settle their new lands in North Carolina, and many of the Moravians answered the call to move south from Bethlehem to Wachovia. An advance group of thirteen unmarried men left Bethlehem for North Carolina in October 1753 to start the settlement and prepare the way for the arrival of families from Europe and Pennsylvania. Arriving on their new lands in mid-November, they immediately began to erect their first settlement, Bethabara. Within a year the settlers at Bethabara were operating a carpenter's shop, a flour mill, a pottery, a cooperage works, a tannery, a blacksmith's shop, and a shoe shop to serve the needs of the Moravian settlers who soon followed.[6] The quest for piety in the face of fierce persecution as well as settlement on the American frontier created a sense of community among the Moravians of Wachovia. Community was also created in the local congregation, with its common experiences and beliefs, its distinctiveness, and its homogeneity and exclusivity. The Moravians lived their lives as members of an international community of congregations of the Unitas Fratrum in North Carolina, Pennsylvania, and Europe.[7]

The immigration of the Moravians to the North Carolina piedmont was part of a larger population movement into the region during the mid-eighteenth century. Between 1729 and 1755 the population of North Carolina increased from about thirty thousand to eighty thousand. Most of the growth before mid-century filled in unsettled areas in the tidewater regions and pushed settlement into the piedmont. During the second half of the eighteenth century, thousands of English, Scots-Irish, and German immigrants moved into the North Carolina piedmont and mountains, seeking new opportunities and lured by popular accounts of the abundance of good land available for settlement and a mild climate. On his journey across the colony, Bishop Spangenberg observed that in the western portions of North Carolina near the mountains people from Virginia, Maryland, Pennsylvania, New Jersey, and New England had settled. These settlers were "sturdy farmers and skilled men" who traveled down the Great Wagon Road from Pennsylvania into the North Carolina backcountry with horse and wagon and cattle. They settled in North Carolina because, in Bishop Spangenberg's words, "they wished to own lands and were too poor to buy in Philadelphia or New Jersey."[8] In the North Carolina backcountry they found a crude society still living at a bare subsistence level, raising a little corn, and relying primarily on the hunting of game for food. For the first Moravian settlers in North Carolina the isolation of the backcountry and its sparse settlement posed severe challenges. From Wachovia the Moravians had to go three hundred miles south over troublesome paths to Charleston, South Carolina, or north to Boling's Point, Virginia, on a branch of the James River, also about three hundred miles away, to obtain those items they could not produce themselves. Like other immigrants to the backcountry, the Moravian settlers also discovered the lack of craftsmen near their settlements. Until Bethabara was built, the nearest store or blacksmith was about sixty miles from the site of settlement, and the nearest mill was almost twenty-five miles away. But the German and Scots-Irish immigrants brought with them the ways of farming and the craft skills they had learned in their homelands, enabling them to create in the hilly backcountry an economic and social life that revolved around small farms producing grains and raising livestock.[9]

Despite their isolation the Moravian congregations prospered in the backcountry as more of the Brethren made the trek from Pennsylvania and as non-Moravians settled nearby. To relieve the strains of increased population on the Bethabara community, a second town, Bethania, was built three miles away. However, neither Bethabara nor Bethania was to be the primary town of Wachovia because, from the beginning, Salem was planned as the central town. The site of Salem, six miles from Bethabara, was chosen in 1765 after a careful exploration of the central portion of Wachovia. Construction of the new town began in the winter of 1766, and during the first year there arrived from Germany a small company of settlers consisting of a contingent of Moravians recruited by Friedrich Wilhelm von Marshall, an influential member of the Bethlehem congregation involved in the early planning of the new settlement. Following the establishment of Salem as the principal town and center of Moravian society in the South, many Moravians moved from the North to organize new congregations in Wachovia. In 1769 several German families settled in the southwest corner of Wachovia as the Friedberg congregation. At Friedland, in the southeast corner of Wachovia, fourteen German families who arrived in 1770 from York County in the province of Maine established a settlement. Several English families, who for many years had belonged to the Brethren, came to Wachovia from Frederick County, Maryland, in 1772 and established the Hope settlement in the southwestern corner of Wachovia where they worshiped in

English instead of the traditional German of the other Moravian congregations.[10]

In the years after its founding, Salem congregation grew and prospered, from 132 people in 1773 to 316 people in 1807. Of the 316, almost all of whom were German, 233 lived in the village while eighty-three lived on their farms in the nearby countryside. By 1807 Salem had developed as an orderly and peaceful village, its physical layout reflecting the respectful piety of the Moravian congregation. Located half-way up a hill near the center of Wachovia, Salem had a main street running north along the crest of the hill which was bisected by parallel streets stretching from east to west and smaller cross streets. Life in Salem revolved around the central square bordered by four streets, along which the principal buildings and houses of the town were erected. On the northeast corner the Moravians built a fine brick church with the village clock in the steeple that struck the hours and quarter-hours for the townspeople. The church was the principal building in the congregation town and held special significance for the Moravians of Salem as a symbol of the unity that bound the Brethren together and made them a community. Also on the east side of the square was the Single Sisters' House where many of the unmarried women and girls of the congregation lived and boarded. Near the Single Sisters' House was the Girls' School. Across the square, on the west side, were the Single Brothers' House where the unmarried men and older boys lived and boarded and the Boys' School. On the southwest corner of the square the congregation store was located. In 1807 the growing population of the countryside found in Salem a post office, house of a physician with an apothecary, pottery shop, toy shop, tannery and leather dressery, as well as the shops of local artisans which included a shoemaker, tailor, baker, carpenter, cabinetmaker, glover, hatter, saddler, wheelwright, tinner, turner, gunsmith, blacksmith, silversmith, watch and clock maker, and a tobacconist. In the neighborhood around Salem several mills, including paper, oil, saw, and grist mills, operated on the banks of the Middle Fork and other small streams. Whereas the other settlements of Wachovia remained small farming communities, Salem rapidly became the largest town and commercial center of the northwest piedmont of North Carolina. Though Moravian leaders had planned that the settlement would be self-supporting through a blend of subsistence farming and small-scale artisanal manufacturing, within twenty years of its founding Salem had become a community where the crafts and trade predominated.[11]

Life in Salem revolved around home, workshop, and the community. Strolling down the streets on summer evenings, people visited; in the tavern, shops, and on the street, they gathered for informal conversation that covered the important topics of the day. Salem shoemaker Henry Leinbach, probably like most artisans in Salem, regularly filled his days with working in his shop, hunting, fishing, beekeeping, playing ball and chess, and drinking and conversing with friends at the tavern. Leinbach still found time to attend militia musters, participate in congregational administrative affairs, attend Moravian worship services, and occasionally go to nearby rural neighborhoods for camp meetings. Visitors to Salem were impressed by its "order and general air of neatness" exhibited by the paved streets swept clean and the houses with their small gardens facing the street. The Moravian congregation was often viewed by other southerners as quaint and exotic. Juliana Connor of Charleston, South Carolina, visited Salem in July 1827 and saw in the Moravian community a way of life she believed was much like that of Washington Irving's Sleepy Hollow. To Miss Connor the Moravian village was

> like an admirably constructed piece of mechanism in which each part or member has certain duties that are punctually performed, the springs are concealed—the motion and effects only are visible—they live in a world and are governed by laws of their own creation, independent of and distinct from all other society and their views extend but beyond the hill which forms their natural boundary—but in kindness and politeness divested of all etiquette, they are not excelled.[12]

Wherever they settled the Moravians' purpose was to cultivate "simple, unfeigned Christian discipleship . . . where religion remained the central factor of life." Though the Bible was regarded by the Moravians as the sole source of all religious truths, the Moravians stressed religious piety and ethical conduct more than obedience to a specific set of beliefs. Constantly striving to emulate that love of humanity Christ demonstrated by his sacrifice on the Cross, religion for the Moravians was a social experience in which fellow believers were united as a community of brotherly love and guided by a spirit of cooperation and willingness to work together. The Moravians sought to create in Salem a community where all of the members of the congregation were joined together as a large family. In Friedrich Marshall's words, "A Congregation-Town differs from other Congregations in that it is more like one family, where the religious and material condition of each member is known in detail,

SOUTHWEST VIEW OF SALEM NORTH CAROLINA

Fig. 1.1. Southwest view of Salem with the congregation's mill in the foreground. Painted in 1824 by Moravian artist Daniel Welfare. Courtesy of the Wachovia Historical Society.

where each person receives the appropriate . . . oversight, and also assistance in consecrating the daily life."[13] In the congregation community life was lived within a framework of personal relationships between kin and friends with one set of values. As in the congregational towns of seventeenth- and eighteenth-century New England, family, church, and town defined the milieu of Salem where public and private spheres of life merged under church direction, and an adult male's social roles as father, neighbor, church communicant, farmer or artisan, and town official were united. In the Salem congregation the spiritual and material condition of each member was known explicitly, and each communicant received counsel and aid in realizing the commitment to God which the Moravians demanded. Thus, all relationships in the congregation, whether legal, commercial, or personal, were carried out within the context of the Moravians' love of God and of all people.[14]

The ethos of brotherly love and cooperation that guided the Moravian community reflected what was real to the Moravians and was expressed in the social structure of the congregation which governed social relations in Salem. The Moravians perceived through their particular worldview that Christians were in a special relationship with God because of Christ's sacrifice for humankind, and that God was the compassionate, loving father of humankind and also the chief elder of the Christian church. The social structure of the congregation community reflected this reality. The patriarchal relationship between God and humankind was recreated in the community between the elders and the members of the congregation on one hand, and on the other hand in individual families where the father was the head of the household and exercised patriarchal authority over family members.[15] This patriarchal authority expressed itself through congregational institutions like the administrative boards and the choirs of the community as well as through the individual families and households.

The bonds of community were strengthened by the congregation government and its system of authority that brought everyone under the auspices of a patriarchal social order and congregational rules that governed all aspects of life and preserved exclusivity and homogeneity in the community. Having no civil institutions, Salem was governed by three agencies that had rather vague and often overlapping spheres of authority. The Aeltesten Conferenz, or Elders Conference, chaired by the local minister, was concerned with the spiritual affairs of the congregation and had the responsibility of ensuring that all of the administrative boards and officials in its jurisdiction functioned effectively and harmoniously. The Elders Conference in Salem represented the direct line of authority that reached down from the Unity Elders Conference at Berthelsdorf through the Provincial Elders Conference in Wachovia. Members of the Salem Elders Conference were appointed by the Unity Elders Conference. The Congregation Council concerned itself with the broader issues and matters which affected the long-term prospects of the congregation, such as changes in the congregational rules. Originally elected annually by the adult males of the congregation, the Congregation Council was reformed in 1832 to include all of the adult male members of the congregation. Hence the Congregation Council provided the adult males of the town with a voice in community affairs. The Aufseher Collegium, whose seven members were elected by the Congregation Council, exercised authority over secular affairs. The everyday matters of town administration were vested in the Vorsteher, or warden, and the Aufseher Collegium. Through these institutions the Moravians attempted to maintain consensus in the community.[16] Representing the interests of the town's shopkeepers and farmers, congregation authorities through the 1820s pursued policies which promoted the goals of the church and furthered the purpose of the congregation settlement.

An ancillary institution of congregational authority and spiritual over-sight was the Choir—an association to which particular segments of the congregation belonged. There were separate Choirs for children, boys, girls, older boys, older girls, single men, single women, married men, married women, widows, and widowers. The Choir system grew out of the practical considerations which the Moravian congregations in Europe and America confronted and answered the need of the Moravians to guarantee places in the community for the congregations' increasing num-bers of young adults. In the Choir house of the Single Brethren, the young adult men of Salem boarded together under the oversight of a Pfleger, who provided spiritual leadership. There the congregation's young men pursued their individual crafts, including shoemaking, hat-making, cabinetmaking, and dyeing as journeymen or apprentices. Single women in Salem lived in the Single Sisters' house under the direction of a Pflegerin and worked as milliners, seamstresses, and spinners. But as the congregational villages overcame the uncertainties of frontier settle-ment and were safely established on a firm basis, the Choirs evolved into primarily spiritual institutions to provide members with fellowship and spiritual support.[17]

Authority in the congregation community resided in the adult males who served on congregational administrative boards, headed households, and were masters of workshops. The congregation leadership relied on fathers and master craftsmen to pursue the moral imperatives of the congregation and to guarantee that order and peace reigned in the town. The heads of households and master craftsmen were responsible for the conduct of those in their homes and shops—their children, apprentices, and journeymen. This responsibility blended well with the organization of work and production in Salem, as the master craftsmen exercised a fatherly authority over their journeymen and apprentices. Thus, the structure of artisanal production in Salem augmented the authority of the formal congregation agencies. Family authority extended beyond the household and into the community because authority within the family was regarded as integral to the authority of congregational agencies. This frequently was evident when the congregation's "house-fathers," or heads of households, and masters were occasionally called upon to assert their authority over the town's youths. In 1824, when the Aufseher Collegium was concerned about the noisy and disorderly conduct of many of Salem's boys who habitually gathered around the village square, a meeting of the masters and house-fathers addressed the problem and sought solutions. Rowdyness among the town's youths was a persistent concern of the congregation elders. On New Year's Eve in 1810 several young men of the congregation gathered and fired their rifles on the town streets, disturbing the peace and offending the residents. To make an example of such disrespectful behavior the Elders Conference excluded the young men from all congregational privileges. In 1812 a letter from the Elders Conference of Bethlehem was read to the Salem congregation asking the members to refrain from "worldly manifestations of joy" on the Fourth of July. The letter was not well received by several of the young men of the congregation who showed their disdain for such restrictions on their behavior by sticking cockades in their hats. The Aufseher Collegium decided that before the next Communion the recalcitrant young men would be asked to consider their "spirit" and advised that "if they have no liking for the Unity it would be better for them to leave of their own free will." The Aufseher Collegium noted with pleasure on July 7, 1812 that on the Fourth of July "all was quiet and orderly." There was growing concern over youthful morality and the behavior of unsupervised young men and women, so that the masters and house-fathers were urged by the elders of the congregation to maintain greater order in their homes and not to permit unnecessary meetings of young men and women.[18] Standards of conduct within the congregation, an important responsibility of patriarchal authority in Salem, are a revealing artifact of early nineteenth-century community culture. The congregational vision of the Moravians emphasized standards of behavior that did not compromise the church's ideal of service to God. Drunkenness, laziness, and debt, believed by the Moravians to be interrelated, were serious offenses. Cockfighting and circuses, frequent challenges to congregational moral standards, were not deemed worthwhile and moral activities for the Moravians.[19]

Throughout the first quarter of the nineteenth century the village of Salem remained a community united by a single religious vision. Like most towns during this period, life revolved around daily personal contacts with family, friends, and neighbors. The combination of patriarchal social, economic, and political structures with the congregational vision of pious service to God imbued Salem with a distinct community culture

in the eighteenth and early nineteenth centuries. The vision remained
through the first quarter of the nineteenth century, defining a life of piety
apart from the corrupt world which surrounded the congregation. It
animated the cultural life of the community expressed in the experiences,
values, behavior, and institutions of the Moravians in Salem. The religious celebrations and activities which filled the lives of the communicants were integral parts of this culture. The rituals of worship in the
Moravian church were a constant reminder to members of the Salem
congregation of their special relationship to each other, to other congregations of the Unitas Fratrum, and to God.[20] Preaching, reading-meetings,
communions, marriages, and music performances were regular events
which brought the congregation together and reaffirmed the common
ethos and personal relations that united the communicants. As the annual
diaries of the Salem congregation illustrate, every week of the year was
punctuated by religious services which brought the congregation together
daily for prayer, litanies, the liturgy, and the reading of the Unity
newsletter and communications from Herrnhut and other congregations.
The festal days of the Unity were of special importance. May 12 was set
aside for the observance of the founding of the Renewed Unitas Fratrum.
The observance commemorated the day that the first Moravians from the
ancient Unitas Fratrum in Bohemia arrived on Count Zinzendorf's estate
for the laying of the cornerstone of the first prayer-hall in Herrnhut. May
12 also commemorated the recognition of the Unitas Fratrum as an
ancient episcopal church by the English Parliament which admitted the
Moravians into all British lands and colonies. July 6 was especially important as it commemorated the martyrdom of Jan Hus and celebrated
the sacrifice of those martyred for witnessing for the church of Jesus. In
all of the congregations there were festal days for each Choir which
strengthened the spiritual meaning of the Choirs, commemorated their
establishment in Herrnhut, and celebrated the covenant between church
members and God. Special days were set aside for each Choir: April 30
for the widows; May 4 for the Single Sisters; June 4 for the older girls;
July 9 for the older boys; August 17 for the children; August 29 for the
Single Brethren; August 31 for the widowers; September 7 for the married couples. The Choir festivals were celebrated with hymns, prayer,
and Choir litanies that reminded members of the merits which Christ
bestowed upon those who belonged to each particular Choir. The litanies
called Choir members to consider the doctrines of the Trinity and the

Atonement through Christ's sacrifice. The persistent theme of Moravian belief—the crucified Christ—was the message conveyed in the Choir celebrations.[21]

The ritual of the Love Feast was an integral part of the Choir celebrations as well as other significant worship services. The Love Feast demonstrated the "agape" of the early Christians, that Christian love that united all of the faithful regardless of wealth, rank, or status in the community into a true brotherhood. The Love Feast, a joyous occasion, one of the most anticipated events in the life of the congregation, was a common meal associated with church celebrations and religious services that had a symbolic meaning found in the ceremony of breaking and eating bread together. In Salem Love Feasts were held to celebrate the anniversary of the founding of the congregation, Choir festivals, Christmas, the admission to communion of youths and new members of the congregation, the dedication of new congregations, New Year's Eve, days of thanksgiving, Unity commemorations, and birthdays of longtime members and servants of the congregation. On the occasion of the Love Feast, members of the congregation were called to renew and reaffirm the spirit of brotherly love that made them a special community and to remember the presence of God's Spirit among them.[22]

Through the Elders Conference, Aufseher Collegium, and Congregation Council, the social, economic, and religious life of the town was regulated so that no one would profit at the expense of another, everyone would enjoy the necessities of life, and harmony would reign.[23] In practical terms these aims were achieved by the lease system and the regulation of all economic activities in Salem. Congregation authorities could enforce the town regulations by revoking an individual's privilege to reside in the town and by expelling recalcitrant members from the congregation, thereby denying them the opportunity to practice their religion. These sanctions generally proved to be effective means of regulating conduct in the town. Yet, such measures could be self-defeating if an issue was allowed to rend the congregation into factions. For this reason Moravian authorities followed a policy of accommodation and compromise to preserve unanimity in the community. Controversies in Salem over the regulation of the trades and property holding were resolved by including all adult male members of the congregation in the decision-making process to achieve a consensus.

The lease system allowed the church to determine who could live in Salem and to regulate the conduct of the townspeople. The Salem congregation leased land from the Unitas Fratrum, which held title to most of Wachovia. The Salem lot was about three thousand acres, roughly all of the land within a three-mile radius of the town. Within the village of Salem lots were leased to individuals and any improvements made were owned by the individual who made them.[24] Thus, the household head in Salem might own his house, but it was built on land owned by the congregation and rented to the homeowner. This arrangement insured the church's control over membership in the Salem community and guaranteed that property holding in Salem would be closely bound to the spiritual condition of the residents, as Thomas Christman learned. In 1829, Christman announced that he had accepted the tenets of the Baptist faith, declared that he was no longer a member of the Unitas Fratrum, and refused to allow his child to be baptized. The Aufseher Collegium, acting under the congregation rules, ordered Christman to sell his house to a buyer approved by the rules or leave it in the care of a resident appointed by him. In any case, Christman was ordered to leave town. After four months Christman had not sold his house and had demonstrated no intention of doing so, thus forcing the congregational authorities to take further action. Matters relating to leases involved the possible conflict of congregational rules and civil law, posing tricky problems for congregation authorities in Salem. Christman's hesitancy in leaving Salem forced the Elders Conference to decide whether to pursue a civil action in the county court, specifically a writ of eviction. The Elders Conference decided instead to keep the matter under church authority and recommended to the Aufseher Collegium that the congregation purchase Christman's house, which it did in January 1829.[25]

While leases helped congregation authorities maintain the type of community the Moravians sought, there were occasional confrontations between individual members of the congregation and the church authorities that centered around how the leased lands were used. Disagreements with the Aufseher Collegium over the types of buildings erected, improvements made, and the actual provisions of the leases themselves occurred now and again. In a controversial case in 1834 Frederic Schuman was accused of "overstepping the privileges of his lease" by constructing buildings on the tract which the Aufseher Collegium had not authorized. For this reason the Aufseher Collegium decided to end Schuman's lease. After a bitter fight in which Schuman threatened to take legal action against the congregation authorities, the matter was resolved when the parties reached a compromise, and Schuman received a new lease on the property he occupied.[26] The issue of the leases, a cornerstone of the congregational town system, remained a regular point of contention between individuals and church authorities into the 1840s.

From the beginning of Moravian settlement in America economic activities in the congregations had been regulated by church boards to guarantee the survival and well-being of the congregations. In the early years of settlement during the mid-eighteenth century the general economy, or *Oeconomy*, directed the practice of the trades in the congregations. Under the *Oeconomy* artisans practiced their crafts for the benefit of the congregation, providing the necessities of life for the congregation with all profits going into the congregation's treasury in return for a wage. But, in 1772 when Salem was established as the *gemein Ort*, or principal congregation town of Wachovia, the *Oeconomy* was closed and a more "private" economy emerged in which the married men as heads of households worked for themselves and kept the profits their shops and farms produced. Many of the crafts which had been carried on as congregation activities in the Single Brothers' House in Salem gradually became the private enterprises of individual artisans. In 1812 the saddlery which Christian Wageman had carried on in the Single Brothers' House was taken over by the Single Brother Heinrich Rudolph Herbst when Wageman married and moved from Salem. Herbst carried on the saddlery shop "on his own account." Nevertheless, the congregational boards continued to regulate the trades, determine who could own a shop, and set prices for goods. By restricting competition and regulating prices and the quality of workmanship, the leaders of the congregation sought to protect the ability of each member of the congregation to make a living. Certain crucial economic activities—the general store, tavern, tanyard, and pottery—were owned by the congregation's economic agency, the diacony. But, private initiative under the strict regulation of the Aufseher Collegium was permitted in the other trades.[27]

The local artisans were the central characters in the economic life of the town during the eighteenth and early nineteenth centuries, when the economy was limited by poor transportation facilities and trading relationships were largely local—usually between family, friends, and neighbors. Salem's master craftsmen, working in small shops alongside their journeymen and apprentices, produced articles for trade in the local community and with the farmers of the surrounding countryside. In this town-centered economy, involving production for the local market and with little outside competition, the status of Salem's artisans was rela-

TABLE 1.1

*Real Property of Salem
Artisans in 1832*

Acres	Percentage
Under 50	80.9
50 to 100	14.3
101 to 499	4.8
Over 500	0

Sources: Minutes of the Aufseher Colle-
gium and Minutes of the Aeltesten
Conferenz, 1828–32, Fries et al., *Re-
cords*, 8: passim; Stokes County, List of
Taxables, Salem District, 1832,
NCDAH.

tively secure. Because the artisan owned his tools, the raw materials used
in production, and the product of his labor, the price he sold his wares
for was the wage he received for his labor and that of his journeymen. In
this work setting the functions of merchant and producer were united in
the same person. Remuneration for productive labor was tied directly to
the price of the article paid by the consumer.[28] As long as competition
was restricted and quality maintained, the price of finished goods and
services remained tied directly to the costs of production, and there was
little threat to the status of the skilled artisan in Salem.

Most Salem artisans combined farming with their trades. In 1827 the
congregation leased lots adjoining the village to members of the congregation for an annual rent of from fifty cents to seventy-five cents an acre.
Consequently, property holding among the townspeople of Salem was
widespread, with 88.5 percent of Salem's residents holding property in
1835. Among Salem's artisans 67.7 percent held property, though 80.9
percent held less than fifty acres. The landholdings of Salem's artisans
were likely to be town lots in Salem, with a few acres near town for
growing food crops. Table 1.1 illustrates the distribution of property
among Salem artisans.[29]

The congregation's economic regulations and a strict system of apprenticeship were crucial to the continued success of Salem's artisan shops
and to the maintenance of the congregational way of life. Under the
congregational rules each master craftsmen in Salem was granted the
privilege to work in his craft as long as the needs of the community,
as determined by the Aufseher Collegium, were served. Congregation
authorities allowed in a particular trade only the number of artisans

capable of supporting themselves and their journeymen. If there were too many artisans in a trade, the Aufseher Collegium denied permission to applicants who wished to work in that occupation, either as masters, journeymen, or apprentices. When Theophilus Vierling petitioned the Aufseher Collegium in 1833 for permission to enter the shoemaker's trade in Salem he was turned down because master shoemakers were already plentiful. Charles Cooper's application to open a cabinetmaking shop was denied for the same reason; he was advised to learn chairmaking instead. Conversely, when Salem was without the services of a wagonmaker in 1831, the Aufseher Collegium sent John C. Blum to Pennsylvania to inquire in the congregations there for a good wagon- and carriagemaker for the town.[30]

To guarantee the prospects of artisans in Salem, only communicants of the Unitas Fratrum were allowed by the congregation rules to settle in Salem and pursue a trade. Moravian records contain numerous cases of artisans seeking to start their trades in the town but who were denied that opportunity because they did not belong to Salem's congregation. In one case, Levin Belo and Eli Reich petitioned the Aufseher Collegium in 1847 for permission to open a shop in Salem. Belo, a saddler, and Reich, a shoemaker, wanted to join together and rent part of the old congregation pottery for their shops. The Aufseher Collegium had no objections to Belo's plan since he was a member of the congregation; but because Reich was not a member of the Salem congregation he was not allowed to set up a shop.[31]

The Aufseher Collegium was continually called upon to deal with the matter of masters hiring workers who did not belong to the congregation. In 1827 the Aufseher Collegium reaffirmed the regulation that no "outside" young man was to be employed in the trades when a son in the congregation was available. In 1838 the Aufseher Collegium reprimanded Emanuel Reich for hiring a "strange" apprentice in his shop without obtaining permission. When Philip Reich employed Joshua Ball to learn the tinsmith's trade, it was under the express condition that if Ball, who was apprenticed for two years, did not comply with the congregation rules, he would be dismissed. While the Aufseher Collegium did not demand the dismissal of Ball, it did express its concern that so many strangers worked in the shops of Salem. Congregation authorities believed that the chances of the town's youths to find suitable employment were lessened. The restriction on "outside" apprentices and journeymen protected Moravian artisans from the competition that an increased number of craftsmen would have created. It also limited the competition the town's young men faced in securing apprenticeships or employment. However, when the needs of the town warranted and when there were no suitable Moravians available in particular trades, exceptions were made. Thus John Vogler, a silversmith, was allowed to engage his nephew from Salisbury as an apprentice.[32]

Apprenticeship proved an effective means of regulating both the quality of workmanship and the future of the congregation. Through apprenticeship the young men of the town were introduced to their responsibilities as tradesmen and citizens of the community, and the time spent as apprentices was a vital part of the education of Moravian youth. The Salem *People's Press* advised the town's young men that apprenticeship was the most important stage of life through which a mechanic passes because he can become the master of his trade only through the strictest attention. The editor of the paper advised apprentices to persevere, be studious, and attentive.[33] The apprentices' obligation to hard effort, perseverance, and attentiveness to his craft was matched by the masters' obligation to educate and provide for their young students as they would for their own children. In a typical apprenticeship bond, John Henry Stultz was bound to L. F. Eberhart to learn the blacksmith's trade. Eberhart agreed to

> teach and instruct, or cause to be taught and instructed . . . to read, write and to cipher . . . , and give him a Bible and 40 dollars . . . and give him two suits of freedom clothes homespun. And that he will constantly find and provide for said apprentice . . . sufficient diet, washing, lodging and apparel, fitting for an apprentice . . . [34]

Because apprenticeship was so vital to the well-being of the trades and thus the congregation, it was strictly regulated by congregation authorities. Few outsiders were admitted to apprenticeships and those who were met strict standards of morality. Non-Moravian apprentices had to demonstrate a strength of character that convinced the Aufseher Collegium that they posed no threat as corrupting influences on the town's youths and that they would be upstanding and productive members of the community. To this end the Aufseher Collegium required that it be notified before master craftsmen hired journeymen or apprentices. Generally, the authorities acquiesced if the proposed boy or young man was of the congregation and if they were convinced that the employer was qualified to instruct the youth adequately in the craft. In September 1824 John Ackerman, a cooper, asked for permission to employ John Spach as an apprentice in his shop, but the Aufseher Collegium denied the request because Spach was not a member of the Salem congregation. The Collegium reiterated that it would not break the congregation rule which forbade the hiring of "outsiders" as apprentices. But, in January 1837 shoemaker Emanuel Reich was permitted to employ an apprentice who did not belong to the congregation on the condition that the young man was to be on probation and if he did not abide by the congregation rules then Reich would have to dismiss him immediately. Often, the status of a particular trade in Salem was a factor in admitting a youth to an apprenticeship. When William Hull moved from South Carolina to Salem in 1827 and tried to secure an apprenticeship for his son, the Aufseher Collegium offered young Hull apprenticeships in either shoe-making or tailoring since they were the only trades with openings.[35]

The quality of workmanship was a primary concern of Salem's master craftsmen and congregation authorities. Before a journeyman was allowed to open his own shop in the town, the master craftsmen in his trade and the Aufseher Collegium considered the quality of the applicant's work, the number of artisans already in the trade, and the ability of the applicant to make a suitable living at his craft. In 1832 Christian Eberhard's application to work on his own account as a master shoemaker drew objections on two points. First, the Aufseher Collegium believed that there were already too many shoemakers in Salem. Second, some master shoemakers who knew Eberhard's work were concerned about its quality and his ability as a shoemaker. In denying the petition, the Aufseher Collegium advised young Eberhard to perfect himself further in his craft as a journeyman in one of the other shops in town.[36]

The congregation rules allowed artisans to price goods and services in relation to the cost of raw materials and the labor required in production so that the master craftsmen and his journeymen received a fair return for their labor. In Salem an artisan could not undercut the prices charged by other artisans and thereby gain an advantage in the trade. Additionally, the regulation of prices guaranteed the community that needed goods and services would be available at affordable prices. Thus, no one in the congregation would benefit at the expense of others. The Aufseher Collegium was always concerned that the necessities of life be available to all of the Brethren with as little hardship as possible. In 1809 when economic conditions were unsettled because of continuing tensions between the

United States and Great Britain and money was scarce in the country-side, thus driving up the prices of commodities, the Aufseher Collegium resolved that the prices for food should be kept "uniform" as far as possible. The Collegium believed that the present price of two shillings per bushel of corn and $3.50 to $4.00 per hundred pounds for hog meat should be maintained. The practice of regulating commodity, especially food, prices continued well into the nineteenth century. In July 1826 a committee of the Aufseher Collegium reached an agreement with the town's butchers to stabilize prices of meat. However, when the prices and quality of workmanship in a particular trade did not meet the Aufseher Collegium's standards, the authorities occasionally sought the remedy in competition. Because of frequent complaints about the quality and prices of Christian Winkler's baked goods, the Aufseher Collegium seriously considered James Hall's petition to open a bakery. Many in Salem believed a second bakery would offer competition and force Winkler to lower prices and improve the quality of his product. Winkler was warned that unless he offered better and cheaper baked goods, a second bakery would be permitted to open. Because Winkler was given a second chance, the Aufseher Collegium denied Hall's petition.[37]

With competition in Salem regulated and thus prices and wages stable and secure, the work routine of Salem's artisans remained casual, reflecting the preindustrial character of the crafts during the first third of the nineteenth century. Work in the shops was done by hand with the artisan completing all of the production processes in crafting raw materials into a finished product. Consequently, production was task oriented, time was measured by how long it took to complete a task in the manufacturing process, and the artisan had control over his own work pace. The pace of work in this preindustrial setting was usually uneven as the artisan mixed work and leisure during the workday, as the daily work routine of Salem shoemaker Henry Leinbach illustrates. On Mondays, Leinbach spent the day cutting out the leather for shoes which his apprentices and journeymen assembled. On the other days, Leinbach usually spent his mornings in the shop, but come the afternoon and he was out fishing, hunting, walking, playing "corner-ball," or, in wintertime, ice skating. Masters and journeymen, during the course of a day's work, customarily took a "daily lounge" where they gathered at a local tavern, the courthouse, or a store like Winkler's bakery for drinking beer or brandy and conversing on the important topics of the day.[38] In this setting close personal relationships developed between master craftsmen

TABLE 1.2

Distribution of Real Property, Stokes County, 1820

Acres	Property Owners	Percent	Cumulative Percent
0	17	22.4	22.4
1–50	5	6.5	28.9
51–100	8	10.5	39.5
101–200	23	30.3	69.8
201–300	9	11.8	81.6
301–500	10	13.2	94.8
Over 500	4	5.3	100

Sources: Stokes County, List of Taxables, 1820, NCDAH; 1820 Census, Population Schedule manuscript microfilm, Stokes County, North Carolina.

and their journeymen and apprentices which extended beyond the shops and daily work routines. Sharing a common status as members of the congregation, and, thus, entitled to a voice in the administration of town affairs, there was little to divide journeymen and masters. With competition limited and prices regulated, there was no reason for masters to decrease their journeymen's wages in order to lower prices so that they might gain a competitive edge over other craftsmen. For their part, Moravian journeymen found they could realistically aspire to be masters and heads of households in the congregation.

The early success of the artisans and shopkeepers of Salem was promoted by the role of Salem as an important commercial center in Stokes County. Salem anchored a local economy that brought together the craftsmen and farmers of the countryside and villages of Stokes and neighboring counties. The hilly country, gray sandy loam soils, and heavy forests combined to make the northwest piedmont of North Carolina a region of small family-run farms that produced grains and raised livestock for local consumption and a small-scale export trade. Most Stokes farmers, as Table 1.2 shows, owned two hundred acres or less, which they farmed with their own labor and that of their sons or hired helpers. Only 14.5 percent of property holders in Stokes County in 1820 owned slaves. As Table 1.3 illustrates, Moravian farmers in Stokes County, on the average, owned even smaller farms. In the Moravian settlements of Bethania, Bethabara, and Salem, 51.7 percent of the farmers owned farms that encompassed one hundred acres or less, while 78.1 percent owned farms of two hundred acres or less.[39] A few large plantations using slave labor sprouted along the fertile bottom lands of Yadkin

TABLE 1.3
*Distribution of Real Property among Moravians
in Stokes County, 1820*

Acres	Property Owners	Percent	Cumulative Percent
0	16	14.5	14.5
1–50	16	14.5	29.0
51–100	25	22.7	51.7
101–200	29	26.4	78.1
201–300	12	10.9	89.0
301–500	8	7.3	96.3
Over 500	4	3.7	100

Sources: Stokes County, List of Taxables, 1820, NCDAH; 1820 Census, Population Schedule manuscript microfilm, Stokes County, North Carolina.

River tributaries. Some farmers did accumulate great wealth growing tobacco for the export market. One such wealthy planter was John Mecum who, upon his death, left an estate valued at $3,142.26 and included over two thousand pounds of tobacco and seven slaves. It appears that Tucker Moore was just as successful because his estate also included two thousand pounds of tobacco and eight slaves.[40] But Mecum and Moore were exceptions, since most Stokes farmers were yeomen farmers who owned less than two hundred acres which they worked without the aid of slave labor. Until the postbellum era, the upper piedmont of North Carolina remained an area of small farms employing few slaves and relying on white family labor to produce corn, tobacco, wheat, fruits, cattle, hogs, and whiskey.

Lacking broad, deep rivers running from the piedmont to the coast, farmers in the countryside around Salem in the early nineteenth century found few markets beyond the local community readily accessible to them. Most of the commerce of the piedmont moved either south down the roads of the Yadkin and Catawba river valleys into South Carolina and on to Charleston, north through the Shenandoah Valley to Philadelphia, or east to Fayetteville and then down the Cape Fear River to Wilmington, thus giving Salem a central location along important trade routes in the North Carolina upcountry. The Moravians used roads that connected the rural villages with each other and the backcountry with Pennsylvania, going regularly between the Wachovia settlements and the Moravian congregations of Pennsylvania. These roads, however, were primitive, little more than paths that cut across farm fields and the dense piedmont forests, so that the movement of goods and people was "slow, difficult, and expensive." Even under the best of conditions a trip from Salem to Fayetteville took three full days of traveling from before sunrise to after sundown; under poorer conditions, the trip could be longer. Because of the poor state of transportation the lives of most North Carolinians revolved around their own neighborhood and county, relations being limited primarily to kith and kin.[41]

Given these conditions, backcountry farms in the early nineteenth century participated in the world market on a limited basis. Moravian farmers like other backcountry farmers grew large quantities of corn and smaller quantities of rye, oats, and barley as well as raising cattle, hogs, and sheep. However, in their limited involvement in the export market, these farmers looked to wheat as a crop that earned cash. Wheat yielded higher profits for Stokes farmers than corn: an acre of wheat in the late eighteenth century brought forty-five shillings compared to thirty-six shillings an acre for corn. At the end of the eighteenth century there was a growing trend in the Carolinas toward greater wheat production as farmers realized its commercial possibilities, and the Carolina backcountry developed as part of an "irregular" wheat belt that stretched from New York south through New Jersey, Pennsylvania, Maryland, Virginia, and the Carolinas.[42] While most wheat continued to be consumed in the local market, its increased cultivation answered the greater demand for wheat and flour in overseas markets. The Moravian settlers regularly traded their tallow, deerskins, bread, butter, wheat, and pottery in exchange for salt, iron, coffee, sugar, and other items. By the early nineteenth century external trading relations were becoming more regular as new outlets from the Moravian settlements were opened. In 1810 the Elders Conference of Salem decided to open up trade with Norfolk, Virginia, after a Mr. Curtis of that city had offered to serve as the Moravians' agent there for a 2.5 percent commission on the goods he handled. The Moravians began sending meal from the Salem mill to Norfolk in exchange for other goods. With the blazing of new roads, in the early nineteenth century Salem became one of the largest towns and most important commercial centers in the North Carolina piedmont.[43]

The immigrants who filled the North Carolina backcountry turned to each other to acquire necessary goods and services and thus were bound together in relationships that strove for local self-sufficiency rather than individual self-sufficiency. For these settlers it was difficult to achieve true self-sufficiency since to do so would have meant either giving up the goods one couldn't produce oneself or investing precious time and effort to produce these goods. Though Stokes County farmers may not have been fully in and of the capitalist market economy since they did not seek profits at every turn, they did not conform fully to the long-accepted view of the upcountry yeomanry as largely aloof from commercial relations. There emerged in the Stokes County countryside during the late eighteenth and early nineteenth centuries a diversified economy of farming and crafts that wove the inhabitants together into networks of local exchange. These farmers engaged in a number of ancillary activities which brought in cash and enabled them to purchase what they could not produce themselves. Stokes County farmers Solomon Helsabeck and John Conrad are examples of the interdependencies that emerged between piedmont settlers in the local market. Solomon Helsabeck supplemented what his farm produced by using his team and wagon to haul wheat, oats, hay, wood, and planks for neighbors in return for cash or farm commodities. John Conrad earned cash by making shoes and selling bacon and corn to his neighbors.[44] Public documents from the early nineteenth century reveal the degree to which the people of the backcountry were linked together by personal debt and credit arrangements. With the unavailability of banks and credit, the people of Stokes County turned to each other for cash and credit as well as for goods, farm commodities, and services. Credit took the form of cash advanced to the debtor or the carrying of debts on the account books of artisans who allowed for future payment for the goods they sold or the services they rendered. Of thirty-three estate inventories from 1814 to 1818 examined, eighteen or 54.5 percent had outstanding debts which the administrators of the individual estates had to settle, while seventeen or 51.5 percent of the estates had money owed to them which had to be collected. The estate of William Cardwell, a prosperous Stokes farmer, is illustrative. When Cardwell died in 1813, he had debts amounting to $402.75, but his estate had assets that included eleven slaves, four horses, eleven head of cattle, sixteen head of sheep, thirteen hogs, plus $433 in cash received from those to whom Cardwell had loaned money.[45] Among some Stokes County farmers and artisans there was often a desire to earn profits from the investment of capital, even if the capital was loaned to neighbors. Johanna Krause of Salem frequently lent money to her neighbors in sums that ranged from $10 to $375 at interest that varied from 2 to 5 percent. In 1814 Krause lent Salem miller Van Nieman Zevely $100 at 5 percent interest, which Zevely may have used to finance his new wool carding mill that opened in 1815. Nathaniel Schober, a Salem storekeeper and farmer, purchased stock in both the State Bank of North Carolina and the Cape Fear Bank in hopes of earning dividends as well as profiting from the increased value of his shares. When he died in 1818 he had $700 invested in the shares of the two banks.[46] The small farmers who worked their own land still sought security and independence through the production of grains and livestock and the trade of small surpluses and homemade products in the local market. These yeomen valued independence, equality, and self-respect along with customary ways of life which emphasized personal relations with neighbors.

The surrounding countryside was a rich market for Salem's artisans and shopkeepers who carried on a lucrative trade with the steadily increasing population of the North Carolina piedmont. Several roads ran out from Salem to villages in the countryside which gave the congregation's artisans a wider market for their goods and services and the townspeople ready access to the products of the neighboring farms. Edmund Blum, a Salem coppersmith, provided copperware to fellow members of the Salem congregation, as well as to farmers living in the surrounding communities of Germanton, Midway, Mocksville, Muddy Creek, and Waughtown. The congregation store in Salem offered the Brethren and their neighbors a wide assortment of goods imported from as far away as Europe and from merchants in Philadelphia, as well as from the nearby commercial centers of Petersburg, Virginia, and Fayetteville, North Carolina. Fueling an active local economy, Stokes County farmers turned to village gunsmiths, copper- and tinsmiths, shopkeepers, and physicians for the goods and services they could not provide themselves. In February 1809, two people from distant settlements found the effective care of Moravian physician Samuel Benjamin Vierling. Anna Hart came to Salem from Hillsborough, ninety miles east, for Dr. Vierling to remove a cancerous sore from her tongue. John Johnson came from his home fifty miles away in Randolph County to have Vierling remove a growth from his side.[47] Dense networks of exchange united the people who lived in Stokes County and neighboring counties.

As the Brethren moved through the daily round of living that brought them into regular contact with outsiders in the countryside, they were always conscious of the fragility of the life of piety they sought and the special community which they hoped to foster. The growing number of non-Moravians in the neighborhood of Salem in the early nineteenth century made it difficult for the Moravians to remain apart from the corruptions of the outside world and preserve their own standards of morality. Francis Joseph Kron, a native of Germany, reported in 1835 that a widespread immorality characterized the Yadkin Valley of North Carolina. Drunkenness, gambling, disregard for the Sabbath, and fighting were prevalent among the people of the region. Kron observed that "within a circle of eighteen miles where perhaps thirteen families dwell I could count as many as twenty illegitimate children, some the offspring of widows, others of single never married women, and others, too, intruders in lawful wedlock." Kron's attitude toward non-Moravians in the countryside was consistent with the perceptions of other early Moravian settlers. A German minister named Roschen noted in the eighteenth century that the English and Irish settlers in the North Carolina backcountry were "lazy, dissipated and poor, live in the most wretched huts and enjoy the same food as their animals." The Moravian elders of Salem, quite conscious of the apparent immorality that lurked beyond the town limits, were adamant that these influences be kept out of the community. The Aufseher Collegium constantly found evidence of the inroads of corruption among Salem's inhabitants. The agents of immoral behavior almost always turned out to be non-Moravian apprentices, journeymen, or domestic servants. In one instance the Aufseher Collegium warned the congregation that it was not showing enough discretion in the hiring of domestic servants; girls were hired even though little was known of their "former way of life." According to the Aufseher Collegium there were several maids who had shown a "great lack of discipline and moral conduct." The authorities resolved that the greatest vigilance must be shown regarding the admission of non-Moravian servants to the congregation.[48]

In their worship services and congregational diaries the Moravians often expressed anguish that the conduct of their own lives did not match the gravity of Christ's sacrifice for humanity; indeed, there was much anxiety over whether they were worthy of Christ's love. In looking back over the events of the previous year the elders of the Wachovia congregations in 1809 "sorrowfully acknowledged" the Brethren's sins and shortcomings and expressed "painful concern over those in our congregations who have turned away from the true spirit of Christ and the Unity." Though no one thing or series of particular events led the elders to this conclusion, they expressed a general sense that the community in 1809 lacked the measure of faith exhibited by the original settlers of Wachovia. In the annual Memorabilia of the Congregations, which all members of the Wachovia congregations would read or hear in their worship services, the elders prayed, "Humbly conscious of our many defects and shortcomings, how can we feel worthy of the refreshing enjoyment of the love and care of our Father, the grace and mercy of our Redeemer, and the nurture and comfort of the Holy Spirit, given to all those among us who heartily wish to do the will of God and live to His honor and joy?"[49]

In the end, however, the greatest threat to the community culture of the Moravians was not the corruptions of the outside world, but, rather, the commercial success Salem enjoyed as a market town in the piedmont. The Moravians soon sensed that the achievement of their objective that the village serve as a commercial center might subvert the religious mission of the congregation. The Moravian desire to serve the countryside and to influence it in a way that would raise the spiritual level of its inhabitants also had the opposite effect of the countryside influencing the Moravian community and diverting the Moravians from their mission. In the eighteenth century few Moravian leaders doubted that the ethos and objectives that informed the Salem experience conformed to the realities of an era in which they lived. However, the men who determined the fortunes of the Moravian community from the 1830s on realized that circumstances had changed, and that the traditional theocratic ideals that shaped Salem had grown increasingly out of step with existing conditions.[50] Throughout the antebellum period decisions were made by the community leadership that seriously weakened the Moravian church discipline. Loopholes in policies, relaxed enforcement of regulations, and the accumulation of precedents which compromised principles raised doubts regarding the true nature of the Salem community. By the 1840s, as a market economy intruded into the North Carolina piedmont, new tensions emerged in the community as many craftsmen perceived that changing economic conditions might not be beneficial to their livelihoods. By mid-century, as the world was changing around them, new conditions overwhelmed the original aims of the eighteenth-century Moravian fathers.

CHAPTER TWO

The Congregation and a Changing Economy

Beginning in the late 1820s there was a growing recognition among the Moravians that economic circumstances in the piedmont countryside were changing. Salem and its neighboring countryside were becoming more deeply enmeshed in a market economy that stretched beyond the boundaries of surrounding counties. As people produced an increasing proportion of their total output for exchange rather than for use in the household, they adopted new ways of behavior that demonstrated the influence of a new ethos emphasizing individualism and the private pursuit of opportunity and wealth.[1] Some of the town's successful shop masters observed new opportunities in deeper involvement with the market. Among this group of Moravians there arose a new awareness of entrepreneurial possibilities which promoted a mentalité quite removed from the congregational vision. But the emergence of the market in the daily lives of the Moravians generated hard times and divisive social and political tensions in Salem.

The transformation of the Moravian community occurred against the backdrop of a changing agricultural economy in the piedmont countryside during the antebellum years, made possible by the improvement and expansion of transportation facilities. During the second quarter of the nineteenth century Salem developed trading relations with northern cities and western towns as shipments traveled from Boston, New York, and Philadelphia by steamboat to Petersburg and by wagon from Petersburg to Salem. Salem's two textile mills in the 1840s shipped their cloth and yarn north to consignees in New York and Philadelphia, and west to

TABLE 2.1

Agriculture in Stokes and Forsyth Counties, 1840, 1850, and 1860

	1840	1850	% Change	1860	% Change
Corn (bu.)	423,970	572,320	+35.0	550,845	-3.8
Wheat (bu.)	74,989	56,739	-24.3	241,248	+325.0
Tobacco (lbs.)	596,103	442,986	-25.7	2,064,482	+366.0
Cotton (lbs.)	56,481	0		121,600	

Sources: Compendium of the Sixth Census. 1840; Statistical View of the United States. Compendium of the Seventh Census. 1850; Report of the United States in 1860. Compiled from the Original Returns of the Eighth Census, vol. 2.

Mississippi, Louisiana, and Texas. By mid-century railroads and plank roads linked the piedmont countryside with the fall-line commercial towns that provided gateways to the national and world markets. The Fayetteville and Western Plank Road ran northwest from Fayetteville through Salem to Bethania in northern Forsyth County. The road provided Salem with an important connection with the North Carolina Railroad at High Point, enabling Salem and its neighboring countryside to benefit from the expansion of a rail network in the Carolinas and Virginia during the late antebellum years. The North Carolina Railroad which passed through nearby Greensboro and High Point, and the Richmond and Danville Railroad, with its terminus at Danville, Virginia, provided better connections between the Carolina backcountry and eastern commercial and manufacturing centers. By the Civil War few communities in the Atlantic seaboard states were completely isolated from the forces of the national economy.[2]

With easier access to markets than in earlier years, by mid-century Stokes and Forsyth county farmers, who had once devoted their efforts to producing food crops for household consumption and trade in the local market, had become increasingly attuned to the market demand for their farm products. These farmers turned to producing cotton, tobacco, and wheat for trade in regional and national markets, as Table 2.1 shows. However, as these numbers demonstrate, the march toward market involvement was not without detours. When economic conditions in the countryside were difficult, as in the 1840s when cash was scarce and farm commodities brought low prices, Stokes farmers retreated from the market and looked to greater self-sufficiency as a means of family household security. Stokes County farmers relied on corn to get their families through the hard times. During the 1840s corn production increased 35 percent from 423,970 bushels in 1840 to 572,320 bushels in 1850, while production of wheat and tobacco—the principal market crops—declined. Wheat production dropped 24.3 percent from 74,989 bushels to 56,739 bushels, and tobacco production dropped 25.7 percent from 596,103 pounds to 442,986 pounds.[3] When economic conditions rebounded in the 1850s, Stokes and Forsyth county farmers once again sought profits in the market. In the 1850s corn production in Stokes and Forsyth counties decreased slightly by 3.8 percent from 572,320 bushels in 1850 to 550,845 bushels in 1860, but the production of wheat and tobacco experienced explosive expansion. Wheat production rose 325 percent from 56,739 bushels in 1850 to 241,248 bushels in 1860, while tobacco production expanded 366 percent from 442,986 pounds in 1850 to 2,064,482 pounds in 1860. Cotton production boomed, rising from a few hundred pounds in 1850 to over 121,600 pounds in 1860. Despite its cyclical nature, a clear trend emerged of greater commitment to production for the market in Stokes and Forsyth counties between 1840 and 1860. During these years there was a net increase in production of wheat of 300.7 percent, of tobacco 340.3 percent, and cotton 115 percent. At the same time corn production showed a net increase of a modest 31.2 percent by comparison. During the 1850s per capita corn production actually dropped from 29.7 bushels to 23.8 bushels.[4]

Commodities from piedmont farms were likely to be shipped to Fayetteville and Petersburg, the important commercial centers of the region, which provided entry into the regional and national markets. The convergence of prices for some agricultural products in these market towns offers further evidence that a market economy in certain agricultural commodities was evolving. In March 1851 the price for wheat was nearly the same in Salem ($1.00 a bushel), Fayetteville ($1.00 to $1.10 a bushel), and Petersburg ($1.00 to $1.05 a bushel). In March 1856 wheat sold for $1.25 a bushel in Salem, Salisbury, and Fayetteville. In June 1856 wheat was selling for $1.00 a bushel in Salem, Salisbury, and Fayetteville. In contrast to wheat, corn prices varied significantly from community to community, which suggest that prices for corn were set in the local market where it was consumed. In March 1851 corn sold for fifty to fifty-five cents per bushel in Salem, eighty-five to ninety cents in Fayetteville, seventy cents in Petersburg, and ninety cents to $1.00 in Cheraw, South Carolina. In March 1856 the price for corn in Salem was fifty-five to sixty cents, fifty to fifty-five cents in nearby Salisbury, and seventy-five cents in Fayetteville.[5]

TABLE 2.2

Distribution of Farm Size by Improved Acres, Forsyth County, 1850

Acres	Farms	% Total
1–24	18	10
25–49	79	42
50–74	48	26
75–99	11	6
100–149	19	10
150 over	11	6

Source: 1850 Census, Agriculture Schedule manuscript microfilm, Forsyth County, North Carolina.

Market production made farming more intensive as the number of improved acres, or land being cultivated, increased to produce more surplus for exchange. Between 1850 and 1860, acres of improved farmland in Forsyth County increased 40 percent from 51,873 to 72,509. As more farm acreage was brought into production, the value of farms increased. The cash value of Forsyth County farms reported in the federal censuses increased 98 percent from $593,197 in 1850 to $1,174,800 in 1860. As Tables 2.2 and 2.3 show, farmers in Forsyth and Stokes counties worked small farms for which the farmer's family generally provided sufficient labor. In Forsyth County the mean farm size in 1850 was 59.5 improved acres. Most farms, however, were about thirty improved acres. Table 2.2 illustrates the distribution of Forsyth County farms by improved acres. In Stokes County in 1850 the mean size of a farm was 64.6 improved acres, and, as in Forsyth County, most farmers worked farms of about thirty improved acres.[6]

TABLE 2.3

Distribution of Farm Size by Improved Acres, Stokes County, 1850

Acres	Farms	% Total
1–24	18	15
25–49	49	42
50–74	26	22
75–99	5	4
100–149	10	8
150 over	10	8

Source: 1850 Census, Agriculture Schedule manuscript microfilm, Stokes County, North Carolina.

TABLE 2.4
*Distribution of Slaveholding in Forsyth
County, 1850*

Size of Slaveholding	Farmers	% Total
1	4	24
2	4	24
3	2	12
5	1	6
6	1	6
7	5	29

Source: 1850 Census, Slave Schedule manuscript microfilm, Forsyth County, North Carolina.

The shift toward greater production for the market necessitated a larger supply of labor to work the fields, and, between 1820 and 1860, Stokes and Forsyth county farmers came to depend more on the labor of slaves. Between 1820 and 1860 the number of slaves in the two counties increased 92 percent from 2,204 to 4,233. Between 1840 and 1860 the number of slaves jumped 57.8 percent. While the number of slaves in the northwest North Carolina piedmont grew over the course of the antebellum period, few farmers in Forsyth County relied on slaves to help them work their farms. Only 9 percent of Forsyth County farmers included in a sample drawn from the federal census of 1850 owned a slave, and, as Table 2.4 shows, of those who did own a slave, 48 percent owned just one or two slaves. However, 41 percent of the county's slave-owning farmers owned five or more slaves, and the mean size of slave holdings in Forsyth County was 3.76. The largest slave holdings belonged to farmers who farmed one hundred improved acres or more. Six of the seven farmers in the sample who owned five or more slaves farmed one hundred improved acres or more, while six of the ten farmers who owned three or fewer slaves farmed less than seventy-five acres. No farmers in the sample who worked less that twenty-five acres owned a slave.[7]

As farmers shifted an increasing share of their effort and resources into producing for the market, more households went into the market to acquire the necessities of life as well as those articles that made life more comfortable and enjoyable. With cash earned from the sale of market crops or through the trade of corn, beef, or fruit with a local shopkeeper or craftsman, many households acquired needed articles like cloth, molasses, books, shoes, and whiskey. The value per capita of household manufactures (defined as those goods once made in the household or on the farm) reported in the federal censuses provides a measure of this changing consumer behavior during the decades before the Civil War. There was a steady decline in the per capita value of household manufactures between 1810 and 1860. In 1810 the per capita value of household manufactures in Stokes County was $2.40. By 1840 the value had dropped to $2.00, and in 1860 the per capita value of household manufactures in Stokes and Forsyth counties was $1.64. By the eve of the Civil War Stokes and Forsyth county households were embracing an economic orientation that contrasted sharply with that of households sixty years earlier in what was then the Carolina backcountry. After the hard times of the 1830s and 1840s, farms were producing more and farmers were able to get their crops to market much more easily than at any time in the past because of the plank road and nearby railroads. As farming in the countryside shifted toward the market, business in Salem prospered and many shop-keepers were pursuing new opportunities, establishing shops, and buying new equipment. The Salem *People's Press* reported in 1851 there was a new impulse to local business and improvement was the order of the day for Salem businessmen.[8]

Piedmont farmers sought opportunities where they found them, sell-ing or trading their surplus wheat, corn, and orchard products for cash, other commodities, or articles produced by local artisans or manufactured in distant factories. These produced for the market when conditions allowed them to realize profits and family financial strategies. In the early 1830s when a continued drought drove up prices for the decreased sup-plies of wheat and corn, Stokes County farmers pursued greater profits by keeping their crops off the market in hopes of driving up the prices still higher and improving their advantage in the market. Henry Leinbach of Salem noted in his diary that in the summer of 1830 the people of Salem were greatly concerned about the availability of wheat and its price as a result of the farmers' actions. In nearby Bethania the Moravian minister there recorded in the congregation's diary that in the winter of 1831 there was a "pressing need" for corn among the poor people of the countryside, but yet "many" farmers were holding corn off the market for a better price.[9]

As in other southern communities during this period, the greater involvement of the Stokes County countryside in the market, as well as economic ties that stretched beyond the local community, had a profound impact on local farmers, artisans, and shopkeepers as greater concentra-

TABLE 2.5

Distribution of Wealth in Stokes County, 1820–45

Rank	1820		1845	
	Value	*Share*	*Value*	*Share*
Top Decile	$47,785	46.8%	$41,444	47.4%
Second Decile	14,261	14.0	16,873	19.3
Third Decile	9,469	9.3	5,080	5.8
Fourth Decile	8,090	7.9	7,261	8.3
Fifth Decile	9,105	8.9	6,200	7.1
Sixth Decile	2,390	2.3	3,587	4.1
Seventh Decile	4,757	4.7	3,188	3.6
Eighth Decile	3,579	3.5	2,716	3.1
Ninth Decile	2,063	2.0	579	.7
Tenth Decile	598	.6	583	.7

Source: Stokes County, List of Taxables, 1820, 1845, North Carolina Department of Archives and History, Raleigh, North Carolina.

tions of wealth emerged which sharpened social and economic stratification.[10] As land became harder to acquire and as more people found themselves in straitened circumstances, there was greater stratification in the social structure. Consequently, between 1820 and 1845 the percentage of propertyless in Stokes County increased from 19 to 32 percent. More people in Stokes County went into debt and found it difficult to recover, sliding into financial insolvency. The percentage of insolvent polls reported in the tax lists rose from 9.2 percent in 1833 to 14.9 percent in 1836, before decreasing to 13.4 percent in 1841. The size of property holdings among most landowners decreased as well. Between 1820 and 1845 the mean size of property holdings dropped from 241 to 178 acres and the median size of property holdings declined from 124 to 66 acres. Among the property holders real wealth became concentrated between 1820 and 1845. As Table 2.5 shows, the poorest third of Stokes County property holders saw its share of the total wealth in the county decline slightly from 6.1 percent in 1820 to 4.5 percent by 1845. By contrast, the wealthiest third of the county's property holders expanded its share of the wealth from 70 percent in 1820 to 73 percent in 1845. However, the middle ranks of property holders suffered only a slight decrease in their share of the wealth, possessing 23.8 percent in 1820 and 23.1 percent in 1845.[11]

The changing economic conditions of the Stokes County countryside had a profound impact on the people of Salem. As the community

TABLE 2.6

Distribution of Wealth in Salem, 1820, 1845

Rank	1820		1845	
	Value	Share	Value	Share
Top Decile	$8,042	31.7%	$13,009	51.1%
Second Decile	3,909	15.4	4,388	17.2
Third Decile	2,800	11.1	3,051	12.0
Fourth Decile	2,700	10.6	2,125	8.3
Fifth Decile	3,230	12.7	1,500	6.0
Sixth Decile	1,018	4.0	330	1.3
Seventh Decile	1,366	5.4	751	2.9
Eighth Decile	1,150	4.5	000	0
Ninth Decile	718	2.8	174	0.7
Tenth Decile	406	1.6	137	0.7

Source: Stokes County, List of Taxables, 1825, 1845, NCDAH.

became more immersed in a broader market economy the distribution of wealth in Salem became more concentrated as some people profited from the new conditions while others suffered losses. As Table 2.6 illustrates, wealth in Salem between 1820 and 1845 became increasingly concentrated at the higher end of the scale. The percentage of propertyless on the tax lists for Salem almost doubled between these years, increasing from 14 to 25 percent. The poorest third of the citizens of Salem suffered as their share of wealth declined from 8.9 percent to 1.4 percent. At the same time the wealthiest third of the community saw their share of wealth increase from 58.2 to 80.3 percent. Significantly, the middle range of property holders, those occupying the fourth through the seventh deciles of wealth distribution, declined from 32.7 percent to 18.5 percent.[12]

A further consequence of involvement in the emerging national economy of the antebellum period was the introduction of manufactured goods from northeastern cities which brought external competition to artisans in the many small communities scattered across the country.[13] Salem's artisans suffered losses from the competition of lower-priced goods arriving from outside the community as the increasing availability of cheaper manufactured goods deterred many in Salem and the surrounding countryside from purchasing the custom-made articles of local craftsmen. Henry Leinbach observed in the early 1830s that demand for custom work in his shoe shop had fallen off, and he increasingly came to rely on retail trade instead of custom-made shoes, producing shoes that were not "spoken for." Becoming more attuned to the changing market Leinbach learned that "exposing shoes to view induces people to buy, otherwise they would not have thought of buying." Despite the efforts of Salem craftsmen like Leinbach to lure customers into their shops, some residents of Salem and Stokes County preferred goods made in the North to locally produced articles. Louisa Belo of Salem wrote her friend Julia Jones in nearby Bethania requesting that Julia order shoes for her when she placed her own order. Louisa favored the shoes of a certain shoemaker at 59 New Street in Philadelphia because these shoes "wear and fit better than any I have ever owned." The effect of these developments was not lost on Salem's artisans. Competition of lower-priced items from manufacturers outside of the community forced Salem craftsmen to cut costs and lower prices to stay in business. Charles Brietz, a Salem tanner, reported to the Aufseher Collegium in 1839 that imported leather sold at lower prices in nearby stores robbed him of his business and forced him to lower his price for finished leather in order to remain competitive.[14]

Salem's artisans faced additional competition from artisans in the Stokes County countryside. During the first half of the nineteenth century Salem's artisans were situated at the center of an expanding region as the northwest North Carolina piedmont grew with new settlers during the second quarter of the nineteenth century. The improvement of transportation facilities and the consequent easier access to markets made the northwest North Carolina piedmont with its small-farm, mixed agriculture economy an attractive region for settlement. From 1820 to 1860 the population growth in Stokes and Forsyth counties outstripped the population increase of North Carolina. The population of Stokes County increased from 14,033 in 1820 to 23,094 (including Forsyth County) in 1860, a 64.6 percent jump. The population of North Carolina grew by 55.4 percent, from 638,829 in 1820 to 992,622 in 1860. The white population of Stokes and Forsyth counties increased from 11,634 in 1820 to 18,557 in 1860, a 59.5 percent increase. Between 1840 and 1860 the white population increased 38.3 percent. While the increased population and enlarged regional market of Stokes and Forsyth counties enhanced Salem's position as a regional commercial center, Salem shopkeepers confronted increased competition from the many artisans among the new settlers. John Conrad, a Stokes County farmer and shoemaker who was not part of the Moravian community at Salem, filled the needs of neighboring yeomen who might otherwise have gone to Salem for their families' shoes and boots. Conrad made and mended shoes for his neighbors for which he received cash or farm commodities as payment.[15] The competition from artisans outside of Salem intensified because these artisans were not constrained in their economic activities by the congregation regulations which governed the conduct of Salem artisans. Consequently, Salem artisans had to compete with artisans who could produce articles at a lower cost, which Charles Brietz had already discovered.

As Salem and its surrounding countryside were integrated into the regional economy, the community was increasingly subject to the cyclical fits and starts of the antebellum national economy which made the goals of security and independence increasingly difficult to meet by traditional means. The downturns in the economy in the late 1820s and early 1840s had a profound impact on the economic fortunes of piedmont farmers, artisans, and shopkeepers. The minister of the Moravian congregation at Salem recorded in the congregation's annual memorabilia that 1827 was a difficult year for the congregation as "hard times" had hit the trade of the village and the community's craftsmen did not do well. The Salem *Weekly Gleaner* in November 1828 reported from the *Niles Register* that in North Carolina "local currency is deranged and money scarce." In the aftermath of the Panic of 1837 in which the national economy went into a depression, business conditions spiraled downward, and the people of Salem and Stokes County suffered the dislocations and hardships of an "almost unexampled depression" in business affairs which was made worse by drought and bad wheat harvests. Many Moravians found themselves in tight financial circumstances and some went bankrupt, including John Leinbach, a prominent member of the congregation at Salem who served many years on the Congregation Council and the Aufseher Collegium. By 1833 Leinbach had accumulated property worth about $2,400 and his holdings included 228 acres of land, an oil mill, a sawmill, cotton gin, and numerous buildings. Leinbach, however, had made some bad business decisions as well as overextended himself, incurring more debt than his income could cover. Leinbach lost all of his property in a sheriff's sale. John Leinbach's son Henry noted that while his father's case unfolded other members of the congregation found themselves in the same circumstances. David Clewell, a bookbinder, was sued for his debts and all of his property was under execution of judgments by the court. Salem shoemaker Emanuel Reich was in debt for about $1,400, and he had nothing but his house, about $100 in outstanding accounts, and $100 in the bank. Philip Reich was in debt upwards of $1,100, all of which was invested in his house, shop, and stock.[16]

While many Salem shopkeepers suffered as the external market economy impinged on the local community, some of the town's ambitious shop masters like William Fries perceived new entrepreneurial possibilities that promoted a worldview quite removed from the congregational vision of cooperation and the subordination of individual interests to the mission of the congregation. Johann Christian Wilhelm Fries arrived in Salem in the fall 1809 from Herrnhut and, after a year and a half as a joiner in the Brothers' House, became the master of the shop. In the fall of 1811, Fries, at the age of thirty-five, married Johanna Elisabeth Nissen and became a member of the congregation as a head of household. Quickly earning the reputation of a respected member of the congregation, he was elected to the Congregation Council in 1815 and to the Aufseher Collegium in 1819 and 1821. By 1819 William Fries acquired a farm, and in that year he reported to the tax collector property of thirty-two acres valued at $150 and a town lot in Salem valued at $400. Four years later Fries's farm had grown to 162 acres valued at $470. By the late 1820s William Fries had accumulated enough capital to make some speculative investments. However, in these investments Fries found only financial troubles which put him in a precarious financial situation and strapped for cash in the late 1820s when one of his investments, the Cape Fear Bank, failed. Fries wrote his son Francis about conditions in Salem that "the times are very bad with us. Our business goes very slowly because money is so scarce."[17] Fries's financial situation in the late 1820s and early 1830s forced him to look for new sources of income which would enable him to continue to improve his status in the community.

Many Salem artisans, whether they were trying to survive in a more competitive market or confidently pursuing new opportunities, responded to the new economic conditions by pursuing individual interests and profits at the expense of the cooperative ethos of the congregation community. These artisans engaged in activities in their shops that did not conform to congregational regulations. Some entered into partnerships in an effort to gain a competitive edge, while others hired slaves to work in their shops. The conduct of some artisans provoked antagonisms among members of the congregation which emerged in the 1830s and 1840s in all areas of community life, but most noticeably in economic affairs. Challenges to the congregational regulation of the trades escalated as the community faced the hard times of the late 1820s and 1830s. During these years many of the shopkeepers of Salem engaged in what the Aufseher Collegium called "secret trading," that is, selling in their shops articles which were deemed by the congregation authorities not to be a legitimate part of the trade of their particular craft or shop. Recognizing the increased incidence of illegal trading the Aufseher Collegium realized that it must take action to maintain the congregational economic order. In February 1829, the Aufseher Collegium held meetings with the adult members of the congregation to discuss openly the issue of illegal trading. The Collegium hoped to convince the Brethren of the congregation that the established economic order in Salem worked to the benefit of the congregation and all of its members. The Elders Conference expressed its fear that if the illegal trading was not checked, the greatest single producer of revenue for the congregation, the diacony store, might be harmed.[18]

William Fries was at the center of a controversy that erupted in 1829, engulfing the whole community and prompting serious doubts regarding the survival of the congregation and its special way of life. In 1826 Fries had acquired the congregation's tobacco shop which he ran in addition to his joiner's shop. Reeling from his losses in the bank stocks and the general downturn in business which put him in a precarious financial situation, Fries looked for a way out of his financial difficulty. By selling a variety of goods in his tobacco shop to increase his income, including glass, coffee, and sugar, Fries found himself in violation of the congregation rules. Hoping to make his activities legal, Fries in August 1829 petitioned the congregation authorities for permission to operate a small store in conjunction with his tobacco shop. Fries's request brought into the open the tensions that smoldered under the surface through most of 1829. The Collegium considered Fries's petition and heard numerous charges against individuals engaged in illegal trading in their shops. Fries accused the widow Elizabeth Rights of operating a dry-goods store in her deceased husband's toy shop. The Single Sisters' workshop was accused of selling calico and dry goods in addition to the millinery permitted. David Clewell was criticized for selling in his shop items not usually associated with either a shoemaker's or bookbinder's shop, including toys, coffee, sugar, dry goods, and other items not permitted him by the trade rules of the village. Papermaker Gottlieb Schober complained that Clewell sold stationery which competed with Schober's paper mill. Schober in turn was accused of selling a variety of goods in addition to the paper he manufactured. The situation was frustrating for the Aufseher Collegium because each shopkeeper justified his or her illegal activities by pointing to the illegal activities of others.[19]

As the Aufseher Collegium deliberated on the situation of the trades, Fries waited anxiously for a reply to his petition to operate a dry-goods store. In the meantime, struggling to regain control of the conduct of business in the community, the Collegium reached agreements with Elizabeth Rights, Gottlieb Schober, and David Clewell, who promised not to sell items that infringed on other shopkeepers' business. The Collegium then considered Fries's request. The congregational authorities refused to be intimidated by Fries's threat that he would rather leave the Salem congregation than be continually troubled by the Collegium's meddling in his business affairs. Confident that Fries could make a good living if he ran his tobacco shop "expediently" and engaged in his actual trade as a joiner, the Aufseher Collegium denied Fries's petition and ordered him to sell only tobacco and glass in his shop. When he protested that he had to sell a wider selection of goods to live and that the Collegium's demands were excessive, Fries was told bluntly he could sell his house and move from Salem to where he could do as he pleased. The Collegium regretted that Fries did not examine his true motives in his behavior and "seek the cause of this troublesome situation of his with himself." Fries's personal ambition to acquire greater wealth, which appeared to become an end in itself, was not in harmony with the interests of the congregation. The Collegium believed that if Fries could not realize this and control his ambition, then he and the congregation would benefit if he left Salem. Both the Aufseher Collegium and the Elders Conference recognized that the only weapon they possessed to address the matter effectively was moral suasion, especially appeals to brotherly love and loyalty to the community and its special ideals. The Collegium and the elders hoped to lead the transgressors back to the faithful execution of their duties as members of a congregation community. But, Fries was unrepentant. In a letter to his son Francis, Fries expressed his true feelings of the situation and his belief that some artisans in Salem no longer placed confidence in the authorities to regulate economic affairs in Salem: "We are well and have nothing to complain of if it was not for the silly Collegium that wants to quarrel with us and others all the time. They are ridiculed in the village and think they are the only wise ones."[20] Within months after the public meetings, the Elders Conference lamented that there was still much secret trading among the Brethren. Undaunted by the denial of his petition, William Fries, demonstrating a greater ambition than could be satisfied by the joiner's trade and a small tobacco shop, pushed ahead with his plans to expand his business endeavors. Fries surreptitiously offered customers of his tobacco shop a variety of "small wares," including coffee, sugar, molasses, spices, nails, glass, and paints.[21]

The congregation authorities found it impossible to break the spirit of private enterprise in Salem. Some members of the governing boards of the congregation like William Fries, David Clewell, and John Christian Blum, those individuals whose lives were expected to provide examples of how members of a congregation community should subordinate private interests to the well-being of the community, frequently violated the trade rules and even advocated the abolition of those rules which restricted private business activities. In the fall of 1831 Salem was divided once more over the issue of trade as the Aufseher Collegium heard complaints of William Fries again engaging in illegal trading. Called again before the Collegium for this trade, Fries petitioned once more for permission to continue this dry-goods trade, but he promised that he would not enlarge this trade by carrying additional items which might compete with the trade of other shopkeepers and artisans in the village. At the same time the Collegium considered John C. Blum's request that he be permitted to sell stationery and books in his print shop. The requests by Fries and Blum prompted other tradesmen in the town to request permission to expand their businesses to carry additional items for sale. Gottlieb Schober again protested encroachments on his business and told the Collegium that if Blum's request was granted then he would have to expand his business along other lines as well, especially since David Clewell continued to sell paper and blank books in his bookbinder's shop. The Collegium had a monumental dilemma to settle as peacefully as possible. It recognized that to allow the free pursuit of individual business endeavors would endanger the concept of a congregational community itself as private interests asserted dominance over congregational interests. If Blum was given permission to sell all the various articles associated with book printing, stationery and blank books primarily, his trade would harm that of Schober and Clewell. If the Collegium acceded to Fries's request and allowed him to sell those goods which he had sold illegally, then more people in the congregation would be hurt as Fries's business infringed on the trade privileges of others.[22]

At its meeting on the evening of November 28, 1831, the Aufseher

Collegium considered the request of Blum and Fries. Against a backdrop of continued secret trading in the community, during the early 1830s meetings of the Aufseher Collegium were often contentious as the issue of "free trade" in the village continually demanded attention. During these years times were difficult for Salem shopkeepers, patience among many of the townspeople was thin, and complaints against shopkeepers who continued to violate the trade rules provoked heated confrontations among the Brethren. Henry Leinbach captured the spirit of these days in his diary where he noted pessimistically in the spring of 1830 of his experience in the Aufseher Collegium, "after an hour and a half's talking the meeting separated without producing anything except warm words." The meetings of the Aufseher Collegium during November 1831 were confrontational, with short tempers and heated words. At the meeting of November 7 Henry Leinbach exchanged "warm words" with fellow Collegium member John C. Blum over the trade issue. According to Leinbach, Blum was for "free trade" in the community — that is, unregulated business activity. Out of frustration and in a fit of rage, Blum, who apparently felt out of touch with other Collegium members on this issue, left the meeting saying that he should resign from his office. Henry Leinbach noted in his diary later that at this meeting: "We had a knotty question before us, which seemed to drag the free trade system at its tail." John Blum, not wanting a confrontation, withdrew his petition. The Collegium then considered Fries's petition. In its deliberations the Collegium referred back to the meetings of August-September 1829 when this issue was debated. At that time the Collegium had stressed the benefits for all and the advantages accruing to the congregation from the congregation diacony. After considerable discussion the Collegium decided to affirm the existing trade regulations and refuse Fries's petition.[23]

Through the 1840s many Salem tradesmen continued to challenge the congregation rules by engaging in illegal trade. Phillip Reich, a Salem tinsmith, complained in September 1845 that Edmund Blum, a coppersmith, sold in his shop tin and iron made by Alex Hauser, who was not a member of the Salem congregation. Reich contended that Blum's illegal trade damaged his tinsmith business. This development surprised the authorities because Blum, who had only recently begun his trade in Salem, was so soon violating the congregation rules. A member of the Aufseher Collegium was sent to discuss the matter with Blum, but it did not appear that Blum intended to discontinue his activities. The authorities reminded Blum that he was granted only the operation of a coppersmithy, and all other activities had to cease. By the middle of October, after continuous pressure from the authorities, Blum promised to sell out and discontinue his trade in tinware. However, by the end of the month another complaint was made against Blum that he continued to engage in the trading of tinwares. In fact, Blum was accused of having just received a resupply of iron sheeting from Fayetteville—an obvious indication that he had no intention of ceasing his illegal trade. Even after being notified that unless he refrained from violating the orders of the Aufseher Collegium he would have to give up his shop, Blum apparently remained undaunted. The tenacity with which Edmund Blum defied congregation authorities and the repeated talk around town that several tradesmen deliberately violated congregation regulations forced the Aufseher Collegium to reassert its control over Salem's economic activities. It was suggested that the Elders Conference settle the matter once and for all by acting in accordance with the congregation rules and excluding from the Salem congregation those who refused to comply with the regulations. The elders of the congregation agreed, but only after those members accused of misconduct were summoned before the Aufseher Collegium, given a "serious" talk, and allowed time to consider their violations and the possible consequences.[24]

In December Blum appeared before the Aufseher Collegium to discuss his refusal to discontinue the trade in iron and tinwares. Blum stated in his defense that he was not able to make a living without trading in iron and tin because there was not enough work as a coppersmith. He did believe, however, that trading in sheet-iron wares belonged to his trade. Blum was willing to give up the tinsmithy if he could make a living as a coppersmith only. The Aufseher Collegium was apparently unimpressed with Blum's explanation and informed him that he would have to give up the iron and tinsmithing trade. Ed Blum was in a difficult position. Not able to make a go of it as a coppersmith alone, he had to find another means of making a living and this put him in direct violation of congregation regulations. To violate the rules meant not only risking the loss of his trade and home in Salem, along with his membership in the community, but also his status as a communicant of the Unitas Fratrum. In this way secular orders were reinforced by spiritual sanctions that were severe penalties for a devout member of the congregation. Facing this disastrous consequence of his actions, Edmund Blum decided to sell his tin supply and restrict his activities to the coppersmith's trade.[25]

The controversy which arose over slaveholding in Salem was part of the larger question regarding the role of individual enterprise in the community. During the first quarter of the nineteenth century there was growing pressure from shop masters to relax the slave rules as an increasing number of Moravians accepted slave labor as important to the prosperity of the trades and the economic success of the community. Through the 1820s and 1830s William Fries was repeatedly at odds with the authorities because of his ownership of slaves. In 1823 Fries was accused of keeping two female slaves in his Salem home which violated the congregation rules prohibiting the employment of slaves in Salem without the permission of the congregation authorities. In March 1831 Fries was accused of purchasing a female slave for the purpose of starting "a kind of Negro speculation" in Salem. Even after the slave rules were relaxed in the 1820s to allow the hiring of slaves as day laborers, individuals like William Fries who sought a larger share of economic autonomy violated the slaveholding regulations with increasing frequency.[26]

The Unitas Fratrum did not regard slavery as, on principle, irreconcilable with church teachings or with Christianity. Slavery was an economic problem rather than a theological issue, and the controversy revolved around the system of labor the congregation would use. Slaves were originally introduced to Salem during the late eighteenth century when free labor did not meet the needs of the congregation. Through the first two decades of the nineteenth century slaves continued to be used where free labor was unwilling to work. In 1811 blacksmith Henry Sensemann, unable to find an apprentice or journeyman to help him in his shop, was permitted by the Aufseher Collegium to hire a slave with blacksmith skills. Moravians also hired slaves to work as farm laborers, domestic servants, and servants in the local tavern which the congregation owned, particularly since young Moravians would not fill positions as servants which carried the stigma of "negro work." A meeting of the heads of households and shop masters in 1814 recognized the need to use slaves in these jobs because "it is not customary to use white persons as hostlers or servants in a tavern, and [it is] also impossible for lack of persons who are willing to serve in these capacities."[27]

Though slaves were allowed in the community when their necessity could be demonstrated, Moravians remained uncomfortable with their presence because of the impact slaves might have on the community. Moravians feared that employing slaves in the trades might take jobs from Moravian youths. Some Salem artisans responded to competitive pressures by lowering the costs of production and employing slaves and apprentices instead of journeymen. But in the early nineteenth century the values of the community in conjunction with the opposition of united artisans prevented other artisans from using cheap sources of labor. In 1816 cabinetmaker J. F. Belo, exasperated with training apprentices only to have them leave his employ when their apprenticeship ended, petitioned the Aufseher Collegium for permission to acquire a young slave to learn cabinetmaking and work permanently in his shop. The Collegium took an unambiguous and unyielding stand, declaring that Belo's plan "would lead to the ruin of our economic constitution." Declaring that it was only right that an apprentice who becomes a journeyman should seek to set up a shop for himself, the Collegium concluded that "anyone who refuses to take apprentices because of this cannot expect us to sacrifice the welfare of the whole town for his benefit." The administrator of the congregation's land stated that if anyone did what Belo proposed he would be obligated to cancel the individual's lease and force him to leave town. In 1819 when Christian Brietz took in a slave youth to teach him tanning, the Collegium ordered Brietz to end the arrangement. Congregation authorities would not allow slaves to displace free labor from the trades.[28]

Moravian authorities also perceived in slavery a threat to the morality of the Moravians and their way of life. Admitting that the limited use of slaves was occasionally necessary, Moravians believed that the presence of slaves in Salem had a pernicious effect on the young people of the congregation. The authorities feared that with widespread use of slave labor in Salem the young women of the congregation would become "work-shy and ashamed of work," and among the young men "there would be increasing difficulty in holding growing boys to the learning of a profession, in restricting them from dangerous tendencies, and in leading them into outward morality and inward growth in good." In 1814 the heads of households and shop masters advised members of the congregation to consider the "seeming advantage . . . and convenience in keeping Negro slaves, with the greater disadvantage to the outer and inner welfare of the congregation."[29] Consequently, the Moravians of Salem had to balance the labor needs of the community with the moral well-being of the congregation.

Cognizant of changing conditions in Salem, community meetings between 1814 and 1847 attempted to adapt the slave rules and make them more relevant to the social and legal realities of North Carolina and the economic circumstances of Salem. Moravian leaders could never ignore that North Carolina law and custom favored ownership of slaves. Consequently, the controversies over slaveholding that arose in Salem during the first half of the nineteenth century marked the continuing efforts of the Moravians to adapt their congregational culture to the society of the North Carolina piedmont. The 1814 meeting, reacting to the fears of many Moravians of the impact of slavery on the congregation community, first unanimously reaffirmed the community's commitment to the spirit of the eighteenth-century rule that prohibited the ownership or hiring of slaves. Then the meeting redefined the rule and made it more flexible to meet present realities by allowing exceptions to be approved by the Aufseher Collegium, the Elders Conference, and the majority of the Congregation Council. The meeting opened the door a little wider to slaveholding by its provision that if necessity is proven, then permission could be granted to hire, but not purchase, slaves.[30]

The effect of the 1814 resolution regarding the slave rules was to encourage the increased employment of slaves in Salem. Between 1816 and 1825 the number of slaves in Salem increased from seventy-nine to ninety-six. By 1820, however, the increased employment of slaves in the trades alarmed the Aufseher Collegium, which proposed new slave rules that addressed the threat to white labor in the congregation. The Collegium proposed that the trades be practiced exclusively by the residents of Salem, that is, the Moravians of the Salem congregation. The Congregation Council adopted this proposal, with new rules to put it into effect, by a vote of forty-three to five. The slave rules adopted in 1820 provided that no slaves were to work as skilled labor in the trades, future petitions to employ a slave in Salem had to specify whether the slave would be owned or hired, and bonds had to be posted to guarantee that the slave would be removed from Salem if the Collegium deemed it necessary. The net effect of the 1820 rules was to recognize the importance of slaves as day laborers and domestic servants. The new rules actually made it easier to employ slaves in Salem as long as the authorities were notified and the appropriate bonds posted.[31]

The gradual loosening of the slave rules encouraged greater use of slaves, which combined with the continued disregard for the slave rules to convince many Moravian leaders of the increasing futility of regulating slave labor in Salem. In February 1845, at a meeting of the Council, textile manufacturer Francis Fries proposed that all slave rules be abolished since he believed they existed only on paper and were continually violated in every respect. Fries's proposal would put everyone on an equal footing with himself and remove an important obstacle to the future growth of his mill by abolishing congregational regulation of the number of slaves he hired and the manner in which he used them.[32] After two decades of discontent and disregard of the slave rules, the Congregation Council attempted to amend the 1820 rules to make them conform more realistically to circumstances in Salem and draft new rules to which the townspeople would adhere. These developments, of course, implied that the existing slave rules were not relevant to community needs in the 1840s.

Francis Fries had received special permission in 1839 to employ slaves as unskilled laborers in his textile mill, though authorities initially balked at Fries's request. Fries had told both the Aufseher Collegium and the Elders Conference that the work done in his Salem mill would be done by laborers who merely tended the machines while the weaving would be done on his father's farm outside of Salem. Fries convinced the authorities that the slaves in the mill would be filling the same positions they always had as unskilled and semiskilled laborers. Hence, according to Fries, his proposal did not violate the congregation's rule that no slave was to be employed in Salem in a trade for the purpose of pursuing or learning that trade. In their search for workable compromise the authorities found this explanation satisfactory and agreed that Fries was not in violation of the 1820 regulations. But the Elders Conference feared that the operation of the mill with slave labor would set a precedent for other proprietors who would want to use slaves rather than the town's young people in their trades. Congregation authorities were careful to note, however, that the permission granted Fries was not to be considered a precedent and they reaffirmed the existing slave rules. Fries wanted to make better use of the labor of several young slaves growing up on his father's farm who "were not earning their board there." But as soon as he was financially able, Fries began to buy slaves of his own.[33]

Ironically, Fries's turn to slave labor was a response to the Aufseher Collegium denying him permission to build boarding houses for the white operatives he hoped to employ in his mill. Congregation authorities by the early 1840s had serious reservations about the influx of more non-Moravians into Salem, but the Aufseher Collegium denied the application for fear of establishing a precedent if the rules were waived to permit one member of the congregation to construct houses on his property for non-Moravian workers. Many in Salem, however, correctly interpreted Fries's proposal as serving Fries's private interests and, after a discussion which included a consideration of the possible harmful impact of slavery on the community, voted down the proposal forty-one to nine. However, two weeks later the Congregation Council addressed the slave rules again and took a firm stand in favor of slave labor in Salem in rejecting a resolution, by a vote of thirty-six to three, that no more slaves, owned or hired, be brought into Salem.[34]

For the Moravians 1845 was a critical year. As the votes in the Congregation Council demonstrate, the congregation was divided over the issue of slave labor in Salem. A majority in the congregation favored the regulated use of slaves in the town, while an influential minority led by Francis Fries advocated the unregulated use of slave labor. Still a small minority remained against any slaves in Salem. When in February 1845 the Congregation Council reaffirmed the 1820 slave rules five members of the Collegium, all of whom favored little or no regulation of slaves, resigned from the Collegium. Between 1845 and 1847 few slaveholders agreed to serve on the Aufseher Collegium where they would have to enforce the slave rules. Exasperated by the futility of attempting to amend the slave rules to please the majority of the community, and frustrated by the continued disregard for the rules, the Elders Conference turned to the central governing body of the Unitas Fratrum, the Unity Elders Conference in Berthelsdorf, Germany, for its opinion on the slave issue and for advice on how the congregation rules could be enforced. In July 1845 the Unity Elders Conference replied that the Aufseher Collegium, the Elders Conference, and the Congregation Council of Salem should stand firm with the congregation rules and meet violations of the rules with the termination of leases. The Elders Conference in Salem, in accordance with the recommendations from the Unity Elders Conference, admonished the Collegium to enforce the rules firmly.[35]

The instructions of the Unity Elders Conference temporarily defused the slave rules controversy. However, active consideration of the issue was revived at a meeting of the Congregation Council in January 1847, when a proposal was offered to abolish the slave rules of 1820. By this proposal anybody would be able to employ any number of slaves in

Salem without having to post bonds. Since the congregation retained some control over the conduct of residents by the lease agreements householders signed which obligated them to abide by the decisions of the Aufseher Collegium and the Elders Conference, the congregation boards still could set guidelines that determined how slaves might be employed and those slaveholders who did not abide by the decisions could lose their leases. The boards could still regulate the participation of slaves in trades and expel slaves for misconduct, but those who wanted to own or hire slaves no longer needed the prior permission of the Aufseher Collegium. The proposal passed the January 8 meeting of the Congregation Council by a vote of twenty-three to one. A second meeting however revealed the deep divisions in the congregation regarding the slavery issue. With more townspeople in attendance the resolution was sustained, but by a closer margin, in a vote of thirty-one to twenty. By the 1840s, however, the community consensus regarding the employment of slaves in Salem was changing as Moravian shopkeepers came to believe that the freedom to own and employ slaves in the workshops of Salem was critical to economic expansion in the community. Hence with the eventual abolition of the rules pertaining to slaveholding in Salem, the Moravians purchased entrepreneurial freedom with a greater commitment to slave labor as the change in the slave rules allowed Moravian slaveholders more freedom to own and employ slaves. Francis Fries turned increasingly to slave labor in his mill afterwards. Forced to rely more heavily on slaves in his mill, Fries by 1850 owned twenty-three slaves and ten years later the F. and H. Fries Company owned forty-seven. Thus, slaves made up about one-half of Fries's mill work force.[36] For Fries the slave rules had been an impediment to the operation of his woolen mill.

The experience of the Moravian community of Salem points to contradictions in antebellum southern society. By the late antebellum period the "tentacles of capitalism" were gripping many areas of the South, bringing new ways of thinking and acting and a new worldview. Among those Salem artisans and incipient entrepreneurs, like Francis Fries, who challenged the congregation's regulation of slaveholding and led to the revision of the slave rules, there was a growing commitment to the liberal values of individual freedom, private property rights, and the pursuit of personal economic opportunities free of external restraints at the same time as there was a greater commitment to slavery. The individual's unrestrained right to own slaves was a driving force in the reform of the congregational order in Salem. Francis Fries demonstrated the belief that the unregulated freedom to own and employ slaves in pursuit of profits represented the freedom to use one's property without interference from other individuals or congregational agencies. Hence Fries did not regard his property rights in his slaves as conditional on the rules of the congregation; rather they represented absolute property rights which were necessary for profitable business enterprise. For Fries the commitment to the unregulated ownership and employment of slaves meant that his individual rights were primary while duty or obligation to the rules of the congregation was secondary.[37] In challenging the slave rules Francis Fries attempted to establish the preconditions for entrepreneurial success in an economy that was becoming increasingly market directed.

Once the slave regulations were abolished, it was easier for shopkeepers to question the efficacy of other aspects of the congregational order in Salem, in particular those rules that regulated trade. In a discussion in December 1837 that resulted from the decision to turn over the two congregation stores to individuals to be run as private enterprises, the Aufseher Collegium considered whether Salem citizens were permitted to open stores "on their own risk and account" after the two congregation stores had been sold. The congregation regulations, which all adult male members of the congregation had signed and were thus obliged to obey, stated that "nobody is permitted to carry on a trade of any kind or any other business without having reported his intentions, ways and means, his limits etc. to the Collegium and the Elders Conference, and has obtained permission by both conferences." The Collegium believed that up until this time the rules had been observed, though with some difficulty in recent years as William Fries's behavior illustrates. The Collegium maintained that it was obligated to safeguard the right of each Brother who had established himself in his trade, and who would suffer great loss if too many Brethren were permitted to establish themselves in the same trade. But with Salem's deeper embeddedness in a regional market, the regulations became a symbol of a past era when the community was a congregation with a mission in the wilderness. An alternative for an artisan who was not prospering in his trade was to abandon the trade for a more lucrative endeavor. Some Salem craftsmen realized that there were greater profits to be made in merchandising than in artisanal production, as the experience of Edward Belo demonstrated. In July 1840 Edward Belo, a joiner, petitioned the Aufseher Collegium for permission to open a dry-goods store. The authorities realized that Belo was apparently having some difficulty making a living at his trade, but they were concerned that if Belo opened a store he would probably harm the business of the already established shopkeepers who, in self-defense, would begin to sell articles reserved for the artisans. Such a development would further undermine the "good old order" of each trade operating within its established bounds. The question of Belo's application was presented to a conference of the shopowners of Salem because of the interest several master craftsmen had in its outcome. The conference advised the Aufseher Collegium that the store had to be considered on an equal footing with the other trades and that merchants as well as other tradesmen would have to keep within the bounds of their trades to avoid harming each other's business. The Aufseher Collegium had to consider also whether another store could exist in Salem. Since it was believed that the town could support another store and that Belo would not have to borrow much capital to begin business, the authorities consented, with the conditions that Belo give up his joiner trade and not enter into a partnership with any stranger or person living outside of the community.[38]

Because Salem's artisans and entrepreneurs, like William Fries and his son Francis, sought an unfettered freedom to respond to economic opportunities and pursue profits, it was quite apparent to a growing number of Moravians that the old regulations would have to be modified or abandoned if the town's economy was to adjust to the emerging market economy. In January 1849 the congregation authorities faced up to the changing economic conditions that made Salem's special way of life difficult to maintain. As the Congregation Council considered the efficacy of the rules governing the trades in the community, it recognized that those rules, broken repeatedly in recent years, had become little more than a dead letter. The Council also understood that "present day conditions" made it difficult to enforce the rules without causing great hardship for many members of the community. The Council saw that, in part, this state of affairs resulted from the increased availability of manufactured goods which could be sold more cheaply than local artisans could produce them. Consequently, many items were available in Salem and the nearby countryside which were produced in factories, whereas once they could only have been the product of a "specialized trade"—that is, an artisan shop. Given this state of affairs, a citizens' committee proposed the abolition of the trade regulations. When the Congregation Council considered the regulations, forty of the fifty congregation members present voted to abolish all the rules regulating the conduct of the trades and to guarantee complete freedom of trade. Thus, individuals who wished to open a shop in Salem no longer needed the permission of the Aufseher Collegium and the Elders Conference.[39]

The abolition of the trade rules allowed some Salem craftsmen to turn to the more profitable business of merchandising. By 1850 the number of merchants in Salem had doubled, rising from three in 1840 to six. The significance of these new merchants is demonstrated by their role as middlemen in commercial relations between producers and consumers. Increasingly, by mid-century, the people of Salem and the neighboring countryside turned to merchants who offered a wide variety of goods for cash sale or barter. Salem merchants Boner and Crist, Edward Belo, and A. T. Zevely offered residents of Salem and the neighboring countryside a wide assortment of goods which not so long before had been acquired from local artisans or made in the home. Advertisements in the Salem *People's Press* illustrate the growing sophistication in consumer tastes and the demand for more luxury goods. In September 1851 Edward Belo advertised spring and summer goods "which have been selected . . . in all the important considerations of quality, style, and prices." Belo's stock included "Gentlemen's, Youth's and Boys wear" such as "French vest of [English], Belgian and American cloths of all grades and colors; Cassimeres, Sattinets, Tweeds, Jeans, French and English Drab D'Etes, cassimerettes . . . Satin, silk, marseilles and cotton vestings . . . silk and linen [handkerchiefs]; fancy and plain silk, linen and cotton cravats and ties." For women, Belo offered "Ladies Dress Goods" of "Great variety, which in point of magnificence, quality and richness of style, stands unrivalled." The stock included "rich chamelion black, mode and fancy colored silk, foulard and Florence silk, silk poplins and lustre . . . high colored, taney, figured and plain Thibet cloths mohair lustre, mou-lin de lains . . . " To satisfy a growing demand for well-made stylish goods from the North, the firm of Boner and Crist advertised a "large, fashionable and varied stock of Fall and Winter Goods" received direct from New York, Philadelphia, and Baltimore. Boner and Crist offered its customers not only "Ready-made clothing" but also "A Large Stock of China, Glass and Queensware, Hardware, Cutlery . . . and Northern Castings."[40]

By the late 1840s the majority of adult male members of the community were ready to change the rules on slaveholding and the congregation regulation of business activities. Some of the town's ambitious shop masters recognized new opportunities in the broader market which stretched beyond Stokes County. The entrepreneurial spirit that emphasized innovation and profit seeking was evident in Charles Brietz, Edward Belo, and Francis Fries who in 1845 resigned from the Aufseher Collegium over the enforcement of the slave rules. These entrepreneurs engaged in varied business activities for the purpose of making profits for themselves. Brietz, also a slaveowner, was a tanner who by 1850 had expanded into shoemaking. Belo, a cabinetmaker, owned a foundry, an oil mill, and a dry-goods store. In 1850 Belo owned four slaves, which he increased to eleven by 1860. By 1859 Belo was reported to be worth between $40,000 and $50,000 and to own real estate valued at about $10,000. Francis Fries owned and operated a textile mill that was capitalized at $55,400 and employed forty-seven operatives, as well as a paper mill, a tannery, and a general store. In 1847 Fries was listed in the tax rolls as the owner of two lots in Salem valued at $4,500 and nine slaves. In 1859 he was reported by the R. G. Dun and Company to be worth between $75,000 and $100,000. Fries took a leading role in promoting transportation improvements that connected Salem to the regional and national markets. Fries was one of the "prime movers" who initiated and built the Fayetteville and Western Railroad which connected Salem to Fayetteville on the Cape Fear River. He was an original investor in and director of the North Carolina Railroad in the 1850s. Francis Fries's attitude toward life provides insight into a way of thinking that diverged radically from the communal ethos of Christian brotherhood the Moravians valued. His was an attitude of complete self-absorption and individualism. Fries wrote:

> I owe my success in business to economy, unceasing perseverance and industry in giving to every detail my personal attention. Early in life I never attended to anything that I did not consider my own business . . . nor to look after public matters, nor the concerns of individuals, further than they were in connection with my own affairs. I relied on myself, I depended upon myself, I took care of myself.[41]

Those shopkeepers who challenged the congregational rules that regulated trade in Salem won increasing support from the congregation's young men. In the 1820s and 1830s William Fries and John C. Blum were repeatedly elected to the Aufseher Collegium, and in the 1840s Francis Fries emerged as the respected leader of the younger men in the community. Those who challenged the congregation's regulation of trade expressed the frustration of the young men who saw few prospects for themselves in Salem. Many of them believed that the trade rules impeded their opportunity to establish themselves as proprietors and householders in the congregation. During the late 1820s and 1830s many young Moravians were forced to leave Salem due to the lack of opportunities for them there and emigrate to other communities. Single Brother Charles Kramer, who worked as a journeyman saddlemaker in the shop of Henry Herbst, was forced to leave Salem in the fall of 1829 and go to nearby Lexington to find work in his trade when Herbst could no longer employ him. The Aeltesten Conferenz lamented that on completion of their apprenticeships many of the congregation's young men experienced difficulty in finding a position as a journeyman in a Salem shop and were forced to "go out into the world and are lost to the congregation." The situation continued into the 1840s. Between 1838 to 1847 only 40 percent of Salem's apprentices listed in the congregational records remained in the town working as journeymen or masters in the trades to which they apprenticed. The situation was frustrating for the young men in the congregation and during the mid-1830s that frustration erupted into open opposition to the elders of the congregation. In January 1834 the young men caucused and put together a slate of candidates which they supported for election to the Aufseher Collegium. Their ticket carried the day and the incumbents, with the exception of Henry Leinbach, were turned out, while new men, among them Francis Fries, were put on the Collegium.[42] Those newly elected tended to be younger members of the congregation as well as shopkeepers who had in the past challenged the regulation of business activity.

Of course, not everyone in Salem embraced the new order that was emerging in the community during the 1830s and 1840s. Other Moravian artisans in the community, however, uncomfortable with the market economy and its ethos of risk-taking private acquisitiveness, remained loyal to the special way of life of the Moravian congregation that emphasized harmony, brotherhood, and the subordination of private interests to the common well-being of the congregation. After the resolution abolishing the slave rules passed, a number of townspeople attending the meeting of the Council expressed their belief that matters in the congregation town had degenerated to the point that "many Brethren let themselves be guided merely by their own private interests, and that therefore everybody objects stubbornly to any regulation, which would hamper his private interests." The minister of the Salem congregation prayed that, "We may through grace keep in view the high goal of our calling to be a congregation of Jesus which first acts according to the kingdom of God and his righteousness . . . and may not judge merely from worldly interest." Henry Leinbach spoke eloquently for those who opposed the changes occurring in Salem and who hoped to preserve the congregational way of life. The tensions that rended the congregational community during these years as well as his father's financial troubles prompted Leinbach to comment in 1834 that "it appears there is little love among us any more [sic], indeed I strongly suspect that as a communion we will not hold together long. . . . Times are hard, and many people do not do as they wish others to do unto them." Leinbach understood the essence of the transformation that was coming over many Moravians in Salem and observed that "where money comes in play, our Brotherly love forsakes us immediately."[43] This telling indictment of the community revealed the changing ethos that directed the lives of a growing number of Moravians in Salem.

In contrast to William Fries and his son Francis, Henry Leinbach and the townspeople who expressed their concern for the changes that occurred in Salem represented a commitment to the old order that valued the sense of a special community united by a single vision of brotherly love and the subordination of private interests to the mission of the congregation—the service of God. Leinbach remained a shoemaker, working alongside his journeymen and farming his fifty-one acres outside of Salem. A man of modest wealth, he never owned a slave. Along with a decreasing minority of townspeople in Salem at mid-century, Leinbach was not led merely by the pursuit of financial gain, though financial security for his family was not unimportant, but he continued to keep before him a sense of and a commitment to what he believed were more important social and cultural goals.[44] Embracing a precapitalist mentalité that valued security and independence and abhorred unnecessary risk in the pursuit of profits, Henry Leinbach valued the love and harmony of the congregational community more than the profits and wealth of capitalist business endeavor that drove William and Francis Fries.

Salem was changing rapidly after 1825, moving from the theocratic congregation village united by a single religious ideal and social ethos to a secular commercial town caught up in an extensive trading network. By the late 1840s, a consensus had emerged in Salem that fundamental changes in the character of the community were due. Divisive tensions over the regulation of trade and limits on the ownership and employment of slaves in the village shops generated the energy for fundamental changes in the Moravian community. Promoting individual autonomy at the expense of communal values, Salem's artisans sought to remove economic activity from congregational regulation so that the individual might utilize capital, land, and labor as economic conditions demanded, a freedom that was essential for capitalist economic development. These artisans reacted to the emergence of a market economy by questioning the efficacy of the traditional way of life in a congregational community. Leading this transformation to a new moral economy with new ways of behavior were the town's ambitious shopowners and entrepreneurs like William Fries, Francis Fries, and Edward Belo; their identity as Moravian was complemented by an awareness of themselves as autonomous individuals driven by their ambition to acquire private wealth. In the community that was emerging by mid-century, the market assumed greater importance than congregational agencies as an instrument of social discipline and character modification, producing individuals who were rational and calculating in pursuit of profits.[45] Taking their cue from the market, these men looked to new money-making ventures by which to increase their wealth.

CHAPTER THREE

Manufacturing and Community in Salem

As the Moravians considered the efficacy of congregational regulation of business affairs, several of the ambitious entrepreneurs of Salem, among them Francis Fries, John Christian Blum, and Edward Belo, saw a new future for the community in textile manufacturing. These men advocated the establishment of a mill and made the initial capital investment. By investing in Salem's first textile mill these entrepreneurs expressed an early confidence in manufacturing and a deeper involvement in an economy that extended beyond the boundaries of Salem and its neighborhood. Like the contemporaneous effort to limit church control of economic activity, the mill-building campaign in Salem was a response to new challenges and the pursuit of new opportunities. Driven by the need to revitalize the village economy in the 1830s, prominent Moravians in Salem responded to popular claims in the South that textile manufacturing offered impressive profits as well as the opportunity to stimulate the lagging economy of the region.[1] The decision to build a textile mill in Salem had a profound effect on the Moravian community as the introduction of textile manufacturing brought large numbers of non-Moravians into the community and eventually altered the community culture of Salem.

During the early summer of 1836 several of the townspeople of Salem pondered whether a cotton factory might bring greater prosperity to their community. Those Moravians with the financial resources to invest in the stock of a textile mill were lured by the expectation of handsome dividends, especially as cotton prices after the mid-1830s plunged. Across the

South as the price of cotton fell entrepreneurs seeking new investment opportunities were lured to manufacturing by improving transportation facilities that made the movement of manufactured articles less costly, as well as by the high prices for textiles, and capital began to flow into textile mills.[2] In Salem, mill advocates argued that the proposed textile mill offered important benefits to the community, especially as mill hands with cash in their pockets from the regular wages earned in the mill brought relief for the depressed trades in the community. Several well-attended meetings of interested investors were held in June and articles of association were drawn up. A committee was appointed to look into the proposal further, secure additional information about a spinning mill, and consider a prospective site for the mill. The committee located what it believed was the best site for the mill in a field just west of Salem beside the recently laid out Shallowford Street which it hoped might be acquired from the congregation and held in fee simple (i.e., legally purchased) rather than on lease.[3]

The congregation authorities moved cautiously during the summer and fall of 1836 on the mill proposal. Though wary of the precedent established by allowing the mill to hold property in the congregation town in fee simple, the Aufseher Collegium relented and offered two and one-half acres on the proposed site west of the town to be held in fee simple. Congregation authorities regarded this as an extraordinary arrangement and not a precedent, since the factory was meant to promote trade in Salem. However, the congregation authorities believed it wise that the Congregation Diacony should maintain firm control over the mill by acquiring substantial stock in the company. When the Salem Manufacturing Company made its original issue of 250 shares of stock at $200 a share, Theodore Shulz, the warden of the congregation, subscribed for one hundred shares in the congregation's name which made the Salem Congregation Diacony the largest stockholder. The balance of the stock was acquired by twenty-nine citizens of Salem. Among the largest shareholders in Salem's first industrial venture were planter and physician Dr. Frederic Schuman, printer John Blum, joiner and merchant Edward Belo, William Fries, and Francis Fries.[4]

Not all members of the community were enthusiastic about the mill as some villagers were not convinced of the benefits of textile manufacturing in Salem. Instead, they regarded the mill as a threat to the Moravian way of life, fearing the mill's impact on the morality and institutions of the community as large numbers of non-Moravians would come as mill operatives. The creation of a manufacturing enterprise under private control and largely independent of congregational direction provided further evidence to some that the special Moravian congregation community was changing forever. These concerns found official expression in a resolution passed by the Elders Conference in November 1837 as the Salem Manufacturing Company mill was about to open. Since the mill was located on land held in fee simple adjacent to the congregation village the Elders feared that "great hindrances could accrue to the observance of our Congregation Regulations and Congregation Discipline." Addressing these fears the Aufseher Collegium inserted into the deed transferring the land to SMC a clause, "that nothing is to be permitted on the premises of the cotton factory which is counter to the letter and the spirit of the Congregation Regulations of the settlement of Salem."[5] Opposition to textile manufacturing in Salem was much like initial opposition to the early mills in other communities. Rural communities in Massachusetts were ambivalent toward early mills as many townspeople not employed in the mills saw the manufacturing establishments imposing "novel and unpleasant pressures on their lives." In Salem, however, the proponents of textile manufacturing and the mill owners were members of the Moravian congregation, and the mill was regarded by most as promoting the community's economic interests. So local antagonisms over issues regarding the mill were generally muted, though there were some controversies over the mill's use of slaves, water, and woodlands.[6]

Despite this ambivalence there was enthusiasm for benefits the mill supposedly offered the community. This enthusiasm enabled the stockholders of the Salem Manufacturing Company to accumulate a capital investment of $50,000 and set out to build a mill in the summer and fall of 1836. The building committee appointed by the stockholders initially sent inquiries to machinery manufacturers in Baltimore, Paterson, New Jersey, and Pittsburgh concerning steam-driven machinery for the mill. On August 6 the building committee sent Francis Fries north to gather information on the equipment the mill required and the machinery available. The committee gave Fries $72.50 for down payments on machinery and instructions to select a steam engine of sufficient power to run 2,160 spindles and thirty-five looms. Fries was instructed to go to Petersburg to gather all possible information from the mills there which might be useful for the Salem mill, including recommendations of engine manufacturers and machinists. Francis Fries returned to Salem in late September and presented to the building committee contracts he had made in the north.

Fries had engaged the firm of Goodwin Clarke and Company of Paterson, New Jersey, for textile machinery. He had negotiated a contract with Watchman and Bratt of Baltimore for a steam engine with power sufficient to drive two thousand spindles and from thirty to forty looms.[7]

After a year of construction under the direction of Francis Fries, who became the superintendent, the mill was almost ready to begin operation in the fall of 1837, and the building committee began recruiting operatives for the mill. The skilled men needed to set the machinery in operation and supervise the operatives who tended the throstles and looms were engaged first. Dependent on the expertise of skilled machinists from the North, there being few southerners with this skill, SMC wrote to its contacts among the northern merchants and machinery manufacturers requesting the names of men who were likely candidates to be supervisors in the mill. The board of directors hired Thomas Siddall, a highly recommended Englishman working as a carder in Philadelphia, as the principal machinist. The board of directors offered Siddall a two-year contract with a salary of $900 a year plus $100 a year for board. In October Siddall arrived in Salem with his family and set about installing the machinery. Siddall recognized immediately his importance to SMC, and from the beginning he was able to use his knowledge of textile manufacturing and the threat of withholding that knowledge to improve his situation with the mill. When his contract expired in 1840 the board of directors was anxious to keep Siddall. In his new contract the board of directors gave Siddall fifteen shares of stock not only to keep him with SMC but "also in order to cause him to feel if possible a more lively interest in the welfare of the company."[8]

On November 29, 1837, the SMC mill spun its first yarn. In the beginning, when all of the machinery on hand was put into operation, the mill ran 1,032 spindles turning off about five hundred pounds of yarn per day or three thousand pounds per week and employed about thirty-five to forty operatives. The SMC mill was much like many mills that opened in the Carolinas during the 1830s, three- or four-story brick buildings spinning yarn and weaving some cloth for a regional market. In 1840 the Salem mill ran two thousand spindles and was capitalized at $53,000. By contrast, the average North Carolina mill ran 1,917 spindles, employed forty-nine hands, and was capitalized at $39,812. The average New England mill operated 2,222 spindles, employed sixty-nine operatives, and was capitalized at $51,827. In 1849, after eleven years of operation, the SMC mill was capitalized at $80,000, ran twenty-five

TABLE 3.1
*Profit and Loss of Salem Manufacturing
Company, 1841–49*

	February	August
1841	+2,575.65	-4,320.60
1842	+1,665.04	+3,409.59
1843	+859.83	+639.01
1844	+2,690.13	+3,073.13
1845	+1,796.56	+4,581.39
1846	+3,446.01	+3,095.21
1847	+1,920.71	+2,955.79
1848	-2,156.32	N/A
1849	-1,408.64	-840.32

Sources: SMC, General Meetings, March 14, October 30, 1841; January 29, April 2, October 8, November 5, 1842; April 8, October 28, 1843; March 23, October 5, 1844; March 29, October 11, 1845; March 11, September 26, 1846; April 17, October 2, 1847; March 18, 1848; March 24, November 30, 1849, Fries Mills Collection, Moravian Archives.

hundred spindles and thirty looms, and employed seventeen males and eighty-four females.[9]

The chances were greater for failure than success in the early attempts at manufacturing since there were many obstacles to overcome. The twelve years that SMC operated were difficult for the corporation and its stockholders. Excessive competition created by the opening of so many mills in North Carolina during the late 1830s and early 1840s and the rising cotton prices of the late 1840s squeezed profits. In the first three years of its operation SMC found favorable conditions in which demand for yarn was brisk, cotton prices were relatively low, and income generated by the mill's operation was sufficient to allow the addition of more spindles plus new looms to expand production to meet the demand for yarn and cloth. These conditions enabled SMC to realize a profit of $7,213.34 in 1838, its first year of operation. Despite its initial success, however, the company's financial condition was not as solid as the first years may have indicated. While, as Table 3.1 illustrates, SMC generated operating profits between 1841 and 1847, the mill failed to generate sufficient income to cover both the purchase of cotton and the losses resulting from the bad debts of the mill's consignees. In October 1841 the company showed an operating loss of $4,320.60 for the first half of the year and borrowed a total of $9,000 that year to purchase cotton. In

January 1842 SMC borrowed another $6,000 for cotton purchases, which was followed by additional loans of $3,000 each in April and October and $12,000 in November. During the early years these loans appeared to make good business sense while raw cotton prices were declining, yarn prices were stable, and SMC's yarn and cloth were selling. But, every year through 1849, SMC repeatedly borrowed thousands of dollars to finance purchases of cotton and to alter machinery to produce more coarse yarn or fine yarn to meet the demand of an always-changing market. A glutted market in yarn in the late 1840s further complicated the financial situation of SMC as the prices for yarns dropped drastically. In the fall of 1848 yarn was priced at seventy-five cents per bunch, down from ninety cents, and by the spring of 1849 it was at sixty-five cents.[10]

SMC's difficulties were compounded by the inexperienced and unwise decisions of its management. Mill agents who followed Francis Fries were not astute in marketing the mill's products. Agent William Leinbach, who had little mill management experience, was rebuked in 1841 by the board of directors when he entered into secret contracts with two area merchants for the delivery of ten thousand bunches of yarn "at prices ruinous to the concern." Much of SMC's local trade was conducted in barter as neighboring farmers traded agricultural products like wool, feathers, beeswax, and tallow for yarn and cloth. The mill in turn sold these commodities along with its yarn and cloth. However, Leinbach had taken in barter large amounts of feathers and wool at prices considerably higher than these commodities would bring when sold. Furthermore, throughout its life SMC's management extended credit too freely to consignees who sold the mill's yarn and cloth in the Carolinas, Tennessee, Philadelphia, and New York. In 1846 the financial condition of the mill was further compounded when the firm of Danforth and Hoopes, SMC's important consignee in Philadelphia, failed, owing "large sums" which raised SMC's liabilities by about $10,000. In the fall of 1847 the stockholders of SMC instructed their mill agent Constantine Banner to visit the mill's consignees in western North Carolina and Tennessee to collect debts owed the company. Two years later, in November 1849, the stockholders, alarmed that debtors to the company had "increased considerably," observed that Banner, a man of only brief experience in the textile mill, had not properly carried out instructions and urged upon him "to use all possible diligence" in collecting outstanding debts to SMC. By 1848 the situation of SMC appeared "to be drawing towards a crisis." During the first half of 1849 the mill lost approximately $1,300, and debts owed the company had "increased considerably," by about $2,000.[11]

As early as 1845 many recognized the faltering condition of the Salem Manufacturing Company and that the future held little hope of profitable returns on the stockholders' investment. Indeed the risks were becoming too steep for those Moravians apprehensive of the congregation's major stake in the mill. Fearful of the danger of fire which might destroy the company's assets and aware of the gradual depreciation of the expensive machinery in the mill, the congregation's leaders were concerned about the responsibilities of the stockholders to the company's creditors as well as to the financial health of the congregation as principal stockholder. In August 1849 the mill was dealt a serious blow when one of the boilers burst, causing considerable damage to the engine and shutting the mill from early August to mid-November. The mill's situation was made more difficult by the rising price of cotton as prices for yarn dropped. In November 1849 the board of directors observed that the mill had about four to six weeks' supply of cotton on hand. But with cotton selling for ten cents a pound and yarn selling for not more than fifteen cents a pound, the board questioned whether it was prudent for the mill to continue operation. The stockholders were convinced that the company could hardly continue operation without any reasonable expectation of improvement. The decision was made in November 1849 to discharge the hands, collect the debts, pay the liabilities, and sell the mill. Advertisements for the mill were placed in the *National Intelligencer*, the *North Carolina Standard* in Raleigh, the *Fayetteville Observer*, the *Salisbury Carolina Watchman*, and a Charlotte newspaper. The revival of agriculture in the late 1840s and early 1850s which brought higher cotton prices shifted interest away from manufacturing, and, as the board reported to SMC's stockholders, "manufacturing interests are day by day depreciating in our country." However, in March 1854, after almost a year of negotiating, the stockholders sold the mill to Governor John M. Morehead for $9,100.[12]

The ambitions of SMC's stockholders to revitalize the local economy far exceeded the capacity of the enterprise for success, especially as SMC expanded too rapidly and its expenses outstripped its capital resources. But the failure of SMC was typical of many mills during the early years of industrialization. Insufficient capitalization, combined with incompetent or inexperienced management, caused many mill failures in the North and South during the first half of the nineteenth century. William

Gregg, the antebellum South Carolina mill pioneer, attributed the failure of so many mills to the unwise selection of machinery, insufficient capitalization, and the lack of reliable, efficient, and cheap motive power. A common mistake was overambition, as these early mills attempted to operate on too large a scale given their limited capital resources. Manufacturers who had the patience to start small and grow slowly as their resources allowed, who were innovative and able to create and hold together a network of kinsmen, business associates, and workers, usually survived and built lasting manufacturing companies. Francis Fries successfully followed this formula, making few of the errors that sank SMC.

In 1840 Fries left his position as agent of the SMC mill and, in partnership with his father, planned a steam-powered mill where wool would be carded and prepared for spinning and weaving by the wives and daughters of the area's farmers in their homes, or by slaves on William Fries's plantation outside of Salem.[13] Custom carding, however, proved only a seasonal business, leaving Fries's carding machinery idle much of the time. To keep his machinery fully utilized, Fries expanded the mill by adding spinning and weaving equipment. As his business grew, dyeing equipment and a fulling mill were added. By 1842 Fries was offering a "good assortment of wools, common yarn, stocking yarn ready twisted, and cheap lindseys, and cloths of different colors, qualities and prices." In 1843 Fries added a heavy jean that became the mainstay of his line. Henry Fries joined his brother in the mill and the firm became F. and H. Fries in 1846. Though the firm remained small, employing only seven whites and sixteen slaves in 1847, the business was growing. Francis Fries traveled extensively through the Carolinas and Georgia securing orders for his mill and buying wool. By 1860 F. and H. Fries employed seventy-seven operatives and produced $87,300 in woolen and cotton goods in a market that extended from New York through the South, including consignees in Mississippi, Louisiana, and Texas.[14] With the success of the F. and H. Fries mill, textile manufacturing took root in Salem and propelled the community toward its industrial future.

Textile manufacturing introduced into the Moravian community new modes of production, a new method of organizing labor, and a large, mostly non-Moravian, work force. The Salem Manufacturing Company was the first manufacturing enterprise in the community to concentrate a large semiskilled work force, primarily women and children, in one location for the purpose of mechanized production. There was genuine curiosity among the townspeople about the new order of production which

Fig. 3.1. Francis Fries, son of William Fries, first mill agent of the Salem Manufacturing Company and founder of F. and H. Fries Company. Courtesy of the North Carolina Division of Archives and History.

the mills introduced into the village. The SMC mill stimulated much interest in Salem when it opened in the fall of 1837. In the afternoon of New Year's Day 1838, "large numbers" of the people of Salem strolled down Shallowford Street to the edge of town for their first glimpse inside of the new mill. Management proudly showed off the mill, leaving open the doors and shutters so that the curious could hear the clicking and clacking of the steam-powered spinning frames and observe the systematic order of production as the mill hands, the large majority of whom were strangers to the Moravian community, busily tended to their tasks.[15] The fascination of the townspeople with the mill was in part due to the hopes that textile manufacturing would revitalize the stagnant local economy. But the townspeople were fascinated also because the mill represented an important departure from traditional ways of life and work prevalent in a rural, preindustrial society. The opening of a textile mill in Salem introduced a labor force that differed greatly from that found in the town's artisan shops. The most striking difference was that the mill work force was made up of so many women and children. And the size of the mill work force attracted the Moravians' attention, as many more people worked in the mill than in any single shop in the village. All of the mill's workers were gathered under one roof, enclosed and protected from the natural variabilities of the piedmont climate. Surrounded by the relentless roaring of the steam boiler and the din of the spinning frames, the mill hands tended to their assigned tasks without break or letup in the pace of the machinery. The concentration of non-Moravian workers in both the SMC mill, and later the Fries mill, barely one-half mile from Salem square posed a distinct counterpoint to the congregation town. The life-style and work routines of operatives on "Factory Hill" diverged greatly from what the Moravians had known in their own experiences. The textile mill created in Salem an industrial labor force, mostly white females, centralized in one location, possessing few skills, receiving low wages, dependent on mill management for housing and board, and with little hope of improving their status.

The opening of the Salem mills created an immediate need for operatives. The type of labor used in southern mills depended on what was available in a particular locality, as some mills used all white labor, some all slaves, while many used a combination of both. The managers of the Salem mills, like other mill superintendents across the South, looked to the nearby countryside for prospective employees. Hence most of Salem's mill hands came from the nearby rural neighborhoods of Stokes County,

TABLE 3.2
Sex Distribution of Salem Manufacturing
Company Operatives

	1841	1845	1849
Males	28	28	17
Females	128	116	84
Total	156	144	101

Sources: 1840 Census, Population Schedule manuscript microfim, Stokes County, North Carolina; Francis Fries Memorandum Book, December 30, 1837, F. and H. Fries Collection, Moravian Archives; SMC, General Meetings, January 1, 1838, Fries Mills Collection, Moravian Archives; SMC, Board and Wage Books, 1841–49, Fries Mills Collection, Moravian Archives.

though some came from neighboring Guilford, Davie, and Davidson counties. The families of John Brown and William Collins came from the Stokes County communities of Deep River and Beaver Island, respectively. Eliza Holder and Harriet Stoltz, the daughters of Moravian farmers, entered the Salem mill from the neighboring Moravian communities of Friedberg and Bethania, respectively, while Elizabeth Gallimore came from her family's farm in Davidson County. Some mill hands, however, came from farther away. Martha Vinson came to Salem from Petersburg, Virginia, where she had worked in a spinning mill. The Jesse Lumley family, which supplied numerous mill hands, came to Salem from Wake County but had kinfolk already in Stokes County.[16] Some families were headed by women, widowed or abandoned by their husbands, whose means of subsistence was uncertain in the countryside. Elizabeth Loggins came with her teenage daughters to the SMC mill in January 1838 where the family found lodging and work. From the beginning, SMC regarded families who could furnish at least three or four workers as the most desirable source of labor. In its earliest stages the cheap labor of females and children was crucial to the success of the textile industry, and women played an important role in Salem's first manufacturing venture, as Table 3.2 indicates. Of the 367 employees of SMC between 1841 and 1849, 85 percent were female.[17]

The families that entered the SMC mill were those of small farmers and the landless in Stokes County, the class of people who suffered the most hardships during economic dislocations. They entered the Salem mills from a rural society characterized by small farms in which landholding was widespread. However, in a society of general farming and small landholdings, those without property found it difficult at all times to make a living because wages were low and employment opportunities were few, as emigration from North Carolina during these years demonstrated.[18] The availability of prospective mill workers can be attributed to the changing economy of the piedmont and to the rising tide of propertylessness rolling over the countryside around Salem in the 1830s and 1840s, which made it increasingly difficult for many farmers and laborers to provide for their family's well-being. In the five years between 1835 and 1840, the percentage of propertyless in Stokes County increased from 25.5 to 30.6 percent. The increasing number of insolvent polls in Stokes County during these years offers vivid proof that the scarcity of money and credit, as well as repeated droughts and bad crop years, created difficulties for many people in the countryside. Of eight heads of mill families (seven males and one female) located in the Stokes County tax lists for the years from 1835 to 1840, five owned no property, two owned fifty-one acres or less, and one owned one hundred acres.[19] Impoverished farmers and laborers responded to the mill's offer of regular work, steady wages, and a house to live in for those families that provided three or four operatives for the mill. For families, the decision to move to the mill was likely to be one of economic strategy. Father could find work in the town, maybe temporary jobs around the mill like carpentry or cutting firewood, while the children worked in the mill, and mother spent her days at the house provided by the mill taking care of the needs of her family. In the female-headed households sons and daughters worked in the mill, while their mothers spent their days at home to cook, clean, and wash clothes for the mill hands who boarded in their household. Elizabeth Loggins, whose daughters worked in the mill, took in six mill hands as boarders in the housing provided by the mill. These were the people southern mill owners believed were well-suited for mill work. One Fayetteville mill owner observed in 1846 that "there was a large population of a class whose means of support are very uncertain . . . [whose] labor at cheap rates can always be commanded."[20]

While families entered upon mill work to pursue their objectives of subsistence and independence, the motives of single female mill hands were complex and are difficult to determine conclusively. Young women embarked on mill work because of family financial needs, their own individual financial needs, and their ideas regarding their status within their families and their need for greater individual autonomy. Women working on behalf of their rural families may have gained some power and privileges in their families with the cash they brought home, which gave them additional leverage within the family by the threat of withdrawing their labor and income from the family economy. Regular wages often gave women the chance to escape the social constraints of the rural neighborhood or even leave the parental home. At a minimum, mill work may have given some single women the dignity and self-respect that productive labor brought in a rural society that valued hard work. Hence mill work offered many women a kind of personal independence that was difficult in a patriarchal society, but for most mill work was an extension of the traditional family economy.[21] For the women in the mill, mill work revealed a powerful tension between the tenuous personal autonomy wage work outside of the home promised and the ambition of the family for economic security. Through the antebellum period the household remained the important unit of production in the southern economy, and its family relations reinforced male dominance in society. By law and custom women and children remained dependent on and subordinate to the male head of the household and were expected to labor for the family's subsistence. Consequently, most southern women lived their lives and interpreted their experience within the bounds of male-dominated households. However, as in northern communities during the early nineteenth century, the increasing inability of many southern households to meet the needs of family subsistence drove women and children into work outside of the home.[22]

Those who left piedmont farms for the mill found hard work at low wages. In the SMC mill, hours were long for working days ran from sunrise to sunset during the spring and summer and from sunrise to 7:30 P.M. during the fall and winter. Operatives labored in the mill six days a week, though on Saturdays the mill stopped at 4:00 P.M., making for a workweek of almost eighty hours during the summer and about seventy hours during the winter. Twelve- to fourteen-hour days, which were common for most workers, took a heavy toll on operatives who were in an oily, dusty, and noisy factory tending machinery running at a rapid pace continuously walking and standing. The daily routine for the SMC mill hands was to wake at the company bell before dawn, go to the factory thirty minutes later, and work straight through, except for thirty-minute breakfast and lunch breaks at home, until the mill stopped for the day. In contrast, the smaller Fries mill in its early years operated on a more irregular, preindustrial routine. Relying on custom work and heavily dependent on slave labor that moved back and forth from mill to farm, the industrial routine varied according to the amount of wool brought to the mill by area farmers and the demand for labor on William and Francis Fries's farms. Francis Fries and his workers continuously moved from mill work to farm work, especially during planting and harvesting seasons. At times, however, there was much activity in the mill. On occasion wool would come in to be carded and the mill would run through the night, sixteen hours straight. When there was much work to do in the mill, Fries often gave his operatives time off after the work was completed. On one occasion, after his workers had spent several days spinning nonstop, Fries gave them an afternoon off to go rabbit hunting. On another occasion, Fries stopped the mill at midday so that he and the "boys" could go to the circus.[23]

The traditions of southern rural culture had a profound impact on the early textile mills in Salem. Though the capitalist market was spreading over many areas of the piedmont during the late antebellum decades, the character of social relations among most southerners remained largely customary. These customary social relations emphasized personal face-to-face relations among people who recognized the individual's dignity and independence as a white southerner in a slave society. The mill hands brought to the mill a framework of beliefs that emphasized independence, self-respect, and the economic well-being of the family household. Salem's mill hands viewed mill work from the perspective of the small landholders and landless laborers of the piedmont countryside. These traditions informed the mill hands' perceptions of the mill and influenced their actions that, in turn, shaped the character of textile manufacturing.[24] As southern yeomen and laborers, as well as their wives and daughters, fought tenaciously over the course of the nineteenth century to maintain their traditions and way of life as the emerging market economy swept over the countryside, many turned to the textile mill in search of a greater measure of economic security and, hence, independence.

As in the countryside, the family was the center of life for Salem's mill hands and the importance of the family determined the structure of mill labor as well as management's efforts at creating a productive work force. In antebellum southern society, as in preindustrial society in the North, the family household remained the principal production unit or economic institution. Every member of a domestic household who was able contributed to the household's financial success. In the antebellum South, girls and women as daughters and wives were expected to be "sensible and practical" and learn the skills of sewing, carding, weaving, and spinning in order to contribute to the family's total income. This "farmwife ideal" easily transferred to the mill where women could earn wages to help support their families.[25] As southern whites migrated from the piedmont farms to the mills, they continued to infuse rural traditions into the evolving industrial system. This is demonstrated most clearly by the powerful persistence of family work patterns. Rural traditions determined who worked in the mill, thus shaping the character of the mill work force. The family's decision of which members entered the mill demonstrates that families not only adapted to industrial labor but, through the force of cultural traditions and work habits, modified it. Despite the authority of management over their lives, mill families retained extensive control over the lives of family members. The degree of workers' independence or dependence on mill work, especially in regard to mobility in and out of the mill, was regulated less by mill management than by individual and family needs which were continually changing over the stages of family development. For the mill hands there were different stages in their lives when mill work was more necessary due to the degree of poverty or level of subsistence the individual or their family experienced. Families tended to enter the mills at certain stages of their lives, especially during periods of economic strain, as when their children were too young to earn wages in any job but mill work.[26]

The families of Richard Carmichael and John Brown offer a revealing insight into the dynamics of the family-labor system. In 1838 Richard Carmichael, a landless laborer, brought his family from Germanton to Salem to work in the SMC mill. Carmichael settled his family into a company-owned boarding house. While his wife Sarah, age thirty-eight, tended the family's needs at home, Carmichael's oldest daughters Martha, Salina, and Mary went to work in the mill. As his younger daughters grew older, they too entered the mill. Margaret Carmichael began mill work in 1843 when she turned eleven years old, and her younger sister Louisa entered the mill in 1845 also at the age of eleven. As his daughters went off to work in the mill, Richard Carmichael, age forty-one, found work around the mill chopping firewood for the mill's steam boiler and unpacking bales of cotton in the cotton shed. Carmichael also found work as a carpenter in Salem. In 1840 he was hired as a carpenter to work on the construction of Francis Fries's new wool mill.[27] John Brown, a forty-four-year-old landless farmer, moved his family from Deep River in rural Stokes County to Salem. While his oldest son Henry, age seventeen, was able to find work as a farm laborer, Brown's daughters had virtually no opportunity to find paying work that contributed to the family's subsistence. The SMC mill offered a solution to the Brown family's need for more income. As part of a family financial strategy, John Brown decided which family members would work in the SMC, when, and for how long. Only son Henry who was seventeen years old when the Brown family went to Salem did not work in the mill. Of the five Brown children in the mill, Betsy, age sixteen, Milly, age eight, and Sally, age seven, worked in the spinning room steadily from 1845 to 1849 for SMC. Sons David, age fourteen, and Nathan, age eleven, worked much briefer and more intermittent periods in the mill, probably when the family most needed the added income their wages provided. David worked in spinning only in 1845 and Nathan worked in 1845, 1847, and 1849. In 1850, David at age nineteen and Nathan at age sixteen worked as laborers and attended school. Thus mill work was important at this stage of the Brown family's life, but John Brown did not see the mill as permanent employment for his sons.[28] Thus internal family considerations—generally, economic need—determined who would enter the mill, which son or daughter would begin first, and which members would seek opportunities outside of the mill. Generally, the oldest female in the mill household did not work outside of the home. Instead, she remained to prepare meals, care for the younger children, tend the garden plot, and perform other chores around the house. Both Sarah Carmichael and Matilda Brown stayed at home to perform those tasks. While a family might live in company-owned housing, the parents of the children, not the mill management, decided which family members would work in the mill. Usually it was the oldest sons and daughters in their middle to late teens who entered the mill as operatives. Thus, family factors influenced which members went to work.[29]

As mill work was part of a family's financial strategy, the family functioned as an economic unit, with the wages of all the members going to meet the needs of the family. Consequently, the head of the household received the wages of all family members. That the child worker should turn over his or her earnings to the father was sanctioned in the common law which held that the child owed the father certain services which the father had a right to demand. Thus, the child's wages belonged to the father who had the right to require of him or her labor in return for support.[30] In 1840 Nathaniel Casey and his wife Mary, both fifty years old, lived in a company-owned house on Factory Hill. When they had entered the mill several years earlier, the Caseys provided five workers: Nathaniel, his two sons Fort and William, and two daughters, Peggy and Eliza. Nathaniel Casey was paid for his work as well as that of his children, Eliza and Fort. However, once a child came of age, around eighteen, the father no longer received the wages, even if the child remained in the household. Four of the Casey children worked in the mill alongside their father. But, Eliza, William, and Peggy Casey, being in their late teens and early twenties, were considered by SMC to be board-ers rather than family members. The company paid Nathaniel board for them as it did for Carolyn Hays and Emily Moser. Fort Casey, who was still counted as a family member, was not paid board, but his father was paid the wages for his labor. While the three oldest Casey children were not members of the family in SMC eyes, they probably did contribute to the maintenance of the household.[31]

The organization of labor in the mill and the wages mill work paid reflected the distinctions of gender found in antebellum southern society beyond the mill's walls. Women and older girls worked exclusively as spinners or weavers, jobs which closely conformed to their traditional domestic tasks. Men worked as supervisors, machinists, firemen tending the boilers, and as "hands of all work" doing various odd jobs around the mill. Women were paid the lowest wages in the mill, except for the young boys and girls working as doffers and sweepers. The pay scale in the spinning room of SMC in 1841 ranged from seventeen cents to $1.75 a week. Most of the spinners, young women in their mid- to late teens and early twenties, were paid $1.62 a week, more than what women could make in domestic work, which paid an average of $1.08 per week. The young boys and girls who worked as doffers or swept the floors received seventy-five to eighty-five cents a week. The more skilled adult males, such as mechanics, earned from $2.50 to $4.00 per week, roughly equal to the wages of day laborers. Only supervisors made as much as artisans in Salem, receiving $10 weekly. The wages paid by SMC were comparable to wages paid in other piedmont mills. At the Cedar Falls Manufacturing Company in Randolph County, female spinners were paid $1.50 a week and female weavers $2.50 a week. Salem's mill hands' wages were below the average wages paid mill hands in the North. Female spinners in the Philadelphia mills in 1837 were paid an average of $1.92 a week, while child operatives received between seventy-five cents and $1.00 a week. The wages for North Carolina and Philadelphia opera-tives were significantly below the wages paid in the large mill complexes of Lowell, Massachusetts. There female spinners averaged fifty-eight cents a day or $3.48 for a six-day workweek and male machinists were paid $1.27 a day or $7.62 a week.[32]

Though the mill paid wages for the labor of the family and board of the single hands who lived in the household, much of this money returned to the mill in exchange for provisions which the families purchased from the mill and for rent of the houses where the families lived. Thus mill families found it difficult to accumulate savings which would offer a small degree of independence and security. In 1845 the Casey family purchased from the mill cloth, yarn, wood, tobacco, and shoes. The mill also advanced the Casey family cash and often paid debts incurred by the Caseys to other members of the Salem community. For the month of November 1845 the Casey household was paid $30.86 in wages for Nathaniel and Fort, plus board for the boarders in the household. Casey paid out $32.89 for provisions and rent. In addition, Eliza, William, and Peggy earned $18.74 in the mill. Together with Casey's income as head of the household, the Casey family showed a surplus of $16.71 after provisions were paid for, thus demonstrating the need for several wage earners in the family and the role of the family as an economic unit. For the year, however, the story was different. In 1845 the Caseys earned $223.87 in wages plus $38.50 in payments from SMC for the workers they took in, yielding an income of $262.37. Expenses amounted to $427.77, leaving the Caseys in debt to the company for $165.40. Though the income derived from boarders was important to mill families, it often was not enough to keep the family free of debt to the company. Foreshadowing the postwar lien system that kept poor whites and blacks of the South in perpetual debt to merchant-creditors, the dependence of mill workers on SMC for all of life's necessities created a debtor class over which the company could exercise complete control.[33] Consequently, the economics of the family-labor system benefited the Salem Manufacturing Company because the family provided labor for the mill and often operated a boarding house that took in single mill hands.

Still, mill work did allow some families the opportunity to acquire land, a greater degree of security, and a sense of being a part of the independent southern yeomanry. Of the five heads of mill families mentioned previously who had entered the mill propertyless, four eventually acquired some real property. These property holdings tended to be small, less than seventy-five acres on the average. Mill work enabled Richard Carmichael to acquire a small farm of fifty-one acres by 1840. For a landless farmer who could not read and write, the mill made possible John Brown's eventual mobility into the land-owing class. By 1850, John Brown at age forty-nine was a farmer who owned real estate valued at $239 that probably included about one hundred acres.[34] Many of the families with small land holdings remained close to the mill, using the wages earned through mill work by family members to supplement what the small farm produced. Thus, some boys and girls may have been sent from their father's farms to work in the mill as part of a family economic strategy; therefore, mill work remained tied to the rural economy through the yeoman farm.

Family ties were important to mill hands for companionship, financial security, and as a bridge from the farm to the mill, as mill hands often followed other family members to the mill. The extended family was the family-type most adaptable to industrial labor because it could manage its resources and direct its members into the work force according to its own needs. Additionally, the extended family served the interests of the mill management in its role as a labor recruiter. Once a family was established in the mill it attracted other family members to mill work and served as a base to which these brothers, sisters, cousins, nephews, and nieces came to find work in the same mill. Among the mill families employed by SMC during the 1840s, the Lumleys, Caseys, Collins, and Holders were larger than just the nuclear family of father, mother, and children. The size of the families ranged from six, the number of Fowlers employed in the mill, to seventeen, the number of Lumleys.[35] Unfortunately, due to the closing of SMC in 1849, many mill workers and families were gone when the 1850 census was taken, and it is therefore impossible to determine which workers of the same last name belonged to which households. But kinship and intermarriage between mill families produced a community that offered relief and a sanctuary to those engaged in mill work.[36] In these families the remnants of a preindustrial way of life were preserved as the family stood between the individual and the mill as a buffer that made the transition to industrial work easier.

Family ties carried over into the organization of the work force in the Salem mills. In the SMC mill, family members often worked together in the same department and in the boardinghouses they lived together. Such kinship ties were extensive. For the 153 workers employed by SMC in 1845, there were only fifty-nine different surnames—almost one in three workers shared a common surname.[37] It was quite common for sisters to enter the mill together, or for one to come first, find a place, and wait for a second to follow. For single women with no family present to fall back on for support, their fellow workers with whom they shared life in the factory and boardinghouses became family. The relationship between the nuclear family and boarders in the household was one of an intimate interdependence. Boarders were important to the financial success of the mill family as they provided extra income. Families in mill housing became a surrogate family for single workers in the household where they boarded. Polina and Barbara Tuttle, along with Elizabeth and Emily Kenady, Susan and Elizabeth Crouch, Elizabeth and Aurora Renn, and Martha and Patience Alberson, boarded together in the Richard Carmichael household. Both Polina and Barbara Tuttle worked in the spinning room, Polina entering in 1844 and Barbara following in June 1845. The Caseys all worked in the weaving room of SMC. In this way families determined an informal social network within the mill. In 1841, 42 percent of the operatives in the SMC mill worked alongside siblings or other family members. By 1849 the percentage had climbed to 60 percent, probably for two reasons: the mill's greater reliance on family hands in the late 1840s, and the closing of the weaving operations in 1849 which led to the consolidation of some mill hands into other areas of the mill. This pattern of work was also found in other nearby mills. In the Cedar Falls Manufacturing Company mill, about 80 percent of the operatives worked alongside siblings. This organization of the labor force in North Carolina mills differed from that of New England mills relying on family labor. There mill owners separated family members on the shop floor as a way of promoting management's control over the labor force and diluting family authority over members. However, in southern mills management had to accept family work traditions which were an important part of southern rural culture.[38]

In the mills all of the operatives, family members as well as single hands, found themselves subject to the pervasive discipline of mill management as the Moravians attempted to extend to the mill the community's patriarchal social relations. Mill management endeavored to create a dependable labor force as well to counter opposition from different quarters of the Moravian community that large numbers of non-Moravians in Salem threatened the Moravian way of life. Management desired only "sober, orderly, and moral" mill hands who could provide certification from their "most respectable and trustworthy neighbors" that they were "of industrious habits and unexceptional character." The key to securing such workers, and the foundation of managerial authority in the mill, was company-owned housing. By providing adequate housing the mills attracted the workers they needed and kept wages down. But, most importantly, the family houses and boardinghouses gave the company an unprecedented degree of control over their workers. Once hired and located in mill housing, the workers, especially those belonging to families, were effectively bound to the company and the job, for if they left the mill they would be forced to find other accommodations. SMC held the upper hand in regard to work contracts that kept the families tied to the mill. Families were required to give one month's notice if they intended to quit the mill, which also meant vacating their homes, while the company was obligated to give only one week's notice if a family was being dismissed. Individual autonomy was severely constricted in the mill and in the company houses, for the workers' freedom of movement was regulated and limited by the mill management. When not at work the operatives were expected to remain at their houses, and after dark everyone was supposed to be at home. On election day in August 1838, an important community occasion in the rural culture of the antebellum South, Francis Fries, the mill agent, imposed a "dark curfew" on all mill hands who lived in company housing. All of the mill hands who had spent the afternoon "loose" at the election ground were required to be in the family houses or the boarding house by dark and expected to be ready for work the next morning. If the operative planned a trip of any distance from the mill, the superintendent's permission was required.[39]

Because SMC relied heavily on family labor, the family became the most effective instrument of paternalistic control of the work force. The social system of the mill that lodged families in company housing and reinforced paternal authority in the household fit nicely with the traditional Moravian agencies of social control—the households and workshops of the master craftsmen. Under SMC rules, families had to take in as many boarders as the company requested. The head of the family assumed responsibility over everyone in the household, and was expected by the company to see that all members adhered to the rules. The role of the family was especially important in the case of the single women employed in the mill. Placing single women in family-run, company-owned boardinghouses circumscribed women's behavior and buttressed the traditional patriarchal authority of the Moravians in Salem. Just as Moravian authorities expected shop masters and heads of households to exercise authority over the members of their households, so mill management expected heads of families in the company houses to exercise authority in their households. By holding family heads accountable for the behavior of members of their households, management used the heads of mill families as agents of company authority who regulated the behavior of mill hands outside of the factory.[40]

Keeping the mill workers under the authority of mill management served also to calm fears about the creation of a work force living outside of the traditional community social order. By 1841 the total number of operatives working in the SMC mill during that year equalled about 26 percent of the total membership in the Moravian congregation at Salem in 1840. Furthermore, as many members of the Salem congregation pursued their private interests, often in violation of the congregational rules, there was a greater sensitivity to threats to the moral and social order of the community. While they fought among themselves over the preservation of the congregational system in Salem, the Moravians regarded outsiders living among them with serious doubts. On a visit to four non-Moravian families living in the rural neighborhoods outside of Salem, the pastor of the Friedberg congregation seemingly confirmed Moravian suspicions of their neighbors when he found the families living in "poverty stricken huts and in poverty apparently their own fault. Infinitely greater still is the pitiful condition of their immortal souls. . . . Neither Testament nor Bible is to be seen in their huts and no one of these poor heathens can read." Congregation authorities in Salem were determined in the 1830s to protect the community and its way of life from such pernicious influences they saw in the countryside beyond the village's borders.[41]

Beside introducing a new type of worker and a different organization of work and production, textile manufacturing also introduced new work routines and new concepts regarding compensation for labor. Unlike Salem's journeymen and farm workers, work for the mill operatives was regulated by the speed of the machinery. The mill operatives were the first manufacturing workers in Salem to tend nonhuman-powered machinery producing articles for a market that stretched beyond the local community. Because textile manufacturing was deeply immersed in a competitive nonlocal market economy, the price of yarn and cloth had to be kept low for the company to remain competitive. Consequently, there was competitive pressure to reduce operating costs, especially wages. Therefore, compensation for mill work was determined by market conditions and the profitability of the company rather than by the preindustrial custom in the artisan shop of paying the producer a share of the value of the product. Thus mill work tended to set apart those engaged in it from the rest of the community. The men in the mill found themselves outside of the mechanic culture of Salem, having never served an apprenticeship and with slim hope of upward mobility and ownership of their own shop. The situations of male operatives in 1860 who once worked for SMC and who remained in Forsyth County after the mill closed supports this observation. Of forty-nine male mill hands identified in the SMC time books, seventeen were located in the 1860 census. Most of these men lived an uncertain existence. Seven worked as laborers and four reported no occupation. Ten of the seventeen former SMC operatives owned no real property. One of the seventeen was a shoemaker who owned no real estate. Five of the seventeen men were farmers who owned real estate. Six of the seventeen could not read or write. For the women who made up the bulk of the mill operatives, the distinction was even greater. Wage work drew a sharp distinction between women who did not have to work outside of their family households and women who had to work for wages to support themselves or help support their families. The nineteenth-century ideal of a woman who kept a proper home supervising all of the affairs of the household, and who still found time to enlighten her mind, was impossible for most working-class women, regardless of how hard they might have tried to live up to the ideal.[42] As most Moravian women in Salem continued to work in the homes of their families, or if they were unmarried young women in the homes of other Moravian families, most non-Moravian women in the village worked in the mill. Hence the work experiences of Moravian and non-Moravian women increasingly diverged. The experiences of Salem's textile workers enabled them to create a community of workers apart from the larger Moravian community as Factory Hill became an early vision of Salem's future.

Recognizing that within the congregation village the mill hands living on Factory Hill were evolving into a separate community with different work patterns, distinct family lives in the company-owned boarding-houses, and less than certain prospects for the future, the Moravian congregation leadership undertook efforts of moral suasion through the church to influence mill hand behavior and lead the mill hands in what the Moravians believed to be the proper direction. To this end the local clergy took an active role in ministering to the spiritual needs of the mill hands. There is little doubt that the Moravian pastors in Salem were sincerely concerned for the spiritual condition of the mill hands. As the opening of the SMC mill approached in 1837, the pastor of the Salem congregation noted in the congregation diary the hope that "we succeed also in caring for the spiritual needs of the numerous strangers who come as workers in the factory." Expression of this spiritual concern is evident in the opening of a Sunday school on Factory Hill in 1838 for the benefit of the mill hands and their families, particularly the children connected with the mill.[43] However, the efforts of the Moravian pastors were met with mill hand ambivalence. The mill hands enjoyed participating in the Moravian lovefeasts at Christmas and New Years, and in other celebrations which the church sponsored. The Moravian Sunday school was also appreciated for the educational benefits it provided. Yet, the mill hands rejected other Moravian missionary efforts. In November 1838 a member of the board of directors of SMC, noting the mill hands' desire to attend evening worship services, urged that the mill stop running every other Tuesday evening so that the mill hands could attend the regular Moravian service held on Tuesday night. After about two months it was obvious to the board that the mill hands did not share "that relish for our Moravian service, which was believed to exist," and the mill resumed operation on Tuesday evenings.[44] Many of the mill hands probably found the Moravian worship services foreign, especially since usually the hymns were sung and sermons preached in German. Non-Moravians must also have found the Moravian style of worship chillingly formal and lacking in emotion compared to the fervor of Baptist and Methodist services. But more important, the mill hands probably resented the closing of the mill one night every two weeks which denied them the wages they would have earned had the mill operated.

By contrast, the Methodists were more successful in their missionary efforts among the mill hands, as attendance at the Methodist meetings near the mill demonstrated.[45] The Methodists brought the religion of the countryside to the mill. The preaching and emotional responses of the faithful, seen so often at Methodist camp meetings in the rural neighborhoods around Salem, offered the spiritual nourishment the mill hands sought. The rejection of Moravian efforts among the mill hands and their acceptance of Methodism illustrate that the mill hands drew a line beyond which management and the congregational leadership were not allowed to go in their efforts to direct the lives of their workers. Management exercised broad control over the mill hands' lives in the factory and in the company-owned houses, but the mill hands were determined to retain autonomy over their spiritual lives—the one facet of life they controlled outright. Furthermore, the Moravian church was the established church of the community and the church of the mill owners. Rejection of the Moravian church was also a rejection of one part of the authority of the mill owners. Regarded as strangers by the Moravians, the mill hands were forced to live in houses built around the factory and located beyond the town limits. As strangers, the mill hands were always second-class citizens in the Moravian community. In their rejection of the Moravian church, the mill hands were turning their backs on the institution that conferred on them their lower status in the community. Methodism, however, provided a sense of community to replace the one the mill hands had left behind when they came to the mill.

Throughout the life of the SMC mill, management regarded its work force as unreliable because individual mill hands often were absent for days and, sometimes, weeks at a time. The problem of mill hand absence was especially acute during the early years of the mill's operation when single young women comprised a larger proportion of the work force. The board of directors often complained that the single hands—those not attached to families in the mill—were in the habit of going home and returning when they wanted. Considerable time was lost when the mill could not run at full capacity because of a lack of hands. During the summer of 1838, the mill's first in operation, Francis Fries continually confronted the problem of absent hands. On June 23 Fries could run only some of the mill's machinery because so many of the operatives were out nearly the whole week having the "summer complaint." On the afternoon of June 27 most of the hands were out of the mill fishing. According to Fries, very little business was done that week. Fries found it necessary to get tough with his operatives and informed them on June 29 when he distributed their pay that "after this week I deduct the board of such as are sick from their wages, as I found some were taking advantage of my paying their board." Fries's stern measure had little effect apparently. The next day the mill could run only six frames because so many hands missed work. The problem continued, and in August 1839 Fries reported that the mill was short of hands and several had left unexpectedly, either out sick or gone home.[46] The mill time books illustrate the character of the operatives' inconstant work habits. In 1845 the average number of days per month worked by all operatives in the spinning room was 20.5 days. For single hands, the average was lower, 15.6. There was also a monthly variation, with July and August having the highest average, 22 days, and March and September the lowest, 19 and 18 days, respectively.[47] The mill hands left the mill unexpectedly for a variety of reasons, all of which were linked to the customs of rural preindustrial culture. They left to help their families who remained on farms at planting and harvest times, to attend Methodist camp meetings, to attend the funerals and marriages of friends, family, and fellow mill hands, to go fishing in the summer, and to gather all day at the election field on election days, a customary holiday among the yeomanry.

Quitting the mill to seek employment elsewhere or to return home was an explicit comment by mill hands on what they felt about either industrial labor or mill management. Soon after the mill opened, the board of directors recognized the difficulty management was having retaining the mill hands after they had learned the skills necessary for tending the machinery. The machinist of the mill complained that the mill hands were too "uncertain" which deprived the company of flexibility in regulating the number of hands employed. The time books confirm the machinist's complaint. Of the 151 operatives who were employed in the mill in 1841, only twenty-three or 15 percent were still working for the company in 1848. As was the case with absenteeism, high turnover as mill hands quit unexpectedly made it difficult for the mill to keep all of its machinery running. Often, the mill hands who remained had to tend extra machines, though with extra pay, until replacements for the departed could be hired and trained.[48]

Management's complaints about the unreliability of the mill's operatives must be considered against the backdrop of wage cuts, mill closings, and reductions in the mill work force undertaken by management. SMC's continual cash short situation prompted the company to pay careful attention to costs and the changing conditions of the market, always with an eye to increasing profits in order that the company might deliver on earlier hopes of big dividends.[49] In its quest for increased profits the actions of mill management had a profound impact on the mill hands. In an effort to cut costs the company found it necessary not to run the mill at night, a standard practice during the winter months, and reduce wages by twelve and one-half cents per week. Beginning in 1842 wages fluctuated as the financial condition of the mill varied, and mill hands found their wages increasingly inconsistent. Gillian Ivy, who worked in the spinning room, was a typical case. She saw her wages cut from $1.62 a week to $1.50 in October 1842, restored to $1.62 in April 1843, and cut again to $1.50 in May. The situation of the operatives was made even more difficult by the periodic suspension of part or all of factory operations due to backlogs of cloth or yarn, the fall in yarn prices, or when cotton prices were too high. In the winter of 1842, SMC, like other piedmont mills, suspended its weaving operations, and turned out all of the hands who had been engaged in the weaving room. Again, in 1847 the mill did not operate from September 5 through December 6 because of the large stock of yarn on hand and high cotton prices. The financial situation of SMC was adversely affected and the mill hands found themselves out of work with no regular income when the mill broke down periodically and operations stopped, often for weeks at a time. From July 10 through August 26, 1842, the mill closed for engine repairs. In October and November 1843 the mill did not run for about four weeks, again for engine repairs.[50] With inconsistent wages, layoffs, and shutdowns, mill work was often unreliable, failing to meet the mill hands' expectations of steady work, regular wages, and a dependable income. The unreliability of mill work and the undependability of mill management in its promises to the operatives bred a corresponding unreliability in the mill hands.

By absenteeism and quitting, the mill hands forced management to adapt the mechanized routine of the factory to the customary habits and volition of the operatives. Though Easter and Christmas were recognized by management as holidays when the mill did not run, the mill hands successfully stretched the holidays for several days by not returning from home promptly. In 1837 the board of directors advised Francis Fries to use his discretion regarding the operation of the mill the day after Christmas. The board told Fries: "If the hands seem to expect [a] holiday the contrary might not be insisted upon." Mill hand behavior also prompted management to reconsider its attitude toward the kind of labor that should be employed in the mill. Mill management had believed that a combination of families and young single individuals would be the ideal labor force for the mill. But by 1839 the board of directors of the company recognized that single operatives, or "loose" hands in the terms of SMC, posed too many difficulties in their habit of "going home and returning when they think proper." Consequently, the board of directors decided that the mill should recruit more family hands to comprise the largest proportion of the work force. To this end, the board of directors decided in 1839 to build another family house and, in 1841, to convert the boardinghouse where single hands had been lodged into three apartments to accommodate families.[51]

The personal conduct of the mill hands also challenged the authority of mill management and appeared to confirm the fears of many Moravians in Salem that the operatives would have a detrimental effect on community morals. SMC continually reported difficulties with its employees living in the boardinghouses, where management believed that the excessive consumption of liquor was rampant. The situation was made worse by the lack of deference by the mill hands toward mill management. Management viewed its operatives as often contentious, refusing to abide by the mill's rules, and openly disrespectful of management's authority. The board of directors expressed its exasperation with the mill's operatives and declared that the company could no longer be subject to the "whims, caprices, and insolence" of its employees. Francis Fries found it necessary in 1838 to dismiss Washington Barrow because of his "unwillingness to work out." In 1841 the board of directors felt compelled to admonish the mill hands that it and the president of the company "should be treated by those engaged in the establishment with due respect [and] that at the same time becoming respect is due to the Superintendent of the establishment."[52]

The managers of the Salem textile mills saw two possible solutions for creating a reliable and productive work force. The first, which carried with it many problems in the congregation community and was thus embraced reluctantly, was the replacement of undependable and sometimes defiant white workers with slaves hired from the neighboring countryside. The second solution which carried few risks of alienating many in the congregation community was to adapt the factory routine and management policies to meet the expectations of the mill hands. But this alternative worked to weaken the mills' financial condition as well as sometimes impede the mills' productivity in a competitive textile market. The turn to slaves to replace defiant workers was a peculiarly southern response to labor problems in the early mills, but in many ways it was not unlike northern mill managers' turn to French Canadians or Irish immigrants to replace often rebellious Yankees. Mill owners in both regions turned to whatever alternative labor source was immediately available. Southern industrialism was distinctive in its extensive use of slave labor. Of the South's total slave population employed in industry, roughly 80 percent were owned by manufacturers while the remainder were hired out for specific periods of time. Though slave labor was not popularly believed to be as efficient as white labor on a daily basis, blacks were regarded as efficient long-run workers because they could not leave their jobs as easily as whites did. A common theme among antebellum manufacturers was that slaves were cheaper, more docile, and dependable than white laborers who were often refractory, frequently left the mill for days without giving notice, and wasted too much time at taverns and attending militia musters and elections. The key to the ready adaptability of slave labor to industrial work, and its advantage over white labor, was its vulnerability to coercive discipline. Additionally, the employer of slaves was not bothered with labor organizations nor with having to bargain over wages with his workers. Given the frequent intractability of southern white workers, slave labor, despite its occasional resistance, could be more reliable.[53]

Upon examination of wage rates paid by SMC to white male employees and rent paid for hired slaves, the use of slaves in the mill does not appear to have brought a compelling economic advantage to the mill, especially in light of the ill feelings within the community toward the increased use of slaves in the village's shops. In 1847 the average monthly pay for semiskilled white male operatives, mostly teenagers, was $6 per month plus board. In the spring of 1847 SMC negotiated an agreement with C. L. Banner to hire four of his slaves. "Old" Aaron was hired at $5 a month to haul wood. Martin, the principal hand in the picking room, was hired for $8.30 a month, while Eli who operated the small picker was hired for $7.50 a month. Lewis was engaged at stripping the cylinders for $5.80 a month. SMC hired Banner's slaves for an average of $6.65 a month per slave. However, before this agreement with Banner, SMC had paid an average of $10.25 a month for the hire of these slaves, which was roughly equal to the wage paid to many skilled white workers. In 1848 the agreement with Banner for the hire of his four slaves cost SMC an average of $8.33 a month per slave.[54] While SMC was spared the cost of boarding the slaves hired for the mill, the company did not realize a significant savings in its labor costs by employing slaves. The only appreciable benefit to SMC from hiring slaves was in the relative reliability of slaves over white labor. Slaves did not have the mobility of white workers, hence they could be bound to a specific place in the mill for a whole year. In this regard hired slaves offered an advantage to SMC.

The presence of a large class of chattel labor gave southern manufacturers a decisive edge over their white laborers because, when needed, blacks were always available to replace white workers.[55] Slaves made effective strikebreakers in southern manufacturing. However, the use of slaves in manufacturing created tensions in the community which were central to the controversy over congregational regulation of the use of slaves in the town. In 1838 SMC was having trouble with the fireman and picker tender, both white, who refused to obey their supervisor, the machinist. To solve the problem the machinist suggested filling these positions with blacks, from whom "more punctual obedience could be enforced." This suggestion brought the mill management face-to-face with the congregation's rules against the use of slaves in Salem and created a conflict within the company's board of directors. The directors reluctantly acceded to the machinist's request. Claiming that the company could not be subject to coercion by its employees who might leave their jobs "in a momentary passion," the directors allowed the employment of blacks as unskilled labor in the engine house and picker room, but the blacks were not to be purchased. Ten years later SMC reaffirmed its commitment to white labor, when it was available. Instead of hiring the teenaged slaves of Constantine Banner, the mill agent, the directors decided that the children of the white families who lived in the company houses and worked in the mill should be given first chance for employment. The company did not want to take any actions which would put whites out of work. Management's preference for white labor reflected the Moravian leaders' fears that extensive use of slaves in Salem in any job would establish a dangerous precedent for the increased employment of slaves in the town's workshops and thus, in the long run, would limit opportunities for gainful employment for the congregation's youths. The employment of slaves was an issue on which the congregation leadership could not capitulate without jeopardizing the authority of the congregation regulations which opposed the employment of slaves in Salem. Therefore, SMC, controlled by the prominent Moravians of Salem, had to remain true to the spirit of the congregation orders.[56] Only as a last resort did the company turn to slaves.

Francis Fries, in contrast, had other ideas about the role of slaves in manufacturing, and in the woolen mill he established after leaving his position at SMC, Fries joined the institution of slavery to the industrial development of Salem and created a mixed work force in his mill of whites and slaves. Fries believed that if slaves were "willing enough" they could make good mill hands, especially those who were too small or not strong enough for field work. Fries believed that it took one to three months to train a slave for spinning. But he was convinced that they could be the equal of white workers because "their stock is never sick, and working them ever so hard seems never to hurt them." Fries gave his slaves extensive responsibilities that provided them opportunities to develop industrial skills and earn money of their own. In the mill they performed all of the production tasks alongside white operatives.[57] As incentive to productive work Fries paid his slaves; Wallace received $5 per month plus a pair of shoes and a coat at the end of the year and Henry was paid $4.16 2/3 per month plus a coat. Some of the Fries slaves took full advantage of their status as wage laborers, working on their own account when not engaged in the mill, demonstrating a sense of independence and self-respect as workers. When emancipated, Ellic had saved and deposited with F. and H. Fries $400 with which he planned to buy his freedom. As was the case for white labor, mill work offered opportunities to black mill hands while it served the needs of mill owners. As on the farm, slaves in the mills adapted to their situation and even turned it to their advantage. The use of slaves in mills was widespread in the 1830s and 1840s, but as cotton prices recovered in the 1850s slave values increased, making them more profitable as farm laborers than mill hands. Thus, in the 1850s southern mills became increasingly the preserve of white labor.[58] That mill management was attracted to supposedly tractable and dependable slaves to complement or even replace white operatives reveals much about the attitudes and behavior of the operatives who worked in the Salem mills and their relations with management.

Mill hand behavior prompted management to reexamine its policies regarding wages paid in the mill. In their dealings with the employees over the issues of wages and regular attendance at work, management came to understand the nature of its relationship to labor and adopted new measures intended to both compel and induce labor to be more dependable. These measures recognized the cash basis of the management-labor relationship and that the mill hands were more likely to respond to positive measures which would bring them greater financial returns than the negative prohibitions which threatened termination of mill employment. Soon after the SMC mill opened, the board of directors recognized the potential among the mill hands for misconduct or "improprieties" which might stop part of the mill and prompt management to submit to the demands of the mill hands. While the board did not explicitly mention the possibility of strikes, the board was concerned that the mill hands know from the start that management would not tolerate any misconduct merely to keep the mill running. Mill hands were forewarned that they risked dismissal. Yet, the mill hands did not respond favorably to these warnings, because absenteeism continued, and the mill could not risk turning out mill hands and cutting back operations. Therefore, the board had to resort to inducements to persuade the mill hands to be more regular and dependable in their work habits. In the fall of 1839 the chief machinist was authorized to raise wages for individual mill hands by twenty-five cents a week. After a year the board recognized that increased wages were not the whole answer, especially when management was forced to cut wages due to competitive pressures from other mills. The board then decided to require all mill hands to sign a written contract which stipulated a definite term of employment, the withholding of two weeks' pay, and the forfeiture of this pay if the mill hand did not remain in the mill for the term of the agreement. To make the contract more appealing to the mill hands, the board stipulated that all employees who worked for a regular length of time without interruption would be entitled to a cash bonus at the end of the year.[59]

The actions of management aimed at creating a more reliable work force in the mill yielded some results. By recruiting more families to replace single hands and by increasing wages, management was able to increase the persistence rate among operatives and, by 1845, employ a more experienced veteran work force. Between 1841 and 1845 the proportion of mill hands belonging to families living in the company-owned houses increased. In 1841 the company employed 146 operatives; eighty-nine, or 61 percent, were family hands and fifty-seven, or 39 percent, were single hands. By 1845 the proportion of family hands in the mill had risen to 64 percent while the proportion of single hands declined to 36 percent. The mill work force in 1845 was also a more experienced, veteran labor force than in earlier years. In 1845, 52 percent of the 143 operatives employed at SMC had worked in the mill at least three years. Furthermore, one-third of the operatives employed in 1845 had been in the mill at least five years. The mill hands were better paid in 1845 despite periodic wage reductions that occurred with changing market conditions and the financial health of SMC. Wages in the mill rose through the 1840s. The average wage in 1841 was $1.36 a week which, by 1849, had risen to $1.58. The increased proportion of family hands and the veteran character of the workers earning a higher wage gave SMC a more reliable work force. Whereas in 1841 only 26 percent of the mill hands employed in the spinning room worked a full year without extended absences, in 1845 53 percent of the spinning room operatives worked the entire year without extensive absences.[60]

Salem mill hands' responses to the early industrial order of the mill demonstrated on the one hand an accommodation to the productive relations found in the mill and, on the other, a rather successful effort to force mill management and the production process to adapt to their needs. But these responses also represent the mill hands' perception that management had failed to fulfill its obligations to those who entered the mill.[61] In their effort to engage profitably in manufacturing in the emerging regional and national market economy, the Moravian investors and managers of Salem's textile mills had to temper traditional notions of patriarchal responsibilities. Textile mill paternalism, with its supposedly patriarchal regard for dependent workers, was incompatible with the demands of industrial capitalism. When confronted with the possibilities of operating losses or even low dividends, the board of directors did not hesitate to cut wages, close down part of the machinery, and lay off operatives. During the life of the mill the board of directors repeatedly cut back or suspended operation of the mill due to high cotton prices, backlogs of yarn, or low prices of yarn. Like the mill owners of nearby Alamance and Randolph counties, the management of SMC demonstrated a calculating attitude with a careful eye toward profits and losses.[62] Such behavior illustrates the inaccuracy of the long-held and overemphasized concept of antebellum textile mill paternalism. The projection of the image of paternal concern for workers had as its purpose strictly economic ends: a sufficient labor force that was dependable, docile, and productive. But the weak link in a paternalistic approach to mill management was management's inability to be dependable and meet its responsibilities to the operatives. The dilemma for these Moravians was that they were not involved with the mill hands in a strictly patriarchal relationship that traditionally characterized Moravian communities, rather they were engaged in an economic relationship between capital and labor. The ironic twist in this story is that the mill hands were the traditionalists holding on to notions of security and independence as well as an expectation of reciprocity in relationships between members of a community, while the Moravian investors and managers of the textile mills were the innovators seeking to promote new social and productive relations. The traditional values, habits, and ways of life which the mill hands brought to the mill clashed with the discipline required of industrial labor as well as with the mill owners' drive for profits. This confrontation between two divergent ethoses informed the mill hands' resistance to management's prerogatives, yielding a complex relationship between the mill hands and management that revolved around the wage contract and the demands of early industrial capitalism. By absenteeism, quitting the mill, and lack of deference toward mill management, mill hands in

Salem, like operatives in other communities, expressed their dissatisfaction with the situation in the Salem mills and attempted to force mill management and the production routine in the mill to meet their needs.[63]

With the opening of the Salem Manufacturing Company mill in 1837 the Moravians attempted to transpose their special way of life into an industrial setting. Yet, in their efforts to engage profitably in manufacturing in the emerging market economy, the investors and managers of Salem's textile mills had to abandon traditional notions of patriarchal responsibilities which were at the center of the congregational way of life and adopt a management style that was responsive to the demands of a competitive market as well as conducive to the accumulation of profits. The mill was a virtual Pandora's box for the congregation community, as its implications for the life of the community were not fully comprehended by early advocates of manufacturing. Textile manufacturing became an agent of change that demonstrated to many Moravians that the congregational order was not compatible with capitalist enterprise. The mill introduced into the congregation town a large non-Moravian work force and promoted new work routines and life-styles. That most of the mill hands were not Moravian reveals the weakening of a common identity among the people of Salem and an emerging differentiation according to religion and ways of living and working. With the largest single group of workers in the community set apart on the edge of town and outside of the Moravian congregational culture, community in Salem was becoming less the product of that sense of shared experience that had united all who belonged to the congregation community than a place or location of residence and work. Factory Hill offered a glimpse of Salem's future as an important textile center in the South.

Community Culture in Antebellum Salem

Increasing differentiation among the Moravians was expressed in the diverse activities that captured their attention during the second quarter of the nineteenth century. The people of Salem embraced temperance societies, fraternal organizations, evangelical religion, and political parties which prompted William Fries in 1831 to comment that Salem was "in many ways going to extremes . . . some for Temperance Society or Sunday Schools, others have become quite military."[1] These activities illustrate the new complexity of life among the townspeople who considered themselves more than just members of a religious congregation. But they also represent attempts to recreate that unity which the Moravian church and the congregation had once provided. Local bonds were strengthened as townspeople joined in organizations that combined mutuality and communal loyalty with self-interest. Fourth of July celebrations, temperance festivals, camp meetings and religious revivals, electioneering parades and rallies, and other events sponsored by and participated in by various organizations invigorated the sense of community among an increasingly heterogeneous population. Such community-building activities formed a buffer to help absorb the shock of dramatic change that accompanied economic transformation.[2] However, this new solidarity tenuously held together Moravians and the growing number of non-Moravians in an increasingly diverse and differentiated community. By mid-century the people of Salem were no longer just Moravians, but mechanics, mill hands, and merchants, Whigs and Democrats, Methodists and Baptists. They were no longer the pure Moravian settler of the eighteenth century, a generation or two removed from Saxony, but a North Carolinian bound to a new environment and the attitudes and ways of life of an evolving market society.

From its founding in the eighteenth century, Salem had been a community of artisans and shopkeepers who practiced their respective trades and farmed small plots of land rented from the congregation. At mid-century over one-half of the working population were artisans or shop-keepers who were likely to have been artisans earlier in their career. These Moravians shared the common experience of manual labor producing the goods necessary to sustain life in the community. The life course of the congregation's men stretched from apprenticeship for boys in one of the village's shops, though employment as a journeyman while in their late teens and twenties, eventually to full participation in the life of the congregation as a head of a household and master craftsman. In a town cut from the wilderness to fulfill a religious mission labor was a virtue, as it was necessary that everyone work to insure the survival of the town. The achievement of creating a community out of nothing enhanced the artisans' sense of self-worth and enabled them to contest the implied social inferiority of manual work pervasive in the South.[3] The Salem *People's Press* confirmed the dignity of manual labor and that the trades were a calling "as noble as the indolence and inactivity of wealth is ignoble." Affirmations of the dignity of labor reflected a commitment to personal independence that derived from and was preserved by honest toil on the soil and in one's craft. Control of productive property—land or a skill—freed men from dependence on others for subsistence and enabled them to enjoy the fruits of their own and their family's labor. This consciousness formed values by which people made moral choices and judged the desirability of events and ideas and shaped an ethos by which Salem residents made sense of their experiences. Still, the emphasis of the antebellum republican ideology of independence and individual liberty remained in Salem as in other communities across the South in an "uneasy juxtaposition" with notions of dependence and community as the Moravians struggled with the implications of this ideology for the congregational way of life.[4]

The articulation of a mechanic identity among artisans born out of similar life experiences in the church and workshops emerged as an instrument of solidarity and a bond of community in a village of artisans and shopkeepers challenged by the market. As economic interests came to define their lives, tensions between masters erupted and harmony within the congregation began to break down. Increased commercialization of economic relations, the quest for profits and financial advantage, and political tensions over state and national issues such as the tariff, taxes, and the distribution of public revenues rent the community in the 1850s. Increasingly, relations within the congregation were not filled with a Moravian sense of brotherly love between communicants. Henry Leinbach observed as early as 1833 that when money was involved, "Brotherly love" vanished quickly.[5] The identification of masters, journeymen, and apprentices as mechanics enabled them to preserve a fragile unity despite changing economic conditions which were creating a dichotomy of interests in the workplace between employer and employee. The mechanic identity motivated artisans to establish social organizations like the Order of United American Mechanics and the Masonic and Odd Fellows lodges as a device for preserving harmony within the community.

Artisans, both North and South, joined together in their respective communities to organize societies which promoted respect, self-esteem, and a sense of brotherhood among skilled workers who shared a common status as producers. Organized primarily for benevolent purposes, providing aid to members in times of illness, as well as burial expenses, these societies occasionally evolved into class-conscious organizations of producers united for the common goals of protecting jobs, obtaining the passage of mechanics' lien laws, higher wages and shorter hours, laws barring the use of slaves in the trades, and preserving the status of skilled workers as producers. In Salem the Wachovia Council of the Order of United American Mechanics and Working Men was established as a benevolent and fraternal society. Meeting every Friday evening in the Salem town hall, the OUAM provided fellowship for Salem's artisans. The Order of United American Mechanics was organized in Philadelphia in 1845 as a patriotic and benevolent society of native white males who united to defend members from the economic competition of immigrants and to aid the widows and orphaned children of deceased members.[6] Little information on this organization survives except for a few notices, resolutions, and references to its participation in community events published in the Salem *People's Press*, but the organization was probably composed primarily of master craftsmen and their journeymen from the different crafts, uniting them in activities outside of their workshops, and helping to promote a common identity among artisans as mechanics. It is likely that the OUAM was established by mechanics who were aware of the tensions inherent in the emerging new economic arrangements and who sought the means to preserve unity and harmony among Salem's artisans.

While the Order of United American Mechanics may have been composed of local masters and journeymen, the rank and file deferred to the more successful and respected shop masters and conferred on them positions of leadership and prestige. In 1854 when member Lewis F. Eberhart died, a resolution of condolence was printed in the *People's Press* with the names of members who formed the committee to express the condolences. Eberhart, age fifty at his death, was a lock and clock maker who owned property valued at $600. The committee was composed of William Hauser, age fifty, a bricklayer who owned $700 in property, and Henry Holder, thirty-eight years old, also a bricklayer, who owned property valued at $600. Henry Holder enjoyed a modest political career in the decade before the Civil War, serving as a town commissioner of Winston in 1859. Holder and Hauser were listed in a postwar business directory as mechanics working on their own account; Holder as a mason in Winston and Hauser as a brick and stone mason in Salem.[7]

Like the Order of United American Mechanics, fraternal organizations such as the Masons and Odd Fellows provided fellowship and a sense of security in the face of the uncertainties of life in the nineteenth century. Fraternal organizations enjoyed great popularity across the South and were important social and recreational institutions in town life. The Independent Order of Odd Fellows dispensed relief to the members and their widowed families, buried lodge members, and educated orphans. As with the mechanics' society, the leadership and prestigious positions in the Masonic and Odd Fellows lodges were filled by the more successful men of the community. From resolutions published in the Salem *People's Press*, the honorary condolence committees were composed of successful mechanics, farmers, merchants, and professionals who were solidly in the middle rank of local society.[8]

The fraternal and benevolent organizations provided meeting places for mechanics and rising entrepreneurs, greater familiarity with each other, and a sense of shared experience. In contrast, large numbers of semiskilled and unskilled men and women in the community, the largest group being the textile mill operatives, were not likely to belong to the Order of United American Mechanics or the Masons or Odd Fellows. Initiation fees restricted membership to those men who could afford to join and support the activities of the lodges. Men at the lower end of the socioeconomic scale of the community, as well as women, were left out of this circle and found their fellowship in more informal ways—in the home, around a fire, in conversation with kin and friends, at church services and activities, and at public celebrations like Independence Day festivities which were popular in Salem.[9] For these townspeople, exclusion from the activities of the mechanics imbued them, too, with a sense of shared experience. Never a part of the mechanic tradition, having never served apprenticeships or worked as journeymen, these workers were set apart from their neighbors. Factory workers occupied the lowest rank and composed a budding class of industrial laborers in which sons and daughters followed their parents into the factories.[10] This divergence of circumstances between the mechanics on the one hand, and mill workers and day laborers on the other, is indicative of emerging class differences within the community during the late antebellum years. In the decade preceding the Civil War, as more non-Moravians moved into the community and as the political controversies of the 1850s grew more intense, strains became more evident in the community.

The fire company and the militia were more inclusive than the benevolent and fraternal orders. All the townsmen subject to militia duty were required to participate in the regular training meetings of the fire company. The Salem Vigilant Fire Company, organized in 1843, was equipped according to state law with firemen's uniforms, an engine, a new hose carriage, ladders, and a ladder wagon with hooks. Though inclusive of a broader spectrum of the town's population, the fire companies still advanced the artisans' and shopkeepers' predominant role in town life. The officers of the Salem Vigilant Fire Company elected in 1857 were young merchants and mechanics, all of whom had a vested interest in the protection of their workshops and stores.[11] The militia did in fact unite men across class lines. By state law passed in 1830, all white males between the ages of eighteen and forty-five were enrolled in the militia and required to participate in a company muster at least twice a year and a battalion muster once a year. On muster day men from all over the county gathered, bringing together people of diverse backgrounds and from different neighborhoods—people who might never have met otherwise. At militia musters in Salem alcohol and political rhetoric flowed freely, while gambling, fighting, and sports entertained the participants. The Moravian records report numerous complaints about the rowdiness of the musters. In one instance it was alleged that John Wessner and John Spach violated congregation rules by engaging in a marksmanship contest for cash. After one muster the evening liturgy of the local congregation was canceled due to the strain of the noisy day. Despite the disorders and rowdiness, the militia companies aided the socialization process that expanded and molded a sense of community and became instruments for the increased politicization of the community. This was particularly important to the semiskilled and unskilled workers who could not afford to join a Masonic or Odd Fellows lodge. Like eighteenth-century militia at the time of the Revolution, the militia in Salem often became a center of political debate and discussion. Henry Leinbach reported that in October 1831 a number of militiamen met after muster to discuss ways of organizing opposition to Andrew Jackson's reelection as president. The incipient Whigs in the militia unanimously elected Dr. Frederic Schuman, a local notable, as a delegate to the Whig convention in Baltimore which intended to nominate a candidate for the 1832 election.[12]

As militia musters demonstrated, consumption of alcohol and a rousing good time were vital elements of public events in Salem. But the increased use of alcohol and the disorders that resulted prompted increasing concern among members of the community as tippling shops opened and a growing number of storekeepers sold strong drink. Believing alcohol to be the cause of the increasing incidence of disorder in community life, the Aufseher Collegium in 1839 agreed that future members would not serve each other alcoholic beverages, in the hope of avoiding all reproach and offence. The public drunkenness and rowdy behavior of many who attended the annual public examinations at the Salem Girls Boarding School led the Aufseher Collegium in 1846 to even stronger measures in prohibiting the sale of alcoholic drink in the local tavern before and during the examination. In 1852 the heads of households and master workmen convened to address the rising incidents of disorder among the town's boys and young men who frequently gathered on Salem's streets and in the village square in the evening to engage in "deplorable irregularities." These noisy gatherings frequently molested passersby, especially women, and disturbed the peace and quiet of the community with "outrageous and profane language." The town's parents and master craftsmen were blamed for not exercising sufficient authority over their sons and apprentices.[13] The temperance movement in Salem was part of a larger process aimed at addressing the social ills in the community—drunkenness, rowdiness, and crime—that might impede the continued development of the town. The movement attempted to maintain respectability in a community in which the congregation authorities could no longer control personal behavior, since a growing proportion of the community did not belong to the Moravian church.

Efforts to alter personal behavior as a means of eliminating drunkenness and public disorder centered in the local temperance societies. The first temperance society in Salem was organized in 1829, but it was apparently short-lived. In the spring of 1842 about sixty townspeople organized a new temperance society in Salem and won the immediate support of the Elders Conference which believed that drinking in Salem was increasing and "Moravian principles" were unable to change such behavior. Through the 1840s and 1850s the Sons of Temperance directed the temperance campaign in Winston and Salem. The most active antebellum temperance organization, it was founded in New York in 1842 and opened its first branch in North Carolina in Raleigh that same year. Initially, the Sons of Temperance was a secret organization with secret handshakes, signs, and symbols, and a total abstinence pledge. The organization also operated as a mutual aid society providing needed benefits for its members. After a membership fee of $2.00, the regular dues were at least six and a quarter cents a week. In return, every bona fide member in case of illness or disability was entitled to at least $3.00 weekly. Each "brother" was also entitled to $30 to defray burial expenses. If the wife of a member died, he was entitled to $15 for burial expenses. To include the women of the town, a Daughters of Temperance was organized in Salem. Temperance celebrations and lectures entertained and educated the people of Salem. Ministers and professional men were well represented and played leading roles in the local lodges or divisions, but artisans and shopkeepers probably made up the largest numbers which gave the movement a decidedly middle-class tint. A partial reason for the temperance society's appeal to the townspeople was the recreational aspect of the movement, as temperance meetings and rallies with their lectures and debates were popular sources of entertainment. The society played a prominent role in community celebrations on Washington's Birthday and Independence Day.[14]

Those who gathered under the temperance standard agreed that intemperance was the root cause of crime, poverty, and idleness, and an evil that undermined the family, the church, and, in the end, the social order.

Peter Doub, a noted Methodist preacher from Stokes County, labeled alcohol the "master agent of Hell." In an address to the Grand Division of the North Carolina Sons of Temperance in 1852, Doub attributed three-quarters of all pauperism, insanity, murders, and other crimes to strong drink.[15] Temperance won converts in a society in transition, and it promoted a way of life that its adherents believed to be conducive to individual success and a stable social order in the newly emerging circumstances of the Moravian town. As the congregational ethos weakened, the townspeople recognized the need for a new moral order that conformed to the economic and social realities that promoted the unfettered expression of the individual will and the pursuit of private interests. Increased drinking and antisocial behavior, like that of some of the young men of Salem during these years, may have been individual responses to the increasing tensions and uncertainties accompanying emerging individualism as traditional community restraints on behavior weakened. Such antisocial behavior may also have been personal responses to the insecurities and uncertainties economic changes wrought as young men found it more difficult to establish themselves in a trade in Salem. Hence efforts to curb such behavior regarded as detrimental to the community focused on reforming the individual character. Moral suasion was the preferred instrument of changing antisocial behavior. A temperance rally in Salem to celebrate Washington's Birthday in 1855 took a firm stand in support of individual liberty and against coerced sobriety: "Morally and physically, man is a free agent, and any law which seeks to control his volition is an insult offered to his dignity and his understanding . . . " This focus on the free will of people and the individual character had a religious appeal that was expressed in the evangelical movement that swept the country during these years. Temperance and evangelical religion were "interwoven responses" to the same fundamental uncertainties and tensions that characterized antebellum American society.[16]

Evangelical religion was important to the larger process of creating a value system and ways of behavior that fit the needs of a new economic order. Sweeping the South during the first third of the nineteenth century and reshaping the culture of the region, the evangelical movement awakened many southerners to the spiritual side of life. Stressing the sinfulness of human nature, a personal relationship with God, salvation through faith, and the need for conversion through inward grace, evangelicals believed the inner regeneration of the individual as the source of salvation. Evangelical religion preached that self-control and self-discipline were essential to the life of piety toward which Christian men and women should strive and answered needs felt by many southerners at a time when the South and the nation were experiencing social, economic, and political changes. A new code of conduct, a renewed sense of community, and a belief in the responsibility of the individual for his or her own salvation constituted a changing worldview as southerners adopted new perceptions of the changing society around them.[17]

It is difficult to determine who in Salem actually participated in the evangelical movement. Given the wide appeal of the evangelical movement in Stokes and Forsyth counties, artisans, yeoman farmers, day laborers, and mill workers were likely participants. As the leadership of the local temperance organizations demonstrates, the new morality evangelical religion promoted found its greatest expression in the lives of the artisans, shopkeepers, and manufacturers of Winston and Salem. For these southerners, evangelical religion might be regarded as an essential element in a general "tightening up" of the moral code because of its compatibility with new values rationalized by the new economic order.[18] The artisan and the entrepreneur found in evangelical religion an ethos that promoted self-discipline, frugality, temperance, punctuality, and diligence—values increasingly necessary to success in a market economy. Though he did not embrace the evangelical faith sweeping the South, Francis Fries did adopt the ways of behavior many artisans and entrepreneurs believed were conducive to success and which evangelical religion promoted. Fries renounced indulgence in such "worldly pursuits" as bowling in favor of an exclusive attention to his business endeavors and his civic, religious, and family responsibilities. Additionally, there was the belief that religion had a place in the workshop and store. The merchant was admonished to deal justly with his customers while the artisan was to execute his work faithfully, for neither would reach Heaven otherwise. Workers were told that "workshop Christianity" consisted of a "religious fidelity" to the employer and his customers, and to slight or neglect the work one was paid to perform was to commit a sin.[19] For those at the lowest levels of southern society, evangelical religion may have had a different meaning and appeal. Mill workers and day laborers who felt isolated or alienated from the community may have embraced evangelical religion for the sense of belonging and hope for the future that enabled them to endure the present. For these southerners, for whom there was not the promise of material success in the competitive market economy, life offered either a day-by-day existence of monotonous grueling labor wherever it could be found, or tending machinery in a dark, dusty, and oily textile mill where the demands of mechanized production made life unpleasant. For those who did not belong to the influential classes in southern society or had only a limited part in the political and cultural affairs of their communities, evangelical religion offered a sense of shared experience with those of like situation and a feeling that they could at least control their spiritual life. For the powerless, salvation was near at hand to be grasped through faith.

Moravian congregations in and around Salem were challenged by the aggressive proselytizing of evangelical preachers. Through the late 1820s and 1830s camp meetings were frequent events in the Salem neighborhood, and the impact of the Methodist meetings did not go unnoticed. The Moravian minister in Salem wrote in his congregation diary in 1826 that many of his flock fled the regular service for a Methodist camp meeting in nearby Bethania. Among the Moravians, young people appear to have been especially susceptible to the lure of the camp meeting. In 1830 the minister at Bethania wrote that most of his congregation, especially the young, had deserted to the Methodist meeting. This same meeting, held in September 1830, provoked a critical observation by the Bethabara minister who complained of the Methodists' noisy ways and religious practices that made a "thoroughly unsatisfactory impression." He believed, however, that members of his congregation attended the Methodist meetings for an occasional change from the everyday routine and for the opportunity to see something new.[20] Writing in the Salem congregation diary, a Moravian minister observed that because of the Methodists' revivals "somewhat more spirit seems to be stirred up." Henry Leinbach recognized the lure camp meetings held for those Moravians who wanted to see and hear something new. At one camp meeting in August 1831, Leinbach observed: "At the conclusion of the sermon there commences a furious noise, uttered in diverse ways; contortions of faces, clapping of hands, jumping and rolling; some scream as though they were run through with a butcher's knife; faces are to be seen shouting glory, glory! in which any thing [*sic*] but happiness is depicted . . . " The scenes at camp meetings did not agree with Leinbach's view of religion. It astonished him that "men of sound sense" could behave in such a manner. Nevertheless, Leinbach believed that he had heard good sermons at the camp meetings he attended.[21]

The evangelical movement that swept the neighborhoods around Salem during the nineteenth century directly confronted the Unitas Fratrum and pointed to the increasing differentiation in local community life. In the late eighteenth and early nineteenth centuries the extension of evangelical religion was spurred by the migration into the backcountry of people who had little or no attachment to the established church, either the Anglican church in older settlements of North Carolina or the Unitas Fratrum in and around Salem. Those most susceptible to evangelical preaching were southerners who were dissatisfied with traditional authority and behavior, which were buttressed by the established religion that evangelicals identified with the elites of stratified communities.[22] In Stokes and Forsyth counties, the Methodists probably gained many new members from those who were recent migrants to the area and who remained outside of the exclusive congregational life of the Moravians in Salem and other nearby Moravian communities. For many who embraced Methodism, the Unitas Fratrum was probably too closely identified with the firmly established elites of the Salem community. Like the earlier Moravians, nineteenth-century southern evangelicals rejected the traditional distinctions based on political power, wealth, or family background. Instead, they sought a new community with no class distinctions but founded on ideological and moral purity, and created by personal experience, baptism, and discipline.[23] This probably explains why Salem's mill hands and the congregation's young people embraced evangelical religion. For the mill hands, the Methodist camp meeting was more friendly and enjoyable than the worship services of the Moravians, which were directed toward the exclusive membership of the congregation, and certainly easier to understand than the German liturgy, sermons, and hymns. For Moravian youths, evangelical religion may have offered a means by which to assert their independence from congregational and family authority over their lives, especially since such authority may have appeared out of touch with the changes occurring in the lives of Salem's inhabitants. Hence evangelical religion had the power to create new bonds of community but also to introduce new identities and greater differentiation into the community. These trends produced occasional tensions and the potential for deep division, as Salem Manufacturing

Company management and congregation elders discovered with the mill hands who embraced Methodism.

Like fraternal organizations, the temperance movement, and evangelical religion, politics was another source of community unity that carried ambivalent implications. By the late antebellum period politics had become an integral part, an "abiding passion" even, of antebellum community culture in the South. The emergence of a market economy in antebellum America created a greater awareness of diverse economic interests and of the direct impact on individuals of government fiscal and banking policies. This recognition of economic interests, along with the democratization of state constitutions in the 1830s, stimulated the development of competing political elites in local communities who were sensitive to the effects, and opportunities, of national and state economic policies.[24] The political culture of the antebellum community reflected the efforts of citizens to gain control over the institutions that directed their lives and to make government more responsive to existing conditions. This political culture was embodied in the emerging party politics of the community and in the involvement of residents of Salem, and the new county seat of Winston, in public political events.

Participation in political parties, clubs, conventions, and mass public gatherings on the courthouse square gave form to this political culture and demonstrated how much a part of community life politics had become by the 1850s. During the 1830s, the majority of adult white males participated in elections as the constitutional reforms of 1835 extended the right to vote. Political contests became a form of entertainment that added spice to everyday life for all of the townspeople. Speeches and debates between political candidates, open meetings to express the sense of the community on important issues, and parades to enlist support for particular candidates involved the whole community in the political process. Public dinners and barbecues brought the people to the courthouse square or the local grove, which served both politicians and preachers, to hear speeches and debates by candidates and party leaders. On his visit to a Whig party gathering in nearby Rowan County in August 1840, Hugh Johnston witnessed several fights, sang campaign songs, and "returned home as sober as I went."[25] For many years, though, popular politics with its electioneering and factions was not welcome in Salem by congregation authorities, as the Brethren resisted anything that would undermine harmony in the community. For this reason, when Van Nieman Zevely considered publishing a newspaper in Salem in 1840, the Aufseher Collegium expressed its opposition because the newspaper would reflect the views of one of the political parties which they believed would be disadvantageous to the community. Even as late as 1856 the pastor of the Salem congregation, in noting that August 7 was "a lively day" in neighboring Winston as town elections occurred, hoped that "brotherly love not become a casualty."[26] Yet, as in other matters facing the community, it was futile for church leaders to attempt to push back the tides flowing into Salem. The heightened political awareness in the community reflected new loyalties and concerns, and offered further evidence of an increasing differentiation in the community as townspeople became Democrats or Whigs.

The emergence of the market and the attendant dynamics of capitalist enterprise divided the community as people had different interests determined by their relationship to the market. In the 1840s and 1850s these divergent interests were expressed in partisan politics which became a vehicle for the expression of both the hopes and the dissatisfactions of various elements of the community. During these years voters in newly created Forsyth County, as in North Carolina as a whole, developed a strong sense of identification with the Democratic and Whig parties and their respective symbols, as the two parties often offered the electorate contrasting policies on national and state issues. The two parties offered real alternatives to voters, hence political alignments illustrated real differences of attitudes and opinions. During the antebellum years, elections in Stokes and Forsyth counties were sharply contested between the Whigs and Democrats as each party represented a distinctive ideology that derived from worldviews shaped by the beliefs, fears, and hopes of voters as well as particular assumptions about government, society, and the economy.[27]

During the 1830s and 1840s the Whigs were the dominant party in North Carolina because they were able to link in voters' minds national political issues with state and local concerns. While most economic policy issues such as banking and subtreasury schemes may have been too complex for most voters to comprehend fully, historical evidence suggests that large numbers of North Carolina voters, especially merchants, manufacturers, artisans, and commercial farmers in the towns and underdeveloped areas of the state, particularly in the west, were won over to the Whig banner. These voters supported the party's program to promote economic development through state-chartered banks and corporations and public-financed improvements in transportation facilities. The Whig organization in Forsyth County and the party's state convention consistently advanced an activist role for government, calling for the public funding of common schools and internal improvements, and the equitable distribution to the states of revenue derived from public land sales to fund these projects. In particular, the Whigs promoted manufacturing and commerce, becoming the party of "liberated capitalism" which promoted policies designed to "preserve an enlightened republican government and an expanding commercial economy." The Whig party presented a vision of a diversified and differentiated society in which individuals profited or lost, rose or fell, in a fluid social and economic order according to their own abilities.[28]

In Forsyth County the Whigs had a diverse membership, but they tended to win the support of voters who competed in the market economy. Among Forsyth Whigs, 53 percent tended to be engaged in trade or other market activities, either directly as producers or middlemen or indirectly in support functions as lawyers. Only 47 percent of Forsyth Whigs were farmers. Whigs tended to own real property (79 percent), and the mean value of the real property they held was $2,006.07. Forty-two percent of Forsyth Whigs were slaveowners and the mean size of slave holdings was five slaves. Though entrepreneurs like Francis Fries and Edward Belo were prominently represented among Forsyth County Whigs, artisans, shopkeepers, and farmers like David Clewell, Joshua Boner, and Darius Masten were also typical Whigs. Clewell was a Moravian bookbinder who at age fifty owned only his house and shop valued at $700. Boner was a Moravian merchant, a partner in the Salem firm of Boner and Crist. At age forty-two Boner owned real property valued at $3,070 and two slaves. Darius Masten was a farmer, a planter even by Forsyth County standards, who farmed three hundred acres growing wheat, corn, and oats. Masten owned real property valued at $3,000 and seven slaves. As their efforts to dismantle the congregation's authority over the individual pursuit of private interests demonstrated, Fries, Belo, Clewell, and Boner, like their Whig counterparts in other southern communities and in the North, looked to a world of competitive individualism at the expense of community interdependence. They saw opportunities in an expanding market economy and supported government policies that promoted economic development and greater participation in the market.[29]

While those who comprised the Whig party embraced "competitive individualism," other southerners who trusted in notions of personal independence guaranteed by the viability of the household economy and the self-sufficiency of the local community perceived threats to their way of life in the emergence of the impersonal market. These southerners tended to regard with anxiety the tendencies of the market which the Whigs defended—risk, increasing debt, growing dependence on the market, and a higher incidence of insolvency and propertylessness.[30] Many who gathered under the Democratic party banner were suspicious of entrepreneurial enterprise if it promoted by special privileges one group over another. Democrats hoped to preserve what they believed was the simple and direct relationship between wealth and labor, and minimize or even eliminate risk from commerce. Democrats sought to constrain commercial and industrial development within the moral, economic, and political ethos of agrarian democratic society. North Carolina Democrats generally opposed initiatives necessary for the operation of a capitalist economy. They tended to limit the privileges of state banks, opposed chartering corporations, and denied the authority of state government to promote and finance internal improvements. Piedmont Democrats from the 1830s took a firm and consistent stand for conservative and limited government, a "rigid construction" of the Constitution, and opposition to monopolies and special privileges, exemplified by the Bank of the United States and the protective tariff, which benefited the few. The party resisted the distribution to the states of revenue derived from public land sales out west and proposed that these revenues should be used by the federal treasury to pay the public debt.[31]

The characteristics of Forsyth County Democrats reflected the party's ideology. Men like Samuel Alspaugh, a twenty-five-year-old farmer who owned real property valued at $400, Solomon Transou, a fifty-five-year-old farmer who owned sixteen slaves and real property valued at $5,000, and wagonmaker J. M. Vawter who at age thirty-six owned a house and shop valued at $375 belonged to the Democratic party because of the party's commitment to a vision of America as a republic of independent proprietors of small farms and enterprises. Of Forsyth Democrats, 70 percent owned real property and 67 percent were farmers. These Democrats were on average not as wealthy as their Whig neighbors. The mean value of their real property was $1,224.81. These Democrats were also somewhat less likely to be slaveholders than Whigs, but those Democrats who were tended to own more slaves because of their involvement in agriculture. Forty percent of Forsyth Democrats were slaveholders, each owning an average of six slaves. The composition of the Forsyth County Democratic party was not as diverse as the Whig party and its members were less likely to engage in commercial or manufacturing enterprises. Only 26 percent of Forsyth Democrats were engaged in nonagricultural activities and of these, 23 percent were artisans and 3 percent were lawyers. As the statistics reveal, the makeup of the Forsyth County Whig and Democratic parties reflected the respective membership, interests, and ideology of the state and national parties.[32]

The 1850s were politically eventful years in North Carolina, and the Democrats and the Whigs offered the people of Forsyth County clear choices on a variety of issues important to the interest of the county and its citizens. The public stance and composition of the parties and the votes they won contribute to an understanding of what the population of Winston and Salem considered important and what hopes they had for themselves in the future. Through the 1850s the two parties sparred over public funding of internal improvements, public education, and universal white suffrage. Through the 1840s the Democrats resisted projects that would increase public expenditures and hence the authority of government, opposing public support of internal improvements and education while the Whigs promoted state aid for improvements.[33] An examination of the election results for the years 1852–56 provides insight into the appeal of the two parties in Forsyth County and Winston Township (which included the town of Salem). In state elections the Democrats consistently carried Forsyth County, their strength being in the rural neighborhoods of small farmers and farm laborers. The Whigs carried Winston Township, with the commercial classes of Winston and Salem.[34]

Assuming that loyalty to a party and its principles carried over from the senatorial to the gubernatorial election, the vote of those owning less than fifty acres can be determined by subtracting the vote for senator from the vote for governor. This procedure illuminates how workers and petty proprietors voted. As Tables 4.1 and 4.2 illustrate, from 1852 to 1856 there was an increasing tendency in both Winston Township and Forsyth County to vote Whig, probably because the Whig party supported a constitutional convention to reform the suffrage laws and because of the party's stand in favor of distribution of public land revenues to pay for internal improvements and public education. During these

TABLE 4.1

Distribution of Gubernatorial and Senatorial Vote, Winston 1852–56

	1852		1854		1856	
	vote	%	vote	%	vote	%
Governor: Total						
Whig-American	300	53	334	57	356	56
Democratic	262	47	253	43	277	44
Governor: Nonpropertied Vote						
Whig-American	193	52	240	58	263	57
Democratic	175	48	172	42	198	43
Senate:						
Whig-American	107	55	94	54	93	54
Democratic	87	45	81	46	79	46

Sources: *People's Press*, August 7, 1852, August 5, 1854, August 5, 1856.

years there was a corresponding loss of votes for the Democrats, even while they continued to carry the county. Table 4.1 shows that in 1852 the free suffrage issue probably gained many votes for the Democrats. Of the nonpropertied voters, the Democrats took 66 percent of the vote in the county and 48 percent in Winston Township. But as the Whigs repeatedly campaigned for a convention to address the free suffrage issue, they cut into the Democrats' strength. The Democrats' share of the vote of workers and small proprietors dropped in the county from 66 percent in 1852 to 61 percent in 1854 and 57 percent in 1856, and in Winston Township from 48 percent in 1852 to 42 percent in 1854 and 43 percent

TABLE 4.2

Distribution of Gubernatorial and Senatorial Vote, Forsyth County 1852–56

	1852		1854		1856	
	vote	%	vote	%	vote	%
Governor: Total						
Whig-American	356	38	468	42	570	42
Democratic	571	62	644	58	803	58
Governor: Nonpropertied Vote						
Whig-American	164	34	240	39	360	43
Democratic	312	66	375	61	471	57
Senate:						
Whig-American	192	43	228	46	210	39
Democratic	259	57	269	54	332	61

Sources: *People's Press*, August 7, 1852, August 5, 1854, August 5, 1856.

in 1856. The election results show that, regardless of the issues in a particular election, the Whigs consistently garnered over one-half of the votes of the workers and petty proprietors of Winston Township. This pattern was not true in the county, where the Democratic vote at times was overwhelming. The loyalty to the Democratic party among the small farmers, artisans, and day laborers of the rural neighborhoods might have been due to the perceived threat of the market to their way of life. These people probably voted Democratic in support of the party's longtime stance on banking, public expenditures, and special privileges of corporations as well as issues regarding equal political rights and the dignity of common people. This may account in part for the support the Democrats enjoyed among slightly less than one-half of Winston Township's workers and petty proprietors, but most of these seemed to vote Whig because of that party's historic support of commerce. In their support of the banking system, internal improvements, the tariff, and industrial development, the Whigs best represented small-town commercial interests.[35] The nonpropertied voters, including many shopkeepers, may have voted Whig for the above reason but also because of the political reforms which the party advocated. The Democratic party in Winston Township probably attracted those who felt their interests to be different from the wealthier Whigs. Those in Winston Township who voted with the Democratic party probably did so because of their ties to the yeoman culture of the countryside. These Democrats may have been mill workers and day laborers who still regarded themselves as rooted in the land, but with ambitions someday to own a farm and maybe a few slaves.

By the end of the 1850s partisan politics had created deep divisions in the community that were often expressed in personal animosities. The breakup of the Whig party and the resulting party realignment, the secession controversy, and the hardships of the Civil War found members of the community bitterly at odds with each other. With the disappearance of the Whig party and the rise of the American party, politics in Salem became more vicious and personal. The dissolution of the Whig party removed a source of stability in local politics that enabled townspeople to disagree over issues without that disagreement weakening the bonds of community. The Democratic party was itself divided into factions that could not be disciplined and held together without the threat of a strong opposition party.[36] Francis Fries who had left the Whig party for the Democratic party mourned the demise of the "old high tone" of the

Whig party and the rise of "political brigands" among the ruins of that party. Fries observed in 1859 that for the first time in Salem the leaders of the Opposition party—former Whigs and Know-Nothings who opposed the Democrats—"make party a test in town elections, and denounce every man who would not go the whole stripe lost and unworthy of Whig support. . . . The motive and precedent are bad and nothing is calculated to render this community odious with the county and the state more than such spirit of proscription." One member of the community complained to the *People's Press* that there was a "Court-house-clique" that ruled the county and local politics through edicts much like the cotton barons of the eastern counties.[37]

In 1849 the outside world drew even closer to the congregation community, ending the separateness that the Moravians originally sought in settling in the Carolina backcountry. The increasing population of Stokes County demanded the creation of a new county. The General Assembly divided Stokes County and reorganized the southern half into Forsyth County. The population of Forsyth County in 1850 was 11,168, reflecting a 43 percent increase in the portion of Stokes County reorganized into the new county.[38] Because Salem was situated at the center of the new county, the recently appointed Forsyth County commissioners applied to the Aufseher Collegium for thirty-one acres adjacent to the village on which to build the new county seat. The Collegium, believing that the establishment of the county seat so near Salem would have a profound influence on the congregation community and hence not inclined to assume the responsibility for ruling on the commissioners' request, referred the matter to the Congregation Council. In a series of meetings in February and March 1849, the Congregation Council discussed the location of the county seat and recognized that the formation of a new town might have a considerable impact on Salem's economics and morals. By the end of March a clear consensus had emerged that the location of the county seat close to Salem would have a positive impact on the Moravian community, and the Collegium unanimously accepted a proposal to sell the commissioners a tract adjacent to the northern boundary of Salem, with the conditions that the courthouse had to be located in the middle of this land and that streets laid out on this land were to be a continuation of Salem streets. The Congregation Council resolved by a

Fig. 4.1. A winter view of Salem Square with the Congregation Church and Salem Female Academy, around 1850. Lithograph of drawing by E. A. Vogler. Courtesy of the Wachovia Historical Society.

vote of fifty-seven to ten that the courthouse be built as close to Salem as possible. The county commissioners accepted the proposal and requested fifty-one acres which would be adequate to lay out three rows of town lots and four streets. With the approval of the Aufseher Collegium, the congregation sold Forsyth County fifty-one and a quarter acres at five dollars per acre. On January 15, 1851, the General Assembly named the new county seat Winston. Until the new courthouse for Forsyth County was built, the county court met in the Salem concert hall.[39]

Some members of the community saw ill foreboding in these developments. In the annual memorabilia of the congregation, Salem's pastor recorded his fears for the future of the congregation community:

So we look forward to many things in the future which can have consequences for Salem as a congregation of the Savior and particularly as a settlement congregation, that we are unable to foresee at present. May our dear Lord in the exceeding riches of His grace and truth overrule all for good. . . . Much has occurred during the course of this year which is not compatible with the glory of our Lord or the welfare of immortal souls. Rather to a regrettable extent it has been a hindrance to this high goal.[40]

As the pastor's comments illustrate, the creation of Forsyth County and the location of Winston so close to Salem created apprehension among many in Salem about the economic and moral influences that the county seat would exert on the congregation. These fears were not unfounded, since antebellum county seats in North Carolina were often the sites of "wildness and rudeness, intemperance, ferocity, gaming, licentiousness, and malicious litigation," as large numbers of people flowed into the county seat from the outlying areas. The pastor of the Salem congregation noted that when the county court met, large numbers of people crowded into the town and the increased sale and consumption of alcohol on these occasions led to conduct that was not compatible with the spirit of a community of saints.[41] Once again, as in the controversies over slaveholding and the congregation's regulation of the trades, the community was divided. Conservatives among the Moravians feared that new settlers would move in, bringing with them ideas which might conflict with the ideals of the Moravian congregation and threaten the remnants of the Moravian way of life. But pro-development businessmen in the congregation believed that the new settlers to the county seat would have a rejuvenating effect on Salem. Francis Fries along with F. C. Meinung, a law office clerk, John Vogler, a silversmith, Christian Reed, a carpenter, Solomon Mickey, a cooper, David Collins, a bricklayer, and merchants Jacob Tise and John P. Vest were among several Salem artisans and merchants who saw new economic opportunities in the new village and became original property owners in Winston. Thus while some Moravians looked backward, fearing the disturbing influence of the nearby county seat, others—among them the growing commercial interests of Salem—believed that locating the county seat several miles away would hurt Salem economically because a new town would grow up around the courthouse. This fear was justified because most of the towns of North Carolina were significant only as the seats of municipal functions for their respective counties. The county seats of antebellum North Carolina flourished because it was convenient to carry on commercial affairs where public business was also conducted.[42]

With the county seat Winston located only a few hundred feet to the north, Salem quickly prospered as the commercial center of the new county. In February 1851 the Salem *People's Press* reported "a new impulse" energized the town's businesses and that "the march of Salem is decidedly onward." During the 1850s a cohesive entrepreneurial class emerged to play a leading role in the lives of Salem and the new county seat, Winston. These men engaged in intensive efforts to create the conditions conducive to the further development of Salem and Winston as well as the neighboring countryside. Expressing the desires of these businessmen, the *People's Press* in the early 1850s consistently championed the cause of turnpikes, plankroads, and railroads in the piedmont. Salem's Whig newspaper noted that the area's grain sold at "almost unprecedented high prices" as large quantities were sent to Fayetteville and on to Wilmington and foreign markets because of grain failures in Europe and tensions between Russia and Turkey. But, according to the *People's Press*, Forsyth farmers still relied for the most part on local markets due to the inadequacy of internal improvements in the piedmont. The newspaper lamented that Forsyth farmers were at a disadvantage compared to farmers in the western and northwestern states who, though more remote from the seaboard, benefited from better transportation facilities which gave them access to lucrative foreign markets.[43] Francis Fries and a group of entrepreneurs that included merchants Edward Belo, Robert Gray, and S. B. Allen were at the center of the development movement. During the early 1850s these men initiated and invested in a number of schemes to construct roads to connect the surrounding countryside to Salem and to outlets to the national and world markets through Fayetteville or Petersburg. These men were also involved in the creation of the Salem Savings Institution to provide the community with capital for further investment in development.[44]

The men who led this development movement constituted an elite which directed the cultural, economic, and political affairs of the community. In Salem, the elite composed the congregation's Aufseher Collegium and the town's municipal government. Between 1841 and 1861 only twenty-six men served on the governing bodies of the town. In fact, there was a significant carryover from the Aufseher Collegium to the town's secular municipal government which was established in the late 1850s after the state legislature vested municipal government in a town board of commissioners and a mayor. Of those who filled these offices between 1841 and 1861, one-half were artisans and the remainder professionals, merchants, manufacturers, and farmers. All of those who served on the governing boards were property owners and 35 percent were slaveholders. However, only 15 percent of the artisans who formed this elite owned slaves, while 85 percent of the manufacturers and professionals were slaveholders. The three manufacturers owned a total of sixty-three slaves. In Winston the situation was much the same. Artisans made up

55 percent of the town commission in 1859 and 1861, while merchants were 27 percent of the commissioners. Thirty-six percent of the commissioners owned slaves, but only one artisan on the commission owned slaves. As with the commissioners and congregation authorities of Salem, all of the Winston commissioners were property holders. This elite owed much of its position to the changing economic order of the community. As successful mechanics, merchants, and manufacturers they thrived in the new competitive market that disrupted the lives of others not so fortunate. As men of capital and property they were set apart from the mass of workers and shopkeepers of Winston and Salem. It was the possession of wealth and, concomitantly, political and economic power, that distinguished these men as a class.[45]

By the middle of the decade Salem's entrepreneurial elite could see both positive evidence of development and the potential for even greater growth. In "A Ramble about Town" in 1856, the *People's Press* found in Salem: three gunsmith shops; three cabinetmaker's shops; two jewellers; three copper, sheet-iron, and tin-plate establishments; three shoemakers; three blacksmiths; one extensive tanyard; two coopers; five confectioneries; two tailors; one hatter; one saddler; one chairmaker; one bookbinder; two coach-making establishments; two Daguerrean galleries; one potter; several carpenters; two steam cotton mills; one steam woolen mill; one steam flouring mill; a steam saw mill; a water-propelled paper mill. In 1856 Salem was the home of over twelve hundred people.[46]

As Salem grew many of the townspeople recognized that the community was leaving behind the congregational way of life. There was also the recognition that the time was drawing near when the remaining structures of the congregation community would have to be dismantled and town government reorganized to meet the demands of new circumstances in Salem. In April 1854 thirty-six householders petitioned the Salem Aufseher Collegium for the abolition of the lease system in the congregation town.[47] The implications of the petition were profound for the congregation. The petitioners were, in effect, asking for the dismantling of the congregation system which had given life in the community its special character. The petitioners sought the transformation of Salem into a secular town governed by the laws of the State of North Carolina. The lease system had been the keystone of the congregation system which enabled church boards to exercise authority over members of the community and enforce compliance with the congregation regulations.

Without the lease system, congregation authority would have no meaning because conformity to the rules of the congregation could not be coerced through the threat of revocation of a householder's lease and the surrender of his or her house or shop. Furthermore, without the lease system congregation authorities could no longer preserve Salem as a homogeneous community of the Moravian faithful. In the future, anyone who wanted to move to Salem would be able to acquire a house and workshop and establish him- or herself in the community. Hence the congregation as a unified community in Salem with a common purpose would cease to exist.

The abolition of the lease system grew out of the recognition by congregation authorities that there were repeated violations of the congregation rules by Moravians in Salem who rented and sold rooms, houses, and shops to non-Moravians without the proper permission of the authorities. Such behavior demonstrated the futility of enforcing the congregation rules and regulations. The situation compelled the Collegium to confess that it was no longer able to enforce the rules and regulations when members of the congregation did not voluntarily comply. The Collegium concluded that "to depend upon forceful measures to deal with every breach of them [rules and regulations], even supposing that such were available, could perhaps ultimately lead to more harm for the congregation than benefit." Two specific paragraphs in the regulations demanded attention if the congregation authorities were to address the petition before the Collegium. Section V, paragraph 3 stated: "Every member of the congregation is bound to abstain from undertaking any thing, which might prove injurious to the spiritual or temporal welfare of another." The Collegium concluded that this section was phrased too loosely and was open to many interpretations, thus it should be deleted. Section V, paragraph 4 stated: "Should anyone persist in transgressing the rules and regulations of the congregation, or even prove guilty of seducing others, such an one is to be excluded from the congregation; [and] in the latter case, if possible, to be removed from this place." The Collegium proposed deleting the phrase "in the latter case, if possible, to be removed from this place" since it had been essentially a "dead letter" as its enforcement had been rare.[48] At the January 28 meeting of the Aufseher Collegium a consensus emerged from the discussion that these rules had not been adhered to for years. Indeed the Collegium admitted that for a number of years now the state of affairs in regard to the continual preservation of the congregational settlement or—what might in some sense have the same significance—of the lease system had become, if not entirely impracticable, yet at least so involved in difficulties and deficiencies that under the present state of affairs one would yield to a delusion— though one which many find pleasure in cherishing—if one would consider this still to be a true congregational settlement.

The Collegium recognized that this state of affairs had resulted from earlier decisions to rescind the regulations on slaveholding and the con- duct of the trades, because of the circumstances which derived from the expansion of trade and commerce. The present situation in the congrega- tion was also attributed to the growth of the town in recent years. Finally, after much consideration and debate, the Aufseher Collegium on January 31, 1856, adopted a resolution calling for the abolition of the lease system in Salem and proposing that lots in the town be held in fee simple. The Collegium's resolution announced, "And whereas further a stronger [and] more determined disinclination manifests itself in a considerable portion of the members of the Congregation, to be governed by rules [and] regulations which, strictly observed and carried out, would interfere with their temporal concerns, [and] deprive them in some degree at least of that free [and] untrammeled action so necessary to the successful pursuit of business." On November 18 the Congregation Council of Salem voted by a majority of more than two-thirds to approve the amendments to the Salem congregation regulations which the Aufseher Collegium and the Aeltesten Conferenz had proposed in February. The next day the Provin- zial Helfer Conferenz ratified the decision of the Congregation Council to abandon the lease system. Now anyone, regardless of "religious qualifi- cation," could become a citizen in Salem, buy a lot for a house, shop, or store, and not be subject to the ecclesiastical jurisdiction that had once governed the town.[49]

As the Aufseher Collegium noted in its deliberations over the lease system, Salem by the mid-1850s was in truth no longer a congregation community in the sense that it was a place where members of the Mora- vian congregation, isolated from the direct influence of others, could practice their faith and devotion. The Collegium observed that non- Moravians were a considerable presence in the town, and the numbers bear this out. Given the *People's Press* estimate that the Salem population in 1856 was just over twelve hundred, the Moravian congregation, which numbered 676 persons at the end of 1852, made up only about one-half of the town's total population. Hence the congregation system of order and authority which was so dependent upon voluntary compliance among the faithful was no longer relevant in the community that had evolved by 1856. The townspeople recognized that new forms of order and authority were necessary to hold the community together. A town meeting on November 28 adopted resolutions presented by Francis Fries petitioning the General Assembly for the incorporation of the town of Salem. The town meeting elected a committee of five prominent businessmen—Francis Fries, Edward Belo, Rufus L. Patterson, C. L. Banner, and E. A. Vogler—to advance the townspeople's cause with the state legislators. On December 13, 1856, an act to incorporate the town of Salem was ratified by the General Assembly.[50]

As the people of Salem embraced new loyalties that supplemented their identity as Moravians, these loyalties often came to represent factions that occasionally divided the community. Community solidarity weakened as the bonds of community created by the ethos of the congregation dissipated. But these new loyalties might also be seen as an attempt to forge a new sense of solidarity among those who embraced different interests. Intense tensions divided Salem as its people dismantled the congregational system, and community had to be recreated, separate from the congregational ethos, out of the conditions that existed there during the antebellum years. The activities of fraternal organizations, temperance societies, evangelical religion, and partisan politics illustrate the circumstances in Salem resulting from increasing differentiation in the congregation community that prompted the dismantling of congregation authority over life in the town in the 1850s. Despite the stresses and strains introduced into the community by the townspeople's new interests and loyalties, it would be inaccurate to see in the differentiation described here evidence of declension among the Moravians of Salem. The declension model so popular with historians of the religious communities of seventeenth- and eighteenth-century New England reveals little of and in fact misinterprets the nature of the Moravians' experience in Salem. That they dismantled the congregational structures of life in Salem and embraced the civil and economic institutions of a secular society does not demonstrate a decline in piety or religious feeling among the Moravians. While the people of Salem embraced the economic changes that were occurring around them, they held fast to their religious faith. They were no less Moravians for creating a municipal government in Salem or joining the Odd Fellows, Masons, or Sons of Temperance. They still felt their faith and worshiped as their fathers and mothers had, attending services and religious celebrations, hearing the liturgy, and singing the hymns. But by the 1850s their lives were more complex in a world that was changing around them. Moving from the simple and homogenous congregation village toward the heterogenous complexity of a municipality, the community at Salem was changing to meet the realities of this new world.[51]

The Community at War

The community that had evolved by the end of the antebellum period was unable to contain divisive tensions that occasionally erupted in partisan local politics and that surfaced in the unsettled conditions of the Civil War years. These years revealed the costs to the community of the new identities and interests among the townspeople. Without the old communal ideal of subordinating private ambitions and interests to the spirit of brotherhood and the common good of the congregation, social tensions and disorders plagued the community as the townspeople competed in the market for scarce goods and challenged each other for positions of power and influence. The experiences of the people of Winston and Salem during the Civil War reveal the tenuous ties of community after the rapid economic and social transformation of the 1840s and 1850s as the tension and stress of war uncovered the depths of division in the two towns. The open avowal of partisan politics and the unfettered pursuit of private wealth which emerged in the 1850s had weakened the bonds once cemented by community consensus in the congregation town. With internal divisions in Winston and Salem evident on several levels, it was difficult for the people to unite in support of the political and military aims of the Confederacy. Traditional deference to community elites eroded during the 1860s as many members of these elites continued to support the Confederate cause while the common people became dissatisfied. The people of Winston and Salem, like their fellow North Carolinians, experienced the war in many different ways as the war's impact on their lives differed according to their specific situations in society. As the burdens of war weighed more heavily on North Carolinians, they grew more and more critical and discontented with the losses they suffered and the hardships they endured, until bitter opposition to the war and the Confederate government erupted.[1]

The deep divisions in the community were evident in the hard-fought and closely contested elections of 1860 when members of local political factions increasingly turned to personal attacks against each other. While fears for the survival of the Union and the preservation of southern rights occupied the thoughts of the people of Forsyth County and North Carolina, state and local elections in August 1860 centered on state issues and the differing policies of the Democratic and Whig/Opposition parties. Against the backdrop of national politics, the two parties continued to disagree over the distribution of public land revenue and internal improvements. But the taxation of slaves emerged as a new issue, with the fearsome potential of dividing both parties along sectional lines and communities by class. North Carolina's increasing need for revenue in the 1850s had led to rising taxes for most of the state's citizens, but especially for those who were compensated for their labor in wages, salaries, and fees—generally artisans, laborers, and professionals. Ad valorem taxation, the taxation of all property, including slaves, on the basis of its value, shifted the tax burden more equitably to wealthier property owners, especially slaveholders. In 1860, the Whig/Opposition party picked up the ad valorem issue and made it a centerpiece of the party's appeal to voters as an issue of fairness and equality among white men. The Democrats opposed ad valorem taxation as a dangerous issue that divided slaveholders and nonslaveholders. The taxation issue stirred up much interest in Forsyth County. Francis Fries, now a Democrat after the demise of the Whig party and chairman of the Joint Finance Committee in the General Assembly, wrote to Judge Thomas Ruffin, a wealthy planter and prominent Democrat, that ad valorem taxation was popular among his constituents and advocated by many. Fries's brother Henry wrote from Salem in June 1860 about the great excitement generated by the coming election, which produced such intense feelings and hot debate that one had to keep one's views close to the vest. Henry Fries believed that the ad valorem issue would win as many supporters as free suffrage had in the 1850s. The Whig/Opposition promotion of ad valorem taxation as an issue of equality among free white men proved successful in painting the Democrats as favoring wealthy slaveholders at the expense of the majority of North Carolina taxpayers. The *People's Press* put the issue in terms that the people of Winston and Salem could appreciate: "Is it right and proper that the owner of a tract of land or a house in town pay five dollars tax on it, while the owner of a slave worth a thousand or fifteen hundred dollars pay only one dollar and fifty cents tax? . . . this glaring inequality and injustice should be remedied."[2]

In Forsyth County and across North Carolina fears for the Union and southern rights as well as ad valorem taxation brought out the vote in August 1860. Over 80 percent of the state's adult white male population cast a ballot. Running on concerns for southern unity and still holding the sympathy of North Carolinians for the party's support of free suffrage in the 1850s, the Democrats were able to hold onto the governor's office. In Forsyth County, though, the Whig/Opposition party won the vote for governor and elected a state senator and one member of the House of Commons. The Whiggish *People's Press* saw a moral in the vote:

> That a majority of the people, including many noble and whole souled Democrats as well as Whigs, are determined no longer to be borne down and ruled by the despotism of Democratic leaders and officeholders. . . . These leaders espoused the cause of Breckinridge, the candidate of W. L. Yancey and other Disunionists . . . and they met with a signal rebuke from the people of Forsyth.[3]

The presidential election in November 1860 shifted the voters' attention to sectional issues, and both the Democratic and Whig/Opposition parties presented themselves to Forsyth County voters as the best defenders of slavery and southern rights, thereby acknowledging a popular commitment to these issues. At the party's state convention in March 1860, North Carolina Democrats expressed their concern for the defense of southern rights, the preservation of slavery, and the "rise of a sectional and fanatical party" in the North. The party's platform asserted the constitutional rights of every United States citizen to take his slave property into national territories. North Carolina Democrats believed that their party offered the only hope of achieving the unity of action necessary to defend the constitutional rights of southerners and preserve the Constitution and the Union from the "aggressive and unprincipled" Republican party.[4]

The Opposition party, made up of former members of the Whig and American parties as well as disgruntled Democrats, affirmed its determination to maintain the rights of southerners in slavery. But it believed that the protection of those rights was best guaranteed within the Union. Calling for loyalty to the Constitution and the laws of the Union, the party steered a moderate course to present a contrast to the fire-eating radicalism of the southern-rights Democrats. The Opposition charged the Democrats with keeping up a "systematic agitation" of the dangerous and emotional issue of slavery and of violating long-established compromises between the conflicting interests of North and South. According to the Opposition party, the Democrats stirred sectional feeling in the South which fostered sectionalism in the North and provided the impetus for the rise of the Republican party.[5]

In the presidential election of 1860 Forsyth County voters confronted bewildering choices, reflecting the inadequacy of partisan politics in moderating passions and healing deepening divisions in the community. The Democratic party in 1860 split into two sectional factions and offered voters two candidates for president: Senator Stephen Douglas of Illinois and Vice President John C. Breckinridge of Kentucky. Southern moderates in 1860 coalesced with elements of the former Whig-American party to support the candidacy of John Bell of Tennessee for president. The Constitutional Union party, looking to the "old Whig strength" to bring about the "restoration of lost harmony," offered voters a conservative alternative to the disunionism of the Breckinridge Democrats.[6]

The Salem *Western Sentinel* endorsed Breckinridge, calling the election a battle for the Constitution and the last chance to avoid a defeat which would be "disastrous" for the Democratic party and the southern people. The Salem *People's Press* endorsed Bell and called upon Forsyth's citizens to "put a quietus to the threats of Disunion." Forsyth County magistrate Rufus L. Patterson, son of a prominent piedmont planter and politician and himself an aspiring merchant and manufacturer in Salem, regarded a vote for Breckinridge as a vote for secession. Patterson wrote a friend in October 1860 that he intended to abandon the Democrats to vote for Bell, not because he intended to join the Constitutional Union party, but because he believed that "in the present distracted condition of our country my vote for that ticket will prove more effective in establishing a Union sentiment in North Carolina than if it were cast for either Breckinridge or Douglas." Patterson was put off by the southern Democrats' demagogic claim that southerners' rights were violated if slavery was prohibited in the western territories. Patterson believed that thoughtful men would see through this issue. "The monstrous absurdity about our rights being taken away in the territories etc. being sufficient cause for breaking up the best government in the world cannot deceive those who are really patriots," Patterson wrote to his friend and fellow Democrat J. W. Alspaugh. Patterson was forthrightly "a Union man" who could not vote for Breckinridge because those who wanted to destroy the Union had lined up behind Breckinridge. William A. Lash corroborated Patterson's view of the Democrats. Lash observed that "everyone who voted for Breckinridge is looked on and counted as a secession man." In the local press, Breckinridge was labeled the secession candidate, and many Forsyth County voters apparently believed this despite the efforts of Breckinridge's supporters to portray their candidate as loyal to the Union.[7]

The combination of the secession issue and the old statewide political controversies of the 1850s—distribution of revenues from the sale of public lands, ad valorem taxation of slaves, and a strong commitment to internal improvements—spurred a large number of Forsyth County's citizens to abandon the Democratic party for the Whig/Opposition party in the 1860 elections. In the local municipal elections in Salem Whigs swept the Democrats from office, capturing the mayor's office and the board of commissioners. Democrats Francis Fries, Edward Belo, and Rufus Patterson were turned out. The victors were identified as former Know-Nothings; "several of them naturally so," according to Patterson. These elections in such difficult times stoked hot emotions. Francis Fries expressed his frustration: "Such is the desperation and recklessness of the Opposition, and such the spirit of some would-be leaders in Salem, that some of the best men have espoused the Democratic cause. Ed and Lewis Belo, Henry Fries, E. A. Vogler [all, along with Fries were former Whigs], and others . . . have taken a decided stand." According to Fries, local members of the Whig/Opposition slandered and defamed their political opponents. Fries observed:

> the leaders of the know nothing party have the effrontery to declare that in Politics, as in horse trade, all things are admissible and fair, and misrepresentations and falsehoods are the order of the day. Not only do they pursue a man whom they consider in their way into the social circle, but they hunt down any one [*sic*] whom they consider friendly to such a man.[8]

In the state elections in August 1860, the Whig/Opposition party garnered 50.3 percent of the vote, up from 42 percent in 1858. This represented a significant loss for the Democrats, who had garnered 58 percent of the county's vote in 1858 but only 49.7 percent in 1860. The Democratic candidate for governor won 49.7 percent of the county's vote, while Breckinridge took 44 percent of the presidential vote. The Whig/Opposition gubernatorial candidate garnered 50.3 percent, while Bell won 52 percent. Of course, Bell split the pro-Union, antisecession vote with Douglas, who took 3 percent. Therefore, the antisecession candidates won 55 percent of the vote to Breckinridge's 44 percent. The Democratic vote declined from August to November by 5.7 percent, while the Opposition gained 5 percent.[9] The voters who cast ballots for the Whig/Opposition party in August supported the Constitutional Union party in November, and some Democrats deserted their party in November instead of voting for Breckinridge.

As the secession crisis of the winter and spring of 1861 swept the Deep South, North Carolinians were quite calm and moderate on the prominent sectional issues, and the political climate remained pro-Union. Because it maintained many ties to the economy of the northern states and to the Union, North Carolina had few ties to the cotton-growing Deep South states that spewed forth the radical rhetoric of secession. Furthermore, two-party competition in North Carolina between the Democrats and the former Whigs continued to lessen those anxieties over the protection of southern rights and way of life. North Carolinians were not so tied to the Democratic party to believe that its defeat in national politics signaled the pending destruction of southern rights. They knew from their own experiences in the 1840s and 1850s that political parties rise and fall and that parties and policies change with each election. With such confidence born of experience, the results of the national election in 1860 did not seem as dreadful as the reactions of the one-party states further south implied.[10]

The vote for the Constitutional Union party in November 1860 provides some indication of the extent of Union feeling in Forsyth County. Over one-half of the citizens of Forsyth County proved unwilling to vote for a Democratic candidate who was even suspected of holding anti-Unionist sentiments, even though the county was a Democratic stronghold through the 1850s. Consequently, Forsyth County voted overwhelmingly against secession in 1861. Many Moravians in Forsyth County embraced Unionist sentiments until Abraham Lincoln's call for troops, because they found it difficult to sunder familial and ecclesiastical relations with their Pennsylvania brethren who had nourished the Wachovia congregations for over a hundred years. Many no doubt shared

Rufus Patterson's unwillingness to see the Union destroyed merely because a Republican president had been elected. Patterson believed Abraham Lincoln should be given a chance to prove himself, and if Lincoln committed no "clear, wilful, and palpable violation" of southern rights, citizens should submit to his government. For Rufus Patterson, "dissolution is a remedy for no evil—it will bring ten thousand evils where we now have one." B. L. Bitting echoed Patterson's sentiment when he wrote John F. Poindexter, a prominent Forsyth County Whig, of his hope "that the extremists of the South will become more calm and desist from any rash acts, at any rate until we see what Lincoln will do."[11]

The Union spirit ran strong in Forsyth County in the winter of 1861. On January 4 the largest meeting ever assembled in the county gathered at the courthouse to express the sentiments of the people of Forsyth County on the secession crisis. The *People's Press* noted the bipartisan character of the meeting with the participation of prominent Democrats like Rufus Patterson, who served as the chairman of the proceedings. According to the newspaper, "all the classes were represented" which gave the meeting more than ordinary weight. The meeting unanimously adopted resolutions which pronounced secession "to be an abandonment of all rights in the Union, and no remedy for a single grievance complained of." The meeting also resolved that "while the Resolutions show the intention of the people to stand by the Union and the Constitution, yet they firmly demand an observance of all its provisions by the North." Most of Forsyth County's citizens apparently shared the belief of the *People's Press* that North Carolina's interests were best served in an alignment with the more moderate border states of Virginia, Maryland, Tennessee, Kentucky, and Missouri. They were willing to take a "wait-and-see" stance toward the Lincoln administration, but they remained vigilant of any threats to the South's rights and interests. The meeting was moderate in tone, even conciliatory toward the new administration, but firm in resolve that the people of Forsyth County would brook no interference with their constitutional rights. While stating that secession, even if peaceably effected, was not an "appropriate and adequate remedy" for southern grievances, the meeting recognized the right of resistance by force to "unauthorized injustice and oppression" on the part of the Lincoln administration.[12]

While the seven states of the Lower South seceded in reaction to Abraham Lincoln's election to the presidency to form the Confederate States of America between December 1860 and February 1861, the General Assembly gathered in Raleigh and debated the state's course. In North Carolina, as in Arkansas, Virginia, and Tennessee, a majority of citizens refused to leave the Union after Lincoln's election. The Unionists believed that until Lincoln acted unconstitutionally, as in coercing the seceded states, North Carolina would remain in the Union. But secessionist Democrats in the General Assembly called for a convention to consider how North Carolina would respond to the Republican victory. The Unionists, mostly Whigs, were able to put off the secessionists' proposal until passions cooled. Eventually the legislature passed a bill that called for an election on February 28, 1861, to decide for or against a convention and to elect delegates to that convention. In the vote, a little over one-half of the state's voters rejected the proposed convention and gave the Unionists a two-third majority among the delegates chosen.[13] Revealing the extent of Union spirit among the county's citizens, the people of Forsyth County voted against having a secession convention, 1,409 to 286. In Winston and Salem the vote against a secession convention was 925 to 171. Even more telling of the conservative feeling in Forsyth County and Winston and Salem was the election of Thomas J. Wilson and Rufus L. Patterson, both "sound and true Union men," as delegates to a secession convention if one were to convene. The Forsyth County vote followed a pattern established across North Carolina. The region of the state that was most intensely Unionist was the central and upper piedmont. But, generally, the strongest Whig counties tended to be the strongest Unionist counties, while the strongest Democratic counties tended to be secessionist. Forsyth County, however, had long been a consistent Democratic county but had voted overwhelmingly against secession. Most of the Democratic counties that voted Unionist were those located along the Virginia border, while most of the Whig counties that voted secessionist were situated along the South Carolina border. Thus interstate social and economic relations were quite strong in influencing the way people regarded the secession crisis, and Forsyth County's consistent Unionism reflected its Moravian ties to Bethlehem and Philadelphia.[14]

Until the Confederacy's attack on Fort Sumter the people of Forsyth County remained loyal to the Union. Ironically, on the evening of April 12, 1861, before news of the attack on Fort Sumter earlier in the day reached Winston and Salem, a Union meeting was held with representatives from neighboring Davidson, Yadkin, and Surry counties. The meeting recognized that "agitators and advocates of war and disunion are combining to thwart and defeat the recently expressed will of a large majority of the people of this State." The meeting resolved that now was the time "when the conservative, industrial masses, without reference to their past party association, should also peaceably unite and firmly combine their influence and energies to meet the threatening attempts at revolution and civil strife in this State." Suddenly, though, circumstances changed and events raced toward crisis. The next day, President Lincoln issued his fateful call for seventy-five thousand soldiers to meet the insurrection. Lincoln's action was widely regarded in North Carolina as coercive and unconstitutional, and the course was fixed.[15] Lincoln's call for troops crystallized public opinion in Forsyth County in support of the Confederate cause.

The reasons why citizens of the Upper South eventually cast their fortunes with the Confederacy are complex. In a region where slaves were few, preservation of slavery alone was not an issue capable of leading people to contest the constitutional government of the Union. In Forsyth County, slaves made up only 13.9 percent of the population in 1860. There were only 297 slaveholders in a white population of 10,710, or 3 percent. Though the future of slavery in the Union was a powerful question in the years before Fort Sumter, the motivating factor that prompted most nonslaveholding southerners to transfer their loyalty to the Confederacy concerned the liberties of free men. Many southerners regarded secession as an effort to create a southern nation that held onto the traditional values of the American nation which had been corrupted by an industrializing and urbanizing North. It was a fight to resist submission to "the yoke of despotism" which would mean "servile subjugation and ruin." One North Carolinian was "willing to give up my life in defence [*sic*] of my Home and Kindred. I had rather be dead than see the Yanks rule this country."[16] For the president of the Confederacy, Jefferson Davis, the fight was to preserve the "sacred right of self-government" that the American revolutionaries had fought for in 1776. Davis captured the southern motivation best when he said, "All we ask is to be let alone." Hence southerners were fighting, they believed, to defend home, hearth, and family against a plundering invader. As one nonslaveholder in the Confederate army told his U.S. Army captors, "I'm fighting because you're down here." While the perceived coercion that the federal government exerted on the South changed the issue from slavery to a question of popular liberty in the minds of southerners, the fact is that without slavery there would not have been the rise of the abolition movement and the success of the Republicans as a regional political party. Without these developments southerners would not have been compelled to defend their distinctive society, culture, and way of life against northern attacks. But among the nonslaveholding majority of North Carolina society there was a strong sense of being southerners and free men, and a corresponding determination to defend their homes and resist northern aggression until death rather than submit to tyranny. Martha Wilson expressed her fears for her home and family to her friend Julia Jones:

> I cannot think the Yankees will whip us in the end but every prospect points toward a lengthy contest and I shudder to think of the trials we will probably have to contend with. I fear our houses will be burnt and our provisions taken from us . . . may the Lord avert it and give us brave arms and stout hearts to continue to bear all . . .

Once the war began, the people of Forsyth County united, "ready to oppose aggression and defend their homes' firesides to the last." [17]

Immediately after Fort Sumter, Governor Ellis convened the General Assembly. The legislature quickly called for the election of delegates to a convention which would open in Raleigh on May 20. The convention met, passed an ordinance of secession, and ratified the constitution of the Confederate States of America. The election of delegates to the secession convention uncovered deep rifts among the townspeople of Winston and Salem. Bitterness, innuendo, and name calling ruptured the community of the two towns, while factions formed and debate became shrill. Thomas J. Wilson and Rufus Patterson were elected by a wide margin again as they had been in February. The secessionists in the community were very bitter over their second loss, and prominent secessionists took the defeat personally and responded in kind. Rufus Patterson, who remained a committed Unionist, was the butt of much abuse from secessionists who called him an abolitionist and a "Black Republican." Patterson's wife, Louise, offers a vivid description of sentiments in the community: "The secessionists have been very bitter since their defeat[.] I have never seen such bitterness as they can cherish in this place, if you differ with certain persons in politics or other matters, they take it as a personal insult and grow cold sometimes [and] not speak[.]" [18]

Once secession was accomplished, the people of Winston and Salem began mobilizing for war. Across the South mobilization to defend the Confederacy from the Union invaders was largely a local "do-it-yourself" affair as amateurs prepared for the bloodiest conflict in American history. Local communities and prominent wealthy individuals organized and equipped companies of volunteers which were eventually incorporated into state militia to form active regiments that became the backbone of the Confederate army in the early months of the conflict. Across the countryside and in the towns and cities of the South young men expecting a "short and glorious war" flooded recruiting offices to get in on the fun and glory before it ended.[19] Two volunteer companies from the Salem vicinity, each numbering fifty men, were organized. One adopted the name of "Forsyth Riflemen" and the other the "Forsyth Grays." As the men of Winston and Salem enlisted, the Winston town commissioners appointed a committee to consult with local gunsmiths on the "practicality of changing the flint muskets now in the possession of the town, into percussion muskets." The women of the community also rushed into the excitement of mobilization and preparation for war. In Salem the women gathered at the Odd Fellows and Temperance halls to make uniforms and put together other war supplies for the two companies. On June 17 the first two companies left Salem to join the Confederate army at Danville, Virginia. The volunteers were sent off with solemn ceremony and public prayers in the town square, imparting a sense of unity of purpose to the community. The *People's Press* expressed the feeling of the moment in its description of the event:

> It was truly a solemn and affecting scene to witness this religious ceremony on the eve of the departure of our brave Volunteers to a neighboring state . . . surrounded as they were by a large number of distressed and weeping relatives and friends. And at the close of the ceremony, when the order of march was given, a scene presented itself which will long be remembered: It was the parting of husband and wife, brothers and sisters, parents and children, perhaps forever. A large number of persons accompanied the Volunteers to the "Bridge." . . . At the final parting there, cheer upon cheer rent the air in honor of those brave men who were going forth to peril their lives in defense of southern soil.[20]

Loyalty to a common cause against tyranny, a readiness to make individual sacrifices for the common good, and confidence that "right" was on the side of the Confederacy unified the community in the summer of 1861. As the volunteers marched off to war, a sense of common experience shared equally by everyone soothed past differences and erased old grudges. If only briefly all were now southerners fighting for their rights as free people and to defend their homes and families.

The people of Winston and Salem and Forsyth County, like North Carolinians across the state, experienced the war in different ways. For many merchants and manufacturers the war brought difficult times in which to do business, but it also brought new opportunities for profit. With the mobilization of troops the F. and H. Fries Company sold goods that included swords and cloth for uniforms to equip and clothe numerous volunteer companies that included both the Forsyth Riflemen and Forsyth Grays as well as companies from other communities like the Allegheny True Blues and the Alamance Volunteers. It was not long, however, before the hardships of war were evident in Forsyth County. The army drained the county of its farmers, artisans, and laborers. Wartime economic policies and the decline in industrial and agricultural production led to shortages and inflation which made life more difficult for those remaining at home. Finally, the political policies of the Confederate government, some necessary for the prosecution of the war effort, soured morale and fed disaffection. Within eighteen months, the enthusiasm and confidence that had greeted North Carolina's secession had given way to war-weariness, bitterness, and outright disloyalty.[21]

With so many of the county's farmers and farm laborers in the army, there was much suffering in Forsyth County. Women, children, and old men left at home had to bear the brunt of planting and raising a crop. Consequently, shortages in basic foodstuffs soon appeared. As volunteer companies were mobilized in May 1861, county authorities stepped in to provide assistance to soldiers' families. The justices of the peace of the Forsyth County Court of Pleas and Quarter Sessions appropriated funds to provide monthly assistance to soldiers' families. However, by the following spring such assistance for all of the families of soldiers was proving to be a greater burden than the county's resources could support. When the conscription act passed by the Confederate Congress in 1862 retained all volunteers for the duration of the conflict, the county court estimated that as many as twelve hundred men from Forsyth County might be called to service. Since the monthly assistance originally appropriated "would entail an enormous debt upon the county, entirely disproportionate to an ability to pay, and would therefore be a great hardship upon a community already heavily taxed . . ," the court discontinued all monthly payments. But the court believed that no one should suffer and everyone should have the necessities of life. To provide relief to those families in need, the court created the Board of Sustenance to consider applications for relief from families in need and to provide the necessary assistance. The Board of Sustenance under the leadership of its president, E. A. Vogler, was authorized to procure agricultural commodities and funds for the relief of distressed families. At the height of the conflict in 1863–64, the Board of Sustenance spent about $192,359 to assist 1,568 wives or children of Forsyth County's soldiers.[22]

The greatest hardship affecting everyday life in the community was scarcity of the necessities of life—food and clothing—and the rapid inflation in the price of all items. By the fall of 1863 conditions in Forsyth County were desperate, after two years of crop failure resulted from untimely freshets which flooded meadows and washed away grain and a continued drought in the latter part of the crop season. The Board of Sustenance reported "a most deplorable condition" that without assistance from the state or Confederate governments there would be much suffering and the "horrid fate of actual starvation." The shortage of foodstuffs was exacerbated by the number of men from Forsyth County serving in the army, taken away from the county's farms and leaving no one to produce the much-needed food. The shortage of manpower was especially acute in Forsyth County because there were few slaves and few large farms there. Most of the farmland was owned by small farmers, many of whom had been called into service leaving their fields untilled and their families unprovided for. Martha Wilson expressed the popular fear of seeing so many men drafted into the army when hunger and hardship were so prevalent in the countryside: "I cannot help thinking its [sic] rather a hard thing to submit to. I know many who have crops and no one to tend them but themselves. . . . It seems to me they can as well serve their country by making bread as any way."[23]

Hardships at home created additional burdens for soldiers at the front. Desertions were rampant as men received letters from their wives telling of the hardships at home. J. C. Zimmerman wrote of one soldier whose wife "wrote to him that her children was [sic] crying for bread and she had not a mouthful to give them nor a cent of money." The situation was made worse by the fact that the army would not pay the soldiers so that they could send home a few dollars. Confederate soldiers regularly wrote home advising their wives in matters related to setting out a crop and keeping the farm productive so that their families might survive. While away in the army, Zimmerman remained involved in the operation of his farm, advising his wife when and how much to plant, and how much a day laborer should cost to help her around the farm. Zimmerman's letters to his wife reveal the detailed attention soldiers away from home paid to their farms. In one letter Zimmerman gave his wife specific instructions regarding the farm:

> I think if you could sow some wheat it would be best even if you had to give a dollar in one day a good hand ought to put in a bushel or more a day[.] If you can see how your [*sic*] going to get wheat cheaper another year than to raise it is more than I can see . . . a hand ought to sow six bushels a week and if it was to come good it ought to make forty or fifty bushels and it would cost six dollars to have it sown this fall. . . . I should like to know how you are saving fodder and how the meadow was whether you had any of it cut. . . . I want you to butcher and sell what cattle you cannot keep this winter . . . if I do not get to come home next spring to make a crop we will be entirely broke up.

At other times Zimmerman told his wife to sell livestock when she needed money and to "keep all the grain you can and save it with care" if the family was to survive. Zimmerman stressed the importance of getting in the crop in order to keep the farm and as a means of survival.[24]

High prices for agricultural commodities and the declining value of Confederate currency further intensified the hardships caused by shortages. From October 1861 to March 1864, the general price index in the South climbed at a rate of 10 percent per month. Money steadily decreased in value and by April 1865 the general price index had outstripped its prewar base by 92 times. In comparison, wages increased only tenfold while wholesale prices rose fortyfold. Consequently, real wages were only one-third of their prewar level. In Winston and Salem the cost of all of life's necessities rose steadily while Confederate money lost value. In May 1861 Louise Patterson complained of the high prices for groceries: coffee and sugar each sold for twenty-five cents per pound, and bacon from eighteen cents to twenty cents per pound. In the first fall after the war began Mary Denke was frustrated that "everything is going up in price, and those that charge do not know how to go high enough." As the war dragged on, commodity prices rose steeply. The F. and H. Fries Company in 1862 paid thirty cents a pound for bacon, $2 a bushel for corn, and $3 a bushel for wheat. By 1865 the Fries company was paying $1 per pound for bacon and $25 per bushel of corn. E. A. Vogler, the Confederate impressment officer in Forsyth County responsible for procuring farm commodities for the army, complained of having to pay the same high price for corn.[25]

In this crisis many people in Forsyth County took advantage of the situation to profit themselves. In a circular addressed to the county's farmers, E. A. Vogler stated that although taxes were heavy, some of Forsyth's farmers could and ought to spare more of their produce to the county and to soldiers' families. Vogler believed that farmers were hoarding grain and that he was forced to pay $200 for a barrel of flour, or $20 to $25 for a bushel of corn, when some neighboring county commissioners were paying much less for grain in their counties. Vogler asked the farmers what good is this grain in the hands of those who hoard their surplus and refuse to sell it to the county, the soldiers' families, or the country's poor without demanding exorbitant prices. Vogler warned that if surplus grain were not sold at reasonable prices, he would impress it, to which he knew, "the majority—the poor and soldiers' families in particular—would say amen." Many farmers justifiably disputed Vogler and argued that they were forced to keep their grain to trade for leather, cotton yarns, and other goods which they needed to farm and survive. Across the Confederacy merchants and manufacturers were buying farm commodities and holding them until scarcity and inflation brought as much as a triple return on investment. By demanding trade in kind and refusing to accept Confederate notes, these businessmen created greater hardships for the impoverished who had to barter what little they had for other necessities.[26] The F. and H. Fries Company regularly traded yarn for farm commodities, continuing a practice that was standard in the cash-short rural economy since the mill's opening in the 1840s. In August 1862 the mill sold to one customer nine bundles of yarn worth $27.00 for one and one-half bushels of corn, thirty-five and three-quarters pounds of bacon, thirty-nine pounds of lard, and $1.58 cash. The scarcity of yarn and the higher price it commanded in the market prompted many manufacturers to increase output. Rufus Patterson in January 1862 decided to start up the machinery of his Wachovia steam mills to spin cotton thread. While Patterson and other manufacturers saw themselves filling a demand for a scarce article, some people in Winston and Salem saw these activities as war profiteering. In a letter to his father Patterson angrily commented that "every man who is pursuing an honest calling and realizing profits is denounced." Across North Carolina textile manufacturers were accused of taking profits two or three times prewar levels on the products they sold. Governor Zebulon Vance accused wool manufacturers of "fixing enormous profits" on the wool they produced, a charge that Francis Fries vehemently denied. These charges prompted eighteen mill owners to convene in Greensboro in December 1862 and agree to charge no more than 75 percent profit on the cost of manufacturing yarn and cloth. The manufacturers' convention set the price for cotton yarn from $2.75 to $3.75 per bunch and thirty to thirty-five cents per yard of cloth. F. and H. Fries agreed to sell cotton yarn to soldiers' wives and widows at $3.50 per bunch in March 1863. Regardless of whether farmers, merchants, and manufacturers reaped extraordinary profits on scarce goods, the popular perception that they did had a damaging effect on the community. The rural tenant classes and the urban wage earners experienced the greatest hardship while those of higher economic standing, particularly those who owned slaves, appeared to suffer least.[27]

As the losses of war mounted and hardships multiplied, social disorder erupted in Winston and Salem that revealed the desperation and frustration of many people. In the winter of 1863 the *People's Press* felt it necessary, due to the "extensive number" of fires, to warn town officials to bolster the night patrols; "too much caution cannot be exercised in these times to guard against fires and robberies." The newspaper called for the appointment of a dependable policeman since "in these revolutionary times . . . property is evidently not as secure as formerly, judging from the frequent robberies and fires which have occurred lately." Burglaries of smokehouses were common as scarce meat was taken. Food riots were widespread across the South in 1863. In nearby Salisbury and neighboring Yadkin County, there were riots as women broke into stores and removed food and other necessities. In April 1865 the F. and H. Fries mill and warehouse were broken into by Stoneman's troops. As Union soldiers opened the doors, a "mob" which had gathered rushed into the factory, not only taking finished goods, but also cutting down cloth still on the looms and cutting the belts which drove the machinery as well. The mob consisted of "all kinds of folks, reputable and disreputable—men, women, and children." Much of the mill property was found in the possession of persons John Fries thought were "good and friendly neighbors."[28]

Events and group actions that expressed the hopes, desires, discontent, and suffering of the people reveal much about popular feelings in Winston and Salem. The increased number of burglaries and fires, and the looting of the F. and H. Fries factory and warehouse, were evidence both of severe hardship and increased popular disaffection with the war and those identified as supporters of the Confederacy. Mundane events which many historians have ascribed to the hardship and suffering of the poor assume greater significance when they are examined within the context of widespread discontent and intense class feelings. Looting and burglaries were not simply rash acts by the miserable poor, but they could be expressions of larger, more deeply felt ideas of right and wrong. The deepening poverty exacerbated class tensions and a campaign of violence was waged by impoverished and suffering yeomen, workers, and soldiers' wives who took matters into their own hands to get what they believed was "socially just and rightfully theirs."[29]

The riots and looting in the South were statements by the poor about the war, the people who supported the war, and the market economy which encouraged speculation and profit taking. The actions of the crowds in Winston and Salem, as well as individual thefts, arson, and vandalism, might be regarded as frustrated expressions of traditional values. Hostility toward merchants and manufacturers, who were popularly believed to be better off as a result of their not making equal sacrifices and because of their supposed holding back of needed goods or charging of exorbitant prices, might have reflected a popular protest against entrepreneurship and its ways—speculation, profit taking, maximizing advantage, and accumulation of private wealth, especially in wartime. Such attitudes and actions demonstrate that through the mid-nineteenth century in America the emerging market economy was still shaped by customary community standards of behavior. Riots and looting on a large scale were legitimized by old ways of thinking and moral and legal precepts prohibiting both the hoarding of needed commodities and speculation for higher profits. Strapped North Carolinians considered speculation and hoarding to be offenses because they were exploitative and raised the price of needed provisions. Such popular actions were a final attempt to reimpose an older moral economy over the evolving free market economy.[30]

As economic hardship sapped the morale of southerners, the policies of the Confederate government further antagonized the common people. There was a growing belief in North Carolina that the Confederate government was moving rapidly toward a military despotism that would deprive the southern people of their liberty. Conscription, suspension of the writ of habeas corpus, the impressment of farm animals and produce by the army, and the enactment of a 10 percent tax-in-kind levied on farmers alarmed those who were making the greatest sacrifices for the

Confederate cause. The *People's Press* warned that the small group of "reckless and designing" men who controlled the Confederate government favored a military despotism. The newspaper hoped that the people would not remain silent but, instead, would "be vigilant and zealous in the protection of their rights and liberties."[31] By 1863 many in Forsyth County may have wondered who the real enemy to liberty was. Disaffection with the Confederate cause was expressed vividly by some in Forsyth County. After almost a year and a half of war, J. C. Zimmerman wrote to his wife of Confederate soldiers' unhappiness: "All the soldiers are getting tired of the war . . . if we don't obey we are punished severly [*sic*] and have to do worse than a negro under a mean master." Zimmerman, who had returned to his farm by 1864, wrote to a friend of his feelings about the war and those who supported it: "The hot head secesh [*sic*] about here glory in the duration of the war as long as they can keep out. God help the contentious ignorant creatures for they need it [;] they will receive their reward in due time." Many simply felt that the southern cause was not worth dying for. G. W. Poindexter wrote that if he had $100,000 he would "give it all to get clear of this horrible war, but I have not enough to get a substitute." He advised John Dalton to hire a substitute for his son because "it will be better for him to pay 2000 dollars for a man to come in the place of George than to let him be killed in this war."[32]

Opposition to the war also found expression in the organization of secret societies like the Order of the Heroes of America which was active in the northwest piedmont counties of North Carolina. The presence of the HOA and the degree of Union sentiment in the region around Forsyth County were well known early in the war. In January 1862, the Richmond *Examiner* warned of disloyalty in Randolph, Guilford, Davidson, Davie, Yadkin, Wilkes, and Forsyth counties. One unidentified Salem merchant claimed to know of persons in the community who continually corresponded with the Lincoln government. E. B. Petrie, a member of the HOA, testified that the society enjoyed an extensive membership and broad support in Forsyth County. Though the evidence is sparse—due to the secret nature of the society—the Heroes of America apparently had a class orientation, or so its enemies claimed. Loyal Confederates believed that the organization was composed of those radical Unionists whose loyalty to the federal government expressed their hatred for the political and social elite that ruled both North Carolina and the Confederacy. Many secessionists believed that members of the order were recruited from the lower elements of the community by promises that the property of Confederate supporters would be divided out to HOA members once the Union achieved final victory.[33]

Though the HOA was active in its opposition to the Confederacy and no doubt enjoyed the support of many Tarheels, most citizens of Forsyth County expressed their opposition to the war effort in more passive ways. Thus, the class tensions revealed during the war must be understood within the context of community-wide opposition to the war by 1863. The class tensions evident in Winston and Salem during the war were expressed by hard-pressed yeomen, mechanics, and laborers who bore the brunt of military service and whose families subsisted on the border-line of survival. It was these Tarheels who held the strongest feelings against Confederate politicians, military officers, and businessmen who profited from wartime commerce. But the protests of these unfortunate citizens was but one expression of widespread disaffection with the Confederate government and the war effort. The larger community consensus in Winston and Salem was one of war-weariness and a desire for peace. Most who were disillusioned and ready for peace expressed their feelings by attending rallies which demanded peace and by voting for candidates who advocated ending the war.

As the war progressed, a gulf widened between the views of the slaveholding wealthy citizens of Forsyth County and nonslaveholding yeomen and workers, spawning intense political dissension. Even as events turned against the South, the secessionists began to look for more extreme ways to oppose the Union. J. F. Shaffner, a prominent Salem physician and son-in-law of Francis Fries, believed that upon the defeat of the Confederate army southerners might resort to "scouring the country and carrying on a guerrilla warfare, at least worry out our numerous foe, and compel a most reluctant acknowledgement of our independence." As matters were becoming desperate for the Confederacy in 1863, Shaffner was heartened by rumors of disaffection toward the Lincoln government in the Midwest. Shaffner believed that "a separation of the States of the Upper Mississippi Valley from the Eastern States of the Lincoln Government, and the erection of a third independent Empire, appears now an irresistible consequence." But while members of the upper class were still hoping for victory and the success of an independent Confederacy, disaffection was spreading among the common people. Early in the war there was disloyalty to the Confederate cause in Forsyth County, including talk of resisting the military draft. By the fall of 1862 many of those serving in the Confederate army were tiring of the war and their treatment in the army.[34] Army life was harsh and there was constant danger, not only from enemy bullets and bayonets but also from the treatment received from the officers. J. C. Zimmerman wrote to his wife that it was "no wonder you see and hear tell of so many coming home the way they are treated here [;] a man can eat all [he] gets for a days [*sic*] rations at one meal [and] they won't send one off to the hospital until there is no chance for them to get well." As the burdens of war weighed more heavily on North Carolinians, they grew more critical and discontented with the losses they suffered and the hardships they endured until a bitter opposition to the war and the Confederate government erupted.[35]

By 1863 support for the war effort was waning in Forsyth County. Two years of death, destruction, hardship, and misery had taken their toll, and Confederate defeats at Gettysburg and Vicksburg brought "unprecedented gloom." There was a growing realization of the futility of further military struggle, so that people in Forsyth County, like other southerners, grew attentive to any glimmerings of peace sentiment in the North. The peace sentiment in North Carolina blossomed in the summer 1863 as many influential newspapers called for peace on any terms which weren't degrading. William W. Holden, editor of the *North Carolina Standard* and prominent political figure, expressed publicly his belief that if southerners would accept terms of peace on the basis of the existing United States Constitution, then they could avoid emancipation of the slaves and confiscation of property which might follow defeat. Holden's appeal gained popular support and spurred the many peace meetings held across the state in July and August. In neighboring Davidson County, a mass meeting protested the "improper and unjust" treatment North Carolina had received at the hands of the Confederate government and resolved that it was necessary that all of the county's men then at home remain there to produce the "necessaries of life" and promote the agricultural interests of the state. The citizens of Davidson County went on record as favoring peace "at any time it can be effected on honorable terms."[36]

In Winston on August 26, 1863, over twelve hundred citizens packed the grove outside of the courthouse to address the issue of peace and to protest secession and its cost in lives and property. The meeting accused those who led the state into secession of demanding "the last man and the last dollar in persistence of their fruitless and destructive policy which has well nigh proved the downfall and ruin of the South." Convinced that continued fighting would bring no solution, the citizens demanded a fair and honorable settlement which would secure their property. The people believed that the only ones who favored continuing the fight were the "speculator and extortioner, and the high paid officers, civil and military, who are fattening on the carnage of war and the destruction of civil and religious liberty." On the other side, local loyalists to the Confederacy convened in September of 1863 and reaffirmed their support of the Confederacy and the war effort. The meeting resolved that "a reconstitution of the Old Union is a thing impossible, and an idea incompatible with the dearest rights and interests of the South." Only about twenty-five people attended the loyalist meeting.[37]

The degree of dissatisfaction was illustrated by the support Forsyth County gave to William W. Holden's gubernatorial campaign in 1864. Both Holden and Governor Zebulon Vance were "peace" candidates for governor, but Vance advocated attempts to make peace in cooperation with the other Confederate states while Holden was labeled the "peace-at-any-price" candidate who advocated a separate peace for North Carolina. Holden favored a state convention which would seek an armistice with the Union while protecting the state from the encroachment of "arbitrary power." Vance attacked the convention proposal as a first step toward reconstruction. He was convinced that a convention would lead North Carolina out of the Confederacy and into the Union, consequently involving the state in a war with the Confederacy. Vance positioned himself before the electorate as an antisecessionist with his attacks on the secessionist Democrats and as a peace candidate with his urging to Davis to initiate peace negotiations with the North. Thus Vance focused his effort on securing the votes of the old Unionists.[38] Vance's efforts were successful as he won 80 percent of the total statewide vote. In Forsyth County, however, the vote was much closer, as Vance took 54.5 percent of the vote to Holden's 45.5 percent, indicative of the deep divisions within the community and stronger Union sentiment. But the vote totals do not tell the complete story. The army vote gave Vance his victory in Forsyth County. The civilians of the county, wearied by the sacrifices and hardships of the war, and uncertain of its true purpose, gave their votes to the "peace-at-any-price" candidate, Holden. The message of the people of Forsyth County was clear—peace. That the unpopularity of the war was so widespread and the desire for peace so strong were indicated by the failure of the Democrats—the party which took North Carolina out of the Union—to field a candidate for governor in 1864.[39]

Hopes for peace were fed by a steady diet of rumors through the fall of 1864 and the winter and spring of 1865. As each rumor came and went, unfulfilled despair grew deeper, times got harder, and, in their disillusionment, some in Forsyth County abandoned even the necessary work of getting in the crop. When the Confederacy accepted defeat in May 1865, hope returned. On May 20, the fourth anniversary of North Carolina's secession, the flag of the Union was raised above the courthouse in Winston in a joyous celebration. The *People's Press* reported that "in obedience to the wishes and feelings of the loyal citizens of Forsyth County, Saturday the 20th of May was set apart to raise the Union flag, which during four years of tyranny, under a bogus government, had been prohibited to float from the dome of the Court House." The Salem newspaper described the emotion of the proceedings: "As the flag reached the top and spread its ample folds to the breeze, a shout went up. . . . The joy was so overwhelming, that many of the old and young shed tears of joy freely, as cheer after cheer went up in honor of the occasion. It was the proudest day in the history of Forsyth County."[40] The enthusiastic reporting of the *People's Press* on the surrender of the Confederacy and the return of peace, it must be remembered, was one-sided and reflects the attitudes and feelings of the many former Whigs and members of the Constitutional Union party who were always conservative Unionists and who wanted peace immediately. Though there was a significant number of Forsyth County residents who still remained loyal to the Confederacy, there can be no doubt of the depth of war-weariness and desire for peace in Forsyth County as well as North Carolina in 1865.

In Winston and Salem the demands of war revealed more starkly than previous events the differing worldviews of members of the community. While Whigs and Democrats disagreed over government policies and channeled those disagreements into a partisan political party system, entrepreneurs like Francis and Henry Fries and Rufus Patterson differed from small farmers, artisans, and workers in matters of behavior and social values. The stresses and demands of war demonstrated that entrepreneurial values of risk, speculation, profit taking, and private accumulation of wealth were often not consistent with community well-being and traditional notions of right and fairness. The war revealed the potential for deep class divisions in the community between capitalists who pursued economic opportunities and profits, and those members of the community who found themselves increasingly dependent on manufacturers, merchants, and commercial farmers for employment, wages, and those necessities of life which they could no longer produce for themselves. In the postwar period, as entrepreneurs further transformed the community by integrating the local economy more completely with the regional and national market economies, the tensions the war uncovered became a permanent feature of community life as members of the community increasingly came to see themselves as distinguished by class and race.

Out of the conflict arose a new order. The antebellum economy crumbled as its system of labor was swept away by emancipation and as many southerners recognized the need for a diversified economy of manufacturing and commercial agriculture. In its place arose a society and an economy based on free labor. Though North Carolina would remain primarily agricultural until well into the twentieth century, one prerequisite of industrial production was now available—an abundant supply of cheap labor. In time, as cotton prices declined, the planters would join in the march to industrialism and become heavy investors in local manufacturing ventures. No sooner was the last shot fired before the calls for a New South, removed by time and ideology from the antebellum South, were made in the region's press and on the stump by aspiring young politicians. The Civil War indeed marked a watershed for Winston and Salem.

Postbellum Winston and Salem:
The Emergence of a Business Class

Immediately after the guns were silenced, the bitter experience of the Civil War led many southerners to search for an explanation for what had happened and to fix the blame for the disaster. In trying to understand what had gone wrong, they focused on the differences they perceived in northern and southern societies, and many concluded that southern agrarianism was no match for northern industrial power. These southerners believed that if the South were to resume its former place in the Union it would have to adopt new ways. Manufacturing, not agriculture, appeared to many the key to future prosperity and power in America. Newspaper publisher J. D. B. DeBow told his southern readers that the keys to southern recovery were economic diversification with manufacturing and small farms which would stimulate immigration.[1] The Salem *People's Press* joined the broad chorus of postbellum southern advocates for change, and urged a policy of industrial development and the expansion of manufacturing. People in North Carolina were counseled to cast aside their "brooding preoccupation" with past events, let bygones be bygones, and see the error of old ways. In 1871 Governor Tod R. Caldwell took up this theme in the governor's annual message to the General Assembly, describing the present condition of North Carolina as "disorganized" and warning that "thousands of persons with millions of capital have been deterred from settling among us." The governor reminded North Carolinians, "It behooves us all to throw the mantle of

Fig. 6.1. Main Street, Salem, in 1866. Photograph by Henry A. Leinbach. Courtesy of Old Salem, Inc.

oblivion over our differences and devote our energies to raising up our beloved commonwealth from the low estate into which she has fallen."[2]

The early years after the war were difficult for the people of Winston and Salem as well as for those in the surrounding countryside. The 1870s brought sporadic rather than steady economic growth as Forsyth County continually swung between prosperity and hard times. Local newspapers reported that business was "dull" in 1871, but trade was "rapidly on the increase" in 1873 only to "stagnate" again in 1876. These unsettled economic conditions led to serious financial difficulties for many businessmen in Winston and Salem. Of fifteen businessmen who were in business before the war, nine (60 percent) were seriously injured financially by the war and the difficult conditions of the late 1860s, according to the R. G. Dun and Company of New York, the leading credit reporting agency of the time. Of the nine businessmen, five (56 percent) eventually failed. Merchants suffered most from the hard times as people had little money to spend. Of the nine hard-pressed businessmen, four were merchants, including Edward Belo, two were confectioners, two were involved in a sawmill and lumber operation, and one was a bookseller. The six successful businessmen either survived the war with their finances largely intact or they prospered by selling goods to replace those lost during the war. Of the six, one was a manufacturer and merchant, Rufus L. Patterson, three were carriage or wagonmakers, and one was a prosperous confectioner of long standing in the Moravian community, William Winkler.[3]

From the ruins of defeat there emerged an entrepreneurial class in Winston and Salem involved in manufacturing and mercantile enterprises. It demonstrated a strong commitment to industrial development as the key to prosperity and southern progress. Entrepreneurs new to Winston and Salem, men like tobacco manufacturer Richard Joshua Reynolds, arrived in the 1870s from neighboring counties in North Carolina and Virginia to augment the leadership of the Moravian businessmen who had directed the early years of economic expansion before the war. These men, the sons of antebellum planters, yeomen, merchants, and mechanics, advocated the reconciliation of sectional differences, racial peace, and, with far-reaching implications, a new economic and social order in which manufacturing and modern, diversified agriculture would revitalize the South. Because scarcities of manufactured articles and rapid wartime inflation enabled manufacturers to accumulate financial surpluses which they used to finance the refurbishing of their mills, southern manufacturing, unlike southern agriculture, recovered from wartime damage rather rapidly and prospered. Between 1869 and 1899 the total output and total value added in manufacturing in the South rose more than six times, while capital investment expanded by ten times. During these years the value added per southern worker increased by more than 50 percent. Between 1869 and 1889 value added per worker grew at 2.5 percent annually.[4] In Winston and Salem the businessmen who led the economic recovery created the urban industrial community, managing its firms and factories, establishing its banks and savings institutions, and building its waterworks, electric power facilities, and municipal railroad. They built the boardinghouses and tenements that gathered into working class neighborhoods the workers they recruited and employed in their tobacco factories and textile mills. These men initiated and promoted efforts for new transportation lines to connect Winston and Salem more firmly to the piedmont countryside and to the national market that encompassed America at an accelerating rate after the war. With these efforts this entrepreneurial class came to dominate all aspects of civic life in Winston and Salem and attempted to create an environment conducive to economic growth, prosperity, and social stability.

The railroad was the key to the economic development of Winston and Salem after the war as economic activity quickened and the population grew rapidly. Across the postwar South, railroads expanded into new areas of the piedmont, connecting more towns and providing direct links to the North. In early 1868 a railroad meeting in Forsyth County attended by prominent lawyers, manufacturers, merchants, and farmers, resolved that the county subscribe $100,000 for the extension of a line from the North Carolina Railroad, which ran from Raleigh to Charlotte via Greensboro. The proposed extension, the Northwestern North Carolina Railroad, would run from Greensboro through Winston, Salem, and Mt. Airy to the Virginia line. Later in the same year the Constitutional Convention sitting in Raleigh chartered the Northwestern North Carolina Railroad, and Salem merchant Edward Belo was elected president of the new railroad. Upon completion it stirred much excitement in the community. On July 12, 1873, a warm Saturday afternoon, a large crowd gathered on the heights above the newly built railroad bridge and on the banks of the creek below to watch as the first train on the new line slowly crossed the bridge to be greeted by the Salem Brass Band.[5]

The connection of Winston and Salem with North Carolina's rail system marked the extension of the process of market involvement that had begun in earnest in the late antebellum years, though market integration in the 1870s and 1880s progressed at a greater pace and infiltrated much more deeply into the local economy. Across the southern piedmont, from the end of the war through the turn of the century, the market established its domination over people's lives.[6] In Forsyth County during the immediate postwar decades, there was continued movement toward greater involvement in trade and commercial agricultural production. Local farmers embraced commercial agriculture by producing more tobacco, wheat, and corn. As Table 6.1 shows, between 1850 and 1890 tobacco cultivation in Forsyth County increased by more than a factor of thirty and the production of wheat by more than a factor of three, while corn declined 29 percent. The change toward commercial production is further illustrated by the shift in the ratio of commercial crops—tobacco and wheat—to corn, the leading crop for household and local consumption. In 1890 the tobacco/corn ratio was 6.46 and the wheat/corn ratio .53. By comparison, in 1850 both the tobacco/corn ratio and the wheat/corn ratio were .1. The shift toward commercial farming is illustrated

TABLE 6.1

Annual Production of Wheat, Corn and Tobacco on Forsyth County Farms for the Census Years 1850, 1870, 1880, 1890

	1850	1870	1880	1890
Crop Production:				
wheat (bushels)	40,735	66,678	77,082	132,895
corn (bushels)	349,320	173,146	335,164	248,436
tobacco (pounds)	49,880	76,569	822,788	1,607,323
Farms:				
number	996	1,272	1,871	2,088
acres improved	51,873	114,125	79,350	79,954

Sources: Statistical View of the United States. Compendium of the Seventh Census, 1850; Statistics of the Population of the United States. Ninth Census. Volume 1. 1870; Statistics of the Population of the United States at the Tenth Census. 1880; Report on the Statistics of Agriculture in the United States. Eleventh Census. 1890; Report on the Population of the United States at the Eleventh Census. Part 1. 1890.

also by the changing use of farmland in Forsyth County. In 1870, as the hardships of the postwar period meant poverty and the threat of starvation, Forsyth County farmers put more land into production to meet the need for food commodities. Under these conditions the county's 1,272 farms brought an average of eighty-eight acres into production as compared with fifty-two acres in 1850. As the tobacco economy took off in the 1880s and Winston's tobacco factories demanded large quantities of leaf, Forsyth County farmers attempted to meet that need at the expense of general farming. Farmers concentrated on the production of Bright leaf tobacco which was labor intensive, requiring careful attention at different stages in the crop season and as much as 370 hours of labor per acre. Tobacco cultivation required fewer acres than general farming or the production of food crops. In 1880 Forsyth County farmers were producing an average of 488 pounds of tobacco per acre. Forsyth County's 2,088 farmers in 1890 cultivated a mean of thirty-eight acres. By 1880, 36 percent of Forsyth County farmers produced tobacco, up from 4 percent in 1850. At the same time the number of farms increased 64 percent, from 1,272 to 2,088. As the number of farms increased during the 1870s and 1880s, so did the proportion of landless blacks and whites working other people's land as tenants, increasing from 16 percent in 1880 to 27 percent in 1890.[7] Tobacco grown on Forsyth County farms, as well as on the farms of eight nearby counties in North Carolina and Virginia, was sold to Winston tobacco manufacturers, while grain was sold to local merchants in exchange for cash, credit or household items, clothing, and farm implements.[8]

A second aspect of the integration of Winston and Salem into the national market was urban growth and the transformation of the economic structure of piedmont towns. After the war the number of towns in North Carolina with populations greater than five hundred rose from twenty-three to 129, and the piedmont's share of these towns increased from one-third to one-half. Economic development and population growth in Winston and Salem were mutual interactions; each fed the other as more businesses and factories demanded more labor and increased population demanded more jobs and services. The increasing commercialization of the countryside and more extensive exchange relations produced greater demand for manufactured articles, which in turn promoted an increase in the number of mercantile enterprises in Winston and Salem. Local merchants imported many consumer articles manufactured outside of the local community for consumption by farmers who were no longer self-sufficient. By the 1880s a vibrant urban-rural trade had developed which led to a greater diversification in the economic activities of Winston and Salem, as Table 6.2 illustrates. Merchants in the piedmont were particularly well situated to take advantage of the opportunities the national market economy offered. Table 6.2 also shows that between 1872 and 1884 the number of general stores in Forsyth County more than tripled. Retailing became more specialized as merchants filled specific needs of consumers. While there were no clothing or hardware stores listed in an 1872 business directory, by 1884 there were four of the former and three of the latter. The increased number of stores in the two towns provided retail outlets for many local manufactories, like the F. and H. Fries Company. On the other hand, the increasing population of factory workers provided the numerous mercantile enterprises with a large clientele. This pattern of economic growth and change that transformed the southern piedmont during the immediate postwar decades was quite similar to that which transformed rural New England forty years earlier.[9]

The increasing integration of local communities into the national market economy was a key element of southern industrialization in the late nineteenth century. The key to the success of Winston and Salem as an emerging southern industrial center in the 1880s was the creation of manufacturing enterprises that could take advantage of the particular circumstances of the society and economy of the piedmont. Because the South did not possess adequate capital, nor the pool of skilled labor necessary for a diverse manufacturing economy, the region's economy

TABLE 6.2

Business Establishments in Forsyth County: 1850, 1872, 1884

	1850	1872	1884
saw mills	13	7	10
grist mills	22	17	26
coppermills	5	0	0
tin smiths	1	3	3
shoemakers	7	2	1
cabinetmakers	2	3	5
chairmakers	1	0	0
carriage- and wagonmakers	6	5	14
bakers	2	0	3
tanneries	7	3	6
wheelwrights	2	0	0
plow makers	1	0	0
saddle/harnessmakers	3	1	6
blacksmiths	3	0	1
potters	2	0	2
gunsmiths	2	1	1
lime kilns	2	0	0
distillers	3	0	3
cigarmakers	1	0	0
tailors	0	0	2
tobacco factories	1	2	29
cotton & woolen mills	2	2	2
paper mills	1	1	0
blind, sash, door makers	0	1	2
ready-made clothing	0	2	4
hotels, saloons, restaurants	2	7	16
shuttle & spoke factory	0	0	1
well fixtures	0	0	1
millwrighting	0	0	5
marble works	0	0	1
winemakers	0	0	1
building contractors	0	0	3
confectioners	2	0	3
brickmakers	0	0	4
hosiery makers	0	0	1
tobacco auctioneers	0	0	5
tobacco warehouses & brokers	0	0	11
insurance	0	0	3
merchants: total	13	37	108
general store	0	16	50
grocery	0	8	14
drug	0	2	4
clothing	0	0	4
hardware	0	0	3
specialty	0	11	33

Sources: 1850 Census, Population Schedule manuscript microfilm, Forsyth County, North Carolina; 1850 Census, Manufacturing Schedule manuscript microfilm, Forsyth County, North Carolina.

was at a decided disadvantage relative to the diversified and complex industrial economy of the North. For southern manufacturing to take hold and prosper, southern entrepreneurs had to focus their efforts and limited resources on those activities by which the region could compete, by offering the national economy products which were in demand and which the northern economy could not produce as efficiently. In short, southern manufacturers had to carve out their own niche in the national economy. They did this by creating an industrial base that was tied closely to the region's agricultural economy, processing its staples into manufactured products in labor-intensive enterprises that depended on labor control and low wages. Postwar southern entrepreneurs embraced textiles and tobacco which proved to be the engines that drove southern industrialization until well into the twentieth century.[10]

Postbellum manufacturing in Winston and Salem saw the transposition of antebellum production techniques and business structures pioneered in the textile mills to other areas of the local economy. The employment of larger work forces of low-skill and low-wage laborers, task differentiation, and the use of steam-powered tools proved that the innovative structure of production in the textile mills could be adapted to other industries. Partnership was another innovative business practice borrowed by entrepreneurs from the practices of the early textile mills. Before the war, partnerships were primarily limited to those enterprises which demanded large capital outlays for machinery, raw materials, and labor costs, the most prevalent example being textile mills. But as entrepreneurs sought ways to expand their businesses to survive and to take advantage of new opportunities, the pooling of resources into a single firm was appealing and met the need for additional capital. Local merchants also realized the benefits of partnerships. Since capital was in greater demand, mercantile firms assumed a larger role in the southern economy as sources of credit, and partnerships among merchants helped to meet these needs. In the decades after the war business enterprise became more concentrated, with two or more principals joining together in an endeavor. In 1868, a North Carolina business directory listed only six partnerships in Winston and Salem, mostly among merchants. By 1886, however, the number of partnerships had grown to thirty-two, including three in the trades, seven in manufacturing, and two in mercantile enterprises. For example, N. D. Sullivan's general store was a partnership of Sullivan, R. Stanley, Stephen Hodgin (also a merchant), and Israel Robinson. Merchants played a leading role in starting and capitalizing new business enterprises, especially in manufacturing. In Winston, Hamilton Scales's tobacco factory was a partnership of Scales and merchants P. A. Wilson and Albert Gorrell. W. F. Bowman and Company, a Winston spoke and handle manufacturer, included as partners Robert Gray and James A. Gray, merchants.[11]

The F. and H. Fries Company was quite typical of the textile industry in North Carolina that survived the war years and prospered in the late nineteenth century. A great many mills operating in the piedmont after 1880 were established before the war as family enterprises and then enjoyed significant postbellum success. The antebellum roots of many mills was an asset to North Carolina's postwar economic growth as a number of communities had a manufacturing tradition which ensured a trained work force and experienced mill management, which, along with the survival of the mills, formed a nucleus for the further growth of the 1880s.[12] The textile mill Francis Fries built in the early 1840s survived its founder's death in 1863 and continued as a family enterprise until well into the twentieth century. Its success can no doubt be attributed to Francis Fries's willingness to include his younger brother Henry in all aspects of the mill's operation. Consequently, the mill made a sure recovery from war and enjoyed impressive growth through the remainder of the nineteenth century. This success came after a slow start immediately after the war, since machinery had to be replaced or repaired, and cotton and wool had to be procured. But business grew as demand for Fries products was heavy, and by the fall of 1871 the mill was running day and night and hiring extra hands. Purchasing cotton and wool from North Carolina, South Carolina, Virginia, and in some northern markets, F. and H. Fries manufactured cotton yarn, cassimeres, satinets, kerseys and linseys, and sheetings for sale primarily in a regional market that encompassed the Carolinas and Virginia. Products from the Fries mills also penetrated the national market on a small scale with shipments going to New York, Chicago, Philadelphia, Georgia, Mississippi, and Texas, and the international market with sales of sheetings to China. But, as mill management reported to the U. S. Treasury Department in 1886, "the aggregate of these shipments is small compared with the home trade." Henry Fries and his nephews met the increased demands for yarn and cloth in the 1870s and 1880s by continually expanding the mill and installing the latest model frames and looms as well as more powerful and efficient engines. In 1870 the Fries cotton mill had run 528 frame spindles and employed twenty-seven operatives, mostly females, while the woolen

Fig. 6.2. Henry W. Fries of the F. and H. Fries Company, brother of Francis Fries and son of William Fries. Courtesy of the North Carolina Division of Archives and History.

mill employed fifty hands, mostly males, ran 606 spindles and twenty-six looms. The new Arista cotton mill, built in 1880, ran 3,394 spindles and 102 looms when it opened. In 1886 the F. and H. Fries mills employed 184 operatives; eighty-five white males, nine black males, and ninety white females. The value of the annual product of the Fries mills rose from $157,410 in 1880 to $288,948 in 1885.[13]

The postwar expansion of the Fries mills brought prosperity and change to Salem, but the tobacco factory was the vehicle that took Winston from a small county seat to an important manufacturing center. The southern tobacco industry developed because local entrepreneurs took advantage of ready access to an abundant raw material and expertise born from their long experience in producing and marketing plug and twist chewing tobacco. Tobacco manufacturers prospered because they turned out a product that was unique in the national market economy, which protected them from the ruinous competition of northern producers. The explosive growth of tobacco in the North Carolina piedmont during the 1870s had its origins in the cultivation of Bright leaf tobacco that was particularly well-suited to the siliceous soils of the region. The development of flue curing techniques to replace the old Virginia method of curing by open fire enabled North Carolina producers to offer a thin, milder-tasting yellow leaf that satisfied the increasingly sophisticated tastes of tobacco users. Bright tobacco was widely embraced by farmers in the piedmont counties of North Carolina along the Virginia border, where the soil was too thin for successful general farming. Ironically, the Civil War proved a boon for the tobacco growers and manufacturers of Bright tobacco in the piedmont. The thousands of Union and Confederate soldiers who passed through the state had the opportunity to sample the mild tobacco that was grown in only a few piedmont counties. After the war, their demand for more North Carolina Bright tobacco proved a catalyst for the state's new industry.[14]

Winston's tobacco manufacturers sprang from the tobacco-growing farms and the small tobacco factories that dotted the tobacco belt of the Virginia and North Carolina piedmont. Ambitious young men off the region's farms saw opportunity in what had been a small sideline to tobacco growing in the antebellum and immediate postbellum years. Combining their foresight and talent with capital most often provided by small-town merchants, they established the small manufacturing firms that gave birth to one of the South's leading industries. The tobacco industry that made Winston and Salem an important southern industrial center started in 1870, when Hamilton Scales in partnership with merchant Peter A. Wilson opened a small plug chewing tobacco factory. Scales's early efforts received a big lift in February 1872 when the first tobacco auction held in Winston took place in a renovated livery stable

Fig. 6.3. Winston's first tobacco warehouse with Nissen wagons of tobacco farmers lined up. Courtesy of the Forsyth County Public Library, Winston-Salem, North Carolina.

that T. J. Brown and his partners A. B. Gorrell and Peter Wilson had converted to a tobacco warehouse. Brown, a native of nearby Caswell County, ensured the success of his venture by purchasing tobacco seeds and teaching the area farmers to grow Bright tobacco. Scales and S. M. Hobson opened another tobacco warehouse in 1873 to guarantee a regular supply of leaf for their factory. With the sale of raw tobacco in Winston and the completion of the railroad from Greensboro, other tobacco manufacturers soon opened factories in the town.[15] R. J. Reynolds was one of those early entrepreneurs to recognize Winston's potential in tobacco manufacturing.

Richard Joshua Reynolds, the son of a prominent Patrick County, Virginia planter, started as a boy growing and manufacturing tobacco on his father's plantation. Reynolds began manufacturing on his own in a log cabin in Patrick County in 1873. But soon after he saw a new opportunity. In 1874 Reynolds sold this small factory, along with his brands and trademarks, to his partners and moved to Winston. According to Reynolds, he was attracted to Winston by "the benefit of railroad facilities,

Tobacco brake, a scene during Tobacco selling Season, Winston-Salem, N. C.

Fig. 6.4. Tobacco-selling season outside of Brown's Tobacco Warehouse. Courtesy of the Forsyth County Public Library, Winston-Salem, North Carolina.

and on account of this town being located in the center of the belt in which the finest tobacco in the world is grown." [16] Reynolds was joined in Winston by other entrepreneurs who saw in the town the same promise of success. W. L. Brown and R. D. Brown came to Winston in 1876 to establish the Brown and Brother factory. Having started manufacturing tobacco in neighboring Davie County, the Brown brothers, like Reynolds, soon realized that Winston with its tobacco market, tobacco warehouses, and railroad connection was the emerging center of tobacco manufacturing in the piedmont. In April 1878, P. A. Miller, S. A. Woodruff, and William Wood arrived from nearby Surry County to open a tobacco factory with capital supplemented by $5,000 borrowed from F. and H. Fries on a real estate mortgage. In 1883, William Taylor, who grew up in Richmond during the Civil War and worked with tobacco manufacturers there and in Lynchburg, arrived to open his factory which he operated in partnership with his brother Jack. While Winston was of little importance as a tobacco market before 1879, and plug manufacturing did not take firm root until the mid-1880s, these modest beginnings eventually grew into an industry which in 1888 included twenty-two factories and employed four thousand workers.[17]

The early endeavors at tobacco manufacturing were small affairs requiring little capital for startup since the processing of chewing tobacco was largely handwork until the late 1880s. Reynolds's first factory was typical of these early enterprises. When Reynolds arrived in Winston in the fall of 1874, he had startup capital of about $7,500, some of which had been furnished by his brother-in-law and silent partner, A. M. Lybrook. In October Reynolds purchased from the Moravian congregation a one hundred-foot lot on Depot Street on which he built his first factory, a frame building thirty-eight by sixty feet which cost $2,400 to erect and equip. With a small work force of two full-time assistants and twelve helpers, Reynolds launched his business. In the early years Reynolds, always strapped for operating capital, made it on small loans from his family and from local banks. By 1879, R. J. Reynolds Tobacco Company occupied a three-and-a-half story brick factory and employed 175 hands. The firm of Brown and Brother, founded in 1876, also started small. By 1879, W. L. Brown and R. D. Brown owned "one of the largest, best built, and best equipped tobacco factories in the South," employing 225 hands in a brick factory 50 by 130 feet, four stories high, and mechanized with a twenty-five horsepower steam engine.[18]

By the mid-1870s Winston tobacco manufacturers began to differentiate their products by experimenting with flavorings, using creative attention-getting packages to gain an advantage over competitors, and aggressively promoting their product. Many manufacturers believed that a wide range of brands offered greater opportunities for success, and in 1887 *Connorton's Tobacco Brand Directory of the United States* listed forty-three brands of plug and twist tobacco and thirty-three brands of smoking tobacco produced in Winston. R. J. Reynolds offered Sam Jones' Vest Chew, named for a popular evangelist. Brigham Young and Missing Link were sold by P. H. Hanes, while T. L. Vaughn offered chewers Otto of Roses and Dewdrop. The innovation and aggressiveness of Winston manufacturers enabled them to increase their share of the market when Virginia manufacturers were being squeezed out by Burley tobacco products made in Kentucky. But Winston manufacturers themselves felt pressure from chewing tobacco made with Kentucky Burley because of its capacity to absorb more of the sweetener tobacco users preferred. To meet this threat, the Winston manufacturers used saccharin, much sweeter than sugar, as a flavoring. Southern tobacco manufacturers

Fig. 6.5. Richard Joshua Reynolds, founder of the R. J. Reynolds Tobacco Company. Courtesy of the North Carolina Division of Archives and History.

Fig. 6.6. Factory 256, R. J. Reynolds Tobacco Company. Courtesy of the Forsyth County Public Library, Winston-Salem, North Carolina.

blazed new paths in marketing a consumer product that established brand-name recognition and consumer loyalty. To introduce his product, William Taylor offered samples of his Stars and Bars to Confederate veterans en route to a reunion in Richmond.[19] Winston manufacturers further distinguished themselves by aggressively marketing their brands in the small markets of the southern backcountry generally ignored by Virginia manufacturers. Some manufacturers, though, looked beyond the southeast for markets. Brown and Brother marketed its products in all of the southern states and in eastern and midwestern markets that included Maryland, Pennsylvania, Kentucky, Indiana, Illinois, Michigan, and Missouri. R. J. Reynolds also concentrated his efforts in the North and Midwest, thereby establishing the Reynolds name in the national market. Reynolds believed that the keys to "unqualified success" were making a "good product" and aggressive advertising, especially in local newspapers, to promote his brands.[20]

In its earliest stages tobacco manufacturing was an uncertain venture.

Because start-up costs were low, the large number of tobacco manufacturers in North Carolina and Virginia ensured fierce competition which led to many failures. While Winston flourished as tobacco manufacturing expanded, individual tobacco manufacturers found the going rough and success uncertain. Winston's first tobacco factory, Hamilton Scales and Company, illustrates the precariousness of new business enterprises in the hard times of the 1870s and the bonds of debt that united Winston's entrepreneurial class. Hamilton Scales's firm began as a subsidiary of the Winston mercantile firm owned by Peter A. Wilson. Wilson, once described as a merchant tailor, owned a general store and a flour mill which he acquired in partnership with Robert A. Gray from Rufus L. Patterson in 1865. In 1870 Wilson entered into a partnership with Scales to manufacture tobacco, with Wilson probably providing most of the capital. The firm must not have met Wilson's expectations for profits because in January 1872 he withdrew from the partnership, leaving Scales and Gray as the principals. Wilson was reported by the R. G. Dun and Company to be worth at least $10,000, mostly in real estate, one-half of which was mortgaged to cover heavy debts. Scales and Gray collapsed in 1874 which left Wilson "somewhat embarrassed." Scales, however, recovered from this failure and was back in business by 1876 manufacturing tobacco with J. A. Bitting and W. A. Whitaker as silent partners. Pleasant Henderson Hanes and John Wesley Hanes had experiences similar to Scales as they endeavored to establish themselves as tobacco manufacturers in Winston. The Hanes brothers came to Winston from neighboring Davie County in 1872 to open a factory. The Haneses, joined by their brother B. F. Hanes, along with T. J. Brown and Mocksville tobacco manufacturer P. N. Dulin who took a financial interest in the firm P. H. Hanes and Company, built a two-story factory. Hard times struck immediately when Dulin died and the firm had to settle his financial interest with his heirs. Strapped for capital the firm struggled on until the factory burned in its second year of operation. Because the firm owed considerable debts and had little insurance, Brown withdrew from the firm. The Hanes brothers continued the firm, renting a factory in Greensboro until a new building could be erected in Winston. The firm recovered, grew, and prospered, despite the withdrawal of B. F. Hanes to start his own business and a second fire in 1893. When the R. J. Reynolds Tobacco Company acquired the firm in 1900, P. H. Hanes and Company produced five million pounds of tobacco products.[21]

The business of the tobacco manufacturers was further complicated by the dominant position commission merchants held in the market system and by fierce competition. T. L. Vaughn complained of a particular merchant in New Orleans who sold Vaughn's tobacco at a very low price and then charged a 10 percent commission. The bad debts of many merchants plagued Winston manufacturers. John Moore lost $1,200 when the firm of Warren and Bush of Montgomery, Alabama, failed. Many of the Winston manufacturers, including R. J. Reynolds and P. H. Hanes, began their career as tobacco peddlers and saw firsthand the troubles that plagued their trade. It was common for the tobacco peddler, who was often the owner of the factory, to tour the South with his product for several weeks, always maintaining contact with his factory so that new stocks could be sent to him by rail. As a youth of only sixteen or seventeen in Virginia before the war, Reynolds peddled tobacco manufactured in the family-owned factory. In later years Reynolds remembered how he drove a wagon-load of tobacco products through the mountains of western Virginia into east Tennessee and Kentucky, trading the tobacco for anything of value to make a profit. Occasionally, after all of the tobacco was gone, he even traded his horses, harnesses, and wagon, returning home with cash which was always needed. Hamilton Scales, on one trip, traveled to Charleston, then Savannah, Macon, and Atlanta, in that order, peddling his plugs. In Savannah he was afraid to show his tobacco because the city required payment of a $25 tax. Even so, Scales found the city well supplied with tobacco, for he had been preceded by other peddlers. To Scales, selling tobacco was an "up-hill business" of which he quickly tired, while he never grew tired of being in his factory overseeing production.[22]

Though many firms enjoyed only a brief existence, the industry took firm root in Winston and quickly became the backbone of the local economy. Winston's and Salem's thirty tobacco factories in 1885 produced plugs and twists which were sold across the United States and in England. Within fifteen years of the opening of the first tobacco factory, the pace of tobacco production in the Winston factories was regarded as an economic barometer for the community. When factories were running day and night in December to close out the season's work and to meet the strong demand for their product, many took it as a sign of "better things ahead, a prospective increase in trade and a general awakening in the business of our towns and section."[23] But the greatest impact of the industry was in the people associated with it. The factory owners cooperated with the successful shopkeepers, merchants, and professionals of the two towns to alter the local economy by their business activities and came to direct community affairs.

The key development in the economic history of Winston and Salem was the growth of an influential entrepreneurial class which guided the postwar economic expansion of the two towns. In no area of community life are the differences between Winston and Salem so evident as in the composition of their respective business elites. In Salem there was continuity as the antebellum business enterprises of the town formed the core around which the postbellum economy was built, and Salem's post-war business leadership had deep antebellum roots. Of forty-two business proprietors in Salem in 1878, thirty-one were either successful antebellum tradesmen or the sons of antebellum tradesmen.[24] The remainder came to the community sometime in the late 1860s and 1870s. Thus, by the 1880s Salem had a long-established entrepreneurial class around which the town's economic and political life evolved. Men like Edward Belo, Henry Fries, Rufus L. Patterson, Julius Mickey, and Jacob Tise added to their antebellum holdings and pursued a number of business endeavors after the war. Salem's leading industrial family also expanded its activities after the war. Henry Fries, who became the head of the family enterprises after Francis died in 1863, not only reinvested F. and H. Fries's profits into enlarging and improving the company's mills, but he also branched out, owning a grist mill and, in partnership with Rufus Patterson, a general store. Julius Mickey and Jacob Tise began their careers as artisans in Salem. Mickey, a tinsmith described as "a pushing man" and "energetic," eventually owned a grist mill and a general store, plus real estate valued at $5,000 in 1874. Jacob Tise, a blacksmith, successfully expanded his business activities. In 1850 Tise operated a small shop employing two journeymen, but by 1867, he had started manufacturing wagons. In 1869 his combined blacksmithing and wagonmaking business employed six hands. With the wealth accumulated from these enterprises, Tise opened a store and engaged in business as a merchant. By 1878 he had added a grist mill and real estate to his holdings. R. G. Dun and Company reported that Tise owned a "brick block" which contained six stores plus at least six houses. In December 1879 Tise, who was described in the Dun credit ledgers as a self-made man of good business habits, "close saving and industrious" who had "worked his way up," was estimated to be worth $35,000 to $40,000.[25]

While Salem's postwar proprietors emerged from the antebellum merchant and mechanic class, Winston's proprietor class was made up of men who moved to the newer and faster-growing Winston during the 1870s and 1880s as the tobacco industry developed. Of the tobacco manufacturers listed in a 1877 business directory, only one was living in the town in 1870. Among Winston proprietors only eleven of thirty-eight, or 29 percent, were established in Winston before 1870. Those businessmen who came to Winston brought some capital with them, as R. J. Reynolds did. That the average age in 1880 of those who started tobacco factories was thirty-nine suggests that they had spent ten to fifteen years in other trades or businesses and accumulated the capital necessary to begin tobacco manufacturing. Mercantile enterprises were often the springboard to tobacco manufacturing, as six of fourteen tobacco manufacturers in Winston in 1877 were also involved in merchandising.[26] For these men, industrialization that complemented the advantages of readily available raw materials produced by the region's agricultural economy was the key to southern progress. Tobacco manufacturing provided them with the opportunity to participate in the early stages of the region's industrial transition. Though the postwar business elites of Winston and Salem had different origins, there was a consensus among the business leaders that they increase their own trade and make Winston and Salem a growing commercial and manufacturing center.[27]

Thus Winston and Salem had a solid entrepreneurial core around which newcomers coalesced and a vital business class emerged. United by membership in trade organizations, fraternal societies, business endeavors, and politics, the business and political leaders of Winston and Salem shared a common identity and formed an elite that exercised unparalleled influence over community affairs. This business class, like the postwar commercial elites that emerged in other piedmont communities, regarded their community as a complex of interlocking organizations which promoted the civic and economic progress they considered crucial to individual prosperity and the welfare of the community. The dominance of civic, economic, and political affairs by this proprietor class lent an increasingly bourgeois character to the two towns. These businessmen engaged in efforts to create in Winston and Salem an environment conducive to profitable business enterprise, economic growth, and the advancement of the community. Furthermore, this elite had the effect of uniting the two towns into a single community that transcended the municipal boundaries. It was no mere coincidence that during the 1880s Winston and Salem came to be regarded as the "Twin City."[28]

Within the growing black community in the 1880s and early 1890s a vital entrepreneurial and professional class also emerged to provide leadership. Black entrepreneurs established businesses that were not just confined to the black neighborhoods but served the whole community and competed with white businesses in downtown Winston. Black businessmen prospered in their ownership of cafes and restaurants, grocery stores, dry cleaners, billiard parlors, jitney and taxi services, funeral parlors, and insurance companies. Black tradesmen—brickmasons, shoemakers, blacksmiths, undertakers, and barbers—served black and white clienteles. William Scales exemplified the black entrepreneur in Winston. Scales came to Winston as an uneducated laborer to work in the tobacco factories, but by 1895 he had opened a cafe and a poolroom. Scales prospered in downtown Winston and diversified his activities, becoming a realtor and owning a grocery store, a bonding agency, two theaters, and a funeral parlor. Scales invested in the Forsyth Savings Bank, and his wealth eventually approached $250,000. Black professionals—lawyers, physicians, educators, and ministers—provided leadership in Winston and took the initiative to create institutions of uplift and progress for the black community. Dr. Henry Humphrey Bell, Winston's first black physician, John S. Fitts, Winston's first black lawyer, and Simon Green Atkins, an educator, arrived in Winston in the early 1890s and mobilized the black community toward moral and social uplift and political involvement to give it an important voice in the affairs of Winston.[29]

In business affairs the community's entrepreneurs of both races promoted activities that furthered the interest of economic development, like their counterparts in other southern communities. To guarantee the growth and prosperity of Winston and Salem this business class promoted tobacco manufacturing. To induce more growers to sell their tobacco in the Winston market, a Board of Tobacco Trade was formed in the early 1870s to protect the interests of the local tobacco industry and to pursue good relations between manufacturers and growers. The board appointed a committee of arbitration to settle disputes between manufacturers and farmers over prices. In January 1879, tobacco dealers M. W. Norfleet and Thomas Barber and merchants W. B. Carter and S. E. Allen published in the Winston *Leader* a letter to the tobacco growers of western North Carolina and the border counties of Virginia promoting the advantages of Winston. Citing the large number and variety of stores where farmers could easily spend their new cash from tobacco sales, the letter urged the growers to sell their tobacco in the Winston market. In

1884, R. J. Reynolds, James A. Gray, Frank Fries, and Henry W. Fries joined with other merchants and manufacturers to organize the Orinoco Warehouse Company with a capital stock of $30,000 to erect a warehouse for the purchase, storage, hauling, and sale of leaf tobacco.[30]

Leading tobacco men like R. J. Reynolds, M. W. Norfleet, P. H. Hanes, and W. L. Goslin joined together with other community manufacturers, merchants, professionals, and newspaper editors like J. F. Shaffner, Henry Fries, George Nissen, James E. Gilmer, and J. W. Goslin to establish the Forsyth Immigration Society in the mid-1880s to recruit additional farmers to settle permanently in Forsyth County to grow tobacco for the town's factories. In a pamphlet describing ·Forsyth County, its soil, products, climate, and trade, the immigration society told prospective farmers and farm tenants of the "superior quality of tobacco grown in the area and the number of tobacco factories in Winston." The society invited the inquiries of planters who had more land than they could successfully cultivate and intended to match landless farmers with landowners to work as tenants and sharecroppers.[31] Increased immigration offered the towns' entrepreneurs many benefits. More farmers in the area producing tobacco would provide more leaf for Winston factories and thus, presumably, lower prices for the new leaf needed by manufacturers. Secondly, more farmers would increase the demand for good farmland, therefore making it more valuable for its owners. For the merchants and mechanics, additional farmers earning an income from tobacco would mean more customers and more money circulating in the local economy. However, some members of the community were wary of possible unintended consequences of the effort to attract immigration to Winston, Salem, and Forsyth County. The Winston *Union Republican* in 1887 recognized the need to attract additional labor for the towns' growing factories, workshops, and stores, but considered that this need should not be filled at the expense of the moral well-being of the community. Horrified at the "general mess that is building up the great West so rapidly," the *Union Republican* reminded its readers:

> We are content with a steady natural increase and the occasional higher moral class of emigrants that from time to time deem proper to unite their fate and fortune with us. . . . We have room and a hearty welcome for good law abiding citizens, rich and poor, who are willing to lend an influence and work, and for these alone. Such additions to a community and the South are beneficial.

Despite such concerns, businessmen across the South created local agencies to solve the need for labor which they believed the postwar industrial program would supposedly create.[32]

In October 1885, manufacturers R. J. Reynolds and John W. Fries joined with other businessmen to organize a chamber of commerce to advance the interests of business enterprise in the community. The new chamber was dedicated to promoting internal improvements, encouraging immigration, collecting and disseminating information about the community, and addressing the threat that Winston and Salem might be bypassed by future railroad development. In an effort to safeguard the economic future of the town, the members of the chamber began a campaign in the fall of 1885 to secure a connection with the planned Roanoke and Southern Railroad, which would give Winston and Salem direct connections with the western Virginia tobacco-growing counties. R. J. Reynolds joined with other businessmen to organize a company for constructing a railroad from Martinsville, Virginia, located in a prime Bright tobacco-growing area. In 1887 the General Assembly incorporated the Salem-Winston and Dan River Railroad Company to build a line from the towns of Salem and Winston to connect with the Cape Fear and Yadkin Valley Railroad. Tobacco manufacturers R. J. Reynolds and W. L. Brown, textile manufacturer F. H. Fries, and merchant James E. Gilmer sat on the new company's board of directors. By the early 1890s Winston and Salem had rail connections through Davie County to Wilkes County and into southwestern Virginia that carried lumber, iron ore, tobacco, and county produce from the region's small farms.[33]

The town's leading businessmen were also instrumental in creating financial institutions that were necessary for successful business enterprise. Several of Salem's foremost merchants, artisans, and professionals, among them Edward Belo, Israel G. Lash, Peter A. Wilson, and John W. Alspaugh, organized the People's Building and Loan Association of Salem in 1871. Two banks were organized during these years, the First National Bank of Salem and the Wachovia National Bank in Winston. In 1889 merchant S. E. Allen, tobacco manufacturers W. A. Whitaker and T. L. Vaughn, and textile manufacturer Henry Fries joined other investors to organize the Winston-Salem Building Loan Association to accumulate funds sufficient to enable members to build or purchase homes or to invest in any business they deemed advantageous to them.[34]

Winston's and Salem's business leaders took an active role in creating the infrastructure that served the economic development of the community. Adequate supplies of pure running water, electric power, and a street trolley system were important to the production of goods, the transportation of people and products within the community, and the quality of life in the two towns to attract workers to the factories and customers to the tobacco warehouses and mercantile establishments. In the 1880s a group of merchants and manufacturers that included S. E. Allen, W. L. Brown, R. J. Reynolds, and P. H. Hanes formed the Winston Water Company with a capital stock of $16,000 for the purpose of supplying Winston with water. Merchants, tobacco manufacturers, and professionals including D. H. Starbuck, T. L. Vaughn, J. A. Bitting, and James E. Gilmer, who were the officers and directors, organized the Winston Electric Light and Motive Power Company in 1887 to bring electric power to Winston. In 1889 local businessmen incorporated the Winston and Salem Street Railway Company to build an electric trolley system. The list of fifty-four investors in the new corporation reads like a who's who of the business class in the community and includes: tobacco manufacturers T. L. Vaughn, W. A. Whitaker, J. A. Bitting, and T. J. Brown; textile manufacturer Frank Fries; merchants S. E. Allen, Joseph Rosenbacher, James E. Gilmer, and W. B. Carter; and professionals Eugene E. Gray and Thomas J. Wilson, both attorneys. These men came together again in numerous development and investment companies to acquire land and build new homes and factories to bring about a growing and prosperous Winston-Salem. The Twin City Development Company, formed in October 1890, and the Winston Development Company, formed in November 1890, were the vehicles by which this elite mobilized its capital and energy to direct the growth and development of the twin cities and invest in its business enterprises.[35] Table 6.3 identifies the business elite of Winston and Salem. These men were identified as those who owned business enterprises and who played important roles in the community's civic and business associations as well as in political activities.

The postbellum elites of Winston and Salem were formed of those individuals who held the most influence over their neighbors which imbued them with power in the community.[36] The power of this elite was exercised on two levels—the economic and the political. On the economic level there was an elite which at points intersected with the political elite but which primarily exercised its power as proprietors of Winston's and Salem's business enterprises. This elite guided the towns' economic development through the establishment of trade associations,

TABLE 6.3

Postbellum Business Elite of Winston and Salem

Name	Occupation
S. E. Allen	merchant
John W. Alspaugh	attorney
Thomas Barber	tobacco leaf dealer
Edward Belo	bank and railroad president
J. A. Bitting	tobacco manufacturer
T. J. Brown	tobacco manufacturer
Charles Buford	railroad agent
John C. Buxton	attorney
John W. Fries	textile manufacturer
Henry W. Fries	textile manufacturer
A. B. Gorrell	tobacco leaf dealer
James A. Gray	merchant and banker
P. H. Hanes	tobacco manufacturer
John W. Hanes	tobacco manufacturer
C. A. Hege	agricultural implements manufacturer
G. W. Hinshaw	merchant
R. B. Kerner	attorney
Israel G. Lash	bank president
D. P. Mast	attorney
M. W. Norfleet	tobacco leaf dealer
C. J. Ogburn	tobacco manufacturer
J. L. Patterson	attorney
R. J. Reynolds	tobacco manufacturer
T. L. Vaughn	tobacco manufacturer
W. A. Whitaker	tobacco manufacturer
M. N. Williamson	tobacco manufacturer
Thomas J. Wilson	attorney
C. B. Watson	attorney

Sources: North Carolina, vol. 10, 463–553, R. G. Dun and Company, Collection, Baker Library, Harvard University Graduate School of Business Administration; *Branson's North Carolina Directory*, 1877–78, 113–16; *Southern Business Guide*, 1883–84, 685–700, 1885–86, 693–706; Forsyth County, Record of Corporations, vol. 1, 14–16, 46–48, 53–54, NCDAH.

immigration societies, banks, and savings and loan associations and played an important role in organizing, funding, and directing civic activities and agencies to improve the quality of life in the community. R. J. Reynolds headed a campaign in the late 1870s for increased property and poll taxes to support public education. He also contributed large sums of money to fund the establishment of the Slater Hospital for the black citizens of Winston and Salem and to establish a college for blacks

in Winston. John W. Fries, son of Francis Fries and president of the
F. and H. Fries Company, played an active role in civic and church
affairs.[37] But this elite's most important power base was in its role as
employers. As thousands of people immigrated to Winston and Salem in
the 1870s and 1880s to work in the tobacco factories, textile mills, shops,
and stores, the power and influence of this elite grew sharply.

The political elite consisted of people who served as magistrates of
Winston Township and as decision makers in local party politics. A
sample of the community's political elite was drawn from the executive
committee of the local Democratic party which dominated in local elections and from the appointed magistrates of the township. Of the forty-
eight men in the sample, twenty-eight were located in the 1870 census.
This elite was propertied, with the average holding in real estate being
$3,542. While merchants and shopowners formed the backbone of the
elite, three were tobacco manufacturers who had come to Winston in the
early and mid-1870s to open their factories. Of the forty-eight, twenty-
one served in the municipal government of either Winston or Salem.
During the years between 1865 and 1887 there was remarkable consistency in town government in the two towns, further indicating the power
the business class held in the community. In Salem during these years
forty-two men filled 136 places on the town commission with an average
tenure of three terms. Town government in Salem had a distinctive
mechanic flavor as craftsmen who had made the transition to shopowner
held the largest number of positions on the town commission. Of the
forty-two officeholders in Salem, thirty-five were located in the 1870
census and of these, sixteen had mechanic origins. The second largest
group, merchants, had twelve officeholders. Of course, most of the mechanics were proprietors, owning their own shops and employing others.[38] There was a continuity in elite domination in Salem from the
antebellum years to the 1880s. A business class of small proprietors
evolved out of the artisan tradition of shop-owning master craftsmen, but
because many of these artisan and merchant proprietors were engaging in
diversified economic activities after the war, it is highly unlikely that they
still worked in the shop beside their employees. Instead, these proprietors
were evolving into a managerial class which directed business activity and
was concerned with returns earned in diverse enterprises.

In contrast, Winston's town government was in the hands of merchants and manufacturers. In Winston forty-nine men held 114 places
on the town commission with an average tenure of two terms. Town

government was slightly less stable in Winston than in Salem as newcomers poured into the town and quickly established themselves. Of the forty-nine officeholders, fifteen were merchants and sixteen were manufacturers, ten of whom were tobacco manufacturers. Only five of Winston's elected leaders were mechanics. Large-scale manufacturing gave Winston a character distinct from Salem. Rather than being the center of long-established artisanal trade, Winston became the home of manufacturers and merchants who settled in the town after the war. Of forty-five businessmen in Winston who were listed in *Dobbins' 1890 Historical Sketch of Winston-Salem, N.C.*, as tobacco manufacturers, leaf dealers, and warehouse proprietors, thirty-six had come to Winston and Salem from elsewhere in North Carolina and Virginia to open their businesses. That these tobacco entrepreneurs established a place for themselves in Winston and quickly won the acceptance of their neighbors reveals the somewhat different attitudes toward industrialization held by southerners and northerners. Studies of northern industrialists who emerged in the 1870s have revealed local attitudes inimical to men new to the community who opened factories which were deemed disruptive to established economic and social relationships. These new industrialists often did not readily achieve high social status in the community.[39] In Winston the situation was different because tobacco manufacturers were in the vanguard of an industrial movement seen by many southerners as a solution to the South's perceived weakness. The rapidly growing tobacco industry of Winston fit nicely with the New South boosterism of the aspiring business class in the region's piedmont communities. And the extent of their involvement in community affairs was indicative of the tobacco manufacturers' success at achieving influential status shortly after their arrival.

The merchants and manufacturers who transformed Winston and Salem by their business endeavors were part of a movement across the South in which businessmen responded to the profound changes in the economic direction of the South after the Civil War. With the creation of a labor market after emancipation in which employers were able to mobilize a large reservoir of cheap labor, southern businessmen saw opportunities for profitable enterprises that exploited the region's land, labor, and raw materials. Land and labor were reallocated to produce more cotton and tobacco, and there was energy and enthusiasm for railroads, new manufacturing enterprises, and local economic development. These elites embraced industrialization in order to expand the local economy on which their wealth and power were based. After the war, the principles and directions of entrepreneurial enterprises were transformed by the market, and the investment strategies, entrepreneurial designs, and political programs embraced by the South's business leaders demonstrated the emergence of a new mentalité or worldview among the elite.[40] On the local level, a commercial class united by the desire for an environment conducive to its success directed the affairs of Winston and Salem. The artisan-merchant elite of the antebellum years evolved into a postwar coalition of merchant-manufacturer-professional found in towns of the upper piedmont. This class shared a common status as employers which marked them as different from the larger segment of the community. However, as this cohesive employer class evolved, a working class of factory workers and unskilled and semiskilled laborers emerged in juxtaposition.

CHAPTER SEVEN

Workers in an Industrial Community

The business class that emerged in Winston and Salem after the Civil War to direct the transformation of the local economy created the conditions that profoundly altered the lives of the majority of people living in the community. The process of change and adaptation that occurred in the postwar community reveals the character of industrialization as it occurred in Winston and Salem. Industrialization meant greater diversification of economic activities and occupations as well as local producers turning out goods for a wider nonlocal market. Producing in a wider market meant greater competitive pressures than those which existed in the antebellum economy. In Winston and Salem, as across the southern piedmont, the expanding market economy brought a variety of less expensive goods to southern consumers which had been mass-produced in the North and transported on railroads southerners rushed to build. These goods offered stiff competition to local producers who faced intense pressures to compete successfully in the national market. The drive for greater profits led producers to introduce innovations in the production process that increased productivity and lowered costs. Some advocates of postbellum southern economic development like J. D. B. DeBow regarded workers of both races as well as popular recognition of the dignity of labor to be critical to the South's prosperity and progress. The Salem *People's Press* recognized the importance of hard work to the success and prosperity of the South and proclaimed, "Success to all working men say we, and we hope all the young men and boys will

TABLE 7.1
Distribution of Occupations in Forsyth County 1850, 1880

	1850		1880	
Occupations	frequency	%	frequency	%
Unskilled, Service	87	18.7	550	41.6
Semiskilled	4	0.9	222	16.8
Skilled	67	14.4	120	9.1
Petty Proprietors	282	60.5	321	24.3
Clerical, Sales	9	1.9	49	3.7
Proprietors, Managers	3	0.6	23	1.7
Professionals	13	2.8	30	2.3
Government Officials	1	0.2	7	0.5
Totals	466		1322	

Sources: 1850 Census, Population Schedule manuscript microfilm, Forsyth County, North Carolina; 1880 Census, Population Schedule manuscript microfilm, Forsyth County, North Carolina.

roll up their sleeves and pitch in good earnest and make an honest and respectable living and become independent." The *People's Press* warned employers to respect and reward labor:

> Underpaid labor always revenges itself upon the employer in negligence and waste. The man who cares little for the interests of the master who cheapens the sweat of his brow to the lowest possible farthing, and the work he does is never performed with cheerfulness or alacrity. Getting the greatest amount for the least outlay, never yet paid in the long run.

But for the workers in the crafts, industrialization meant mechanization of some if not all of the production process, task differentiation and the consequent decline in the skill levels of workers, the substitution of wage-earning, semiskilled laborers for skilled artisans, the abandonment of apprenticeship, lower wages, and poorer working conditions as employers attempted to remain competitive. For semiskilled workers in the tobacco factories and textile mills, industrialization brought new opportunities for steady employment and regular wages but also work that was routinized at a pace that workers no longer controlled. During the 1870s and 1880s the people of Winston and Salem had to come to terms with new ways of living and working.[1]

Continuing a process begun during the antebellum years, the expanding market economy had its greatest impact on skilled workers whose presence in the local economy diminished as there were fewer opportunities for employment in local shops and mobility into the propri-

TABLE 7.2
Distribution of Occupations in Winston Township,
1880

Occupations	Frequency	%
Unskilled, Service	117	27.0
Semiskilled	178	41.0
Skilled	57	13.1
Petty Proprietors	19	4.4
Clerical, Sales	31	7.1
Proprietors, Managers	12	2.8
Professionals	14	3.2
Government Officials	6	1.4
Total	434	

Source: 1880 Census, Population Schedule manuscript microfilm, Forsyth County, North Carolina.

etor class. The shops of local craftsmen that had once provided the local community with goods shrank in size as many of these goods were imported from northern manufacturing centers for sale in local dry-goods stores. Consequently, as Table 7.1 shows, the skilled artisans and petty proprietors in Forsyth County who made up 74.9 percent of the work force in 1850 were only 33.4 percent of the workers in 1880. The character of the local work force in Forsyth County shifted as people took manual labor jobs requiring little or no skill. The unskilled and semiskilled segments of Forsyth county's work force increased from 19.6 percent of the working population in 1850 to 58.4 percent in 1880.[2] The change was even more profound in Winston and Salem by 1880, as Table 7.2 shows. Skilled artisans made up only 13.1 percent of Winston's and Salem's work force, while the unskilled and semiskilled segments, mostly tobacco factory workers and textile mill operatives, was 68 percent.[3]

From its initial steps in antebellum Salem with textile manufacturing, industrialization advanced further after the war with the transformation of the crafts, especially in shoemaking, carriagemaking, and tailoring. These trades faced oblivion as crafts in the 1870s and 1880s, since the competition of manufactured articles led younger men to abandon them and production shifted to a small number of larger shops. The shops of tailors, shoemakers, and wagon- and carriagemakers which had once produced consumer goods for the local market contracted in size and activity. Between 1850 and 1880 the number of artisans listed in the census who identified themselves as shoemakers declined from forty-one

Fig. 7.1. View of the Nissen Wagon Works with its large smokestack towering over the plant. Courtesy of the Forsyth County Public Library, Winston-Salem, North Carolina.

to fifteen and tailors declined from nine to four. Those craftsmen who remained at their trades were engaged in repairs and custom work for a limited luxury trade. Production for the market moved from the shops of the master craftsmen to the factory. By bringing together larger numbers of workers under one roof than had been typical in artisan shops and mechanizing important steps in the manufacturing process, these small factories realized efficiencies that enabled them to turn out greater quantities of articles at lower prices and to compete in markets beyond the immediate locale. The Vogler and Pfohl shoe factory illustrates this trend. In 1868 the *People's Press* proudly reported that the shoe factory employed three experienced workmen from the North who worked with local shoemakers to turn out shoes on "the most approved machinery of the kind now in use in the New England States." Vogler and Pfohl in 1870 employed twelve males and five females working year-round turning out one hundred pairs of boots and shoes daily. Salem tailor Peter A. Wilson also made the transition to manufacturing and by 1868 had be-

Fig. 7.2. A Nissen wagon like those produced in the Winston-Salem factory. The wagons were popular with tobacco farmers who used them to haul tobacco to market. Courtesy of the Forsyth County Public Library, Winston-Salem, North Carolina.

come a large manufacturer of ready-made clothing employing over fifty workers. Wilson offered the people of Winston and Salem factory-made clothing using material from the F. and H. Fries looms. Wilson's business was so successful that in 1868 he was looking for ways to extend it further. In the ledgers of the R. G. Dun and Company, Wilson is reported to have been also involved in a general store, a hotel, and a tobacco factory.[4]

Competitive pressures also reshaped the carriagemaking trade in Winston and Salem. Competition from outside manufacturers who used lower-cost convict-leased labor forced many smaller carriage shops in Forsyth County to shut down while other shops reorganized their mode of production to realize greater efficiencies. In 1884 there were seven wagon shops in Winston and Salem, but this number had declined to five by 1886. In the 1880s carriagemaking in Winston and Salem was significantly different from what it had been thirty years before. The decline of carriagemaking as a craft is seen in the decrease in the number of men reporting their occupation as "carriagemaker." In 1850, twenty-three men, including apprentices, journeymen, and masters, identified themselves as carriage- or wagonmakers in Salem, but only three did so in 1880. In the carriagemaker's shop before the Civil War, individual artisans working together made the whole carriage. But by the 1880s, in the larger shops tasks were differentiated as each worker completed just one specific step in the process of making a carriage or wagon and apprenticeship was abandoned. Carriagemakers no longer labored together but were separated in different areas of the shop depending on the task they performed. The organization of production in the Nissen Wagon Works illustrates the changes occurring. The Nissen Wagon Works, in operation almost forty years, was one of the largest in North Carolina. The factory was divided into two shops, the blacksmith shop and the woodworking shop, located in separate buildings. In the blacksmith shop sixteen men worked twelve forges which were arranged around a large smokestack making iron fixtures for the wagons. In the woodworking shop, where about forty-five men worked, a steam-powered engine ran a planer and numerous saws which the workers used to fashion wood used in the wagons. The men working in the wagon works ceased to identify themselves as carriagemakers, but instead they saw themselves as blacksmiths, wheelwrights, or carpenters, depending on their specific role in the production process. Some small shops became even smaller and engaged in only repairs. Though these workers continued to identify themselves as blacksmiths, wheelwrights, and carpenters, it does not mean they were necessarily skilled artisans in those crafts. It is highly likely that they were semiskilled factory workers performing just some of the tasks of those skilled crafts.[5]

As the shops of master craftsmen closed or made the transition to factories, the character of the work force in the crafts changes. The age distribution within each trade reveals its declining status with industrialization. In the crafts which suffered the greatest losses of status the average age of the artisans rose between 1850 and 1880. The average age of carriagemakers rose from twenty-nine to fifty, while shoemakers increased from thirty-two to forty-five and tailors from twenty-eight to fifty-two. Tables 7.3 and 7.4 make the situation clearer. The declining crafts—shoemaking, carriagemaking, and tailoring—stand out as the decrease in the number of men in these crafts aged thirty and under is notable. The decline of young men in this age group is dramatic between 1850 and 1880; from 57 percent to 0 in carriagemaking, from 59.5 percent

TABLE 7.3

Age Distribution in Six Crafts in Salem (Including Winston), 1850

	15–20	21–30	31–40	41+	Total
blacksmith	8	15	5	12	40
%	20	37.5	12.5	30	
carpenter	1	7	8	6	22
%	5	32	36	27	
carriagemaker	5	8	6	4	23
%	22	35	26	17	
shoemaker	8	16	8	9	41
%	20.5	39	20.5	22	
harnessmaker	0	1	3	2	6
%	0	17	50	33	
tailor	1	5	2	1	9
%	11	56	22	11	

Sources: 1850 Census, Population Schedule manuscript microfim, Forsyth County. Age grouping adapted from Hirsch, *Roots of the American Working Class*, 43.

to 20 percent in shoemaking, and from 67 percent to 0 in tailoring. The best explanation for this phenomenon is that in trades receiving orders only for custom work and repairs, only a few master craftsmen remained. This trend is an important indicator of the status of a craft because young men avoided trades where they saw little hope of becoming independent shopowners. The displacement of workers in their teens from the artisanal work force accompanied the aging of those in industrializing crafts. Fewer teenagers found places in the crafts because apprenticeship had been largely abandoned in the declining trades as the remaining master craftsmen, reeling from the competition of manufactured goods available in local stores, did not have sufficient trade to support an apprentice. Furthermore, with the introduction of machinery and task differentiation in certain crafts, it was no longer necessary for workers to know all of the production processes. Apprenticeship came to be regarded as unnecessary as well as inefficient and less profitable.[6]

New arrangements emerged in the place of the traditional apprenticeship that took advantage of young men as sources of cheap labor. Apprenticeship became more informal and less paternalistic as personal ties which once bound the master and apprentice together were replaced by purely economic arrangements. In this new form, the employer assumed less responsibility for the youth's moral condition and education. Traditionally, apprenticeship meant learning the intricacies of a particular

TABLE 7.4
Age Distribution in Six Crafts in Winston-Salem, 1880

	15–20	21–30	31–40	41+	Total
blacksmith	2	9	7	14	32
%	6	28	22	44	
carpenter	3	25	15	26	69
%	4	36	22	38	
carriagemaker	0	0	0	3	3
%				100	
shoemaker	0	3	1	11	15
%	20	7	73		
harnessmaker	3	3	1	1	8
%	37.5	37.5	12.5	12.5	
tailor	0	0	0	4	4
%				100	

Sources: 1880 Census, Population Schedule manuscript microfilm, Forsyth County. Age grouping adapted from Hirsch, *Roots of the American Working Class*, 43.

craft. But by the 1880s apprenticeship had become merely child labor, especially in crafts where machine production was important.[7] The North Carolina Bureau of Labor Statistics reported that after the normal apprenticeship period ended, the young man was released as manufacturers sought to avoid paying a journeyman's wage, and another young man was taken on. Young men who entered a craft under such an arrangement usually struck out on their own to seek employment as "skilled" workers. One Winston printer complained to the North Carolina Bureau of Labor Statistics that "those men who do not serve an apprenticeship but gained a limited knowledge of the business . . . will work cheaper and do much to injure wages." Furthermore, as the agricultural economy of the South stagnated under the burdens of low cotton and tobacco prices and sharecropping, impoverished farmers and farm laborers with few skills other than farming fled the land for the overcrowded urban labor force. In 1888 the North Carolina Bureau of Labor Statistics reported numerous complaints from skilled workmen of "the large number of incompetent workmen who set themselves as proficient to the detriment of those who really are competent." The agreement entered into by Winston stonecutter J. W. Durham with Charles Bennett in 1878 reflects the new circumstances of apprenticeship in the industrializing community. Durham agreed to teach Bennett marble cutting but he incurred none of the obligations contained in antebellum apprenticeship bonds. Durham was not obligated to provide Bennett with food, washing, lodging, and apparel, nor to teach him reading, writing, and arithmetic. Instead, Durham was only to teach Bennett his trade, pay him, and provide him with a new set of tools at the end of the three-year arrangement when Bennett turned twenty-one. In addition to learning the trade, Bennett was to receive $100 annually the first two years and $150 the third year, paid monthly. Durham entered into the same arrangement two years later with John Bennett, Charles's brother. Durham agreed to give John Bennett a new set of tools and to pay him $108 the first year, $120 the second year, $144 the third year, and $330 for the remaining one year and ten months until John turned twenty-one.[8] Although the Bennetts were under contract to Durham for three years, they were, in effect, wage laborers. One has to question the level of skill in the craft the Bennetts attained in their brief tenure with Durham. But, regardless of their actual skill levels, after leaving Durham the Bennetts likely passed themselves off as journeymen stonecutters.

The course of industrialization was uneven in Winston and Salem, affecting some crafts more dramatically than others. While shoemaking, carriagemaking, and tailoring were losing their status as crafts, other trades—blacksmithing, harnessmaking, and carpentry, for example—retained their craft status with varying degrees of success. Blacksmithing was on the wane as a craft but not to the extent of shoemaking, carriagemaking, and tailoring. The number of blacksmiths in Winston and Salem declined by 20 percent between 1850 and 1880. After the war the shops of master blacksmiths were losing their lucrative stove-making and agricultural implements business to shops that specialized just in those items. In addition, these goods could be purchased from local dry-goods merchants who offered a selection of locally produced and northern-made stoves and farm tools. In 1884, C. A. Hege operated the Salem Iron Works, employing eight blacksmiths to manufacture farm implements. R. A. Hamilton sold stoves, no doubt manufactured in the Northeast, in his Salem hardware store.[9] All that was left of the community's blacksmith shops were the custom trade and repairs the local community demanded.

The changing structure of the craft was illustrated by the changing nature of its work force. Those who worked as blacksmiths in 1880 were older on the average than their predecessors in 1850. Between 1850 and 1880 the average age of blacksmiths in the two towns rose from thirty-four to thirty-eight. The number of blacksmiths under thirty decreased from 57.5 percent to 34 percent. Apprenticeship declined in the blacksmith shops as the percentage of teenagers in the craft declined from 20 percent in 1850 to 6 percent in 1880. While blacksmithing had not declined by 1880 to the extent of carriagemaking, shoemaking, and tailoring, there were fewer opportunities in the trade for those who sought to be independent master craftsmen. Consequently, the craft became the province of men over thirty-one years old, 66 percent of those working as blacksmiths. However, the 14 percent increase of men over forty years old in the craft probably indicates the presence of more semiskilled workers who abandoned other occupations to work in the forges of the local wagon works and farm implements shop.[10]

Harnessmaking too resisted full industrialization longer. Though the number of harnessmaking shops in Winston and Salem declined between 1877 and 1884, from five to three, the journeymen harnessmakers maintained some confidence in their future as craftsmen, especially as harnessmaking in Winston and Salem retained its small-shop character. The number of journeymen in the trade actually increased between 1850 and 1880. More important, teenagers still found a place in the trade.[11] While there was competition from imported manufactured leather articles, the three shops that remained apparently found a profitable local trade. The increasing wealth of some tobacco manufacturers, merchants, and professionals stimulated a demand for better-quality harnesses and saddles than those readily available at local dry-good stores.

Carpenters in Winston and Salem between 1850 and 1880 experienced industrialization differently from workers in other crafts. The number of carpenters actually increased over the years. In 1850 there were twenty-two carpenters in the two towns. By 1880 the number had risen to sixty-nine, a 68.2 percent increase. However, though the number of carpenters increased during these years, there were important changes in the structure of the craft. The increase in carpenters is attributable to the frenetic building activity in Winston as tobacco factories were started, stores established, and homes and tenements built to house the growing population. But Winston and Salem carpenters were increasingly being employed as wage laborers by building contractors like H. E. McIver and the partnership of Bowles and Baker in Winston, rather than working on their own as independent craftsmen. Fogle Brothers of Salem was one of the largest contractors in the community, employing seventy-five men in 1884 putting up a tobacco warehouse plus other buildings and homes.[12]

Carpenters maintained the vitality of their craft longer than the other crafts in Winston and Salem. The percentage of journeymen under thirty years old increased from 1850 to 1880, from 37 percent to 40 percent. However, the percentage of carpenters over age forty-one also increased, from 27 percent to 44 percent. The number of men in the thirty-one to forty age group declined from 36 percent to 22 percent.[13] This last fact offers an important insight into the status of the craft and might be explained several ways. First, men in their thirties may not have been as ready to leave their homes and migrate to another town in search of better work. The manual skills and physical stamina of these men were at their peak which made them more productive and, thus, their incomes were probably at the highest levels of their careers. Therefore, the increases in the percentage of men in their twenties and over age forty-one probably represent the influx of semiskilled workers drawn to Winston and Salem by the increased business activity of the two towns. Those men in their thirties might represent the solid core of carpenters who had lived in Winston and Salem for many years, serving their apprenticeships there and working there as journeymen for a number of years. A second, rather contradicting explanation is that the decline in the number of carpenters in their thirties represents an abandonment of either the craft or of Winston and Salem by significant numbers of carpenters who refused to work as employees of the building contractors. The craft was changing, though not as rapidly as other crafts in Winston and Salem.

The experience of artisans in Winston and Salem paralleled what their counterparts in northeastern cities were going through. The introduction of mechanized production and the competition of imported manufactured articles in these cities forced younger men out of many trades. By 1880 cabinetmakers in Poughkeepsie, New York, declined in number due to the competition of more inexpensive factory-made woodwork. Of those who remained in the trade, about one-half were over fifty years old. A similar trend was apparent in Hamilton, Ontario, between 1851 and 1861. In three declining trades in Hamilton, the proportion of artisans under thirty years old dropped notably; from 65 percent to 40 percent of printers, from 48 percent to 23 percent of plasterers, and from 42 percent to 26 percent of painters. The young men of Hamilton knew which trades would not offer the prospect of a secure and profitable career and avoided occupations like tailoring, which was hit hard by competition with ready-made clothing. Finally, in Newark, New Jersey, artisans

TABLE 7.5
Reports from Mechanical and Other Employers, 1888

Firm	Months Operated	Capital Invested	Avg # Employed	Daily Skilled Wage	Daily Unskilled Wage	Workday hrs.
Tailor(1)	12	$10,000	11	$2.50	—	10
Wagon Mfg(3)	12	$27,000	32	$1.38	$0.78	10
Buggy Mfg(1)	12	$ 5,000	9	$1.75	$1.00	10
Printer(3)	12	$ 4,000ᵃ	5ᵃ	$1.41	$0.75	10
Saw Mill Mfg(1)	8	$10,000	14	$2.00	$1.00	10
Painting(1)	9	$ 100	3	$1.50	$1.00	10
Contractor Builders, Sash & Door Mfg(1)	12	—	50	$1.75	$0.75	10
Saw Mill(1)	6	$ 1,300	6	—	$0.72	12
Foundry(1)	5	—	8	—	—	10.5
Marble Works(1)	12	$ 1,000	3	—	$0.75	10
Plasterer(1)	8	—	6	$1.65	$0.75	11

Source: Bureau of Labor Statistics, *Second Annual Report. 1888.*
Notes: ( ) number of establishments in the particular trade reporting.
ᵃ only two establishments reported these figures.

shared experiences similar to those of the artisans in Winston and Salem. Shoemakers and blacksmiths there were, on the average, growing older between 1850 and 1860 as the number of workers under the age of thirty-one declined.[14]

As Winston and Salem industrialized, workers complained of the conditions they endured. Low wages, a more intense work routine that required higher levels of exertion, and long hours on the job elicited the workers' complaints which were documented in the reports of the North Carolina Bureau of Labor Statistics. The *Second Annual Report of the North Carolina Bureau of Labor Statistics*, published in 1888, listed the responses on fifteen questionnaires returned by Forsyth County employers. This report, which Table 7.5 summarizes, offers a glimpse into the condition of labor in Winston and Salem. Artisans in the two towns worked in shops which employed an average of 14.6 men. Of the fifteen firms reporting, ten operated for twelve months and five operated from five months to nine months a year. The average workday was about ten and one-quarter hours.[15]

But the responses of the mechanics to the Bureau's inquiries provide a valuable insight into the condition of labor as the worker perceived it. One cabinetmaker wrote that many workers in Winston and Salem labored eleven to twelve hours, often in the hot sun. A carpenter complained: "In my trade in this place we are worked eleven hours from April 1 to October. The remainder from sun up to sundown, with one and one-fourth hours at noon, except December and January, with three-fourth hour at noon. . . . Our post-office opens after we go to work and closes at the exact time we quit work, making it inconvenient of the laboring man." A blacksmith wrote that his shop worked the "ten hour system—nine hours in winter and eleven hours in summer," which he regarded as too much. Many workers complained that the pace of work in the shop was more intense than previously because mechanization and increased competition demanded greater productivity. According to one blacksmith, eleven hours was too much "the way we have to work." This blacksmith pondered how earlier generations of craftsmen had worked from sun to sun and observed that he had "done more work in the shop in seven years, working ten hours, than our fathers did in fourteen years." This is an important observation because it reveals how some late nineteenth-century workers judged their situation and the conditions of their work lives by an earlier standard. These workers remembered how their fathers and grandfathers had worked, and, in comparison, their own work lives didn't measure up. As the nature of work was transformed, workers felt a sense of loss in the quality of their lives as the work routines of industrial production were more intense, demanding steady, unrelenting effort. To this blacksmith the intense work routines of the postwar period demanded more effort of workers than the longer workdays at a more casual pace demanded of workers of his father's generation. At the age twenty-nine he considered himself "broke down," and if he had to continue as he had been working he would not last long. This blacksmith favored an eight-hour workday which would leave sixteen hours for rest and personal activities. On an eight-hour workday he believed workers could do more work and live longer and better.[16]

For most workers the wages paid for a more demanding and intensive work were "barely enough to live on." Competition between firms exerted a downward pressure on the wages of local workers. One printer reported that in his business every printing office cut its prices which made wages "very low." Consequently, Winston and Salem workers took what they could get. Many mechanics made about seventy-five cents to $1 a day which they had to accept in order that their families might eat.

Wages did not improve much during the postwar years. The 1870 census reported that the average wage paid a day laborer was seventy-five cents a day; carpenters earned $2 a day. The Bureau of Labor Statistics reported in 1888 that the average wage for skilled labor in Forsyth County was $1.63 while unskilled labor received eighty-one cents. Many workers labored for only nine months out of the year, and since house rent and fuel prices were high, debt and misery were widespread. A painter in Salem reported to the Bureau of Labor Statistics in 1888 that the "laboring class" makes up about one-half of the population of Winston and Salem, and its average wages are about $1 a day. For these workers, this painter observed:

> Living is high, house rent is high and fuel is high. Wood is two dollars and fifty cents per cord, and coal in winter is from eight dollars to nine dollars per ton . . . it takes all a poor man can make to live, at the wages he gets, and he generally falls in debt in the winter, and has to scratch throughout the summer to pay for his winter supplies.[17]

While most mechanics were suffering from low wages and barely making a living for their families, a few "master mechanics" did enjoy high wages and significant security. The Salem painter mentioned above reported to the Bureau of Labor Statistics that there were ten to twelve master mechanics in Salem who were paid $2 to $3 per day. Two of these master mechanics worked in the Salem Furniture Factory, probably as supervisors. W. G. Bahnson and R. L. Hege, originally local cabinetmakers who worked a number of years in other towns, returned to Salem to work in the Salem Furniture Factory. Apparently, they were highly skilled cabinetmakers whose work as craftsmen was respected. That the *Union Republican* saw fit to report Bahnson's and Hege's return points to a widening gulf in the ranks of the artisans. Some were retaining their status as respected craftsmen, albeit in a new work setting, while the majority were being reduced to the level of semiskilled factory operatives or laborers. As in other communities that experienced industrialization, the artisan class was being fractured. Most found themselves in conditions similar to the workers in Winston's tobacco factories and Salem's textile mills. As their hopes of becoming master craftsmen and shopowners faded, workers in the crafts recognized their common interests with other wage earners. Low wages, insecurity, and uncertain prospects fueled resentment among journeymen and solidified their conviction that they were rapidly losing ground as mechanics.[18]

By the 1880s the factory workers in the tobacco and textile industries comprised the largest group of workers in Winston and Salem. Fleeing the countryside these southerners, generally poor and uneducated, grabbed the opportunity industrial labor offered; whites headed for the textile mill and blacks for the tobacco factory. With few alternatives in the southern economy for this class of workers, southern manufacturers had few worries about an adequate labor supply in the first two decades after the war. With conditions on the farms poor, opportunities for work so few, and the prospects of the impoverished so bleak, manpower for the South's early industries was readily available. That so many poor whites and blacks migrated to Winston and Salem to take advantage of opportunities in the mills and factories points to the mobility of the poor in the South during the 1870s and 1880s. Though many of the poor of both races were often unable to leave the farms where they worked as tenants, sharecroppers, or laborers because of debt and work contracts, debt peonage did not prevent all southerners from responding to the opportunities of the market. As the swelling urban industrial population of the South during the 1880s illustrates, these southerners moved toward the higher wages and better opportunities the growing cities offered.[19]

Many of the unskilled and semiskilled southerners of both races who sought jobs in the workshops, textile mills, and tobacco factories of the two towns abandoned farms that did not bring the rewards or security they had long sought. With the reorganization of southern agriculture, many southerners were finding it difficult in the 1880s to make a living from farming. Crop prices, high in the immediate postwar years, dropped in the 1870s and remained flat in the 1880s. Increasingly burdened by debt and pressed by merchants who were their creditors, yeomen and tenants struggled from year to year in a deepening dependence on merchants and landlords. As the southern agricultural economy became increasingly commercial, the crop lien, tenancy, and sharecropping became a way of life for those who tried to make a living from the southern soil.[20]

For southerners of both races, the decision to move from farm to factory or mill reflected a choice made after considering available options and with the future in mind. As in the antebellum years, economic need and family economic strategies that sought security and improvement of the quality of life led many southerners to choose mill work over remaining on the farm. For widows with children and few means of support, the mill offered a refuge that guaranteed the family's escape from destitution. For the owner of a small farm, without sufficient resources to survive in the postwar agricultural economy, the mill might have offered his children brighter prospects where steady work earned ready cash and protected the family from the uncertainties of the farm. Some sons or daughters decided on their own that mill work offered a better future than the farm with its unrewarded work and prolonged dependence on parents. All together, those who came to the mills and factories in the towns across the South did so because they realized that farm labor no longer paid for the often back-breaking work it required. In addition, mill and factory offered freedom from continued indebtedness to and control by merchants and landowners. The move to town to work in a textile mill or tobacco factory promised steady work and regular wages which made possible better housing, new clothes, and more plentiful meals. Many southerners, especially young men and women, went to the mill not only to escape the drudgery of farm work but also the sameness of everyday life in the rural neighborhoods of the South. Thus they rejected the romanticized notions of the superiority of farm life which had long been a staple of the southern ideology. For them the mill or the factory was an opportunity for an easier and more secure life and, if the mill was located in a town, certainly a life surrounded by a more diverse group of people than what they would have found had they remained on the farm. This was a powerful allure for the teenaged men and women who made up the bulk of the mill labor force. The decision to enter upon mill or factory work was to evaluate the conditions of one's life, find those conditions inadequate or unsatisfying, and act on a determination to take control of one's life and seek a better situation.[21]

In Winston and Salem, as across the South, the textile mill was primarily the preserve of white workers which reflected the prejudices of the mill owners against blacks and their desire to secure a submissive labor force. Poor whites were in plentiful supply after the war, and mill owners committed themselves to white labor out of the belief that whites had better work habits than blacks and were more adaptable to a regular work routine governed by the pace of the machine. But mill owners also believed white operatives could be easily intimidated with the threat that blacks could fill their places if need be. All of the weavers, spinners, loom fixers, and other employees dealing directly with machinery were white. Blacks, who comprised just 6 percent of the F. and H. Fries work force in 1880, usually filled only menial jobs which were dirty and demanded strenuous labor like sweeping the floors and unloading and unpacking cotton bales. Young single adults and older single women comprised the

TABLE 7.6

Age Distribution of Textile Mill Workers in Winston Township, 1870, 1880

	Male				Female			
	1870	*%*	*1880*	*%*	*1870*	*%*	*1880*	*%*
<14	3	13	11	20	5	16	8	15
15–20	8	35	22	41	17	53	19	35
21–30	4	17	7	13	7	22	17	32
31–40	4	17	6	11	3	9	8	15
41+	4	17	8	15	0	0	2	3

Sources: 1870 Census, Population Schedule manuscript microfilm, Forsyth County, North Carolina; 1880 Census, Population Schedule manuscript microfim, Forsyth County, North Carolina.

largest share of the mill work force. By 1880 single workers over the age of eighteen constituted 76 percent of the work force, and the average age of the operatives was twenty-three. Though females made up the largest part of the mill work force, the number of males increased from 40 percent in 1870 to 47 percent in 1880.[22] Young men between the ages of twelve and twenty comprised 61 percent of the male operatives in 1880, up from 48 percent in 1870, but the proportion of male mill hands between the ages of twenty-one and forty declined from 34 to 13 percent. There was also an increasing number of older women working in the mill. Table 7.6 shows that women between the ages of twenty-one and forty made up 47 percent of the female work force in the mills in 1880, an increase of 16 percent over 1870. The proportion of female mill workers in 1880 over age thirty-one was 18 percent. Many of these women appear to have been single, divorced, or widowed, the last group often accompanied by families. The Hanes family was typical. Melissa Hanes, age forty-one and widowed, kept house while three of her children—Emily, eighteen, Mary, fourteen, and Charles, twelve—worked in the mill. Her eldest child, Elizabeth, twenty-five, shared housekeeping duties with her while William, eleven, attended school. Another widow, Elizabeth Bennett, thirty-nine, found security in a company boardinghouse. John Bennett, sixteen, worked in the mill while Charles, nineteen, worked as a stonecutter. The two youngest children, Lillie, twelve, and Mary, ten, attended school. They shared their household with seven boarders who worked in the Fries mills. The boardinghouse also contained the household of Eliza Holder, fifty-one, widowed, and a former Salem Manufacturing Company operative. Living with Eliza were two sisters, a nephew, and five boarders. During the same period the number

Fig. 7.3. View of Factory Hill and the F. and H. Fries Company mill complex. Housing for the company's employees was situated adjoining the mill. Courtesy of the Forsyth County Public Library, Winston-Salem, North Carolina.

of mill workers who were part of a family unit (either nuclear or extended) declined from 58 percent to 45 percent.[23]

These were southerners living on the margins of their society. For teenagers in the South there were few nonfarm employment opportunities. With apprenticeship declining and fewer teenagers finding positions in the crafts, the mill, along with catch-as-catch-can day labor, offered the only opportunity for work. But the decline in the number of male operatives between the ages of twenty-one and forty illustrates that men in their twenties and thirties had come to recognize the limited prospects of mill labor and sought opportunities elsewhere when they were at the peak of their wage-earning potential. Unskilled labor in the towns' wagon works, machine shops, and sash and door factories which was available to many men who worked in the textile mills paid on the average eighty-one cents a day, six cents to thirty-one cents above what they could earn in the textile mill.[24] For older women the mill was a reliable source of income and security at a time in their lives when they were likely to have family responsibilities. For families employed in the mills there were alternatives in the southern economy. Families were valued by landowners who needed tenants and sharecroppers to produce cotton and tobacco, especially as families were considered to be more dependable than young single wage earners. These families may have moved back and forth from farm to mill as they attempted to strike better deals for themselves with landowners and mill owners.

For many southerners who turned from the farm to the textile mill, the initial encounter with the mill was bewildering. The size of the mill itself was often intimidating to these workers who had never before seen a building of such size. Rising two or more stories and employing under one roof anywhere from fifty to one hundred or more people attentively tending their frames or looms, the mill presented a new world of loud noise and the constant movement of machinery that had no parallel in the new mill hands' past experiences. Work in the mills was long, noisy, and dirty. During the summer months the F. and H. Fries mills ran from 6:00 A.M. to 6:45 P.M., with probably only forty-five minutes off at noon for a meal. During the winter months the mills operated fourteen hours a day, running after dark with gas lamps until electric lights were installed in the 1880s. About twelve hours a day appears to have been the norm for textile mills in the piedmont counties of North Carolina. The industrywide norm was about eleven hours a day. The long hours were spent in unpleasant surroundings where lint and dust hung in the air, clinging to the hair and clothes of the operatives, irritating their eyes, and filling their noses and lungs. The clattering of the machinery was all the operatives heard for twelve to fourteen hours a day.[25]

While the Fries mills in the 1880s were larger, employed greater numbers, and produced yarns and cloth in greater quantities than the antebellum mills, the most noticeable change was in the pace of production. The Fries company continually installed newer and more efficient engines, looms, and spindles which increased the speed of production. The effect of these innovations was to increase the demands on the operatives as they struggled to keep up with the increased pace of the machines. The pace was hectic, for the machinery ran with few stops and workers spent the whole day walking among the machinery, reaching, pushing, and pulling as they tended the looms and frames over which they had little control. The reports of the Bureau of Labor Statistics reveal that factory work was unrelenting and often dangerous. Spinners, mostly older children and teenaged women, tended frames of as many as

104 bobbins a side spinning at 5,000 to 10,000 rpm. Experienced spinners tended six to eight sides arranged on each side of an alley through which the spinner walked checking for and quickly piecing together broken threads. Weavers, mostly older teenagers and young women, had the job that required the most skill in the mill. Working quickly, they adjusted threads on the loom from bobbins and harnesses as warp and woof were woven together into cloth. The fast-paced routine in an environment of exposed running belts and the moving parts of the machines often caused accidents in which mill operatives were seriously injured and maimed. In the F. and H. Fries mill, Ruf Brown, a youth, caught his hand in the feed rollers of a wool picker, crushing a finger badly. Lee Hanes had his hands "painfully scalded" in the dye house of the mill. Noah Outon and his helper, a black youth, were burned severely about their hands, arms, and legs when a carboy of sulphuric acid shattered in the dye department. Since the pace of mill work was set by the speed of the machinery over which the mill hands had little control, the work routine in the mill was a new departure from what these southerners had experienced on the farm, where they had determined for themselves how fast and how hard they worked. On the farm and in their family households southerners had taken frequent breaks during the workday and were able to control their use of time, while the seasons and the weather determined what tasks needed to be completed and when they would be done. Though there was monotony in farm work which pushed the dissatisfied toward the mill, compared to the repetitive activities within the confines of the mill's walls farming offered a diversity of work activities to relieve the day-in and day-out routine of work. Work on the farm was hard and dirty, with heavy lifting, pushing and pulling plows and other implements, and frequently stooping to dig and hoe, often in the heat and dust from sunup to sundown. For some mill hands labor in the mill could be just as heavy and dirty as farm work. The most unpleasant task in the mill, generally reserved for black males, was in the opening and picking rooms, where workers moved and unpacked five hundred-pound bales of cotton, tearing off chunks of raw cotton to be fed into the picker which cleaned the cotton.[26]

The pay for mill operatives was comparable to that received for similar work in the shops and factories of Winston and Salem. One local mechanic who was not employed in the mills reported that the average pay in the Fries mills was about seventy-five cents a day, about what other unskilled work earned. As Table 7.7 shows, in Alamance County in

Fig. 7.4. Operatives employed in the F. and H. Fries mills, probably in the early 1890s. Courtesy of the Forsyth County Public Library, Winston-Salem, North Carolina.

1887, male operatives averaged sixty-nine cents a day while female operatives earned fifty-five cents. Boys and girls earned fifty-two cents and thirty-nine cents, respectively. For skilled workers in the mill the pay ranged from $1.50 a day to $2.25, which was in the pay range for skilled workers not employed in textile mills. In Guilford County a mill foreman reported that he earned $1.50 a day, while a male operative earned fifty cents. In 1887, North Carolina spinners, who comprised the largest group of mill workers, averaged from thirty cents to sixty cents a day and weavers earned from seventy-five cents to $1.25.[27] It is probable that the wages F. and H. Fries paid its operatives were within the range of those paid in Alamance and Guilford counties and across North Carolina. Life in the textile mills may have been unpleasant, with low pay for long hours, but poor whites continued to come into the mill towns from the countryside searching for work. Lured by the hope of a better life, many former farmers looked to the mill. Even the meager wages coming in on a

TABLE 7.7
Textile Mill Wages, 1887 (Alamance and Guilford Counties)

	Daily Wages
Male Operatives	69 cents
Female Operatives	55 cents
Boys	52 cents
Girls	39 cents
Skilled Workers (carpenters, foremen, etc.)	$1.50–2.25

Source: Bureau of Labor Statistics, *First Annual Report. 1887*, 37, 142–43.

steady basis may have been more money than these people had ever seen. A family with two or three members working in a textile mill or tobacco factory could earn an income that easily surpassed what a tenant family could expect.[28]

In contrast to the mechanized production Salem's textile mill hands confronted, the tobacco factory workers in Winston remained in an unmechanized manufacturing setting where handwork persisted until the twentieth century. The predominance of blacks in chewing tobacco manufacturing illustrated the staying power of traditional white southern attitudes regarding the role of blacks in the economy. Southern whites commonly believed that blacks were unsuited for mechanized labor and were most productive in jobs requiring manual labor. Because plug and twist manufacturing was done largely by hand, tobacco manufacturers believed black southerners to be ideal for this type of labor. Consequently black workers found a niche in chewing tobacco production. Reports of the Bureau of Labor Statistics confirm the prevalence of black southerners in tobacco manufacturing. One Winston tobacco manufacturer reported that 80 percent of his employees were "colored," who "for our work are generally better than whites." Winston which remained a center of chewing tobacco manufacturing through the end of the nineteenth century and attracted large numbers of blacks who sought regular wages and an escape from the same debilitating conditions on southern farms which led poor whites to flee to the textile mills. Each spring the "colored population" of Winston increased as the tobacco factories commenced work for the season. By 1884 about thirty-five hundred southerners, most of whom were black, found work in Winston's tobacco factories.[29]

The processing routine in the tobacco factories differed little from the antebellum period when much of the plug and twist manufacturing was undertaken on tobacco plantations with the use of slave labor. Leaf was unpacked from the hogsheads when it arrived at the factory door and treated with steam to make it pliable and easy to remove the midrib. Pickers cleaned the tobacco of trash and separated the best leaves for wrapping the plug and the not-so-good leaves for filling. Stemmers, usually women, working at a fast pace removed the leaf from the stem. After drying until completely dehydrated, the leaf was flavored by immersion in a sugar or licorice solution. In the room where flavoring was added, black men tended large steaming kettles, constantly stirring the mixture with wooden paddles to prevent scorching. After drying the leaf on the roof of the factory, the rollers or lumpers, usually black men, fashioned a quantity of tobacco into either a rectangular cake or a twist which they continually measured, weighed, and trimmed to get a uniform size and weight. With a stemmed, unflavored leaf which each roller's assistant prepared, the rollers wrapped each molded cake in a yellow leaf. After the lump was wrapped it was sent to the prize room where the prize hands placed it in a "shape" which was then pressed to form flat pancakes. After a third pressing, the finished plug was ready for packing and the application of the revenue stamp. Young black boys were employed in the factory to affix tin tags on plugs, place labels and tax stamps on the boxes of the finished products, and run errands. The tobacco factory offered a variety of jobs for laborers—doormen, janitors, truck rollers who moved heavy loads of tobacco through the factory, and coal shovelers.[30]

Work in the tobacco factories, like farm labor, was geared to the seasons. Until the late 1880s, when improved drying machinery proved capable of removing moisture from the finished product, factories operated only during the spring and summer. In 1880, Winston tobacco factories operated an average of six months a year. By the late 1880s, tobacco factories were staying in operation an average of about eight months a year. When the factories opened in the spring the workers would come to Winston from the surrounding countryside and from as far away as eastern North Carolina, South Carolina, and Virginia. Many of Winston's black factory workers remained firmly rooted to their homes in other areas and in the early years of the tobacco industry the factory work force was transient. As the *People's Press* observed: "Winston's colored population, like the leaves, come and go with the summer." One black tobacco worker from eastern North Carolina regularly spent the summers working in Winston, but returned home to his farm in the fall. But the dramatic population growth of Winston between 1870 and 1890 demonstrates that large numbers of the transient workers settled in Winston, and brought their families with them. Many workers came to Winston, worked for a time, and then returned home to gather their families and possessions for a permanent move to the town.[31]

As in the textile mills, work in the tobacco factories was long, with an eleven- or twelve-hour day common, dirty, and often dangerous. In the factory lack of ventilation, high temperatures, and high humidity created unhealthy conditions for the workers, which led to a high incidence of tuberculosis and pneumonia. Poor ventilation and airborne tobacco cuttings caused breathing problems for many workers. Adult workers who fed tobacco into cutting machines spent their working days in a room in which the air was filled with tobacco dust which required them to cover their noses with cloth to keep from inhaling the dust. One factory owner found the tobacco dust "very debilitating," for it kept him "constantly coughing—day and night." Still, he did not think it "unhealthy to most people." Workers in some parts of the factory constantly risked injury. Work in the prize room was dangerous and workers were often injured while operating the presses and rollers there. Frank Pruner, the boss in the prize room of H. H. Reynolds's "Red Elephant" tobacco factory, had three fingers on his right hand severed by one of the machines. The closeness of working and living conditions in the factories and tenements, inadequate housing, and poor sanitation also threatened the workers' health. Around the factories and tenements conditions were often foul. The Winston Board of Aldermen in 1880 reported on the sewage and sanitation conditions and found that Bitting and Whitaker's privy had a "very offensive" smell, while in the hollow behind Brown Brothers Tobacco factory between Church and Chestnut streets the board found cesspools "in such foul condition and so offensive that this secretary is not scholar enough to describe it."[32]

Nevertheless, the tobacco factory did indeed offer the opportunity for impoverished blacks to raise their standard of living. Wages for unskilled men, women, and children in the factory were roughly comparable to the wages paid white unskilled labor in the community at large and in the textile mills (see Tables 7.8 and 7.9). In 1887 unskilled labor in the tobacco factories received an average of fifty-seven cents a day. Table 7.9 shows that women in the tobacco factories were paid an average wage of sixty-four cents a day while children earned fifty cents a day. Semiskilled workers—men working in the screw room, packing room, or as firemen—averaged a little over $1.00. Skilled workers, mostly black, and

TABLE 7.8
Reports from Tobacco Manufacturers, Forsyth County,
1887

Avg. # of Months in Operation	8.4
Avg. Capital Investment	$76,428[a]
Avg. Value of Product	$127,000[b]
Avg. # of Men Employed	82
Avg. # of Women Employed	38
Avg. # of Youths Employed	36
Avg. # of Children < 14 Employed	20[b]
Avg. Total Employed	170
Avg. Workday (hours)	10.9
Wages Paid	semimonthly
Avg. % Adults Read/Write	43[c]
Avg. % Children Read/Write	35[d]
Avg. % Who Own Homes	10.8[c]

Source: Bureau of Labor Statistics, *First Annual Report. 1887*, 158–59.
Note: 8 manufacturers responded to the Bureau's request for information:
[a] 7 responses   [b] 5 responses   [c] 6 responses   [d] 4 responses

supervisors, almost always white, ranged in pay from $1.50 to $2.54 a day. Skilled labor in the trades in Winston and Salem earned on the average $1.63 a day. The highest-paid tobacco factory workers, the rollers who were usually blacks, made $2.54 a day which put them in line with the highest paid wage-earning mechanics. These workers were often paid in a combination of cash and commodities. One firm reported in the 1880 census of manufacturing that it paid its workers in firewood and other provisions equivalent to 10 percent of the wages earned, with the balance paid in cash. Another firm allowed its workers free chewing tobacco. One firm reportedly paid an additional 5 percent over regular rates for overtime work, and, if a full day's work could not be provided, employees were still paid a full day's wage. Though the tobacco factory workers' wages were comparable to those of other workers in the two towns, their work was seasonal, with as much as half of the year idle. One tobacco manufacturer noted that his workers saved almost nothing from their wages and, "consequently when dull season comes in winter, which lasts about three months, they are not prepared for it, and they suffer, unless we make advances to them, which we generally do."[33] The dependence of black factory workers on their employers for help in making it through the off-season potentially bound the workers to the

TABLE 7.9
Tobacco Factory Wages—Forsyth County, 1887

	Daily Wages
unskilled children	$0.50
unskilled women	$0.64
semiskilled men (screw room, packing room, firemen)	$1.00
skilled (carpenters, tobacco rollers, supervisors)	$1.50–2.54

Source: Bureau of Labor Statistics, *First Annual Report. 1887*, 37, 142–43, 154.

factory and circumscribed their freedom to seek more steady and remunerative work.

Except for race the work forces of both the textile mills and the tobacco factories were quite similar demographically. Like the almost exclusively white labor force in the textile mills, the mostly black tobacco workers were young and single. Table 7.10 shows that men under thirty years old comprised 75 percent of the male work force, while women under age thirty made up 95 percent of the female work force. Because tobacco-factory work was seasonal and most workers returned to their homes in the rural communities of North Carolina and Virginia after production stopped, only 31 percent of the males over age eighteen and 40 percent of the females over eighteen were married. In the R. J. Reynolds Tobacco Company factory between June 1879 and May 1880, the only period during these years for which records on workers survive, 110 workers were employed. Of the 110, fifty-five, or 50 percent, were men age fifteen and over, forty-five or 41 percent were women age fifteen and over, and ten or 9 percent were children under age fifteen.[34]

The tobacco factory provided young black men with an alternative to

TABLE 7.10
Age Distribution of Tobacco Factory Workers, 1880

	Male	%	Female	%
14 and under	10	14.9	4	21
15–20	14	20.9	3	15.8
21–30	27	40.3	11	57.9
31–40	11	16.4	0	0
41+	5	7.5	1	5.3
Totals	67	100	19	100

Source: 1880 Census, Population Schedule manuscript microfilm, Forsyth County, North Carolina.

the farm. Leaving the farm for the factories, if only for a few months, was for many young blacks an opportunity to achieve something on their own and for themselves, to escape the stifling conditions in black belt counties where the hopes of black men continually collided with the realities of white economic and social power. The urban factory allowed these ambitious southerners to earn something on their own, regardless of how meager the earnings might have been, and to realize a degree of independence not possible in the old plantation regions. For other black men, the factories offered the chance to earn some cash to take back to their families on the farms. It is quite likely that the decision for a young man to spend six months in the Winston tobacco factories was made in conjunction with the family he left on the farm that needed the additional income to meet obligations there or to accumulate some savings. As the textile mills did for white families, the tobacco factories offered alternatives and opportunities to blacks which farming did not. For blacks in Winston the wage work that the tobacco factories provided imbued them with a sense of having more control over their lives, freeing them from the necessity of having "to be grinning and bowing to whites all the time," as one member of the black community in Winston remembered.[35]

In the twenty-five years following the end of the Civil War, work in America shifted decisively from farm to factory as greater numbers of Americans found themselves engaged in industrial work.[36] In Winston and Salem industrialization transformed the nature of work and created a class of wage-earning workers who shared the common situation of long working hours at low wages, insecure job prospects, and declining status and prestige in the community. The shrinking size of certain trades, a trend toward more middle-aged men entering those trades demonstrating declining skill levels, the decline of apprenticeship, and fierce wage competition provide further evidence that a transformation was occurring in the artisanal economy of Winston and Salem. Yet, while industrialization meant lost opportunities and declining prospects for most of the community's mechanics, it meant new alternatives for many poor whites and blacks mired in the stagnant southern agriculture. This dichotomy of experience illuminates the motivations of the two groups of industrial workers—artisans and factory workers—as they contended with the dominant economic forces in their efforts to improve the conditions of labor in Winston and Salem. The artisans' response to the transformation of production and work was defensive as they attempted to preserve a vanishing way of life. For the impoverished southerners who left the farm for the factory, it was a struggle to preserve their independence and dignity as well as fulfill their expectations of a better life than southern agriculture offered. The emergence of a large working-class population in the 1880s fundamentally altered the social structure of Winston and Salem and reshaped the contours of community for the people living there.

CHAPTER EIGHT

The Industrial Community:
Drawing the Lines of Class and Race

Winston-Salem, with its rapid growth driven by the tobacco industry and an "energetic business climate," offered dramatic evidence of the transformation sweeping across North Carolina that reshaped people's lives. Walter Hines Page, editor of the *Raleigh State Chronicle* and prolific proponent of economic development, proclaimed Winston in 1883 to be a "noisy inland metropolis, possessing every accompanying indication of city-like thrift and go-aheadativeness."[1] Incorporation into the national market economy and the development of tobacco and textile manufacturing reshaped the contours of community. The experiences of the people of Winston-Salem as they pursued their own interests produced a complex urban community characterized by differentiation according to ways of work, residential patterns, and politics. In the postwar southern manufacturing cities like Winston-Salem, Durham, and Richmond, there were deep tensions that occasionally erupted into open conflict in the political arena along class and race lines as southerners struggled to create a new order in a rapidly changing social and economic environment. In this contest workers attempted to promote their interests by improving working conditions and securing their rights as free people. Their employers, on the other hand, attempted to create and maintain a community order that preserved the political power and the authority of the entrepreneurial class to direct the life of the community and promote an environment conducive to profitable business activity. Race became a central factor in the dynamic of

Fig. 8.1. Stores along Liberty Street on Court House Square in Winston. Courtesy of the Forsyth County Public Library, Winston-Salem, North Carolina.

community in Winston-Salem as thousands of black southerners fled the countryside for the city in search of the independence and dignity emancipation once promised. Like white southerners in other towns, the white population of Winston-Salem reacted with a rising fear of the rapidly growing numbers of black southerners who filled the tobacco factories and the proliferating boardinghouses, tenements, and shanties and challenged long-held white notions of black subordination and racial separation.[2] Winston-Salem's rapid postwar growth offers a vivid illustration of the urban expansion that developed across the South as the region recovered from the prostration of its Civil War defeat and railroads linked southern communities into a regional trading network.[3]

The expansion of manufacturing fueled an impressive population growth in the community. The population of Winston Township, which included both Winston and Salem, increased from 1,892 in 1860 to 11,399 in 1890, or 502 percent. The changing composition of the population is revealed by the dynamic growth of the black population which increased from 10 in 1860 to 1,482 in 1880, and to 4,687 in 1890, a 216 percent increase from 1880. By 1880, 54.1 percent of the working population in Winston-Salem was employed in manufacturing.[4] The population increase and its changing composition reshaped the spatial geography of Winston-Salem in the 1880s. Community became increasingly segmented as neighborhoods assumed greater functional, class, and racial characteristics. Two factory districts developed in Winston with the building of the tobacco factories. The largest concentration of factories encompassed eighteen square blocks bordered by Sixth, Depot, Bellews Creek, and Main streets. Within this area were nineteen of Winston's thirty-four tobacco factories. Another concentration of eleven factories was located in a four square block area bordered by Seventh, Cherry, Oldtown, and Third streets. Winston's tobacco factory workers, which the *People's Press* estimated to number about thirty-five hundred in 1884, gathered in tenements and boardinghouses in neighborhoods around the factories. Tenements ran from Sixth and Chestnut streets down to Fifth Street, and also along Third, Fourth, and Fifth streets between Chestnut and Depot streets. The 1880 federal census shows that 79.6 percent of Winston's tobacco workers and 63.1 percent of its laborers lived in the twenty-one square block area bordered by Main, Seventh, Depot, and Bellews Creek streets. Within this part of town 76.5 percent of Winston's black and mulatto population lived. Of the whites in this district who made up 23.5 percent of the population, there were seven manufacturers, four merchants, and five professionals who lived on Main Street on the border of the neighborhood. In contrast, the city's commercial life centered around the Court House Square bordered by Fourth, Liberty, Third, and Main streets. Stores, offices, hotels, an opera house, and private dwellings surrounded the square and extended down these streets. In the twenty-five square blocks bordered by Seventh, Spring, First, and Main streets, 74.2 percent of the white population lived, with merchants, manufacturers, professionals, and skilled workers as residents on the same blocks.[5]

In Salem a small factory district grew up around the F. and H. Fries mills on New Shallowford Road. There the textile mill workers gathered in tenements and boardinghouses around the mills where they worked. The Fries mill was bordered by Elm, New Shallowford, and Salt streets. Tenements extended down First and West Street from New Shallowford Road across from the Arista mill. The 1880 census reports that most mill hands lived within six blocks of the F. and H. Fries mills on Main Street,

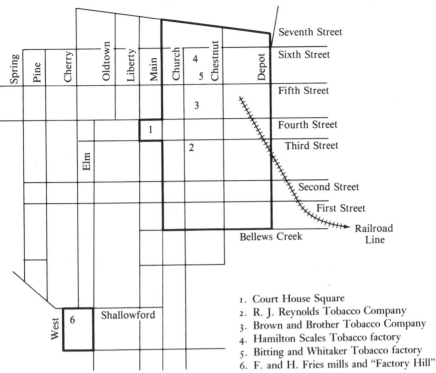

1. Court House Square
2. R. J. Reynolds Tobacco Company
3. Brown and Brother Tobacco Company
4. Hamilton Scales Tobacco factory
5. Bitting and Whitaker Tobacco factory
6. F. and H. Fries mills and "Factory Hill"

Map 8.1. Winston-Salem in 1885

near Cemetery, East Salem, Popular, Cherry, Salt, Elm, West, and Marshall streets, all of which either bordered the mills or were within a few blocks.[6]

Within their separate neighborhoods in Winston-Salem, tobacco factory workers, the textile mill operatives, and day laborers created their distinct subcultures that reflected the circumstances of their lives and their relative status in the community. As industrialization removed production from the home and labor was paid a daily wage for specifically mandated hours of toil, work and life were separated. It was in this separation that workers created their own values and culture as they maintained a degree of autonomy from their employers away from the workplace. Working five days a week from dawn until dusk, and on Saturday until the middle of the afternoon, the social life of the workers centered around their neighborhoods and the family. In their neighborhoods workers created the informal institutions and activities that enriched their lives. Their churches were there along with kinfolk, friends,

Fig. 8.2. Winston Blues baseball club. Courtesy of the Forsyth County Public Library, Winston-Salem, North Carolina.

and fellow workmen. The neighborhood determined one's associates in the informal activities of drinking, chatting, or celebrating holidays or personal events. One printer observed in 1888 that the usual routine for Winston's workers after they left the shops and factories was to go home for supper, then "they go to some store and talk and gossip until time to go to bed." Living in neighborhoods among fellow workers these individuals found the freedom, equality, and respect often denied them in the workshop or the factory.[7]

Outside of their neighborhoods workers in Winston-Salem frequently came together as members of the larger community in the popular culture of the towns. Concerts, minstrel shows, theater, and sports were important ways of entertainment. With admission of fifty cents to seventy-five cents they could attend events like "Thorne's Comedy Company," comedian John Thompson, and "Morton's Big 4 Minstrels with the Brass Band and Orchestra" at Tise's Hall or Brown's Opera House. Workers participated also in community-wide celebrations and events that drew people together across class and race lines. Political rallies and July the

Fourth celebrations were important occasions that brought people together for parades, barbecues, public speeches by town leaders, and fireworks displays. Football and baseball occupied many young men and entertained the community on Saturday afternoons in the spring and summer. These games brought together on the playing fields young men from the different neighborhoods of Salem and a variety of occupations. Fans of the Salem Lightfoot Baseball Club saw F. and H. Fries operatives Walter Barrow and E. B. Waggoman and harnessmaker G. F. Brietz play alongside other skilled workers as well as sons of merchants, manufacturers, and professionals.[8]

While they shared a common status as wage workers and all were dependent on their employers for their livelihoods, the workers of the two towns were divided occupationally and racially. Each segment of the working-class population of the community was united by its own identity and sense of collective experiences. Hence each group of workers addressed the problems of industrial labor from their particular vantage points. The skilled workers, mostly white males, confronted industrialization in the towns' shops and struggled to hold on to artisan traditions as they faced skill dilution, lower earnings, and declining prospects and status. Their reaction to the challenges of industrialization was defensive as they attempted to preserve old ways of work and life.[9]

Like antebellum mechanics the skilled workers of Winston-Salem looked for respect, dignity, and security in such traditional artisanal cultural forms as mutual aid societies, temperance clubs, fraternal organizations, and local political parties. In many cases, however, these artisan institutions served to link artisans to employers and the larger community culture. Both artisans and their bosses, for example, belonged to Odd Fellows, Knights of Pythias, or Masonic lodges. Temperance societies, too, enjoyed the support of the mechanics during the 1880s as the Twin City Temperance Reform Club united them with merchants, manufacturers, and professionals. Self-improvement was the purpose of the Chautauqua Literary and Scientific Circle which met once a month in the Music Hall of the Museum Building in Salem. The twenty-eight charter members of the circle in February 1884 intended "to promote habits of study and reading" among those with limited educational advantages and the development of the "habit of close, connected, and persistent thinking."[10] One printer believed that workingmen must try to educate themselves by reading good books and newspapers like the *New York Herald* and the *New York Times*. In 1888 a group of Winston-Salem merchants, mechanics, and professionals organized the Forsyth Five Cent Bank "to encourage thrift and economy" among the community's working population. The *Union Republican* reported that the bank offered advantages to the laboring class of the community who might save their money for the purchase of a home and greater financial security. Many mechanics recognized that in the industrial community success and security were achieved by adopting ways of behavior that differed from preindustrial times. The new moral code which evolved demanded industry, frugality, and temperance—values that many artisans believed were necessary for the mechanics' success as independent producers in an increasingly competitive economy. Many mechanics who hoped to avoid a life of wage labor adopted these values as a means of focusing their lives on the struggle for upward mobility, dignity, and security. Through self-improvement and temperance the towns' skilled workers defined themselves as part of the local community and found a place for themselves in a changing society. These organizations enabled the mechanics to project the image of stable conscientious citizens whose lives conformed to the emerging middle-class expectations of the business class that dominated affairs in Winston-Salem.[11]

That Winston-Salem mechanics embraced both the ideals of the larger community and those which their particular situation demanded is illustrated by the establishment of the Mechanics' Union in 1886. Operating as a mutual aid society, this association was organized as a cooperative effort to relieve the misery and insecurity which resulted when misfortune befell a mechanic or his family by providing modest financial benefits and aid in the event of emergencies, sickness, and accidents. The Mechanics' Union also embraced and promoted the new morality of the community. It encouraged sobriety among its members and threatened expulsion for any mechanic guilty of habitual drunkenness. The skilled and semiskilled workers employed in the shops of Winston-Salem were sensitive to their loss of control over the production process and the consequent decline in status which accompanied the loss of the dignity of skilled manual labor. As these workers labored long hours in larger, increasingly mechanized shops, they expressed their growing resentment that labor did not receive the respect it deserved. These artisans looked back to the preindustrial past for the traditions of independence, improvement, and mutual aid to interpret their present experiences and fashion ways of shaping the new world of work to meet their needs and expectations.[12] Though white mechanics had grievances against their employers

AT SOUTHSIDE
RR 94

Fig. 8.3. A Fraternal Order of Odd Fellows outing at Southside Park in 1894. Courtesy of the Forsyth County Public Library, Winston-Salem, North Carolina.

and the emerging system of industrial production, these grievances had not yet evolved fully into a class-conscious critique of the industrial system. These workers and their employers remained united by neighborhood ties and relations within institutions like the Mechanics' Union and the cultural affairs of the community.

In contrast to the white mechanics, the textile operatives of Salem found themselves wrapped up in the social system of the textile mill. The mill workers had formed the vanguard of industrial labor in the 1840s and had challenged the authority of the mill owners to maintain control over their lives in face of the paternalistic prerogatives of their employers. In the 1880s, however, these workers had become cautious, trying to balance their need for work and security with the preservation of their autonomy. The mill hands found themselves in a situation similar to that which they had left in the rural areas. Impoverished white families who abandoned tenant farms and sharecropping for the wage labor of the textile mills found familiar relationships in the mill village. On the farms, yeomen and laborers were caught up in a web of personal relations with

Fig. 8.4. Members of a local temperance society in 1894. Courtesy of the Forsyth County Public Library, Winston-Salem, North Carolina.

wealthy planters and landowners who could be very helpful in times of need. This relationship, as it was perceived by both the mill owners and the workers, was easily transferred to the mill, with the company managers filling the place as employer and benefactor. Their experiences on the farm were significant in determining the operatives' response to mill management; they came to the mill accustomed to an employer's paternalism and power.[13] The company-owned tenements in which they lived were symbolic of a relationship based on reciprocity between the mill owner and the operatives, but these structures also demonstrated the dependence of workers. By providing housing, work for the entire family, a company-owned store where the operatives traded, and religious and social activities, mill managers encouraged their workers' dependence on the company. This arrangement robbed the mill hands of the chance to develop a life separate from work, for the company was involved in almost all aspects of employee life.

The textile mills drew operatives into a compact community that centered around the mill, consequently separating them from the larger working class of Winston-Salem. By isolating the operatives in boarding-houses and family houses around the mill, F. and H. Fries management attempted to promote an image of "parental solicitude" toward their operatives which aimed at maintaining control over the mill work force and instilling habits of personal conduct—punctuality, temperance, diligence, reliability, and obedience—that guaranteed the efficient, profitable, and smooth operation of the mill.[14] The president of the F. and H. Fries Company looked after his workers' needs as he perceived them, providing steady work, a regular wage, credit at the company store, and housing, as well as help with whatever extraordinary needs might arise among the workers. The company also looked after the leisure needs of its workers, stopping the mill in 1884 so that the operatives and their families could travel to Raleigh for the state fair. But the concept of reciprocity was essential to management's paternalistic style. The company expected "faithfulness" in its operatives. The mill's Christmas party in 1882 reveals management's approach to maintaining a contented and productive work force. On the Friday evening before Christmas, work stopped and the mill was decorated and lights strung. That Saturday evening management and operatives and their families gathered to dine, engage in conversation, and exchange gifts. The party began with the operatives and their families seated at the south end of a large room in the mill and the proprietors and their guests seated in front. F. H. Fries rose and greeted the operatives, expressing his gratitude for the year's work. Then, according to the *People's Press*, he offered the operatives "good and wholesome advice, impressing upon them that he desired all hands to conduct themselves decently and in order, use no profane language, and lead moral lives." He reminded the operatives that "no reasonable and necessary recreation had ever been denied them and the social and spiritual, and educational improvement of all those who worked in the mills was nearest his heart's wish." Fries told his audience: "The responsibility of the mill work was mutual. The proprietor, bosses, and operatives depended on each other for success, and he counted on their faithfulness in business." Fries concluded by wishing those gathered a Happy Christmas and asked if they were not all happy tonight, which met "with a joyful assent all around." By building company loyalty mill management hoped to reduce absenteeism and turnover, discipline the work force, and inhibit unionization and protest. The *People's Press*, probably expressing the hope of the F. and H. Fries management, reported a "kindred feeling" between management and operatives who seemed happy and contented.[15]

Such solicitude by management toward the operatives probably convinced many of them that the mill president was their only friend, especially as popular attitudes toward mill workers assumed a negative cast. Initially the cotton mill was regarded as a boon to the community specifically and to southern society in general, as it was believed to be the engine of southern economic development and a source of steady work and wages for the region's embattled yeomanry. But as mills expanded to employ larger numbers of operatives and as mill villages grew, popular attitudes in piedmont towns and cities changed. The mill workers who had been regarded as members of the once-proud independent southern yeomanry came to be seen by the nonfactory population as "desperate refugees" fleeing an exhausted land. The emerging middle class of merchants, manufacturers, and professionals in the 1880s and 1890s created its own values, standards of decorum, and a life-style of domesticity and accumulation by which they judged the operatives segregated in mill villages on the edge of town.[16] Mill hands across the South found themselves isolated from the mainstream community of the towns and cities in which they lived and worked. The changing spatial geography of piedmont towns and cities created residential and employment patterns that deepened the chasm between mill and town. In Salem, mill workers, who were isolated in tenements on Elm Street around the factory, had their own community with a place to work, a store in which to trade, and the Elm Street Sunday School, all provided by mill management. In their separate neighborhoods the operatives were looked down upon by the townspeople, including other workers, who referred to mill workers as "lint-heads," "cotton-tails," "factory-rats," and "cotton mill trash." These attitudes were evident in Salem as young toughs from the town often threw rocks through the windows of the operatives' tenements while taunting the mill hands. The separation of the mill village from the rest of the community only reinforced popular attitudes against the mill workers. One mill hand from a mill village in North Charlotte expressed in vivid terms the reality of class divisions that separated mill hands from the larger community: "But we was white trash out here; we was poor white trash because we worked in the mill. We didn't have white-collar jobs, as they called them, like working in a bank or the stores and things like that. 'Poor white trash' they called us." Such condescension toward the mill operatives often had racial implications. One operative observed: "Even the blacks looked down on us, yes they did. Called us white trash." F. and H. Fries management, however, attempted to soothe its

The Industrial Community • 211

employees' hurt feelings and reassured the operatives of their worth and importance in the South's effort to rebuild and prosper through industrialization. Aware of popular feelings toward mill workers, a local Moravian clergyman spoke to operatives and told them "work was honorable in any station of life, and the success of a man depended much upon how he went about it." He denied that mill work was looked down upon and reassured the operatives that factory work was respectable if done faithfully. According to the pastor: "There was no reason why a factory girl could not be as clever, intelligent, virtuous and honest as anyone, and if faithful in her work and social habits she was as good as the best woman in the land, for work was no dishonor, whether done in the office, study, workshop, or factory. The quality of the work alone was the question. . . . Faithful, intelligent work was the main spring of success in all such things."[17]

Though primary documents pertaining to Winston-Salem's textile operatives and their work and life are few and sketchy, the actions of mill management provide some clues to the attitudes and expectations of mill hands. The idea that mill hands completely embraced the paternalistic relationship and were submissive to the dictates of management ignores the essential agency of these workers as free men and women. Paternalism, after all, was management's attempt to legitimize their approach to labor. It was a means of rationalizing their actions to the community, their employees, and themselves. But the everyday reality of management-labor relations in the mills was that to recruit and retain a reliable work force management had to meet the expectations of its employees—regular work and steady wages for most of the family, housing, and security for the future as well as respect and dignity appropriate for independent white southerners. The mill workers, however, were equally pragmatic in their approach to management. Like their antebellum predecessors in the Salem mills, the operatives in the 1870s and 1880s were probably quite effective in shaping management's policies toward them. What might pass as one of management's paternalistic gestures to build employee loyalty—for example, shutting the mill in the fall so the operatives could go to Raleigh for the state fair—may indeed have been a response to a demand by operatives. Or the same gesture might reflect management's recognition that the mills would not operate as so many mill hands took it upon themselves to abandon the looms and spinning machinery for the good times and cotton candy of the fair. In exchange for their faithful and dependable work, the mill hands expected consideration from their employers. With few alternative opportunities in the southern economy, the mill workers were determined to create the best situation for themselves while maintaining as much of their autonomy as possible without losing their jobs.

The tobacco factory workers, the largest single segment of industrial labor in Winston-Salem, also faced challenges to their autonomy as free people. These workers, mostly black males and females seeking opportunities outside of the agricultural economy and sharecropping, saw industrial labor through the prism of hopes stirred by their recent emancipation. After emancipation the former slaves sought to free themselves from their long dependency on and subordination to whites to demonstrate that they were free people. Leaving their homes for Winston's tobacco factories they sought self-respect and personal dignity, freedom of action, and the opportunity to achieve something for themselves by their own efforts. The freed people yearned for the economic independence that made their freedom complete.[18] Once in Winston black workers created their own cultural institutions, many of which paralleled white institutions, to promote racial solidarity and create the means for community in their neighborhoods, where they distinguished themselves from the white community that dominated economic and public life in Winston. Black churches played a central role in welding together a black community. By the early 1890s five churches—a Baptist, a Presbyterian, an Episcopalian, and two Methodist congregations—filled not only their religious purposes, but served as benevolent associations, institutions of racial uplift and social improvement, and training schools for the emerging leadership of the black community. Community consciousness was fostered by fraternal organizations like the Good Samaritan Shining Star Lodge, the Good Samaritan Winston Star Lodge, and the Bloom of Youth Lodge which relieved the destitute, cared for the sick, and provided benevolent aid for their members. Musical organizations like the Gold Leaf Coronet Band and the Gilt Edge Coronet Band brought black musicians into the public life of the larger community to perform at civic functions, including concerts and marching in Winston's Fourth of July parades. A group of young black men seeking education and self-improvement established a debating society in Winston in 1878. A mutual aid society was organized by black workers to offer similar protection to its members and their families as the Mechanics' Union did for white workers. Like their white counterparts, the young men of the black community organized their own baseball club that played on Saturday

afternoons. Since blacks remained largely a transient population through
the 1880s, informal cultural institutions like celebrations that were of
particular importance to black southerners were equally important for
establishing a sense of community among the black population. On January 1 the black population of Winston-Salem came together to celebrate
Emancipation Day which reminded them that they as a community had
a distinctive history. Their common status as freed people imbued them
with an outlook in which independence, respect, and dignity were important.[19] These attitudes proved to be valuable resources in motivating
black workers to join other laborers in the mid-1880s when conditions
prompted the whole working population of Winston-Salem to agitate for
better treatment. Motivated by desires for economic independence and
respect as free people, the black workers were the most aggressive in
Winston-Salem, fervently embracing the Knights of Labor and labor
reform activities.

In the factories black men and women found a familiar paternalism
and mechanisms of intimidation and control similar to those that had
restricted their lives in the countryside. Relations between the factory
workers and their employers reveal a complex process of accommodation
and reciprocity. Some tobacco manufacturers in Winston, like textile
manufacturers, assumed responsibility for providing for the needs of the
black work force in return for loyalty, obedience, and hard work. These
factory owners pursued a benevolent approach to management as a means
of securing a reliable and faithful labor force when labor was often
difficult to recruit and retain. R. J. Reynolds attracted workers to his
factories by paying transportation costs to Winston and providing housing and employment for whole families. The R. J. Reynolds Tobacco
Company promoted its paternalistic management style by offering employment to all seekers who already had a family member working in the
Reynolds factories or household. Eventually, R. J. Reynolds Tobacco
Company established lunchrooms for its workers and provided nursery
schools for the children of women working in its factories. The tobacco
company also built neighborhoods of housing for its employees of both
races to whom it rented with a provision for tenants to purchase their
homes. While R. J. Reynolds might have taken a benevolent approach to
relations with his workers, just beneath the gentle surface of paternalism
lay more coercive forms of labor control that enabled factory management
to take advantage of the seasonal character of tobacco manufacturing and
the resulting financial insecurity and dependence of black workers. These

workers regularly found themselves completely subject to the willful control of their employers who paid wages so low as to keep them dependent. One Winston manufacturer, for example, reported that he had made cash advances to his workers who, he believed, had not saved enough of their earnings to get them through the winter.[20]

Black tobacco factory workers took the initiative to express their sense of self-determination in defiance of the control their employers held over them, assert their independence, and advance a claim for dignity. For their part, black workers sought to remedy the conditions of their dependence. Petitioning their employers for sufficient wages to carry them through the winter, the tobacco rollers of Winston, among the highest-paid workmen in the town, pleaded that they, "as a Laboring Class . . . desire to become citizens, as we are not considered as such on account of the oppression and opprobrium, which we meet day by day." The rollers reminded their employers, "We do not ask riches, nor for high living, all we desire is bread for our wives and our children, and a living man's chance." These workers wanted wages that provided them an "honest living."[21] To the black worker the appropriate solution was higher wages that freed the workers from deprivation in the winter when the factories closed and allowed a sense of dignity worthy of free people. The black tobacco workers correctly perceived that higher wages would enable them to meet their expectations of freedom and release them from their dependence on their white employers. In April 1889 at the beginning of the new production season, the tobacco rollers again attempted to obtain the wages they believed were necessary for the survival of their families by engaging in a general strike. The rollers walked out of the factories when their wages were reduced from $2.00 to $3.00 per hundred pounds to $1.75 to $2.75, while the wages of the hands in the prize room were increased from $1.00 to $1.25 a day. The walkout ended when management read to the strikers the wage schedules of factories in Danville and Reidsville which purportedly showed that Winston rollers were paid higher wages than those in other towns.[22]

While the cultural forms workers used to create a life in Winston-Salem often mirrored the culture of the larger community and utilized many of its values, workers at the same time created institutions emphasizing their rights as free people and promoting the dignity of labor. Significantly, each group of workers, in its own way, interpreted its new experiences from the perspective of its preindustrial past. Skilled workers sought to preserve their independence and the dignity of manual labor, while textile operatives sought security and the sense of neighborly community they valued in the rural neighborhoods they left for the mills. Black workers sought the personal freedom and individual dignity that emancipation promised. The memories of the preindustrial past and their expectations for their future as well as that of their children helped these workers to understand what they faced and to cope with their new situation. Despite the divisions in the labor force during these years there was a growing consciousness among workers that as wage earners they were dependent on their employers for their livelihoods. It was this dependence, plus their relative poverty, that set them apart from the smaller but more influential class of entrepreneurs and professionals and led many of them to share common hopes and values. But it is difficult to speak of a coherent, self-aware working class in southern cities in the late nineteenth century. Class is an elusive concept and class consciousness finds expression in historical events only episodically as workers share a glimpse of their actual situation in the course of events that affect their lives.[23] The situation of the working class in Winston-Salem was complicated by the continuous infusion of people from rural and preindustrial backgrounds. Workers in Winston-Salem did not have the unity necessary to challenge effectively the authority of their bosses as too many workers still believed that they could work a few years in the factories to accumulate the money necessary to fulfill their immediate wants, be they a new suit of clothes or a farm. While many black tobacco workers settled permanently in Winston, a large number still left town after the manufacturing season to return to their farms in eastern North Carolina. Like Salem's antebellum mill operatives, factory workers in Winston-Salem frequently fled the factory for the countryside to help family and friends at harvest or hog-killing season. As in the antebellum mills turnover remained high among factory workers, even well into the twentieth century. In the R. J. Reynolds Tobacco Company factories turnover reached 163.07 percent of the work force in 1923.[24] Still, workers in Winston-Salem in the 1880s acted on an awareness of their situation as industrial workers. Mechanics and factory workers, white and black, shared a sense shaped by events that demonstrated to them their declining status, more difficult working conditions, and the decreasing likelihood of meeting their expectations through manual labor. When they supported "labor tickets" in the 1887 and 1888 municipal elections or responded to the Republican party's pro-labor platform, they demonstrated an awareness of a common identity as producers and sought recognition of the value of that role. They felt a common need to be reassured of their rights as free people, and they were united by common grievances against the industrial labor system. The workers of Winston-Salem seized on the Knights of Labor and labor politics as vehicles through which to demonstrate this common identity, to express their discontent with conditions, and to voice their hopes for the future.

Skilled and semiskilled workers were increasingly aware that changes in the economy of Winston-Salem had adverse effects on their lives and prospects for the future. The once-proud and dignified skilled crafts were being undermined by industrial production and overshadowed by the increasing importance and prestige of the towns' emerging middle class of merchants, manufacturers, and professionals. A carpenter wrote the Bureau of Labor Statistics that the workingman in North Carolina was "less respected and more imposed upon than any other class." A printer wrote that workingmen were in a "bad condition." A painting contractor reported that the condition of workers in Winston-Salem was "growing worse all the time," as their educational, financial, and moral condition were in steady decline. He believed that the workers were "not treated, in many instances, as they should be." These workers were particularly concerned with the number of hours that constituted the workday and the effects of this long day on the quality of their lives and their status as free people. In 1887, the Bureau of Labor Statistics reported mechanics complaining that working twelve to fourteen hours a day precluded any opportunity for self-improvement and education which many workers believed were vital to preserving their rights as free people and as a means of upward economic mobility, or leisure time with their families. Echoing the arguments of many northern workers, one blacksmith argued that God divided time into three equal parts—"eight hours for sleep and refreshment, eight hours to toil and eight for recreation, meditation and serving the Lord." He believed a twelve-hour workday was outrageous and that there should be a law in North Carolina to prohibit it. The Bureau agreed that no one who worked this many hours in one day could appreciate any mental or social enjoyment.[25]

Workers also complained of their employers' attempts to intimidate and coerce them. In the tobacco factories intimidation was sometimes open and acknowledged. It was said that tobacco manufacturers blacklisted any employee who quit in mid-season. A carpenter reported to the Bureau of Labor Statistics in 1888 that the tobacco manufacturers had agreed among themselves that whenever an employee quit one manufacturer, a runner was dispatched to inform the other manufacturers who then refused to hire the employee.[26] Some tobacco factory workers were told by their employers that it was illegal for them to leave their employer to work for another in the same town. Tobacco factory worker T. M. Richardson wrote Governor Daniel G. Fowle in 1889:

> Does the laws of the United States or of N.C. or any town in N.C.[,] me as honest laborer who have never been disfranchies [sic], compell a man if he does not owe his imployer [sic] any thing, if he sees where that he can better him self by working for another man in the same town. My only reason to ask you is this, here in Winston N.C. are several tobacco manu-facturers and they say it is the law and it have had some great efet [sic] on men here.

In the textile mills the threat of dismissal from the job and, consequently, the mill village was no doubt persuasive to mill hands who had nowhere else to go. Intimidation of mill hands, however, was implied by the extensive power mill management exercised over the operatives' lives. Intimidation carried over to the political sphere as well, for some employers tried to influence the way their workers voted. According to a local printer, Winston-Salem workers often were afraid to vote their true sentiments for fear of displeasing their employers. Some employers even told their black workers that they would keep a list of who voted Republican. It is difficult to prove or disprove these charges, and it must be remembered that these allegations were made by workers at the same time that labor was organized for participation in local politics. In 1887 and 1888, workers in Winston-Salem challenged the local elites at the polls and attempted to elect men more sympathetic to labor's cause. Still, workers in Winston-Salem, in the words of a local mechanic, were "too much afraid of their employers."[27]

The Knights of Labor during these years tapped the wellspring of workers' grievances, transforming those concerns into a working-class critique of the industrial order taking shape across the country. From its beginnings in Pennsylvania in 1869 as an obscure organization of work-men, the Noble and Holy Order of the Knights of Labor rose on the tide of the movement to establish the eight-hour workday and the labor troubles of the 1870s and early 1880s. Between the early 1870s and the mid-1890s, two to three million people belonged at one time to the Knights of Labor, and nearly every county in the country had at least one local assembly of the Knights. In the mid-1880s the Knights of Labor appeared to fill the need these workers felt for direct action. The Knights gained the attention of southern workers in 1885 when its strike against Jay Gould's western railroads forced those companies to rescind previously announced wage reductions. Southern workers saw the Knights of Labor as a means of preventing reductions in wages and the loss of jobs.[28] Workers in Winston organized two Knights of Labor assemblies during April and May 1886. Local Assembly 6655 which operated from 1886 to 1889 was composed of black tobacco factory workers and met every Tuesday evening at the Knights of Labor Hall in East Winston; Local Assembly 6485, in existence from 1886 to 1888, was a mixed trades assembly of white workers numbering about 160 members. According to the *Union Republican* the two assemblies stirred much curiosity in Winston-Salem in the months after their organization as they announced their weekly meetings "by chalking Hieroglyphic figures about the towns, denoting month, day, hour, etc." Estimated by the *Union Republican* to number over four hundred workingmen, the two Winston lodges' potential influence immediately aroused concern. The *Union Republican* noted, "Representing labor, we take it the membership is made up of honest men, and that, therefore, whatever conclusions they decide upon will be their honest convictions of duty and right." The paper went on to hope that the Knights "will have the courage of their convictions and vote as they work, in the interests of labor and the laboring man," in other words, Republican. The *People's Press* reported in January 1887 that a Knights assembly was organized in Salem with a lodge room established over H. W. Shore's grocery. This assembly probably included a number of textile operatives.[29]

By enrolling in the Knights of Labor, many workers in Winston-Salem demonstrated their belief that solidarity and concerted action were needed to advance their interests. One local cabinetmaker believed that "trades unions are a good thing when managed by and made up of men who are workingmen." When S. A. Hauser of Winston wrote to the editor of the Fayetteville *Messenger* in 1888 calling for an alliance of laborers and farmers under the Union Labor party banner to defeat a common enemy, he promoted cooperation among those with similar interests. Hence the Knights of Labor and the subsequent organization of trade union locals in the 1890s represent a fundamental shift in the ideology of industrial workers in Winston-Salem from the antebellum free labor ideology which promoted the belief in individual artisanal success and upward mobility to a cooperative ideal that stressed the improvement and security of all workers. The cooperative ideal of the Knights of Labor and the trade unions demonstrated an emerging recognition of the special condition of industrial labor and emphasized efforts to improve the lives of industrial workers through better wages, shorter workdays, and increased opportunities for self-improvement through education.[30] But these workers' protests revealed a continuity with earlier political traditions in America. Utilizing the political inheritance of republicanism and demonstrating a "nostalgia for a preindustrial past," the late nineteenth-century labor movement, including the Knights of Labor, brought to bear on the problems of industrial labor a republican outlook that emphasized equal rights, the close connection between work and the self-worth of laborers, and the security of family and household. The Knights sought "to secure to the workers the full enjoyment in which to develop their intellectual, moral, and social faculties, all of the benefits of recreation, and pleasures of association." In the words of the Fayetteville *Messenger*, the Knights of Labor organ in North Carolina, the Knights of Labor "was founded for the special purpose of assisting the laborers of this land to receive the just fruits of their labor, and a proportionate share of the gains . . . of an advancing civilization."[31] The Knights promoted middle-class standards and expectations of productive work, civic responsibilities, education, a "wholesome" family life, temperance, and self-improvement which expressed the hopes of small shop proprietors and skilled workers seeking to preserve their status and semiskilled workers ambitious to improve their condition. Regarding intellectual and moral growth as essential for the progress of democratic civilization, workers who joined the Knights advocated shorter workweeks which would allow laborers more time for self-improvement and supported efforts like the Blair Education Bill to create a public-funded educational system. To this end the Knights established reading rooms in communities across the country and sent lecturers to educate workers in the cause of labor. The Knights of Labor united those they believed composed the producing classes—shopkeepers, manufacturers, and skilled, semiskilled, and unskilled workers; only bankers, lawyers, liquor dealers, and those employers who did not respect the dignity of labor were excluded. In Winston-Salem the Knights of Labor included newspaper editor L. N. Keith, grocer Henry W. Shore, and laborer Jerry Stockton, along with workers in the wagon shops, textile mills, and tobacco factories.[32]

The Knights of Labor enabled local workers to overcome many of the differences that divided them and to focus their grievances more clearly than before. While the organization never put forward a common political program, it did publicize common complaints. The Knights became involved in politics in almost every community where they had assemblies. Running under the name of "Union Labor," "Knights of Labor," "Workingmen," and "Independents," they challenged the established political order in an attempt to take government out of the hands of local elites. Arguing that the two major parties offered labor no relief from its oppression and disadvantages, workers were advised to abandon the Democratic and Republican parties where elites were entrenched for labor tickets. Reform, they argued, would come, if it came at all, only through a third party of producers, the Union Labor party. The Fayetteville *Messenger* told workers that "the wage-worker has been trampled on and oppressed long enough . . . [and] neither the republican [*sic*] nor democratic [*sic*] parties hold out any hope for the legislation the progressive, thinking laborers are asking." A Winston Knight wrote that he applauded the *Messenger*'s advocacy of the Union Labor party because he had "no more hopes of reform through the Demo-Republican Party than I have of the Mississippi River running towards the north pole."[33]

In the municipal elections of 1886, 1887, and 1888, opposition or labor tickets were offered in Winston-Salem. While the labor tickets did not run on a formal political program, their supporters hoped to elect men who would represent the interests of workers on the town commissions and in the state legislature. These tickets consisted of men from both the Republican and Democratic parties, but significantly they shared the common status of mechanics or proprietors sympathetic to labor's cause. Though the labor candidates had mixed success, with some but never a whole ticket winning, the elections were closely contested as the electorate was sharply divided, which revealed the appeal of labor's cause to many in Winston-Salem. In municipal elections, white voters who still comprised the majority generally supported Democratic party nominees and consequently returned incumbents to office. Both town commissions continued to represent the important business interests of the towns. In Winston the men who sat on the Board of Commissioners were lawyers, merchants, and tobacco manufacturers and dealers. In Salem the commission included mostly proprietors of small shops who had artisan backgrounds, thus maintaining continuity with the leadership of the antebellum community.[34] Although workers never succeeded in electing a labor slate intact, the political effort did mobilize workers and gave them a forum for their grievances.

Though they enjoyed but limited success in Winston-Salem, the local Knights raised a serious challenge to the entrenched political elite of merchants, professionals, and manufacturers, thus demonstrating the need for greater sensitivity to the needs of local workingmen. The merchants and manufacturers in Winston-Salem maintained their control of affairs, either by intimidation, implied or real, or through their prestige and the respect and loyalty they no doubt received from many in the community. Such prestige and loyalty which the elite commanded partially explains the limited success of the Knights locally. While the Knights of Labor engaged in strikes and boycotts across the country as workers sought higher wages and improved working conditions, in Winston-Salem, however, there is no evidence of workers taking such initiatives against their employers during the 1880s, beyond the brief protests by tobacco workers which occurred on two occasions.[35] Workers in Winston-Salem complained privately to the Bureau of Labor Statistics about low wages, long workdays, and undesirable working conditions, but they engaged in few overt protests except for their mixed support of unsuccessful labor tickets in local elections. By controlling jobs, housing, and financial institutions, employers in Winston-Salem exercised sufficient power over their workers to frustrate organized actions by them. Employers apparently allowed workers the measure of freedom to organize Knights of Labor assemblies to dramatize grievances but did not allow actions that would interrupt production. Protest in Winston-Salem during the 1880s remained peaceful and usually confined merely to rhetoric and the organization of the Knights of Labor.

The Knights of Labor had enduring consequences for both blacks and whites in Winston-Salem. For blacks, the Knights was an important vehicle for achieving the dignity they sought and promoting solidarity in the black community. The black workers' local assembly became a center of activity in the black community. Blacks used the Knights' hall to hold a festival to raise money for an organ, bell, and other furniture for their grade school. On July 4, 1887, about two hundred members of the black assembly marched in the annual parade accompanied by their own brass band. When Jerry Stockton, a laborer and influential citizen in the black community, died, the whole assembly turned out for his funeral. For both races the mixed trades local assemblies were crucial in bringing together men from different trades and occupations who shared the common distinction of being wage workers. The most lasting consequence of the Knights of Labor in Winston-Salem, and the agitation of labor in the

1880s, lay in the challenge to the employers' image of themselves as benevolent bosses and the workers as grateful and docile employees.[36]

The limited success of labor politics in Winston-Salem must also be attributed to the failure of the Knights of Labor to bridge racial divisions among workers as well as to its involvement in partisan politics. Ultimately, race was a conundrum for southern labor which made possible only a fragile unity among the workers in Winston-Salem. The Knights of Labor were adopted by the black workers in Winston-Salem as the vehicle to express their hopes and grievances. But, as in other cities, local assemblies in Winston-Salem remained segregated, thus undermining working-class unity. Divided racially, whatever unity the southern working class achieved was likely to be temporary and tenuous. In Winston-Salem as in Richmond, Virginia, and other southern cities, efforts by labor's opponents attempted to divide the workers by racial appeals. In the South, it proved impossible for the Knights of Labor to keep white workers out of the Democratic party and black workers out of the Republican party. While many workers of both races could unite behind labor candidates for local elections in the mid-1880s, they could not sustain that effort under the oppressive weight of southern social traditions. By 1888 the brief interracial unity of workers, underscored by labor's limited success in local political contests, was beginning to waver. By the late 1880s the Knights of Labor had come to be regarded as a black organization. As one southern black observed, "Nigger and Knight have become synonymous terms."[37] The Democratic press in North Carolina, aware of the delicate interracial unity of the Knights, launched a vigorous campaign which depicted the Knights of Labor as supporting social equality. These newspapers warned white workers that the organization would "turn the State government over to the niggers and their worse leaders." As the *Messenger* sarcastically charged, the Knights of Labor were dangerous because "it takes the negro by the hand and calls him brother, recognizing that the interests of the white and black man are identical, and that they must rise and fall together." But reason could not overcome the pervasive fear white southerners had of blacks. To working-class whites, whose status was uncertain in the face of shifting social and economic conditions, black workers could easily appear as a threat. Relations between whites and blacks were further complicated as unskilled whites and blacks found themselves in similar circumstances and competing for the same jobs, especially as white workers blamed the presence of blacks in the local labor market for keeping wages down. One white laborer complained to the Bureau of Labor Statistics, "Negroes should be excluded from all trades, especially bricklaying as they tend to . . . lower a white man's wages until he cannot live by his trade."[38] Whites feared equality with blacks and believed that white workers would be the true losers if such equality came to pass. Political elites in Forsyth County and North Carolina successfully used these fears to divide workers.

Nevertheless, workers in Winston-Salem, blacks and whites, played a critical role in local politics as a fulcrum between the two parties. Within the local party system workers promoted their interests, as Republicans and Democrats tailored their appeals to win the votes of workers who were critical to success. The Republican party rose to power during Reconstruction and controlled politics in Winston-Salem and Forsyth County through the 1870s. Workers and farmers of both races responded to the Republican message on labor, economics, politics, and race which promised a revitalized southern economy and society, and better conditions for poor whites and blacks. Adopting the free labor ideology and rhetoric of their northern counterparts, southern Republicans offered an ideology that lent deserved prestige and status to those who labored and created wealth through their industry. Southern Republicans promised opportunity to those who had been shunted aside or, for black southerners, oppressed in the antebellum economy. In Winston the *Union Republican*, closely aligned with the local Republican party apparatus, consistently defended the dignity and honor of labor and promoted the interests of workingmen. Republicans advocated public education, internal improvements, and prosperous markets as solutions to the South's backwardness and as means of uplift for the mass of southerners, black and white. Recognizing the increasing working-class character of Winston's population, the Republican party through the 1870s and mid-1880s represented itself in Winston-Salem as the party of the workingmen. The party's nominee for sheriff in the 1870s and 1880s, Augustus Fogle, a cabinetmaker, was presented as the workingmen's candidate on the Republican ticket. The *Union Republican* offered Fogle to the electorate as a "representative man of the laboring interests" and warned that to abandon Fogle at the ballot box would be interpreted "as a declaration from you that mechanics and laboring men ought not to aspire to positions of honor and trust." The newspaper challenged the county's workingmen to assert their independence and manhood by voting for Fogle. Consequently, he was elected sheriff four times between 1878 and 1884.[39]

TABLE 8.1

Percentage of Vote by Party in Winston-Salem, 1878–88

	1876	1878	1880	1882	1884	1886	1888
Governor:							
Republican	43.0		47.4		45.2		49.1
Democrat	57.0		52.6		54.8		50.9
State Senate:							
Republican	41.3	52.2	47.4	39.5	40.9	40.8	48.5
Democrat	58.7	43.9	52.6	60.5	59.1	59.2	50.4
Other		3.9					1.1
State House:							
Republican	43.7	52.0	47.6	48.6	43.3	39.2	47.9
Democrat	56.3	45.9	52.4	51.4	56.7	60.8	50.6
Other		2.1					1.5
Sheriff:							
Republican		56.8	51.3	54.5	46.7	41.8	45.4
Democrat		43.2	48.7	45.5	53.3	58.2	53.1
Other							1.4

Sources: *People's Press*, August 8, 1878, November 11, 1880, November 9, 1882, November 13, 1884, November 4, 1886; *Union Republican*, November 8, 1888; Forsyth County, Record of Elections, 1878–1906, NCDAH.

The high taxes North Carolinians paid to fund Republican schemes for development and the prevalence of black Republicans in state and local government gave the Democrats the issues they needed to challenge the Republicans and regain control of North Carolina government in the mid-1870s. Campaigning against "the evils of negro rule" and "Radical extravagance," Democrats appealed to voters who were hard pressed by the high taxes enacted by Republican legislatures to reject Republican "fraud . . . corruption . . . [and] iniquity." Furthermore, Democrats tapped into the emerging popular sentiment for change and improvement by embracing the "New South" program of industrialization, improved and diversified agriculture, education, and sectional reconciliation. As early as 1870 conservatives and Democrats in Forsyth County sounded these themes that eventually worked for North Carolina Democrats. The Forsyth County Conservative Convention condemned the "unparalleled extravagance and corruption, and the profligate waste of the public property and funds that has characterized our state government" under the Republicans. Conservatives and Democrats in Forsyth County attacked the Republicans as the "Civil Rights party" in the 1870s for their sponsorship in Congress of a civil rights bill that would guarantee blacks "full

TABLE 8.2

Percentage of Vote by Party in Winston, 1882–88

	1882	1884	1886	1888
State Senate:				
Republican	43.8	42.7	42.3	49.1
Democrat	56.2	57.3	57.7	49.8
Populist				1.1
State House:				
Republican	47.5	44.9	43.2	48.8
Democrat	52.5	55.1	56.8	49.6
Populist				1.6
Sheriff:				
Republican	49.8	47.1	42.7	46.1
Democrat	50.2	52.9	57.3	52.7
Populist				1.2

Sources: *People's Press*, August 8, 1878, November 11, 1880, November 9, 1882, November 13, 1884, November 4, 1886; *Union Republican*, November 8, 1888; Forsyth County, Record of Elections, 1878–1906, NCDAH.

and equal enjoyment" of public accommodations which included inns, theaters, and public transportation. The Democrats opposed "mixed" or integrated schools which, it was claimed, Republicans supported. The Conservatives or Democrats offered themselves as the most reliable defenders of white supremacy. The Democrats stepped forward as the protectors of white North Carolinians against black southerners' claims of full rights and equality. By appealing to race consciousness, economy in state and local government, and continued progress, the Democratic party recaptured state government in 1876. As most white North Carolinians believed, the Democrats "redeemed" North Carolina from "Negro rule" and the corruption of Republican-led reconstruction government.[40] In Winston-Salem the Democrats won impressive victories in 1876 as Table 8.1 illustrates. Significantly, though, Forsyth County remained a Republican stronghold, as vote percentages in Table 8.3 reveal. White voters in Winston-Salem in a dramatic show of unity contributed to the statewide victory of the Democrats as the rapidly increasing black population in Winston continued to vote Republican.

Even after the Democrats regained power in Winston-Salem and North Carolina, their hold was tenuous as most blacks resisted intimidation and continued to go to the polls where they voted overwhelmingly Republican. Black loyalty kept the Republican party an important force in local and state politics as the threat of the defection of whites to the Republican party could swing election results. In the gubernatorial elections of 1880, 1884, and 1888, the Democrats' largest margin of victory in Winston-Salem was 54.8 percent in 1884. In 1880 the Democratic candidate for governor won 52.6 percent of the Winston-Salem vote and in 1888 50.9 percent. What these numbers show is the impact of race on voting behavior in Winston-Salem. In Winston where blacks made up almost one-half of the population by the end of the 1880s the electorate was split almost evenly between the two parties.[41]

In the mid-1880s issues important to small producers and workers assumed greater weight in local politics. The state Republican platform in 1886 opposed the Democratic government's policy of convict leasing whenever the use of convicts competed with free labor. According to their platform, convict leasing degraded free labor, reduced wages, and threw honest workmen out of work. The local Republican organization also called for extended tariff protection for domestic manufacturers which would encourage local industry and thereby stimulate the circulation of capital and increase opportunities for employment. The Republican message, which catered to the workers' sense of themselves as honest, hard-working producers, swayed the electorate in Forsyth County enabling the Republicans in the elections of 1886 and 1888 to turn small gains made in 1884 into decisive victories, as Table 8.3 shows. In Winston-Salem, as Tables 8.1 and 8.2 illustrate, the Republicans lost by large margins in 1884 and 1886 but narrowed the gap considerably in 1888. The Winston-Salem *Weekly Sentinel*, an advocate for the Democrats, attributed Republican success to the economic distress of the mid-1880s which paralleled a Democratic administration that had promised better times that failed to come and left "people pressed to the wall by dire need."[42] The *Weekly Sentinel*'s assessment was confirmed by a Winston mechanic who reported to the Bureau of Labor Statistics in 1888 that in Winston-Salem the past year "work at all trades had been very dull" which led "a good many carpenters, and some of other trades" to leave for other areas of North Carolina or the country to find employment. In the 1888 elections many workers in Winston-Salem must have taken this mechanic's advice that "if working men will unite, elect their Legislative men and Congressmen, and put a stop to such monopoly laws, and give all men an equal showing, times will be better." This mechanic believed that "until the laboring men agitate, organize, and educate, they need not expect relief." The *Weekly Sentinel* acknowledged that "the cause of labor effected [*sic*] the chances of many aspirants, and politicians, quite gener-

TABLE 8.3

*Percentage of Vote by Party in Forsyth County
(minus vote of Winston-Salem), 1878–88*

	1876	1878	1880	1882	1884	1886	1888
Governor:							
Republican	53.9		51.7		49.5		55.8
Democratic	46.1	48.3		50.5		44.2	
State Senate:							
Republican	51.3	51.6	51.1	40.8	49.1	57.5	55.4
Democrat	48.7	39.5	48.9	56.2	50.9	42.5	44.3
Other		8.9		3.0			.3
State House:							
Republican	52.0	50.4	51.1	46.5	50.1	55.4	55.2
Democrat	48.0	42.5	48.9	53.5	49.9	44.6	44.6
Other		7.1					.2
Sheriff:							
Republican		47.9	51.3	55.2	50.7	52.8	52.5
Democrat		52.1	48.7	44.8	49.3	47.2	47.2
Other							.3

Sources: *People's Press*, August 8, 1878, November 11, 1880, November 9, 1882, November 13, 1884, November 4, 1886; *Union Republican*, November 8, 1888; Forsyth County, Record of Elections, 1878–1906, NCDAH.

ally, have had their eyes opened pretty wide as to the extent of the labor vote."[43] However, despite class and economic issues, race ran as a persistent undercurrent in local politics in the 1870s and early 1880s and emerged as a central issue in the mid-1880s, giving the Democrats the leverage they needed to hold on against the Republican tide in the county.

Local politics in Winston-Salem became much uglier and more menacing in its racist appeals as issues of class and race divided voters. With North Carolinians gripped by a sense of economic and political crisis, newspapers fanned the fires of racism. As the agricultural crisis deepened across the state, with more indebted farmers losing their land to become tenants, sharecroppers, and mill hands, and as urban workers stirred, Democrats invoked fears of "black domination" and asserted white supremacy as the party's cause.[44] The racist tone of local politics developed as the white population of Winston-Salem looked with uncertainty and fear on the rapidly growing presence of a large black population of tobacco factory workers. As potential class divisions in the work place and in the community emerged and found expression in workers' attitudes about the declining dignity of and respect for labor, race became the instrument of solidarity that held the white community together. White solidarity was strengthened as blacks assumed the preponderant role in factory work and established themselves in largely segregated neighborhoods with distinct cultural organizations and leadership. The quest for racial unity among whites in Winston-Salem was consistent with the importance southern whites traditionally have attached to white supremacy. Racial solidarity among whites that spanned class lines and diffused class tensions is a persistent theme in the history of southern social relations that dates back to the beginning of southern society and culture in the seventeenth century. After emancipation whites were increasingly wary of black southerners' claims for independence and respect, and they remained sensitive to any evidence of assertiveness among blacks that suggested social equality between the races. In the 1880s racial solidarity among whites and a tenuous racial control over blacks that reinforced their subordinate status in the community was promoted by racist appeals in local politics that stirred fears among whites of blacks pushing beyond their prescribed roles. Whites in Winston-Salem became increasingly sensitive to blacks' presence in the community and evidence of behavior that confirmed their perceptions of blacks. One member of the white community wrote to the Salem *Western Sentinel* in 1888 that the black men in Winston are "insolent and lazy." According to this observer:

> They will not work, but stand around the street corners, many of them in idleness all day, and depend for a living upon what they can steal. . . . With some exceptions, the negro population of this town are the scourings of the filth of crime and degradation of many cities. . . . They are a shifting, moving, justice-dodging lot that never stay long in one place.

A printer reported to the Bureau of Labor Statistics that the condition of the "colored employees" of Winston "is at a low ebb morally, educationally, and financially."[45] The case of William Houston, a black man who worked for the R. J. Reynolds Tobacco Company, was offered as confirmation of white perceptions of blacks and as a lesson for the black members of the community. Houston was convicted of shooting a woman at a "place of ill-fame" and sentenced to be hanged. The *Union Republican* reported that in an interview Houston desired to "warn his race against drinking, houses of ill-fame, gambling dens, for the result was fatal." As a cure to these problems the white leadership of Winston-Salem advised blacks in the community to work hard and acquire the means of independence, property. The *Western Sentinel* expressed the self-help and independence ideology of the local business class and advocated that Winston's black population seek "honest work and skilled labor" befitting their proper role as a "laboring race." As the "hewers of wood and drawers of water" as "God so constituted them," blacks were advised to be "thrifty and economical" so that they might eventually buy a horse, a dray, a house, and a lot.[46]

The election of 1888 was particularly characterized by racist appeals, as the Republicans and a labor ticket through overt appeals for biracial unity challenged the Democrats. In August 1888 the *Union Republican* reminded Republican voters of how Democratic leaders had little regard for the truth when it came to race and politics. The *Union Republican* reported that Cyrus B. Watson, a prominent local Democrat, "after wading through the usual regulation tirade against the Republican party and a concise survey of the tariff without making even the semblance of an impression on the audience, he tried the 'nigger.' " A Republican from nearby Surry County writing as "Atticus" to the *Union Republican* observed that the Democrats, cornered and confused on every issue, harp on the "white man's party" and "negro rule" issues. Atticus wrote,

Look at S. E. (Social Equality) Cleveland. . . . He came from the North to Washington to teach negro equality. To a White House social gathering . . . he invited and entertained amid other dignitaries a negro and I think his white wife also, He, the first Democrat to sit in the White House in nearly a generation has appointed more negroes than any other President. . . . Why, It becomes a matter of laughter that the Democratic skillet calls the Republican pot black.[47]

The Democratic newspapers kept up a constant barrage of racist appeals to voters to solidify white support of Democratic tickets. The *Western Sentinel* painted a picture of the county Republican convention which met in September 1888 in which "a big negro who, along with five others of his race, sat cheek by jowl with white men of the convention, with their heads over the same tables, and who seemed to be about the biggest men in the pow-wow." The newspaper asked, "You Republicans, who are still white, do you like the picture?" The *Western Sentinel* also reported that on his campaign swing through Winston-Salem Oliver Dockery, the Republican candidate for governor, invited several black men to his hotel room where he entertained them with whiskey, making them drunk. A reporter to the newspaper observed, "One of them became so drunk that he was unfit to work for over a week." Such appeals to racial fears had their intended effect on voters. In the 1888 municipal elections in Winston where the black vote could overcome a divided white vote, the straight Democratic ticket to which most white voters rallied defeated the opposition ticket composed of Republicans, dissident Democrats, and labor candidates.[48]

Despite these tensions black citizens in Winston enjoyed some success in municipal politics. In 1881 Israel Clement, a tobacco roller in Hamilton Scales's factory, was the first black man elected to the Winston town commission. In 1890 a "Colored Men's Ticket" of John B. Gwyn, a grocer, John F. Hughes, a post office custodian, and Rufus Clement, a janitor, defeated its white opposition to win three seats on the commission. By 1894 Winston blacks had elected eight black town commissioners, put Rufus Clement on the local Republican party executive committee, and served as election judges.[49] Through their participation in the Republican party blacks played an important role in Winston politics and government but stirred the enmity of white Democrats.

Politics in Winston-Salem as well as across the South in the 1870s and 1880s was a question of who would hold the power to determine public policy and, consequently, the form society would take. Black southerners, and some whites, supported the Republicans as the party of economic, political, and social change in the South. These southerners voted Republican because of the party's proven commitment to civil rights for the freed people, public education, and a state government responsive to the needs of the masses of southerners so long ignored by ruling elites. White southerners united across class lines to support the Democratic party for complex reasons. The Democratic party during these years was not captive to a single interest but a "disaggregated coalition" of merchants, manufacturers, bankers, planters, yeoman farmers, artisans, mill hands, landlords, and tenants. For upper-class whites, the Democratic party was committed to the continued domination by established elites of politics and government policy and was the ally of railroads, banks, and corporations against the interests of farmers and workers. For common whites, the party offered limited government, reduced government expenditures, and hence lower taxes. Many small farmers, artisans, and laborers, under the shock of rapid social and economic change in the 1880s, may have clung to the Democratic party out of anxiety or even fear for their tenuous status in the postwar South. Democrats successfully used a rhetoric that promoted the party as the protector of the interests and status of common whites against the struggles of black southerners to improve their condition and preserve their political rights. By the appeal of white supremacy and the Democrats' "redemption" of North Carolina from Republican rule and "negro domination," the Democratic party maintained the loyalty of white voters in the 1880s.[50] Racial tensions in Winston-Salem and the overt racial appeals of the Democrats and Republicans proved to be a critical factor in the limited success of workers' efforts to challenge the degradation of industrial labor and secure political leadership which would promote the interests of the working classes of the community.

In the 1880s and 1890s there were no big showdowns between industrial workers and their employers. In fact, the Knights of Labor a the brief appearance of labor tickets in municipal elections might be reg..ded as nonevents given all they failed to accomplish. Workdays remained long, wages low, the power of the bosses undaunted, and mechanization of production continued pushing more workers out of the shops and factories. In the 1890s Winston-Salem saw more intense efforts by aroused workers to confront their employers and win recognition of their desire for more equitable relations between employers and workers. In 1890 both the United Brotherhood of Carpenters and Joiners and the Twin City Typographical Relief Association were organized. While the Twin City Typographical Relief Association appears to have been a benevolent relief society for printers that included employers as well as typographers who worked for a wage, the United Brotherhood of Carpenters and Joiners was a craft union organized to protect the interests of the remaining skilled artisans in the craft. Its purpose was to protect the carpenter trade from the evils of low prices and botched work, to encourage a higher standard of skill and better wages, to reestablish an apprentice system, and to aid and assist members as a mutual protection and benevolent organization. Toward the end of the decade the American Federation of Labor organized the Woodworkers Union of Winston-Salem, and a local of the International Tobacco Workers Union was established. By 1901 there were three craft unions in Winston-Salem with a total membership of around seven hundred.[51] In the tobacco factories workers engaged in several brief strikes from the 1890s through the World War I years and won concessions from factory management. In 1898 workers in the Brown and Williamson factory walked out over a reduction of wages and returned after management restored their wages. In 1899 white and black workers in the Brown Brothers and P. H. Hanes and Company factories walked off the job. R. J. Reynolds Tobacco Company workers staged walkouts in 1900, 1902, and 1914. In 1919 the International Tobacco Workers Union of the American Federation of Labor negotiated a contract with R. J. Reynolds Tobacco Company that raised wages 20 percent, provided time and a half pay for overtime work, and set the workweek at forty-eight hours.[52] The organization of locals of AFL unions in Winston-Salem had a profound impact that signified that many local workers by the end of the nineteenth century were more sophisticated in their understanding of the condition of industrial workers than they had been twenty years before. Recognizing that their status as industrial laborers was permanent, these workers sought through unionization to improve their conditions of work, their remuneration, and their future prospects as industrial laborers.

The significance of workers' efforts is to be found in the implications they hold for the new meaning of community in Winston-Salem. The Knights of Labor, labor politics, and the cultural institutions of the workers' community reinforced this emerging awareness that workers were separate and distinct from the merchants, manufacturers, and professionals of the town who were prospering and tightening their hold on the tiller of community affairs. The urban industrial community that Winston-Salem had become was an arena of subcommunities and subcultures representing distinct identities and disparate and often competing interests. These distinct identities were embraced by merchants, manufacturers, professionals, managers, and clerks who owned or managed the business enterprises, the skilled tradesmen seeking to preserve the dignity of their crafts, and the textile mill operatives and the tobacco factory workers who were dependent on the wages they earned through manual labor. Those who lived and worked in Winston-Salem were employers and employees, Democrats and Republicans, and blacks and whites. Thus the distinctions among members of the urban industrial community were much more complex than those of the congregational community — Moravians and non-Moravians, or members of the Salem congregation and "auswartig" or Moravians from other congregations. In the congregation community that Salem had once been, the roles of the individual as a member of a family, as a citizen, as a member of a church, or as a participant in the economy had been "mutually reenforcing" to constitute collectively a community. But in the 1880s in Winston-Salem these roles which defined peoples' lives were "differentiated and often conflicting."[53] But it was more than this complexity that distinguished the urban industrial community. In the congregation village, community had meant an association of believers who subordinated themselves to the mission of the church to serve their God. The new meaning of community for those who lived and worked in Winston-Salem is to be found in the vision of the urban industrial community as a place of opportunity for individuals seeking success, wealth, security, and independence. The promise of opportunity drew tobacco manufacturers, merchants, artisans, mill hands, tobacco factory workers, and laborers to Winston-Salem, greatly swelling the population between the 1870s and 1890s. Though the fulfillment of personal hopes and the attainment of individual objectives varied among the many individuals, by the 1890s Winston-Salem had become the realization of the vision promoted by antebellum entrepreneurs like Francis Fries and Edward Belo of individual freedom and enterprise.

Conclusion

Across the country in the nineteenth century, industrialization and urbanization introduced new methods of production and marketing and new ways of work. These changes brought to each community greater social diversity and increasing complexity that were expressed in differentiated residential patterns and deeper class and racial divisions. However, industrialization and urbanization were not homogenous phenomena. Though there were similarities of experience between Newark, New Jersey, Lynn and Dudley, Massachusetts, Poughkeepsie, New York, and Winston-Salem, each community experienced these changes in its own way and within the contexts of local conditions. The changes that transformed the villages of Winston and Salem to create the urban industrial city of Winston-Salem define industrialization and urbanization the way they occurred in one community during the nineteenth century.

Winston-Salem evolved out of the congregational community of Salem, as an emerging market economy transformed life in the North Carolina piedmont between the antebellum years and the late nineteenth century. The controversies within the Moravian community over slaveholding, congregational regulation of the trades and constraints on business activity, and the tensions and debates regarding the retention or dissolution of the congregational order in the 1850s reveal the specific impact of the market revolution on one community. Responses to competitive market pressures between producers induced the changes in antebellum Salem which were crucial to the later development of the industrial community. By sweeping away the congregational order in the 1850s, the Moravians of Salem cleared the way for the unleashing of entrepreneurial energies to participate in the market economy and bring about the postwar economic expansion of the community. The experience of the Moravian community illustrates in bold detail the profound impact of economic change on community culture. As the preceding pages have revealed, the urban industrial community, with its diversity and complexity expressed in the subcultures that workers, blacks, and the emerging middle class of businessmen created in their respective neighborhoods and associations, was radically different from the congregation community. The essence of the congregation community was its homogeneity and its single vision and way of life. Social relations in the congregational community were characterized by emotional bonds among the faithful and a mutuality that grew out of the religious mission of the Moravians. Hence in congregational Salem, community was synonymous with the experience of being Moravian.[1]

As Salem was incorporated into a market economy that extended beyond the surrounding rural neighborhood, extra-local relationships and loyalties captured the attention of members of the community as they looked beyond the local town to outside institutions and relationships to satisfy many of their basic needs. By mid-century there was a more varied community culture in Salem, as members of the community looked to national organizations like political parties, benevolent associations, and evangelical religion to meet their needs. Between the 1830s and 1850s the balance within the community shifted as external relationships with non-Moravians increased and as secular goals assumed greater importance in determining behavior. While this was an important stage in the eventual development of the industrial city, Salem had not entirely left behind its earlier community forms. The majority of Salem's residents still looked to their Moravian traditions as an anchor of community as the world around them changed so fast. Thus, even as new forms of social cohesion emerged in Salem, old patterns remained, overlaid with the new but not replaced entirely. The difference was that the "wholeness" or unity that had made Salem distinctive was gone. The Moravians of Salem, like Americans across the country, found themselves struggling with the postbellum economic changes that were transforming the nation and reshaping community life.[2]

Despite the peculiarity of the congregational origins of Winston-Salem, the development of the Twin City was part of a pattern of industrialization and urbanization that typified the South. The advent of a market economy was the critical factor in the urbanization of the South. The post-Civil War expansion of the railroad system in the South connected the interior villages and towns with the regional and national markets and created a network of southern cities that served the regional economy. After 1880 new towns emerged and the region's urban population grew rapidly, especially in towns with populations under ten thousand like Winston-Salem. The mercantile and financial enterprises that served the expanding regional economy concentrated in these new cities. Industrial enterprises that were tied closely to the region's agricultural economy—textile mills, tobacco factories, and wagon works are notable examples—drew to these cities southerners seeking better opportunities than could be found on the land. Accelerating internal migration to the region's towns, especially that of black southerners who abandoned rural areas, fueled this growth of urban populations. Railroads, greater involvement with regional and national markets, population mobility, and the emergence of new cities brought about an "urban revolution" in the South.[3]

By the end of the 1880s Winston and Salem as the "Twin City" constituted an urban industrial community participating in the national economy. In the urban community life was broken into segments as work, family, and town, which in the antebellum community had reinforced personal identities, became mutually exclusive, often conflicting sources of identity.[4] As the Knights of Labor activities of the mid-1880s illustrate, the craftsmen who owned and worked in small shops struggled to preserve the integrity of their trades in the face of changes wrought by industrialization and often opposed the community's large manufacturers and merchants who were regarded by the beleaguered artisans as agents of the changes which threatened their way of life. Furthermore, the emergence of a larger, more heterogeneous working class led to a growing complexity in the community's social structure that generated divisive class and racial tensions. The community then was divided into "subcommunities" of employers and workers, blacks and whites, men and women, in which those with common identities and circumstances pursued interests that often clashed with the interests of other groups. In social and economic relations, the traditional ways and values of the workers clashed with the new entrepreneurial ethos and visions of the factory owners and merchants. Despite the class and racial divisions in the urban industrial community, it was a community nonetheless with a rich culture that expressed the aspirations, ways of living and thinking, and views of the world of a diverse population. But by the end of the 1880s community had a new meaning. The community had become for the people of Winston-Salem the milieu in which competing individuals pursued private opportunities and interests.

Rules and Regulations

To be followed by those living at the Salem Cotton Factory

Article I

1. No family or individual need apply for employment, without at the same time furnishing certificate from some of their most respectable and trustworthy neighbours, that they are of industrious habits and unexceptional character.

2. Families that are employed are considered as engaged for as long a time as they and the employer can agree, but are in no case to leave before they have given the employer one month's notice of their intention to do so.

3. Single individuals are considered as engaged for as long a time as they and the employer can agree, but are in no case to leave before they have given the employer two weeks' notice of their intention to do so.

4. Any one, that wilfully or negligently injures any part of any building or of any machine, will be held accountable for such injury, and the damages deducted from his or her wages.

5. The working hours in the mill will be from sun-rise until sun-set, from the 20th of March until the 20th of September; and the remaining six months of the year from sun-rise until half past seven, except on Saturday, when the machinery will stop at four o'clock.

Article II

1. Persons occupying the family apartments are considered as holding them from week to week, and shall furnish at least five competent hands to work in the factory.
2. They are to take in as many boarders as they are requested to do by the main superintendent, and to furnish them with plain, wholesome and cleanly food.
3. They are to keep their houses clean and orderly, and are to permit nothing to be done in the same contrary to the established rules of the place.
4. They are to take every precaution to guard against fire. They shall not keep their ashes in wooden vessels, nor pour them out on the lot when warm. They shall not carry fire from one house to another in an open vessel, especially when there is any wind. They shall be careful not to let too much soot collect in the chimneys, but burn them out from time to time, during rainy weather.
5. They shall not permit any of their boarders to leave the house at any unreasonable time, or do any thing that is not strictly according to the established rules.
6. If the boarders in any manner misbehave, they shall never fail to remind them of their duty.
7. If their admonitions to such boarders are not regarded, they shall inform the employer of the misconduct of such individuals; and if they fail to do this, they will be considered as encouraging such conduct.
8. They will be held accountable for any thing done in their families.

Article III

1. Individuals engaged to attend the different machinery, will repair to their post punctually when the bell calls them to work, and are not to leave the same until the principal machinist stops the mill.
2. During the working hours they are to act strictly according to the rules of the mills, and the directions given by the superintendents of the rooms in which they are employed.

3. If they cannot attend from sickness or other cause, they are to acquaint the manager of the fact, and of the cause of the absence.

4. Unless called away by business, they are to remain at their boarding houses, and after nightfall especially, every one is expected to be at home.

5. They are not to leave on a visit to any distance without informing the employer of their intention.

6. Every one is expected carefully to avoid all that may tend to disturb the peace and harmony of persons employed in this establishment.

7. Every one is expected most strictly to observe the rules of order and morality, as otherwise his or her presence is no longer desirable.

Source: Salem Manufacturing Company, "Rules and Regulations," Fries Mills Collection, Moravian Archives, Winston-Salem, North Carolina.

Occupational Classifications for Population Sample from 1850 Census

I. Unskilled or Service
  laborer
II. Semiskilled
  apprentice
  welldigger
  sawyer
III. Skilled

carpenter	blacksmith
wagonmaker	gunsmith
coppersmith	tinsmith
baker	shoemaker
silversmith	cabinetmaker
tanner	clockmaker
chairmaker	machinist
portrait painter	tailor
wheelwright	saddler
miller	brickmason
hatmaker	surveyor
cooper	millwright

IV. Petty Proprietor
  farmer
V. Clerical, Sales
  clerk

lime factor
peddler
VI. Proprietor, Manager
merchant
overseer
VII. Professional
clergyman
teacher
physician
VIII. Government Official
clerk of court

Occupational Classifications for Population Sample from 1880 Census

I. Unskilled or Service
   laborer
   farmworker
   servant
   cook
   laundress
   ferryman
   nurse
   hotel porter
   liveryman
   buggy shop worker
   teamster

II. Semiskilled
   tobacco factory worker and factory worker
   mill worker and textile mill worker
   tobacco roller
   tobacco stemmer
   tobacco picker
   wood worker
   barber
   gardener
   well digger

III. Skilled

carpenter	blacksmith
wagonmaker	gunsmith
coppersmith	tinsmith
shoemaker	cabinetmaker
tanner	machinist
tailor	wheelwright
miller	pumpmaker
brickmason	millwright
basketmaker	bootmaker
dressmaker	brickmaker
butcher	painter
harrowmaker	stiller
potter	mattress maker
railroad engineer	florist
milliner	stonecutter
harnessmaker	seamstress
mantuamaker	jeweler
plasterer	printer

IV. Petty Proprietor
 farmer
 grocer
 landlord
 boardinghouse proprietor

V. Clerical, Sales

clerk	bookkeeper
tobacco trader	tobacco dealer
livestock dealer	huckster
furniture dealer	auctioneer
telegraph messenger	salesman
tobacco grader	

VI. Proprietor, Manager
 merchant
 manufacturer
 banker

VII. Professional
 clergyman
 physician
 professor

    editor
    teacher
    lawyer
    journalist
    dentist

VIII. Government Official
    clerk of court
    mail carrier
    government official

Notes

Introduction

1. *Statistical View of the United States. Compendium of the Seventh Census. 1850;* 1850 Census, Manufacturing Schedule manuscript microfilm, Forsyth County, North Carolina; *Statistics of the Population of the United States at the Tenth Census. 1880.* 1880 Census, Manufacturing Schedule manuscript microfilm, Forsyth County, North Carolina; *Report on the Population of the United States at the Eleventh Census. Part 1. 1890; Report on the Statistics of Agriculture in the United States. Eleventh Census. 1890.*

2. The most notable of these monographs which have influenced this study of Winston-Salem are Dawley, *Class and Community: The Industrial Revolution in Lynn;* Johnson, *A Shopkeeper's Millennium: Society and Revivals in Rochester, New York, 1815–1837;* Prude, *The Coming of Industrial Order: Town and Factory Life in Rural Massachusetts, 1810–1860;* and Wallace, *Rockdale: The Growth of an American Village in the Early Industrial Revolution.*

3. These studies include: Hahn, *The Roots of Southern Populism: Yeoman Farmers and the Transformation of the Georgia Upcountry, 1850–1890;* Hahn and Prude, eds., *The Countryside in the Age of Capitalist Transformation: Essays in the Social History of Rural America;* Carlton, *Mill and Town in South Carolina, 1880–1920;* Ford, Jr., *Origins of Southern Radicalism: The South Carolina Upcountry, 1800–1860;* and Siegel, *The Roots of Southern Distinctiveness: Tobacco and Society in Danville, Virginia, 1780–1865.* These studies show that the South was never one society and culture—i.e., a "slave society" with a precapitalist economy and mind-set. Through the nineteenth century the South was diverse in its economies, class structures, race relations, religion, politics, and worldviews. Freehling, *The Road to Disunion: The Secessionists at Bay, 1776–1854,* vii–viii.

4. Freehling, *The Road to Disunion,* vii.

5. Sellers, *The Market Revolution: Jacksonian America, 1815–1846,* 4–5;

Appleby, *Capitalism and a New Social Order: The Republican Vision of the 1790s*, 22; Haskell, "Capitalism and the Humanitarian Sensibility," 550. Karl Polanyi saw in the establishment of a market economy a change in the motives of people in which "gain" replaced "subsistence." Polanyi, *The Great Transformation*, 40–43.

6. The meaning of capitalism has produced much disagreement. As studies of northern society have demonstrated, the transition to a capitalist society was a "complex and uneven" process that cannot be reduced to the single stage of the emergence of a wage labor system, as some historians have argued. Instead, capitalist transformation encompassed a variety of changes that included, in addition to an increasing proportion of wage laborers in the work force, increased agricultural productivity, greater social differentiation, increasing purchasing power, proliferation of retail stores, and the growth of consumer demand. But, more importantly, capitalism developed with the emergence of private property rights which were considered "absolute" in that there were limits beyond which one could not interfere in another's life or property. Clark, *The Roots of Rural Capitalism: Western Massachusetts, 1780–1860*, 14–17; Oakes, *Slavery and Freedom: An Interpretation of the Old South*, xii–xiii, 43–45, 71.

7. Woodward, *Origins of the New South, 1877–1913*, 140–41.

8. *Compendium of the Seventh Census. 1850; Report on the Population of the United States. Part 1. 1890.*

O N E   *The Congregational Community of the Moravians*

1. Gollin, *Moravians in Two Worlds: A Study of Changing Communities*, 1, 4–6; Sessler, *Communal Pietism among Early American Moravians*, 3–11, 14–19.

2. Gollin, *Moravians in Two Worlds*, 5–6; Sessler, *Communal Pietism*, 20.

3. Hamilton and Hamilton, *History of the Moravian Church: The Renewed Unitas Fratrum, 1722–1957*, 169; Surratt, "The Role of Dissent in Community Evolution among Moravians in Salem, 1722–1860," 241.

4. Fries, *Forsyth: A County on the March*, 4–5; Spangenberg Diary, January 8, 1753, in Fries et al., eds., *Records of the Moravians in North Carolina*, 11 vols., 1: 59; Thorp, *The Moravian Community in Colonial North Carolina: Pluralism on the Southern Frontier*, 30; Woodmason, *The Carolina Backcountry on the Eve of the Revolution: The Journal and Other Writings of Charles Woodmason, Anglican Itinerant*, ed. Hooker, 77.

5. Sessler, *Communal Pietism*, 186–87.

6. The advance group of settlers included a minister, warden (church official), physician, baker, tailor, shoemaker, tanner, gardener, three farmers, and two carpenters. Gollin, *Moravians in Two Worlds*, 148; Thorp, "Moravian Colonization of Wachovia, 1753–1772," Ph.D. diss., Johns Hopkins University, 1982, 405; Lefler and Newsome, *North Carolina: A History of a Southern State*, 80.

7. In his influential and provocative studies on the meaning of community in early America, Thomas Bender has observed that local communities in preindustrial America were often characterized by the shared experience that was common to all members of the particular community. Such a community was largely

local in its orientation, with tenuous ties to the world beyond its surrounding countryside. In communities such as those of the Puritans of seventeenth-century Massachusetts and the Moravians in Europe, Pennsylvania, and North Carolina, the individual's decision to join conferred membership and status, not mere presence in a particular geographic location. Bender, *Community and Social Change in America*, 60–66.

8. Lefler and Powell, *Colonial North Carolina: A History*, 96–101; Robinson, *The Southern Colonial Frontier, 1607–1763*, 176–77, 231; Merrens, *Colonial North Carolina in the Eighteenth Century: A Study in Historical Geography*, 27–29, 33, 48, 53–58, 63–66. Spangenberg Diary, September 25, October 28, 1752, in Fries et al., *Records*, 1: 41, 44.

9. Thorp, *The Moravian Community*, 33; Bridenbaugh, *Myths and Realities: Societies of the Colonial South*, 122–38; Lefler and Newsome, *North Carolina*, 77; Gray, *History of Agriculture in the Southern United States to 1860*, 2 vols., 1: 121–23.

10. "Early History of the Moravians," in Saunders, ed., *The Colonial Records of North Carolina*, 5: 1149–52.

11. Wachovia Diary, April 17, 1770, and Friedrich Marshall, "Remarks Concerning the Laying Out of the New Congregation Town in the Center of Wachovia," July 1765, in Fries et al., *Records*, 1: 314, 405–6; "Early History of the Moravians," 1158–61; Thorp, "Moravian Colonization," 43–44, 327–28; Fries, *Forsyth*, 31–32, 123; Johnson, *Ante-bellum North Carolina: A Social History*, 364; Lefler and Newsome, *North Carolina*, 80, 102.

12. John Henry Leinbach, Diary, 1830–43, passim, John Henry Leinbach Family Papers, Moravian Archives, Winston-Salem, North Carolina; Diary of Juliana Margaret Connor, July 21–24, 1827, typescript in Alexander Brevard Papers, North Carolina Department of Archives and History, Raleigh, North Carolina.

13. Hamilton and Hamilton, *History of the Moravian Church*, 169; Gollin, *Moravians in Two Worlds*, 9–18; Sessler, *Communal Pietism*, 32, 100–101, 106–8, 138–54; Marshall, "Remarks Concerning the Laying Out of the New Congregation Town," in Fries et al., *Records*, 1: 313.

14. Bender, *Community and Social Change*, 67–68; Surratt, "The Role of Dissent," 236, 241; Lockridge, *A New England Town, The First Hundred Years: Dedham, Massachusetts, 1636–1736*, 1–7, 13.

15. Results of the Synod of 1818, in Fries et al., *Records*, 7: 3560–62. The social structure of a community is, in Robert Redfield's words, a "system of norms and expectancies," even an ethical system that comprises the ethos of the community. Redfield, *The Little Community: Viewpoints for the Study of the Human Whole*, 45–46; Kroeber, *Anthropology: Race, Language, Culture, Psychology, Prehistory*, 294.

16. Hamilton and Hamilton, *History of the Moravian Church*, 169; Surratt, "The Role of Dissent," 237; Minutes of the Congregation Council, 1820–49, Salem Congregation, Moravian Archives, Winston-Salem, North Carolina (hereafter cited Congregation Council); Minutes of the Elders Conference, 1829–46, Salem Congregation, Moravian Archives, Winston-Salem, North Carolina (hereafter cited Elders Conference); Extracts of Minutes of the Aufseher Collegium,

1831–49, Salem Congregation, Moravian Archives, Winston-Salem, North Carolina (hereafter cited Aufseher Collegium); Minutes of the Aeltesten Conferenz, January 9, 1828, Congregation Council, 1828, in Fries et al., *Records*, 7: 3843–44; Thorp, *Moravian Community*, 81–98. The Moravian quest for consensus and the maintenance of harmony in the Salem congregation was similar to the experiences of Puritan communities in New England during the 1600s. Among the Puritan settlements there emerged a "consensual communalism" as the motivating premise of town life. This consensus was maintained by continued efforts to secure unanimity on issues that threatened to divide the townspeople. In his study of Puritan communities, Michael Zuckerman concluded that unanimity depended upon broad and significant participation in the decision-making process. Because authority in Massachusetts lacked any meaningful coercive instrument in Puritan communities, consensus became the goal of congregation leaders and unanimity the means of achieving that goal. But, for unanimity to be an effective instrument for preserving harmony, the consensus the community searched for had to be less absolute and more accommodative. In Massachusetts, consensus came to be based as much on compromise as conviction. Therefore, as Zuckerman observed, discord had to be resolved through negotiation. Zuckerman, *Peaceable Kingdoms: New England Towns in the Eighteenth Century*.

17. Thorp, *Moravian Community*, 60–63, 77–80; Sessler, *Communal Pietism*, 90–98; Extracts from Salem Board Minutes, January 25, August 23, November 8, 1809; September 11, 1810; January 8, February 5, 1811; November 2, 1818 (hereafter cited Salem Board Minutes), in Fries et al., *Records*, 7: 3091, 3095, 3097, 3122, 3142, 3144, 3379; "Early History of the Moravians," 1159–61.

18. "Memorabilia of the Congregations of the Brethren in Wachovia for the Year 1809," Salem Board Minutes, January 4, 1810, June 30, 1812, May 11, 1813, Salem Diary, June 6, 1823, August 16, 1824, Minutes of the Provincial Elders Conference, February 25, 1824, and Elders Conference, August 4, 1824, in Fries et al., *Records*, 7: 3063–64, 3067, 3117, 3176, 3205, and 8: 3629, 3684, 3695, 3703.

19. Surratt, "The Role of Dissent," 239; Aufseher Collegium, October 18, 1830, September 28, 1833, March 28, 1835, November 7, 1836, in Fries et al., *Records*, 8: 3940, 4087, 4181–82, 4229, 3948.

20. Bender, *Community and Social Change*, 61–62. Geertz, *The Interpretation of Cultures*, 82, 112.

21. Results of the Synod of 1818, Salem Diary, June 24, July 2–9, August 17, 29, September 7, 1809, May 4, 1816, "Diary of the Congregation in Salem, together with Reports from the other Wachovia Congregations in the Year 1818," September 19, 1818, Salem Board Minutes, August 25, 1818, and "Extracts from the Diary of Salem and other Wachovia Congregations in the Year 1820," April 30, May 7, 1820, in Fries et al., *Records*, 7: 3080–81, 3084–85, 3295, 3370, 3377, 3437–38, 3560–62; Sessler, *Communal Pietism*, 99–100.

22. Sessler, *Communal Pietism*, 101, 104–5; Gollin, *Moravians in Two Worlds*, 20–21; Salem Diary, April 1, May 13, December 31, 1809, April 5, 1811, April 2, 1816, December 24, 1821, Salem Board Minutes, August 25, 1818, in Fries et al., *Records*, 7: 3073, 3077, 3089, 3133, 3293, 3377, 3425.

23. Hamilton and Hamilton, *History of the Moravian Church*, 169.

24. Fries, *Forsyth*, 32; Surratt, "The Role of Dissent," 239.

25. Aufseher Collegium, June 16, September 1, November 10, 1828, Elders Conference, October 29, December 3, 1828, in Fries et al., *Records*, 8: 3943, 3847, 3850, 3851. A violation of the Moravian rules of morality was also grounds for revoking a lease. One member of the congregation was told by the Aufseher Collegium that if he did not give up his drinking, he could not remain a householder in Salem.

26. Aufseher Collegium, September 29, November 24, December 9, 1834, February 13, 20, 27, March 2, 1837, in Fries et al., *Records*, 8: 4136–37, 4269–71.

27. Thorp, "Moravian Colonization," 327–28, 405; Salem Board Minutes, April 8, 1812, in Fries et al., *Records*, 7: 3175; Surratt, "The Role of Dissent," 240.

28. Bender, *Community and Social Change*, 66; Lefler and Newsome, *North Carolina*, 300–301; Sydnor, *The Development of Southern Sectionalism, 1819–1848*, 27; Commons and Associates, *History of Labour in the United States*, 4 vols., 1: 34–35.

29. A 20 percent sample of property holders was drawn from the 1835 tax lists for Salem (N = 386, n = 78). Stokes County, List of Taxables, Salem District, 1835, North Carolina Division of Archives and History, Raleigh, North Carolina. Another sample comprised of thirty-one men in Salem who were positively identified as artisans was taken from the congregation records for the years 1828–32 and located in the tax lists of 1832. Aufseher Collegium, Aeltesten Conferenz, 1828–32, in Fries et al., *Records*, 8: passim; Stokes County, List of Taxables, Salem District, 1832, NCDAH.

30. Aufseher Collegium, July 25, 1831, October 14, 21, 1833, in Fries et al., *Records*, 8: 3987, 4088–89.

31. Aufseher Collegium, April 7, 1847, in Fries et al., *Records*, 9: 4963–64.

32. Aufseher Collegium, 1827, March 26, July 31, 1838, in Fries et al., *Records*, 8: 3810, and 9: 4397, 4407, 4538.

33. Salem *People's Press*, May 17, 1851.

34. Stokes County, Apprenticeship Bonds, March 10, 1840, North Carolina Division of Archives and History, Raleigh, North Carolina.

35. Aufseher Collegium, September 20, 1824, June 14, 1830, January 23, February 20, March 19, 1832, March 18, May 13, October 14, 1833, January 23, April 24, October 23, December 24, 1837, in Fries et al., *Records*, 8: 3706–7, 3813, 3937, 4025–26, 4028–29, 4074–77, 4087, 4267, 4272, 4277.

36. Aufseher Collegium, February 20, June 12, 1832, in Fries et al., *Records*, 8: 4028.

37. "Memorabilia of the Congregations of the Brethren in Wachovia for the Year 1809," Salem Board Minutes, 1809, Aufseher Collegium, November 14, 1809, July 10, 1826, June 12, 15, July 8, 1832, in Fries et al., *Records*, 7: 3066–67, 3097, and 8: 3775, 4035–38.

38. Leinbach, Diary, March 3, 4, 5, May 10, November 20, 1830, John Henry Leinbach Family Papers, Moravian Archives; Aufseher Collegium, September 5, 1825, June 16, 1828, August 9, 1830, in Fries et al., *Records*, 8: 3746,

3847, 3939; Hirsch, *Roots of the American Working Class: The Industrialization of Crafts in Newark, 1800–1860*, 9; Johnson, *Ante-bellum North Carolina*, 9.

39. Two samples were used to produce the statistics on farm size in Stokes County in 1820. First, a sample (n = 76) comprised of every tenth head of household was created from the population schedule of the United States Census of 1820, Stokes County. These names were then located in the Stokes County Tax List of 1820. A second sample (n = 120) of Moravian landowners was created by taking every fifth name listed in the tax lists for the Moravian settlements of Bethabara, Bethania, and Salem. Stokes County, List of Taxables, 1820, NCDAH; 1820 Census, Population Schedule manuscript microfilm, Stokes County, North Carolina; Lefler and Newsome, *North Carolina*, 19, 29.

40. Stokes County, Inventory of Estates, 1814–18, 90, 177, 289, 460–61, North Carolina Division of Archives and History. The administrator of Moore's estate informed the Stokes County Court of Pleas and Quarter Session that since the deceased was not in the habit of keeping any book accounts of his business and finances, it was impossible to pay off any outstanding debts.

41. Diary of the Little Pilgrim Congregation, October 24, 1755, Wachovia Diary, April 19, 1767, Salem Memorabilia, 1770, Salem Diary, 1770, and "History of the Building of the Place Congregation Salem, written for the Celebration of the Congregation in Salem, February 19, 1816," compiled by Reverend Ludwig David von Schweinitz; Bethania Diary, March 8, 1825, December 18, 1826, in Fries et al., *Records*, 1: 143, 352, 400, 404, 7: 3045–46, and 8: 3755, 3788; Lefler and Powell, *Colonial North Carolina*, 102; Lefler and Newsome, *North Carolina*, 300–301; Martineau, *Society in America*, vol. 2, 2; Leinbach, Diary, April 16–18, 1830, John Henry Leinbach Family Papers, Moravian Archives; Escott, *Many Excellent People: Power and Privilege in North Carolina, 1850–1890*, 3.

42. Daniel Thorp has estimated that by 1758 wheat accounted for almost 60 percent of the Moravians' total grain output. Thorp, *Moravian Community*, 121; Merrens, *Colonial North Carolina*, 112, 118, 134, 143–44; Robinson, *Southern Colonial Frontier*, 174, 179, 234.

43. Merrens, *Colonial North Carolina*, 159–60; Bethabara Diary, August 18, 1759, December 3, 1765, August 19, 1766, Wachovia Church Book, 1761, Wachovia Diary, April 1768, August 20, October 17, November 6, 15, 1770, Salem Board Minutes, 1810, and Aeltesten Conferenz, March 7, 1810, in Fries et al., *Records*, 1: 212, 234, 307, 334, 413, 417, and 7: 3119; Thorp, "Moravian Colonization," 392–401.

44. Clark, "Household Economy, Market Exchange and the Rise of Capitalism in the Connecticut Valley, 1800–1860," 169–84; Henretta, "Family and Farms: Mentalité in Pre-Industrial America," 3–32; Hahn, *The Roots of Southern Populism: Yeomen Farmers and the Transformation of the Georgia Upcountry*, 32–49; Escott, *Many Excellent People*, xviii, 3–9; Gray, *History of Agriculture*, 1: 122–23, 451–57; Solomon Hilary Helsabeck, Diary, January 24–October 20, 1854, Solomon Hilary Helsabeck Papers, Southern Historical Collection, University of North Carolina at Chapel Hill, Chapel Hill, North Carolina; John Conrad, Ledger, May 16, 1823–September 28, 1827, Conrad Family Papers, Manuscripts Department, Duke University Library, Durham, North Carolina.

45. Every second estate inventory listed in the volume 1814–1818 was chosen for inclusion in this sample (N = 67, n = 33). Stokes County, Inventory of Estates, 1814–18, NCDAH.

46. Stokes County, Inventory of Estates, 1814–18, 1819–23, 44, 161, NCDAH; Memorabilia of the Wachovia Congregations for the Year 1815, Salem Board Minutes, 1811, and Aufseher Collegium, February 6, 1811, in Fries et al., *Records*, 7: 3144–45, 3254.

47. Salem Diary, February 3, 1809, in Fries et al., *Records*, 7: 3071; Edmund Blum, Daybook, 1844–52, Manuscript Department, Duke University Library, Durham, North Carolina; Woodmason, *The Carolina Backcountry*, 77–78.

48. Spangenberg Diary, September 25, 1752, in Fries et al., *Records*, 1: 40–41; Fries et al., *Records*, 9: 4401; Eaton, *The Growth of Southern Civilization, 1790–1860*, 12; Merrens, *Colonial North Carolina*, 58–59.

49. Memorabilia of the Congregations of the Brethren in Wachovia for the Year 1809, in Fries et al., *Records*, 7: 3063–64, 3067.

50. Surratt, "The Role of Dissent," 242, 248–49.

T W O   *The Congregation and a Changing Economy*

1. Charles Sellers offers the most comprehensive view of the evolution of a market society in the United States before the Civil War in *The Market Revolution: Jacksonian America, 1815–1846*, especially 3–33 for a concise overview of the meaning of the market and its impact on people's lives. Kulikoff, "The Transition to Capitalism in Rural America," 120–44; Clark, "Household Economy, Market Exchange, and the Rise of Capitalism in the Connecticut Valley, 1800–1860," 169–89. Ford, "Yeoman Farmers in the South Carolina Upcountry: Changing Production Patterns in the Late Antebellum Era," 17–37; idem, *Origins of Southern Radicalism: The South Carolina Upcountry, 1800–1860*; Oakes, "From Republicanism to Liberalism: Ideological Change and the Crisis of the Old South," 557–62; Weiman, "Farmers and the Market in Antebellum America: A View from the Georgia Upcountry," 627–47; Escott, "Yeoman Independence and the Market: Social Status and Economic Development in Antebellum North Carolina," 275–300.

2. John Jordan and Son to Reverend W. L. Benzien, September 12, 24, 1828, and J. J. Whitney to J. C. Jacobson, April 11, 1836, in Fries et al., eds., *Records of the Moravians in North Carolina*, 11 vols., 8: 3864, 4252; Fries, "One Hundred Years of Textiles in Salem," 12–13; Salem Manufacturing Company, Minutes of the General Meetings, 44, 50, 55–58, Fries Mills Collection, Moravian Archives, Winston-Salem, North Carolina; Salem Manufacturing Company, Minutes of the Board of Directors, 95–96, 103, Fries Mills Collection, Moravian Archives; F. and H. Fries Company, Daybooks #11 and #12, F. and H. Fries Collection, Moravian Archives, Winston-Salem, North Carolina; Taylor, *The Transportation Revolution, 1815–1860*, 74–103, 203; North, *The Economic Growth of the United States, 1790–1860*, 204–7; Lefler and Newsome, *North Carolina: The History of a Southern State*, 348–49, 360–62, 378.

3. Cathey, *Agricultural Developments in North Carolina, 1783–1860*, 105–39, 202–5; Escott, "Yeoman Independence and the Market," 275–300; Beck, "Development in the Piedmont South," 66–67; *Compendium of the Sixth Census. 1840; Statistical View of the United States. Compendium of the Seventh Census. 1850; Report of the United States in 1860; Compiled from the Original Returns of the Eighth Census*, vol. 2; Extracts of Minutes of the Wachovia Provinzial Helfer Conferenz in Salem for the Year 1842, December 5, 1842, in Fries et al., *Records*, 10: 5088–89; John Henry Leinbach, Diary, July 14, 1843, John Henry Leinbach Family Papers, Moravian Archives, Winston-Salem, North Carolina.

4. *Compendium of the Sixth Census. 1840; Statistical View Compendium. 1850; Report of the United States in 1860*, vol. 2. The figure for cotton production in Stokes and Forsyth counties in 1849 appears highly suspect. It is, however, the figure listed in the official report of the seventh census. A 20 percent sample of farms drawn from the 1850 Census, Agriculture Schedule manuscript microfilm, Forsyth County, North Carolina, and five farms o. 2.7 percent of the sample reported producing a total of fourteen bales of cotton or roughly 5,600 pounds in 1849. An important measure of agricultural priorities that lends further evidence of this shift toward market production is a tobacco/corn ratio and a wheat/corn ratio. Adapting the cotton/corn ratio used by historians of southern agriculture to plot the cultivation of market crops with subsistence crops by substituting tobacco and wheat for cotton, the turn to market production between 1839 and 1859 becomes clearer. In 1839 the ratio of tobacco output to corn output in Stokes County was 1.4, but in 1859 when tobacco cultivation expanded, the ratio for Stokes and Forsyth counties was 3.7. The ratio of wheat output to corn output during these years reflected a significant change also, but its impact is not as dramatic as that of tobacco cultivation. The wheat/corn ratio was .17 in 1839 and .43 in 1859. Wright, *The Political Economy of the Cotton South: Households, Markets, and Wealth in the Nineteenth Century*, 166; Ford, *Origins of Southern Radicalism*, 54–88, 375–77; Cathey, *Agricultural Developments*, 105–39.

5. Rothenberg, "The Market and Massachusetts Farmers, 1750–1855," 283–315; Salem *People's Press*, March 29, June 21, September 13, November 15, 1851, March 14, June 6, September 21, November 14, 1856.

6. *Compendium of the Sixth Census. 1840; Statistical View Compendium. 1850; Report of the United States in 1860*, vol. 2. John Beck reports that a similar expansion occurred in Rowan County. There, between 1850 and 1860, improved farm acreage increased 30 percent and the cash value of farms nearly tripled. Beck, "Development in the Piedmont South: Rowan County, North Carolina, 1850–1900," Ph.D. diss., University of North Carolina, Chapel Hill, 1984, 61–67. A sample was created that included every fifth name listed in the 1850 Census of Agriculture manuscripts of Forsyth County (N = 936, n = 187). 1850 Census, Agriculture Schedule manuscript microfilm, Forsyth County, North Carolina.

7. *Compendium of the Sixth Census. 1840; Report of the United States in 1860*, vol. 2. Using the Statistical Package for the Social Sciences (SPSSX), the size of slaveholdings was plotted with the size of farms measured in improved acres. The correlation coefficient equals .29449, with 1.0 being the strongest correlation and

o demonstrating no correlation. 1850 Census, Agriculture Schedule manuscript microfilm, Forsyth County, North Carolina; 1850 Census, Slave Schedule manuscript microfilm, Forsyth County, North Carolina. The sample from the Agriculture Schedule was correlated with the Slave Schedule of the same census.

8. Edmund Blum, Daybook, 1857–1864, Manuscripts Department, Duke University Library, Durham, North Carolina; *People's Press*, February 8, March 29, June 14, 1851, July 1, 1854, April 18, 1856; Tryon, *Household Manufactures in the United States, 1690–1860: A Study in Industrial History*, 176; *Compendium of the Sixth Census. 1840; Report of the United States in 1860*, vol. 2. In his study of the South Carolina piedmont during the antebellum decades, Lacy K. Ford had found a similar transition in the production and consumption patterns of South Carolina households. Ford reports that the per capita value of household manufacture in the South Carolina upcountry in 1840 was one-third of the 1810 level. Ford concluded that "by mid-century, household self-sufficiency in any literal sense was a thing of the past." Ford, *Origins of Southern Radicalism*, 81–84.

9. Leinbach, Diary, July 24, 28, 1830, John Henry Leinbach Family Papers, Moravian Archives; Bethania Diary, February 26, 1831, in Fries et al., *Records*, 8: 4002.

10. Rutman, "Assessing the Little Communities of Early America," 174; Rutman, "The Social Web: A Prospectus for the Study of the Early American Community," in *Insights and Parallels: Problems and Issues of American Social History*, ed. William L. O'Neill, 83; Hahn, *Roots of Southern Populism*, 152–54; Siegel, *The Roots of Southern Distinctiveness: Tobacco and Society in Danville, Virginia, 1780–1865*, 76–92.

11. Stokes County, List of Taxables, 1820, 1835, 1836, 1840, 1845, North Carolina Department of Archives and History, Raleigh, North Carolina. Under the laws of North Carolina, all free males between age twenty-one and forty-five were to pay a poll tax plus a tax on the value of their real and personal property. Harry Watson reminds us that historians must be careful when using the tax lists to determine wealth and not assume that the taxable wealth declared by a property holder was the same as his actual net worth because many forms of wealth— stocks, bonds, and other investments, for example—were not taxed and many taxpayers did not declare all of their property. Watson, *Jacksonian Politics and Community Conflict: The Emergence of the Second American Party System in Cumberland County, North Carolina*, 325–27. However, for the antebellum period, especially when the U.S. Census did not list wealth, the tax lists are the only source that gives a hint to the property distribution in a county. Paul Escott has determined that landless Tarheels composed about 30 percent of North Carolina's adult white population in 1860. Escott, *Many Excellent People*, 9–10.

12. Samples comprised of every fifth name were drawn from the 1825 (n = 73) and 1845 (n = 44) Stokes County Tax Lists for Salem. Stokes County, List of Taxables, 1825, 1845, NCDAH. This pattern of increasing concentration of wealth was repeated in other areas of the South as their economies became increasingly commercial. In his studies of early American communities, Darrett Rutman has observed that social and economic stratification "sharpened" as communities diversified economically and established firmer commercial links to the

world beyond the town's boundaries. Steven Hahn's study of the Georgia piedmont supports Rutman's observation. Hahn found that between 1850 and 1890 the expansion of commercial agriculture in the Georgia upcountry, as well as commercial ties that stretched beyond the local community, led to greater concentrations of wealth. Frederick Siegel as well has documented the same phenomenon in the Virginia piedmont during the antebellum period. Siegel found that in Pittsylvania County, Virginia, located on the Virginia—North Carolina border near Stokes County, the development of commercial agriculture with its attendant economic ties beyond the local community and greater economic diversity within the community produced greater concentrations of wealth in the local community. Rutman, "Little Communities," 174; Rutman, "Social Web," 83; Hahn, *Roots of Southern Populism*, 152–54; Siegel, *Roots of Southern Distinctiveness*, 76–92.

13. Taylor, *Transportation Revolution*, 74–103, 203; North, *Economic Growth of the United States*, 204–7. Siegel's study of Danville, Virginia, demonstrates that the improved transportation system of the late antebellum years caused serious hardships for local artisans in the 1850s as imported manufactured goods competed with goods produced in local shops. Siegel, *Roots of Southern Distinctiveness*, 114–19.

14. Leinbach, Diary, February 17, 1831, January 2, March 19, 1832, January 26, 1834, John Henry Leinbach Family Papers, Moravian Archives; Louisa Belo to Julia Jones, n.d., 1847, February 1, 1849, Jones Family Papers, Southern Historical Collection, University of North Carolina at Chapel Hill, Chapel Hill, North Carolina; Extracts of Minutes of the Aufseher Collegium (hereafter cited Aufseher Collegium), July 5, 1839, in Fries et al., *Records*, 9: 4479.

15. *Census for 1820; Compendium of the Sixth Census. 1840; Report of the United States in 1860*, vol. 2; Dodd and Dodd, *Historical Statistics of the South, 1790–1970*, 38; John Conrad, Ledger, May 16, 1823–September 28, 1827, Conrad Family Papers, Manuscripts Department, Duke University Library, Durham, North Carolina.

16. Memorabilia of the Congregation in Salem for the Year 1827, 1841, 1842, 1843, 1844, Memorabilia of the Bethania Congregation, 1842, 1843, Wilhelm Fries to Franz Fries, March 14, 1828, Salem Diary, December 24, 1809, February 28, 1819, January 19, 1826 Memorabilia of the Congregation in Salem for the Year 1823, and Aufseher Collegium, March 18, October 8, 21, 1833, January 6, February 3, March 3, 17, August 18, 1834, in Fries et al., *Records*, 7: 3087, 8: 3398, 3617, 3768, 3794, 3841, 4074, 4087, 4128–29, 4131, 4135, 9: 4590, 4685, 4713, 4741, 4758; Salem *Weekly Gleaner*, November 25, 1828. Leinbach, Diary, July 20–22, October 28, 1833, January 4, March 19, 1834, July 14, 1843, John Henry Leinbach Family Papers, Moravian Archives; Stokes County, List of Taxables, 1833, NCDAH.

17. Salem Board Minutes, August 31, October 11, November 8, 1809, January 30, February 19, 1811, Salem Diary, October 31, 1809, August 21, 1810, October 13, 1811, February 28, 1819, Memorabilia of the Wachovia Congregations for the Year 1815, Memorabilia of the Wachovia Congregations for the Year 1821, and Wilhelm Fries to Franz Fries, January 12, August 16, 1828, in Fries et

al., *Records*, 7: 3086, 3095–97, 3112, 3138, 3144–45, 3254, 3398, 3466, 8: 3839, 3841; Stokes County, List of Taxables, 1819, 1823, NCDAH.

18. Aufseher Collegium, July 1, 9, 1827, in Fries et al., *Records*, 8: 3809; Minutes of the Aufseher Collegium, February 23, 1829, Salem Congregation, Moravian Archives, Winston-Salem, North Carolina.

19. Wilhelm Fries to Franz Fries, January 28, 1830, in Fries et al., *Records*, 8: 3929; Minutes of the Aufseher Collegium, February 9, 25, August 31, September 7, 1829, Salem Congregation, Moravian Archives. Like William Fries, Gottlieb Schober continually challenged the congregational regulation of trade in Salem. For a thoughtful treatment of Gottlieb Schober's life, see Surratt, *Gottlieb Schober of Salem: Discipleship and Ecumenical Vision in an Early Moravian Town.*

20. Minutes of the Aufseher Collegium, February 9, August 31, September 7, 1829, October 17, 1831, Salem Congregation, Moravian Archives; Minutes of the Elders Conference, February 25, September 2, 9, 1829, Salem Congregation, Moravian Archives; Wilhelm Fries to Franz Fries, March 14, August 16, 1828, November 13, 1829, January 28, 1830, in Fries et al., *Records*, 8: 3841, 3876, 3929.

21. Aufseher Collegium, May 22, 1826, July 9, 1827, and Wilhelm Fries to Franz Fries, March 14, August 16, 1828, in Fries et al., *Records*, 8: 3809, 3841, 3774; Minutes of the Aufseher Collegium, February 9, 23, 31, August 31, September 7, 1829, October 17, 1831, and Minutes of the Elders Conference, February 25, September 2, 9, 1829, Salem Congregation, Moravian Archives.

22. Aufseher Collegium, October 17, 1831, Salem Congregation, Moravian Archives; Aufseher Collegium, November 28, 1831, in Fries et al., *Records*, 8: 3994–95.

23. Leinbach, Diary, March 19, 1830, February 17, November 7, November 28, 1831, January 2, 1832, John Henry Leinbach Family Papers, Moravian Archives; Minutes of the Aufseher Collegium, November 28, 1831, Salem Congregation, Moravian Archives.

24. Aufseher Collegium, September 1, 15, October 13, 30, November 18, December 22, 29, 1845, in Fries et al., *Records*, 9: 4857–61.

25. Aufseher Collegium, December 29, 1845, May 11, 1846, in Fries et al., *Records*, 9: 4861, 4903.

26. Aufseher Collegium, March 21, 1831, in Fries et al., *Records*, 8: 3979; Africa, "Slaveholding in the Salem Community, 1771–1851," 285–86.

27. Aufseher Collegium, January 8, 1811, Minutes of the Housefathers, Masters, and Brethren of the Congregation Council, August 22, 1814, and "To the Dear Brethren of the United Elders Conference in Berthelsdorf," 1845, in Fries et al., *Records*, 7: 3142, 3544–46, and 9: 4820; Africa, "Slaveholding in the Salem Community," 282–84; Fries et al., *Forsyth: The History of a County on the March*, 85–86. In the Salem district of Stokes County in 1825, 12.3 percent of the property holders owned a slave. The average size of individual slave holdings was 1.4 (a 20 percent random sample was drawn from the List of Taxables; n = 73). Stokes County, List of Taxables, 1825, NCDAH.

28. Aufseher Collegium, January 22, 1816, in Fries et al., *Records*, 7: 3301, 3418.

29. Meeting of the House-fathers, Masters, and Brethren of the Congregation Council, August 22, 1814, Salem Congregation, Moravian Archives.

30. Ibid.

31. Stokes County, List of Taxables, 1816–25, NCDAH; Congregation Council, February 2, 24, 1820, in Fries et al., *Records*, 7: 3446–47.

32. Aeltesten Conferenz, July 25, 1827, in Fries et al., *Records*, 8: 3810; Minutes of the Elders Conference, February 10, 1830, February 6, 1845, Salem Congregation, Moravian Archives. The number of slaves employed in Salem before the slave rules were abandoned in 1847 peaked at 109 in 1835. With the economic distress of the late 1830s and early 1840s the number of slaves in Salem declined and averaged about 77. Stokes County, List of Taxables, 1816–45, NCDAH.

33. Aufseher Collegium October 25, November 22, 1839, in Fries et al., *Records*, 9: 4485–86, 4488; Fries, "One Hundred Years," 15; John W. Fries, "Remembrance of Civil War Times," 2, Fries Papers, North Carolina Department of Archives and History.

34. Minutes of the Congregation Council, February 6, 21, 1845, Salem Congregation, Moravian Archives.

35. The five who resigned were Francis Fries, a manufacturer, Henry Leinbach, a shoemaker, Charles Brietz, a tanner, Edward Belo, a merchant, and Solomon Mickey, a cooper. All but Leinbach and Mickey were slaveholders. The entrepreneurial spirit that emphasized innovation and profit seeking was evident in Fries, Brietz, and Belo who engaged in several varied business activities. Fries owned and operated a textile mill, a paper mill, a tannery, and a general store, while Brietz was a tanner who by 1850 had expanded into shoemaking. Belo, a cabinetmaker, owned a foundry and an oil mill. Minutes of the Elders Conference, February 26, 1845, Salem Congregation, Moravian Archives; 1850 Census, Population Schedule manuscript microfilm, Forsyth County, North Carolina; 1860 Census, Manufacturing Schedule manuscript microfilm, Forsyth County, North Carolina; Salem Diary, January 10, March 7, 1845, and Minutes of the Congregation Council, January 10, February 7, 24, March 6, 7, 1845; January 13, 1847, in Fries et al., *Records*, 9: 4831–32, 4839–45, 4957; Minutes of the Elders Conference, July 16, 1845, Salem Congregation, Moravian Archives.

36. Minutes of the Congregation Council, January 2, 11, 1847, Salem Congregation, Moravian Archives; Aufseher Collegium, March 28, 1848, in Fries et al., *Records*, 10: 5225; 1850 Census, Slave Schedule manuscript microfilm, Forsyth County, North Carolina; 1860 Census, Slave Schedule manuscript microfilm, Forsyth County, North Carolina; 1850 Census, Manufacturing Schedule manuscript microfilm, Forsyth County, North Carolina.

37. Fox-Genovese, *Within the Plantation Household: Black and White Women of the Old South*, 55–56; Oakes, *Slavery and Freedom: An Interpretation of the Old South*, 57–71.

38. Minutes of the Aufseher Collegium, December 18, 1837, Salem Congregation, Moravian Archives; Aufseher Collegium, July 16, 1840, in Fries et al., *Records*, 9: 4541–42.

39. Salem Congregation Council, January 5, 1849, in Fries et al., *Records*, 10: 5399–5401.

40. Aufseher Collegium, July 16, 1840, in Fries et al., *Records*, 9: 4541; 1850 Census, Population Schedule manuscript microfilm, Forsyth County, North Carolina; Salem *People's Press*, September 27, 1851, December 11, 1852.

41. 1850 Census, Population Schedule manuscript microfilm, Forsyth County, North Carolina; 1850 Census, Manufacturing Schedule manuscript microfilm, Forsyth County, North Carolina; 1850 Census, Slave Schedule; 1860 Census, Slave Schedule manuscript microfilm, Forsyth County, North Carolina; North Carolina Volume 10, 463, 465, 502, R. G. Dun and Company Collection, Baker Library, Harvard University Graduate School of Business Administration; Ashe et al., eds., *Biographical History of North Carolina from Colonial Times to the Present*, 8 vols., 3: 129–34; Francis Fries to J. F. Shaffner, June 30, 1861, Shaffner-Fries Correspondence, Moravian Archives, Winston-Salem, North Carolina.

42. Minutes of the Elders Conference, October 21, December 2, 1829; January 27, 1834, Salem Congregation, Moravian Archives; Aufseher Collegium, 1838–47, in Fries et al., *Records*, 9: passim; 1850 Census, Population Schedule manuscript microfilm, Forsyth County, North Carolina; Leinbach, Diary, January 24, February 9, 1834, John Henry Leinbach Family Papers, Moravian Archives. Salem's artisans repeated the experiences of Moravian artisans in the congregation community at Bethlehem, Pennsylvania. Through the early nineteenth century non-Moravians were not allowed to settle in Bethlehem and open shops. Since there were no alternative sources of employment in the community labor remained cheap. Therefore, Moravians in Bethlehem who wanted to earn a better living had to emigrate, which many did. Gollin, *Moravians in Two Worlds: A Study of Changing Communities*, 93–95.

43. Minutes of the Congregation Council, January 11, 1847, Salem Congregation, Moravian Archives; Memorabilia of Salem Congregation, 1840, in Fries et al., *Records*, 9: 4527; Leinbach, Diary, October 28, 1833; January 24, 1834, John Henry Leinbach Family Papers, Moravian Archives.

44. Stokes County, List of Taxables, 1847, NCDAH; Henretta, "Families and Farms," 5, 14–29.

45. Haskell, "Capitalism and the Humanitarian Sensibility," 550; Weber, *The Protestant Ethic and the Spirit of Capitalism*, 17–18; Appleby, *Capitalism and a New Social Order: The Republican Vision of the 1790s*, 22.

THREE   *Manufacturing and Community in Salem*

1. Griffin and Standard, "The Cotton Textile Industry in Antebellum North Carolina, Part II: An Era of Boom and Consolidation, 1830–1860," 141, 154–57; Johnson, *Ante-bellum North Carolina: A Social History*, 38–41; Linden, "Repercussions of Manufacturing in the Antebellum South," 318–19; Griffin, "Poor White Laborers in Southern Cotton Factories, 1789–1865," 28–34.

2. Cotton prices which averaged 12.6 cents per pound during the mid-1830s dropped to an average of eight cents per pound in the 1840s. Enthusiasm for mill building ebbed and flowed between the 1820s and 1840s with the price of cotton. During the late 1830s and the 1840s when the mill-building movement was at its peak, almost two dozen mills opened in North Carolina, usually small enterprises in two-story wooden frame structures on the edge of a stream which provided water power. Gray, *History of Agriculture in the Southern United States to 1860*, vol. 2, 691–99; Stokes, "Black and White Labor and the Development of the Southern Textile Industry, 1800–1920," Ph.D. diss., University of South Carolina, 1977, 48, 59, 63–65; Griffin and Standard, "Cotton Textile Industry," 133, 142; Lander, Jr., *The Textile Industry in Antebellum South Carolina*, 25–28, 50.

3. Minutes of the Aufseher Collegium, June 20, 1836, Salem Congregation, Moravian Archives, Winston-Salem, North Carolina (hereafter cited as Salem Congregation, Moravian Archives); Minutes of the Elders Conference, June 29, 1836, Salem Congregation, Central Elders, Minutes, Moravian Archives, Winston-Salem, North Carolina (hereafter cited as Salem Congregation, Moravian Archives); Salem Manufacturing Company, Minutes of the General Meetings, July 5, 1836, Fries Mills Collection, Moravian Archives, Winston-Salem, North Carolina (hereafter cited as SMC, General Meetings, Fries Mills Collection, Moravian Archives); Fries, "One Hundred Years of Textiles in Salem," 10.

4. Extracts of the Minutes of the Aufseher Collegium, June 20, July 6, 8, 18, 1836, in Fries et al., eds., *Records of the Moravians in North Carolina*, 11 vols., 8: 4225–26; Fries, "One Hundred Years of Textiles in Salem," 10; Salem Manufacturing Company, Report of the Building Committee, July 5, 1836, Fries Mills Collection, Moravian Archives, Winston-Salem, North Carolina (hereafter cited as SMC, Building Committee, Fries Mills Collection, Moravian Archives); Salem Manufacturing Company, "A Bill to Incorporate the Salem Manufacturing Company," Fries Mills Collection, Moravian Archives, Winston-Salem, North Carolina; Salem *Weekly Chronicle*, July 16, 1836.

5. Minutes of the Elders Conference, July 20, 1836, November 1, 1837, Salem Congregation, Moravian Archives; Aufseher Collegium, November 1, 1839, in Fries et al., *Records*, 9: 4484; Minutes of the Aufseher Collegium, November 6, 1837, Salem Congregation, Moravian Archives.

6. In November 1839, when Francis Fries proposed building a small wool carding and spinning mill on a lot at the corner of New Shallowford and Salt streets near the Salem Manufacturing Company mill, neighbors objected because they believed that the steam and vapor from the mill would "incommode" them in their homes. Aufseher Collegium, November 1, 22, 1839, in Fries et al., *Records*, 9: 4484–85; Prude, *The Coming of Industrial Order: Town and Factory Life in Rural Massachusetts, 1810–1860*, 158–66.

7. SMC, Building Committee, August 6, 11, September 4, 1836, Fries Mills Collection, Moravian Archives.

8. SMC, Building Committee, November 8, 1836, September 4, October 6, 1837, Fries Mills Collection, Moravian Archives; Salem Manufacturing Company, Minutes of the Board of Directors, November 24, December 6, 1837, Fries

Mills Collection, Moravian Archives, Winston-Salem, North Carolina (hereafter cited as SMC, Board of Directors, Fries Mills Collection, Moravian Archives); SMC, General Meetings, January 21, 1840, Fries Mills Collection, Moravian Archives; Minutes of the Aufseher Collegium, October 9, 1837, in Fries et al., *Records*, 8: 4277; Elders Conference, October 11, 1837, Salem Congregation, Moravian Archives.

9. SMC, General Meetings, January 1, 1838, January 21, 1840, Fries Mills Collection, Moravian Archives; Memorabilia of the Salem Congregation in 1838, in Fries et al., *Records*, 9: 4372; Griffin, "North Carolina: The Origin and Rise of the Cotton Textile Industry, 1830–1860," Ph.D. diss., Ohio State University, 1954, 83, 181; Stokes, "Black and White Labor," 59, 63; Lander, *Textile Industry*, 25–28; Mitchell, *Rise of the Cotton Mills in the South*, 21; Fries et al., *Forsyth: The History of a County on the March*, 98; 1850 Census, Manufacturing Schedule manuscript microfilm, Forsyth County, North Carolina.

10. SMC, General Meetings, January 1, 1838, March 16, 1839, March 14, 1840, March 14, 1841, Fries Mills Collection, Moravian Archives; SMC, Board of Directors, October 26, 1841, September 22, 1846, September 30, 1848, March 24, 1849, Fries Mills Collection, Moravian Archives; SMC, General Meetings, March 14, October 30, 1841, January 29, April 2, October 8, November 5, 1842, April 8, October 28, 1843, March 23, October 5, 1844, March 29, October 11, 1845, March 11, September 26, 1846, April 17, October 2, 1847, March 18, 1848, March 24, November 30, 1849, Fries Mills Collection, Moravian Archives.

11. SMC, General Meetings, March 14, 1841, April 8, 1843, September 26, 1846, October 2, 1847, March 25, 1848, November 30, 1849, Fries Mills Collection, Moravian Archives; SMC, Board of Directors, February 13, 1841, September 22, 1846, Fries Mills Collection, Moravian Archives; SMC, General Meetings, Fries Mills Collection, Moravian Archives.

12. Minutes of the Provinzial Helfer Conferenz, May 9, 1845, in Fries et al., *Records*, 10: 5145–46; SMC, Minutes of General Meetings, January 1, 1838, October 2, 1847, March 18, 1848, November 30, 1849, June 30, 1850, Fries Mills Collection, Moravian Archives; SMC, Board of Directors, April 13, September 20, 1847, September 30, December 28, 1848, March 22, August 8, 1849, December 4, 1849; February 19, March 3, June 22, 1853, March 24, 1854, Fries Mills Collection, Moravian Archives; Salem *People's Press*, March 25, 1854.

13. Fries, "One Hundred Years," 12–13; Griffin and Standard, "Cotton Textile Industry," 134–35; SMC, General Meetings, April 14, 1841, April 8, 1843, September 26, 1846, April 17, October 2, 1847, March 18, 25, 1848, March 24, 1849, Fries Mills Collection, Moravian Archives; SMC, Board of Directors, May 26, September 22, 1846, September 30, December 28, 1848, Fries Mills Collection, Moravian Archives; Lander, *Textile Industry*, 39, 109–10; Stokes, "Black and White Labor," 91; Scranton, *Proprietary Capitalism: The Textile Manufactures at Philadelphia, 1800–1885*, 38; Wallace, *Rockdale: The Growth of an American Village in the Early Industrial Revolution*, 122–23; Francis L. Fries, Diary, Introduction, in Fries Papers, North Carolina Division of Archives and History, Raleigh, North Carolina. In 1850 the Fries mill purchased $1,510 in wool from North Carolina

farmers but spent $37,341 in Philadelphia for wool. John W. Fries, "Remembrances of Confederate Days," 2, Fries Papers, North Carolina Division of Archives and History, Raleigh, North Carolina.

14. Fries et al., *Forsyth,* 99; Griffin, "North Carolina," 182; Fries, "Remembrances," 2, Fries Papers, NCDAH; Griffin, "North Carolina," 183; Aufseher Collegium, March 10, 1847, in Fries et al., *Records,* 9: 4947; Fries, "One Hundred Years," 17; F. and H. Fries Company, Daybooks #11 and #12, Fries Mills Collection, Moravian Archives, Winston-Salem, North Carolina; Eighth Census, 1860, Manufacturing Schedule manuscript microfilm, Forsyth County, North Carolina.

15. Francis Fries, Memorandum Book, December 30, 1837, January 1, 4, 1838, F. and H. Fries Collection, Moravian Archives, Winston-Salem, North Carolina (hereafter cited as F. and H. Fries Collection, Moravian Archives); Minutes of the Elders Conference, December 6, 1837, Salem Congregation, Moravian Archives; Aufseher Collegium, February 26, 1838, in Fries et al., *Records,* 9: 4397.

16. Terrill, "Eager Hands: Labor for Southern Textiles, 1850–1860," 86; Extracts from the Bethania Diary, May 28, 1837, and Aufseher Collegium, February 26, 1838, in Fries et al., *Records,* 8: 4289, and 9: 4397; Francis Fries Memorandum Book, January 4, 1838, F. and H. Fries Collection, Moravian Archives. The 1820 census for Stokes County contains many surnames of mill hands listed in the SMC wage books which suggests that most Salem mill hands were likely to have come from nearby rural neighborhoods. Marriage records show that many operatives had familial ties with counties across North Carolina, including Craven, Cabarrus, Johnston, Rowan, Wake, Orange, Mecklenburg, Nash, Yadkin, Wilkes, and Rockingham counties. SMC, Board and Wage Books, 1841–45, Fries Mills Collection, Moravian Archives; Stokes County, List of Taxables, 1835, 1840, North Carolina Division of Archives and History, Raleigh, North Carolina; 1820 Census, Population Schedule manuscript microfilm, Stokes County, North Carolina; Jackson, *Index to the 1850 Census. North Carolina;* Wynne, compiler, *Wake County, North Carolina Census and Tax Lists Abstracts, 1830 and 1840;* Stokes County, Marriage Bonds, North Carolina Division of Archives and History, Raleigh, North Carolina.

17. 1840 Census, Population Schedule manuscript microfilm, Stokes County, North Carolina; Francis Fries Memorandum Book, December 30, 1837, F. and H. Fries Collection, Moravian Archives; SMC, General Meetings, January 1, 1838, Fries Mills Collection, Moravian Archives; SMC, Board and Wage Books, 1841–49, Fries Mills Collection, Moravian Archives.

18. Stokes County, List of Taxables, 1835, NCDAH. In 1838 the Internal Improvements Convention which convened in Raleigh reported that over 500,000 North Carolinians had migrated to other areas of the country. Twenty years later the 1860 census reported that 30 percent of those born in North Carolina lived outside of the state. Johnson, *Antebellum North Carolina,* 38–41; Linden, "Repercussions of Manufacturing," 318–19; Griffin, "Poor White Laborers," 32–33; Griffin and Standard, "Cotton Textile Industry," 154–55.

19. Memorabilia of the Congregation in Salem, 1841, 1842, 1843, 1844, and

Memorabilia of the Bethania Congregation, 1842, 1843, in Fries et al., *Records*, 9: 4590, 4685, 4713, 4741, 4758; John Henry Leinbach, Diary, July 14, 1843, John Henry Leinbach Family Papers, Moravian Archives, Winston-Salem, North Carolina; Stokes County, List of Taxables, 1820, 1835, 1836, 1840, 1845; Escott, *Many Excellent People*, 9–10; SMC, Board and Wage Book B, 1845, Fries Mills Collection, Moravian Archives; Francis Fries Mill Diary, passim, Fries Mills Collection, Moravian Archives; 1850 Census, Population Schedule manuscript microfilm, Forsyth County, North Carolina; Stokes County, List of Taxables, 1835–40, NCDAH; Wynne, compiler, *Wake County, North Carolina Census and Tax List Abstracts, 1830 and 1840*.

20. Francis Fries Memorandum Book, December 30, 1837, March 14, August 23, 28, 1838, F. and H. Fries Collection, Moravian Archives; 1840 Census, Population Schedule manuscript microfilm, Stokes County; SMC, General Meetings, 1838, Fries Mills Collection, Moravian Archives; SMC, Board and Wage Books, 1841–49, Fries Mills Collection, Moravian Archives; Stokes, "Black and White Labor," 84, 120, 131; Briggs, "Millowners and Workers in an Antebellum North Carolina County," M.A. thesis, University of North Carolina, Chapel Hill, 1975, 50; Quote in Terrill, "Eager Hands," 87.

21. Terrill, "Eager Hands," 84–99; Stokes, "Black and White Labor," 120–21; Briggs, "Millowners and Workers," 78–112; Kennedy, *If All We Did Was to Weep at Home: A History of Working-Class Women in America*, 14–15, 21–22; Prude, *The Coming of Industrial Order*, 89–99; Clinton, *The Plantation Mistress*, 204–5; Lebsock, *The Free Women of Petersburg: Status and Culture in a Southern Town, 1784–1860*, 149; Hagler, "The Ideal Woman in the Antebellum South: Lady or Farmwife?" 414–18. Thomas Dublin maintains that in the Lowell, Massachusetts, mills, evidence does not support the conclusion that financial need drove many women into the mills. Rather, women became operatives for their own reasons, generally to accumulate some savings for personal use. They wanted to earn something of their own, outside and independent of the family economy. Thus, mill work filled the same need for women as migration did for men who had little chance in their native communities to set up on a farm. However, Dublin did note that as large groups of immigrants entered the northern mills in the 1830s and 1840s, economic need did become a motivating factor in mill work. This is borne out by the longer persistence of women in mill work. Dublin, *Women at Work: The Transformation of Work and Community in Lowell, Massachusetts, 1826–1860*, 35–40, 197.

22. Wyatt-Brown, *Southern Honor: Ethics and Behavior in the Old South*, 226–30; Hahn, *The Roots of Southern Populism: Yeoman Farmers and the Transformation of the Georgia Upcountry, 1850–1890*, 30–31; Fox-Genovese, *Within the Plantation Household: Black and White Women of the Old South*, 38–39, 81; Hagler, "The Ideal Women," 405–18.

23. SMC, Rules and Regulations, Fries Mills Collection, Moravian Archives; Wallace, *Rockdale*, 181–82; Terrill, "Eager Hands," 95; Francis Fries, Diary, 1840–42, Fries Papers, NCDAH.

24. Fox-Genovese, *Within the Plantation Household*, 55–56; Genovese, "Yeoman Farmers in a Slaveholders' Democracy," 331–42; Wyatt-Brown, *Southern*

264 • *Three*   *Manufacturing and Community in Salem*

Honor, 62–87; Escott, *Many Excellent People*, xviii, 3–9; Hahn, *The Roots of Southern Populism*, 32–49; Harris, *Plain Folk and Gentry in a Slave Society: White Liberty and Black Slavery in Augusta's Hinterlands*, 5–7, 94–122; Ford, Jr., *Origins of Southern Radicalism: The South Carolina Upcountry, 1800–1860*, 44–95; Oakes, "From Republicanism to Liberalism: Ideological Change and the Crisis of the Old South," 569; Watson, "Conflict and Collaboration: Yeomen, Slaveholders, and Politics in the Antebellum South," 273–98.

25. Briggs, "Millowners and Workers," 101; Lander, *Textile Industry*, 60–61; Prude, *Coming of Industrial Order*, 93; Wallace, *Rockdale*, 66–67, 172; Dublin, *Women at Work*, 93; Kessler-Harris, *Out of Work: A History of Wage-Earning Women in the United States*, 4; Hagler, "The Ideal Woman," 414–15.

26. Hareven, "Family Time and Industrial Time: Family and Work in a Planned Corporate Town, 1900–1924," 188–93, 196, 202; Prude, *Coming of Industrial Order*, 93.

27. Fries Memorandum Book, March 14, August 23, 28, 1838, Fries Mills Collection, Moravian Archives; Francis Fries Diary, April 18, 1840, Fries Papers, NCDAH; SMC, Board and Wage Books, 1841–49, Fries Mills Collection, Moravian Archives; 1840 Census, Population Schedule manuscript microfilm, Stokes County; 1850 Census, Population Schedule manuscript microfilm, Forsyth County, North Carolina.

28. SMC, Board and Wage Books, 1845–49, Fries Mills Collection, Moravian Archives; Stokes County, List of Taxables, 1840, NCDAH; 1850 Census, Population Schedule manuscript microfilm, Forsyth County, North Carolina.

29. Hareven, "Family Time and Industrial Time," 196; Terrill, "Eager Hands," 93; SMC, Board and Wage Book, 1845, Fries Mills Collection, Moravian Archives; Dublin, *Women at Work*, 41.

30. Dublin, *Women at Work*, 174, 177; Wallace, *Rockdale*, 172; Johnson, *Antebellum North Carolina*, 255.

31. 1840 Census, Population Schedule manuscript microfilm, Stokes County; 1850 Census, Population Schedule manuscript microfilm, Forsyth County, North Carolina; SMC, Board and Wage Book, 1845, Fries Mills Collection, Moravian Archives.

32. SMC, Board and Wage Books, 1841–49, Fries Mills Collection, Moravian Archives; SMC, Board of Directors, July 1, 1841, 80, Fries Mills Collection, Moravian Archives; Briggs, "Millowners and Workers," 89; Shelton, *Mills of Manayunk: Industrialization and Social Conflict in the Philadelphia Region, 1787–1837*, 71; Dublin, *Women at Work*, 66. Massachusetts mills competed aggressively to recruit operatives which drove up wages. The wages of southern operatives were lower because of the availability of women, boys, and girls due to the lack of employment opportunities.

33. SMC, Board and Wage Book, 1845, Fries Mills Collection, Moravian Archives. Mill families purchased their provisions from the Salem Manufacturing Company or from local tradesmen; the mill kept a ledger showing how much each family owed on credit, which was deducted from earnings. When Nathaniel Casey purchased meat from Sanford Shultz, a local butcher, the mill paid Shultz

and kept an account of Casey's purchases which was settled on payday. Many New England mill hands found themselves in similar circumstances, with expenses eating up as much as 95 percent of their income. Some also ended up in debt to their employers. Prude, *Coming of Industrial Order*, 91.

34. Stokes County, List of Taxables, 1837, 1840, 1847, NCDAH; SMC, Board and Wage Book, 1845, Fries Mills Collection, Moravian Archives; 1850 Census, Population Schedule manuscript microfilm, Forsyth County; 1860 Census, Population Schedule manuscript microfilm, Forsyth County, North Carolina.

35. Hareven, "Family Time and Industrial Time," 202; SMC, Board and Wage Book, 1841–49, Fries Mills Collection, Moravian Archives; 1850 Census, Population Schedule manuscript microfilm, Forsyth County, North Carolina.

36. Marriages between operatives linked families in the mill village. Sarah Casey and James Holder who were employed in the Salem Manufacturing Company mill in 1841, married in 1842. Sarah Lumley and William Casey married in 1846 after meeting in the mill. On these occasions, large and long-established families of Salem Manufacturing Company operatives came together to create extensive kinship networks in the mill village. Stokes County, Marriage Bonds, NCDAH; SMC, Board and Wage Books, 1841–49, Fries Mills Collection, Moravian Archives.

37. SMC, Daybook 'C,' 1842, Fries Mills Collection, Moravian Archives. Due to the expense of maintaining boardinghouses for the single hands, the Salem Manufacturing Company converted them to family dwellings and boarded single workers with the families. SMC, Board of Directors, July 1, August 6, 1841, Fries Mills Collection, Moravian Archives; SMC, Board and Wage Book, 1844–45, Fries Mills Collection, Moravian Archives.

38. SMC, Daybook 'C,' 1842, Fries Mills Collection, Moravian Archives; SMC, Board and Wage Books, 1844–45, Fries Mills Collection, Moravian Archives; Wallace, *Rockdale*, 60; SMC, Board and Wage Books, 1841–49, Fries Mills Collection, Moravian Archives; Briggs, "Millowners and Workers," 81–82; Prude, *Coming of Industrial Order*, 116–18.

39. SMC, "Rules and Regulations," Fries Mills Collection, Moravian Archives; Francis Fries Memorandum Book, August 9, 1838, F. and H. Fries Collection, Moravian Archives.

40. SMC, "Rules and Regulations," Fries Mills Collection, Moravian Archives; Kessler-Harris, *Out to Work*, 37–38.

41. Extracts of Memorabilia of Salem Congregation, 1840, in Fries et al., *Records*, 9: 4527–32; SMC, Board and Wage Books, 1841, Fries Mills Collection, Moravian Archives; Friedberg and Hope Diary, March 28, 1838, and Aufseher Collegium, January 24, 1842, in Fries et al., *Records*, 9: 4440, 4660; Surratt, "The Role of Dissent in Community Evolution among Moravians in Salem, 1722–1860," 239; Eaton, *Growth of Southern Civilization*, 12; SMC, Board of Directors, 78, Fries Mills Collection, Moravian Archives; SMC, General Meetings, 45, Fries Mills Collection, Moravian Archives.

42. SMC, Wage Books, 1841–45, Fries Mills Collection, Moravian Archives;

1860 Census, Population Schedule manuscript microfilm, Forsyth County, North Carolina; Lerner, "The Lady and the Mill Girl," 5–15; Lebsock, *Free Women of Petersburg*, 146–94.

43. Memorabilia of the Salem Congregation for the Year 1837, Salem Diary, June 7, 1838, and Memorabilia of the Salem Congregation in the Year 1838, in Fries et al., *Records*, 8: 4259, 4388, and 9: 4374; Fries, "One Hundred Years," 11; SMC, Board of Directors, May 8, 1838, Fries Mills Collection, Moravian Archives.

44. Minutes of the Elders Conference, December 11, 1844, Salem Congregation, Moravian Archives; SMC, Board of Directors, November, 1838, Fries Mills Collection, Moravian Archives.

45. Report of the Negro Church in Salem for 1847, August 29, 1847, in Fries et al., *Records*, 9: 4956.

46. Francis Fries, Memorandum Book, June 23, 27–30, 1838, August 5, 12, 22, 1839, F. and H. Fries Collection, Moravian Archives.

47. SMC, Minutes of the Board of Directors, August 15, 1839, November 10, 1841, Fries Mills Collection, Moravian Archives; SMC, Spinning Room, Time Book, 1845, Fries Mills Collection, Moravian Archives.

48. SMC, Board of Directors, February 7, 1838, Fries Mills Collection, Moravian Archives; SMC, Board and Wage Book, 1841–48, Fries Mills Collection, Moravian Archives; SMC, Memorandum Book, October 28, 1838, Fries Mills Collection, Moravian Archives.

49. SMC, Board of Directors, October 26, 1841, September 22, 1846, Fries Mills Collection, Moravian Archives; SMC, General Meetings, January 29, April 2, October 8, November 5, 1842, October 28, 1843, March 23, 1844, October 11, 1845, September 26, 1846, Fries Mills Collection, Moravian Archives.

50. SMC, General Meetings, October 30, 1841, January 29, April 2, 1842, October 2, 1847, March 18, 1848, Fries Mills Collection, Moravian Archives; SMC, Board of Directors, October 1, 1842, November 18, 1843, September 20, 1847, December 28, 1848, August 8, 1849, Fries Mills Collection, Moravian Archives; SMC, Spinning Room, Time Book, 1842–45, 1847, 1849, Fries Mills Collection, Moravian Archives.

51. Francis Fries Memorandum Book, February 7, March 3, 4, April 12, June 23, 27, 29, 30, August 6, 9, 20, October 1, 1838, July 4, August 26, December 25–30, 1839, F. and H. Fries Collection, Moravian Archives; SMC, Board of Directors, December 16, 1837, August 15, 1839, August 6, November 10, 1841, Fries Mills Collection, Moravian Archives.

52. SMC, Board of Directors, July 21, 1838, July 1, 1841, Fries Mills Collection, Moravian Archives; SMC, General Meetings, August 18, 1841; Aufseher Collegium, January 24, 1842, in Fries et al., *Records*, 9: 4660.

53. Dublin, *Women at Work*, 199–200; Prude, *Coming of Industrial Order*, 183–216; Starobin, "The Economics of Industrial Slavery in the Old South," 131–32, 135, 139–40; Genovese, *The Political Economy of Slavery: Studies in the Economy and Society of the Slave South*, 222; Miller, "The Fabric of Control: Slavery in Antebellum Southern Textile Mills," 475; Linden, "Repercussions of Manufac-

turing," 315; Ransom and Sutch, *One Kind of Freedom: The Economic Consequences of Emancipation*, 2.

54. SMC, Board and Wage Book, 1847, Fries Mills Collection, Moravian Archives; SMC, Board of Directors, April 26, 1847, January 25, 29, 1848, Fries Mills Collection, Moravian Archives.

55. Johnson, "Notes on Manufacturing in Ante-Bellum Georgia," 225.

56. SMC, Board of Directors, July 21, 1838, April 26, October 22, 1847, February 5, 1848, Fries Mills Collection, Moravian Archives.

57. Francis Fries to H. W. Fries, May 25, 1860, Fries Family Papers, Moravian Archives, Winston-Salem, North Carolina; Francis Fries, Diary, January 25–October 23, 1841, F. and H. Fries Collection, Moravian Archives, Winston-Salem, North Carolina; Fries, "Remembrances," 2–3, Fries Papers, NCDAH.

58. Francis Fries, Diary, January 4, 1848, F. and H. Fries Collection, Moravian Archives; Fries, "Remembrances," 3–4, Fries Papers, NCDAH; Terrill, "Eager Hands," 86.

59. SMC, Board of Directors, February 7, 1838, October 28, 1839, September 25, October 31, 1840, Fries Mills Collection, Moravian Archives.

60. SMC, Time Books, 1841–45, Fries Mills Collection, Moravian Archives.

61. In her study of the early mills in Manayunk, Pennsylvania, Cynthia Shelton demonstrates convincingly that the "unreliability" of the operatives there must be considered within the context of the mill owners' failure to meet their responsibilities to their employees in providing steady work and regular wages. Shelton, *Mills of Manayunk*, 15–22.

62. Beatty, "Textile Labor in the North Carolina Piedmont: Mill Owner Images and Worker Response, 1830–1900," 490–95; Briggs, "Millowners and Workers," 50, 119.

63. Beatty, "Textile Labor," 485–503; Briggs, "Millowners and Workers," 93–101.

F O U R   *Community Culture in Antebellum Salem*

1. William Fries to Francis Fries, July 30, 1831, in Fries et al., eds., *Records of the Moravians in North Carolina*, 11 vols., 8: 3998–99.

2. Bender, *Community and Social Change in America*, 96–98; Greene, *Pursuits of Happiness: The Social Development of Early Modern British Colonies and the Formation of American Culture*, vii–xiii. Sean Wilentz has ably demonstrated how public rituals and celebrations reveal patterns of significant meaning for members of a community. Wilentz, "Artisan Republican Festivals and the Rise of Class Conflict in New York City, 1788–1837," 37–77.

3. Of 191 inhabitants of Salem who reported an occupation in the 1850 census, 98 or 51.3 percent were artisans or shopkeepers. 1850 Census, Population Schedule manuscript microfilm, Forsyth County, North Carolina; Extracts of Salem Board Minutes, December, 13, 1824, May 5, 1830, in Fries et al., *Records*, 8: 3709, 3936; Johnson, *Ante-bellum North Carolina: A Social History*, 66; Faler,

Mechanics and Manufacturers in the Early Industrial Revolution: Lynn, Massachusetts, 1780–1860, 29–33.

4. Salem *People's Press*, April 28, 1855; Greene, "Independence, Improvement, and Authority: Toward a Framework of Understanding the Histories of the Southern Backcountry during the American Revolution," 12–14. Jack Greene's ideas on independence and individualism in early American society receive thoughtful and provocative elaboration in *Pursuits of Happiness*, see especially 195–97. Ford, Jr., *Origins of Southern Radicalism: The South Carolina Upcountry, 1800–1860*, 50; Watson, "Conflict and Collaboration: Yeomen, Slaveholders, and Politics in the Antebellum South," 280.

5. In this discussion I have accepted Eric Foner's definition of "mechanic" to include masters and journeymen who likely served an apprenticeship, possessed a skill, and probably owned their tools. Of course, as Foner points out in the case of eighteenth-century mechanics in Philadelphia, mechanics were a diverse lot. Their numbers included entrepreneurs directing highly capitalized enterprises, highly skilled craftsmen in the prestige trades of clockmaking and gold- and silversmithing, and many of the somewhat "inferior craftsmen" in trades like tailoring and shoemaking whose work required less skill. Regardless of the status of their crafts in the emerging market economy, these mechanics were united in their belief that the basis of wealth lay in their skills and in their role as a "producing class." Foner, *Tom Paine and Revolutionary America*, 10, 28, 41; John Henry Leinbach Diary, October 28, 1833, John Henry Leinbach Family Papers, Moravian Archives, Winston-Salem, North Carolina.

6. Johnson, *Ante-bellum North Carolina*, 165–66; Linden, "Repercussions of Manufacturing in the Antebellum South," 322; Foner, *History of the Labor Movement in the United States*, vol. 1, 249, 261–64; Schmidt, ed., *The Greenwood Encyclopedia of American Institutions: Fraternal Organizations*, 339–40; *People's Press*, September 6, 1851.

7. *People's Press*, December 30, 1854, March 19, 1858, April 8, 1859, February 13, 20, 1873; 1850 Census, Population Schedule manuscript microfilm, Forsyth County, North Carolina.

8. *People's Press*, May 31, 1851, July 28, 1864, January 26, 1865. Of the 8 members identified from resolutions of condolence in the *People's Press*, there were 4 artisans, 1 merchant, 1 lawyer, 1 farmer, 1 occupation unknown. Of the 4 artisans, 2 were listed as manufacturers in the census of manufacturers in 1850 and 1860. 1850 Census, Population Schedule manuscript microfilm, Forsyth County, North Carolina; 1850 Census, Manufacturing Schedule manuscript microfilm, Forsyth County, North Carolina; 1860 Census, Manufacturing Schedule, Forsyth County, North Carolina; 1860 Census, Population Schedule manuscript microfilm, Forsyth County, North Carolina.

9. Johnson, *Ante-bellum North Carolina*, 162; *People's Press*, July 5, 12, 1851, July 9, 1853.

10. This is readily apparent when the names of the antebellum mill workers of the Salem Manufacturing Company and the F. and H. Fries Company are listed in the 1870 and 1880 censuses as cotton and wool mill workers. These

workers persisted in the mills over the course of their lives and thus constituted a distinct segment of the working class as industrial laborers.

11. Aufseher Collegium, July 12, 1843, in Fries et al., *Records*, 9: 4728; Clewell, *History of Wachovia in North Carolina*, 272; Fries, "Salem Congregation Diacony," 34; *People's Press*, June 17, 1854, May 5, 1855, October 2, 1857. Of the 7 officers elected in 1857, 3 were artisans, 1 a merchant, 1 a clerk, and 2 whose occupations were unknown. They were all in their twenties or early thirties. 1850 Census, Population Schedule manuscript microfilm, Forsyth County, North Carolina.

12. Johnson, *Ante-bellum North Carolina*, 102; Extracts of the Minutes of the Friedberg Committee, February 12, 1839, and Salem Congregation Diary, October 8, 1847, October 11, 1851, in Fries et al., *Records*, 9: 4511, 4952, 10: 5609; Leinbach Diary, October 29, 1831, John Henry Leinbach Family Papers, Moravian Archives; Foner, *Tom Paine*, 64.

13. Aufseher Collegium, March 25, September 26, 1839, March 3, 1846, Extracts of Reports of the Land Arbeiter Conferenz, October 3, 1839, and Minutes of the Heads of Households and Master Workmen, December 9, 14, 1852, in Fries et al., *Records*, 9: 4476, 4483, 4490, 4900, 11: 5745–46.

14. Salem Congregation Diary, December 9, 1829, February 22, April 17, 1842, May 6, 1845, Extracts of the Committee of the Congregation in Bethania, February 22, April 17, 1841, in Fries et al., *Records*, 8: 3875, 9: 4645–46, 4834; Minutes of the Elders Conference, February 9, 23, 1842, Salem Congregation Records, Moravian Archives, Winston-Salem, North Carolina; *People's Press*, February 8, 22, March 1, June 21, October 4, September 27, 1851, January 4, 25, 1856; North Carolina Sons of Temperance, *Proceedings of the Grand Division of North Carolina. Sons of Temperance, 1851*. North Carolina Collection, University of North Carolina at Chapel Hill; North Carolina Sons of Temperance, *Constitutions of the Order of the Sons of Temperance*, 1845, 11, North Carolina Collection, University of North Carolina at Chapel Hill; 1850 Census, Population Schedule manuscript microfilm, Forsyth County, North Carolina; 1860 Census, Population Schedule manuscript microfilm, Forsyth County, North Carolina. Of the 16 officers and representatives to the Grand Division, there were 3 merchants, 5 mechanics, 3 clerks, 2 professionals, 1 farmer, 1 minister, and 1 cotton mill superintendent. All were property owners. Johnson, *Ante-bellum North Carolina*, 168–71; Eaton, *The Growth of Southern Civilization, 1790–1860*, 290.

15. Deems, "What It Has Done, and What We Must Do." Delivered before the Grand Division of the Order of the Sons of Temperance of North Carolina, October 1847; Loveland, *Southern Evangelicals and the Social Order, 1800–1860*, 134–35; Doub, *Address Delivered before the Grand Division of North Carolina. Sons of Temperance. At the October Session. 1852*.

16. *People's Press*, February 24, 1855; Tyrell, *Sobering Up: From Temperance to Prohibition in Antebellum America, 1800–1860*, 4–7; Lender and Martin, *Drinking in America: A History*, 58–66; Rorabaugh, *The Alcoholic Republic: An American Tradition*, 187–222.

17. Rorabaugh, *The Alcoholic Republic*, 189–91; Johnson, *Ante-bellum North*

Carolina, 343; Mathews, *Religion in the Old South,* xiv; idem, "The Second Great Awakening as an Organizing Process, 1780–1830," 23–43; Nye, *Society and Culture in America, 1830–1860,* 285–86, 291; McLoughlin, *Revivals, Awakenings and Reform: An Essay on Religion and Social Change in America, 1607–1977,* 2–8; Boles, *The Great Revival, 1787–1805,* 166–67; Loveland, *Southern Evangelicals,* 69, 135.

18. Relying on the memoirs of prominent evangelical churchmen and a few scattered church records, Donald Mathews found that the majority of evangelicals in the South were yeoman farmers who owned small farms with maybe one or two slaves. John Boles found that the majority were common people who lived a life of hard work and poverty. Mathews, *Religion,* 36–38; Boles, *Great Revival,* 169–70. Methodists and Baptists were aggressive revivalists from 1846 to 1849, but in the early and mid-1850s the Methodists were especially active, and by 1860 the Methodists were the largest denomination in Forsyth County as fourteen of the twenty-seven congregations in the county were Methodist. The Methodist church in particular won the common people by its disregard of ritual and its emphasis on camp meetings, prayers, humanitarianism, religious reform, and education. Loveland, *Southern Evangelicals,* 68; 1850 Census, Social Statistics manuscript microfilm, Forsyth County, North Carolina; 1860 Census, Social Statistics manuscript microfilm, Forsyth County, North Carolina; Lefler and Newsome, *North Carolina: A History of a Southern State,* 392–93; Faler, *Mechanics and Manufacturers,* 101–3.

19. Francis Fries to Henry Fries, June 20, 1860, Francis Fries Papers, Southern Historical Collection, University of North Carolina at Chapel Hill, Chapel Hill, North Carolina; *People's Press,* February 4, 1859.

20. Salem Congregation Diary, September 3, 1826, September 5, 19, 1830, December 4, 1841, Extracts of the Diary of Bethania, September 3, 1830, September 7, 1833, October 27, 1841, Extracts from Diary of Bethania and Bethabara, August 19, 1838, Extracts from Friedberg and Hope Diary, September 9, 1838, and Extracts of Report of the Little Negro Congregation in and around Salem, August, 1846, in Fries et al., *Records,* 8: 3770, 3924–25, 3948, and 9: 4106, 4432, 4444, 4589, 4626, 4914.

21. Leinbach Diary, August 21, 1831, John Henry Leinbach Family Papers, Moravian Archives.

22. Mathews, *Religion,* 14–15, 70. Rhys Isaac has shown that in late eighteenth-century Virginia evangelical religion offered a vehicle for the rejection of the values, life-style, and authority of elites by southerners occupying the lower ranks of society and seeking respect and legitimacy for their ways of life and values. Isaac, *The Transformation of Virginia, 1740–1810,* 161–77.

23. Mathews, *Religion,* 24.

24. Bender, *Community and Social Change,* 102.

25. *People's Press,* March 20, September 11, 1852, July 8, 1854, June 22, 1855, April 11, 1856, June 25, 1858; Hugh B. Johnston to Benjamin F. Bynum, August 18, 1840, in Benjamin Franklin Bynum Papers, Manuscript Department, Duke University Library, Durham, North Carolina; Fries et al., *Forsyth: The History of a County on the March,* 129; Wooster, *Politicians, Planters, and Plain Folk: Courthouse and Statehouse in the Upper South, 1850–1860,* 66–67; Sydnor, *Development of South-*

ern Sectionalism, 1819–1848, 319; Chambers and Burnham, *The American Party Systems: Stages of Political Development,* 11; Norton, *The Democratic Party in Antebellum North Carolina, 1835–1861,* 38; Johnson, *Ante-bellum North Carolina,* 149.

26. Aufseher Collegium, January 13, 1840, and Salem Congregation Diary, August 7, 1856, in Fries et al., *Records,* 9: 4535, and 11: 6008.

27. Chambers and Burnham, *American Party Systems,* 13; Jeffrey, *State Parties and National Politics: North Carolina, 1815–1861,* 7, 65, 118, 121, 142; Oakes, "From Republicanism to Liberalism: Ideological Change and the Crisis of the Old South," 569; Ashworth, *"Agrarians" and "Aristocrats": Party Political Ideology in the United States, 1837–1846,* 1.

28. *People's Press,* December 20, 1851, May 8, 1852, July 15, 1854; Jeffrey, *State Parties,* 68–71, 118, 144–57; Ashworth, *"Agrarians" and "Aristocrats,"* 52–53, 62–64, 73; Kruman, *Parties and Politics in North Carolina, 1836–1865,* 16–17.

29. These statistics were obtained for men identified in the *People's Press* as prominent Whigs who were elected to offices within the party and who served as delegates to district and state party conventions. *People's Press,* December 20, 1851. 1850 Census, Agriculture Schedule manuscript microfilm, Forsyth County, North Carolina; 1850 Census, Population Schedule manuscript microfilm, Forsyth County, North Carolina; 1850 Census, Slave Schedule manuscript microfilm, Forsyth County, North Carolina; Oakes, "From Republicanism to Liberalism," 569.

30. Oakes, "From Republicanism to Liberalism," 562–69.

31. Ashworth, *"Agrarians" and "Aristocrats,"* 30–34; Jeffrey, *State Parties,* 118; *Carolina Watchman,* October 20, 1832, June 14, 1834; *People's Press,* May 22, 29, 1852.

32. *People's Press,* March 20, 1852; 1850 Census, Population Schedule manuscript microfilm, Forsyth County, North Carolina; 1850 Census, Slave Schedule manuscript microfilm, Forsyth County, North Carolina; Kruman, *Parties and Politics,* 25–26; Wooster, *Politicians, Planters, and Plain Folk,* 47–49.

33. Under the 1776 state constitution, only free white adult males who owned a freehold of fifty acres could vote for the state senate. From the late 1830s the Democrats had advocated free and equal suffrage. For the Democrats free suffrage was an issue of equality among citizens of a republic. Reserving the election of state senators to citizens who owned a freehold represented a special privilege that was denied to one group of citizens because of their lack of wealth. Seizing the free suffrage issue, the Democratic party presented itself as the defender of the rights of the common man against the pretensions and special privileges of the wealthy who usually belonged to the Whig party. Free suffrage, thus, was particularly popular in the western counties where small farms predominated. Though it failed in 1852, the free suffrage amendment passed the legislature in 1854 and 1856. In 1857, the free suffrage amendment was ratified by the electorate. Norton, *Democratic Party,* 8, 43, 47–49, 135–37, 166, 169–72, 179–80; Lefler and Newsome, *North Carolina,* 359; Pegg, *The Whig Party in North Carolina,* 114–17, 156–57, 161–63; Johnson, *Ante-bellum North Carolina,* 36; *People's Press,* May 8, 29, June 26, 1852.

34. *People's Press,* August 7, 1852, August 5, 1854, August 5, 1856.

272 • *Four   Community Culture in Antebellum Salem*

35. Cole, *The Whig Party in the South*, 94, 209–10.

36. By the mid-1850s the Whig party in North Carolina was in disarray and some Democrats were frustrated with the politics of their state and national parties. In the summer of 1854 the Know-Nothing movement swept North Carolina with its nativist appeal to stem the flow of immigrants into the United States and warnings against the influence of the Catholic church in elections. By the end of 1855 the Know-Nothing movement and its political organization, the American party, had taken over the Whig party in North Carolina. The Democratic party immediately and correctly characterized the American party as nothing more than the Whig party in disguise. Participants in the Forsyth County American party bear out the Democratic claim. Of the membership in the Forsyth County American party listed in the *People's Press*, none can be identified as Democrats. After the congressional elections of 1857 in which the American party suffered disastrous losses, North Carolinians abandoned the party. The Whigs revived in North Carolina in 1858 as an opposition party made up of former Whig/Americans and disgruntled Democrats who abandoned their party. Jeffrey, *State Parties*, 203–4, 244–63, 271–73; Wooster, *Politicians, Planters, and Plain Folk*, 53; Norton, *Democratic Party*, 43, 47–48, 179–80; *People's Press*, February 3, August 17, 1855, April 11, 1856, April 10, 1857, March 20, 1852, February 15, March 21, April 18, 1856.

37. Francis Fries to J. F. Shaffner, December 23, 1859, Shaffner-Fries Correspondence, Moravian Archives, Winston-Salem, North Carolina; *People's Press*, July 29, 1859.

38. *Laws of the State of North Carolina. Passed by the General Assembly at the Session of 1848–49*, 58–59; in 1840, the district that was reorganized as the new county had 7,805 residents. *Compendium of the Sixth Census. 1840. The Seventh Census of the United States. 1850. Statistical View Compendium;* in 1835 North Carolina was composed of sixty-five counties. In 1861 there were eighty-nine counties. Thomas E. Jeffrey, "County Division: A Forgotten Issue in Antebellum North Carolina Politics, Part I," 314–54.

39. *Laws of the State of North Carolina. 1848–49*, 59–66; Extracts of the Minutes of the Wachovia Provinzial Helfer Conferenz in Salem for the Year 1849 (hereafter cited as Provinzial Helfer Conferenz), April 27, 1849, Extract of the Minutes of the Aufseher Collegium in Salem for the Year 1849 (hereafter cited as Aufseher Collegium), January 29, February 2, March 30, April 10, 1849, and Extract of the Minutes of the Salem Congregation Council for the Year 1849 (hereafter cited as Salem Congregation Council), February 5, March 31, 1849, in Fries et al., *Records*, 10: 5313, 5335, 5339–40, 5404–6; *Laws of the State of North Carolina. Passed by the General Assembly at the Session of 1850–51*, 732.

40. Extract of Memorabilia of the Salem Congregation for the Year 1849, in Fries et al., *Records*, 10: 5391.

41. Salem Congregation Council, February 5, 1849, and Extract of the Memorabilia of the Salem Congregation for the Year 1849, in Fries et al., *Records*, 10: 5391, 5404; Johnson, *Ante-bellum North Carolina*, 117, 148.

42. Fries et al., *Forsyth*, 124–25; Fries, *Forsyth: A County on the March*, 11; Johnson, *Ante-bellum North Carolina*, 116.

43. *People's Press*, February 8, April 5, 1851, February 4, 1854.

44. *People's Press*, December 11, 1852, September 24, 1853, August 19, 1854; *Laws of the State of North Carolina. Passed by the General Assembly at the Session of 1852*, 449; *Private Laws of the State of North Carolina. Passed by the General Assembly at Its Session of 1854–55*, 184, 306–8.

45. *People's Press*, January 8, 1858, January 7, April 8, 1859, January 11, April 12, 1861; R. L. Patterson Diary, January 2, 1860, Patterson Papers, North Carolina Division of Archives and History, Raleigh, North Carolina; Salem Diary, January 5, 1841, January 10, 1845, Aufseher Collegium, January 13, 1851, and Minutes of the Salem Congregation Council, January 10, 1853, in Fries et al., *Records*, 9: 4580, 4831, 10: 5566–67, 11: 5831; 1850 Census, Population Schedule manuscript microfilm, Forsyth County, North Carolina; 1850 Census, Slave Schedule manuscript microfilm, Forsyth County, North Carolina; 1860 Census, Population Schedule manuscript microfilm, Forsyth County, North Carolina; 1860 Census, Slave Schedule manuscript microfilm, Forsyth County, North Carolina; Fries et al., *Forsyth*, 130; Weber, "Class, Status, Party," 182.

46. *People's Press*, November 14, 1856.

47. Aufseher Collegium, April 24, 1854, October 22, 1855, in Fries et al., *Records*, 11: 5875, 5940.

48. Aufseher Collegium, January 14, January 21, 1856, in Fries et al., *Records*, 11: 5977–78.

49. Aufseher Collegium, January 28, January 31, 1856, in Fries et al., *Records*, 11: 5980–82; Provinzial Helfer Conferenz, November 18, 1856, in Fries et al., *Records*, 11: 5975; *People's Press*, November 28, 1856.

50. Aufseher Collegium, January 31, 1856, Extracts of the Diary of the Salem Congregation for the Year 1852, and Provinzial Helfer Conferenz, November 18, 1856, in Fries et al., *Records*, 11: 5743–44, 5975, 5981; "Minutes of the Town Meeting Held in Salem Town Hall, Saturday Evening, November 22, 1856," General Assembly Session Records, November 1856–February, 1857, Box 10, North Carolina Division of Archives and History, Raleigh, North Carolina; *Public Laws of the State of North Carolina. Passed by the General Assembly at Its Session of 1856–57*, 129; *People's Press*, November 28, 1856.

51. Bender, *Community and Social Change*, 96–97; Greene, *Pursuits of Happiness*, xii–xiii.

F I V E   *The Community at War*

1. Escott, *Many Excellent People: Power and Privilege in North Carolina, 1850–1890*, 32.

2. Butts, "A Challenge to Planter Rule: The Controversy over Ad Valorem Taxation of Slaves in North Carolina," Ph.D. diss., Duke University, 1978, 33, 50; Kruman, *Parties and Politics in North Carolina, 1836–1865*, 190–93; Salem *People's Press*, March 16, 23, 1860; H. W. Fries to Francis Fries, June 11, 1860, Patterson Papers, North Carolina Division of Archives and History, Raleigh, North Carolina.

3. Kruman, *Parties and Politics*, 195–96; *People's Press*, August 10, 1860.

4. Kruman, *Parties and Politics*, 180–81; *People's Press*, March 23, 1860.

5. *People's Press*, March 16, 1860; Kruman, *Parties and Politics*, 197; Pegg, *The Whig Party in North Carolina*, 182.

6. Potter, *The Impending Crisis, 1848–1861*, 405–17; Kruman, *Parties and Politics*, 196; *People's Press*, March 16, 1860.

7. Salem *Western Sentinel*, October 5, 1860; *People's Press*, November 2, 1860; Rufus Lenoir Patterson to J. W. Alspaugh, October 3, 1860, Patterson Papers, NCDAH; William A. Lash to John F. Poindexter, November 27, 1860, John F. Poindexter Papers, Manuscripts Department, Duke University Library, Durham, North Carolina. There is some question whether North Carolinians actually identified Breckinridge with secession or merely as the candidate of his party. Those areas of the state that normally voted Democratic did so again in 1860, giving Breckinridge a narrow victory and thus lending credence to the belief that few in North Carolina regarded a vote for Breckinridge as a vote for secession. Furthermore, there is a high correlation between the vote in November and the August gubernatorial election, meaning that North Carolinians tended to vote with the same party in November that they did in August. Escott, *After Secession: Jefferson Davis and the Failure of Confederate Nationalism*, 22–23; Kruman, *Parties and Politics*, 197–99.

8. *People's Press*, November 2, 1860; Rufus Patterson to J. W. Alspaugh, October 3, 1860, Patterson Papers, NCDAH; Rufus Lenoir Patterson Diary, January 2, 1860, Patterson Papers, NCDAH; Francis Fries to J. F. Shaffner, January 11, 15, 1860, Fries and Shaffner Family Papers, Southern Historical Collection, University of North Carolina at Chapel Hill, Chapel Hill, North Carolina.

9. *People's Press*, August 6, 1858, August 10, 1860, December 7, 1860.

10. Escott, *Many Excellent People*, 33–34; Holt, *The Political Crisis of the 1850s*, 219–59, especially 249–51; Kruman, *Parties and Politics*, 180–221. Thomas Jeffrey offers a somewhat qualified view of the strength of two-party competition in North Carolina on the eve of secession. Jeffrey, *State Parties and National Politics: North Carolina, 1815–1861*, 281–312.

11. According to Carl Degler, the Bell candidacy testified to the strength of resistance to secession. Degler, *The Other South: Southern Dissenters in the Nineteenth Century*, 159; Rufus Patterson to J. W. Alspaugh, October 3, 1860, Patterson Papers, NCDAH; B. L. Bitting to John F. Poindexter, November 30, 1860, John F. Poindexter Papers, Manuscripts Department, Duke University Library.

12. *People's Press*, January 4, 1861.

13. Escott, *After Secession*, 27; Kruman, *Parties and Politics*, 201–10; Jeffrey, *State Parties*, 308–9; *People's Press*, March 15, 1861.

14. *People's Press*, March 8, 15, 1861; Kruman found a low correlation (a coefficient of .42) between the proportion of slaves in a county and that county's vote on secession, suggesting little general relationship between the two. But, in studying the number of counties that voted for or against secession, he found that twenty-four of twenty-five secessionist counties had populations containing at least 25 percent slaves. In Forsyth County slaves made up only 13.9 percent of

the population. Kruman, *Parties and Politics*, 211–13; *Report of the United States in 1860. Compiled from the Original Returns of the Eighth Census.*

15. *People's Press*, April 12, 1861; McPherson, *Ordeal by Fire: The Civil War and the Reconstruction*, 145–48.

16. 1860 Census, Population Schedule manuscript microfilm, Forsyth County, North Carolina; 1860 Census, Slave Schedule manuscript microfilm, Forsyth County, North Carolina; McPherson, *Battle Cry of Freedom: The Civil War Era*, 309–10.

17. McPherson, *Battle Cry*, 310–11. For the motivations of Confederate soldiers see Mitchell, *Civil War Soldiers: Their Expectations and Their Experiences*, 1–11; Kruman, "Dissent in the Confederacy: The North Carolina Experience," 295; Escott, *After Secession*, 37–40, 227; Degler, *The Other South*, 167; Martha Wilson to Julia Jones, May 5, 1862, Jones Family Papers, Southern Historical Collection, University of North Carolina at Chapel Hill; *People's Press*, May 3, 1861.

18. Kruman, *Parties and Politics*, 219–20; Louise Patterson to Mrs. S. F. Patterson, May 27, 1861, Samuel Finley Patterson Papers, Manuscripts Department, Duke University Library, Durham, North Carolina.

19. McPherson, *Ordeal by Fire*, 166; idem, *Battle Cry*, 317–18.

20. *People's Press*, May 3, 17, June 21, 1861.

21. F. and H. Fries Company, Daybook #12, May 22–October 28, 1861, Fries Mills Collection, Moravian Archives, Winston-Salem, North Carolina; Escott, *After Secession*, 104–9.

22. *People's Press*, July 17, 1863; S. C. James to Carrie Fries, June 21, 1862, Fries and Shaffner Family Papers, Southern Historical Collection, University of North Carolina at Chapel Hill; Escott, *After Secession*, 108–9; Wiley, *Plain People of the Confederacy*, 39; Forsyth County, County Court of Pleas and Quarter Sessions, vol. 2, 1849–62, 408, 479, 498, and vol. 3, 1863–68, 4, 32, 34, 41–42, 52, 58–59, 68, North Carolina Division of Archives and History, Raleigh, North Carolina.

23. Forsyth County, County Court of Pleas and Quarter Sessions, vol. 3, 1863–68, 41–42, NCDAH; *People's Press*, July 17, 1863; Martha Wilson to Julia Jones, July 1, 1862, Jones Family Papers, Southern Historical Collection, University of North Carolina at Chapel Hill.

24. J. C. Zimmerman to M. A. Zimmerman, August 4, October 20, 27, 1862, August 16, 1863, James C. Zimmerman Papers, Manuscripts Department, Duke University Library, Durham, North Carolina.

25. Minutes of the Wachovia Provinzial Aeltesten Conferenz in Salem for the Year 1864, November 10, 1864, in Fries et al., eds., *The Records of the Moravians in North Carolina*, 11 vols., 11: 6077; Lerner, "Money, Prices, and Wages in the Confederacy," 23–24, 33; Louise Patterson to Mrs. S. F. Patterson, May 27, 1861, Samuel Finley Patterson Papers, Manuscripts Department, Duke University Library; Mary Denke to Julia Jones, October 8, 1861, Jones Family Papers, Southern Historical Collection, University of North Carolina at Chapel Hill, Chapel Hill, North Carolina; F. and H. Fries Company, Daybook #13, August 28, 30, 1862, Daybook #12, January 2, March 27, 1865, loose sheets, Fries Mills Collection, Moravian Archives, Winston-Salem, North Carolina; Confederate

States of America, War Department, "Circular to the Farmers and Citizens of Forsyth County, North Carolina," Broadside Collection, Duke University Library, Durham, North Carolina.

26. "Circular to the Farmers and Citizens of Forsyth County," Broadside Collection, Duke University Library; Wiley, *Plain People*, 41.

27. F. and H. Fries Company, Daybook #13, August 28, 30, 1862, Fries Mills Collection, Moravian Archives; *People's Press*, January 23–24, December 12, 1862, March 6, 1863; Rufus Patterson to S. F. Patterson, February 6, 1862, Samuel Finley Patterson Papers, Manuscripts Department, Duke University Library; Griffin, "North Carolina," 107–8; Francis Fries to Captain C. W. Garrett, December 5, 1862, Thomas Marritt Pittman Papers, North Carolina Division of Archives and History, Raleigh, North Carolina; Wiley, *Plain People*, 36–38.

28. *People's Press*, January 30, March 6, May 22, 1863; Wiley, *Plain People*, 48–49; Tatum, *Disloyalty in the Confederacy*, 22; Escott, "The Moral Economy of the Crowd in Confederate North Carolina," 9; Fries, "Remembrance of Civil War Times," 10–15; Fries Papers, North Carolina Division of Archives and History, Raleigh, North Carolina; Flyer Issued by Henry W. Fries, April 14, 1865, Civil War and Reconstruction Papers, Moravian Archives, Winston-Salem, North Carolina.

29. Escott, "Moral Economy," 2–3, 7.

30. Writing about the economic and social transformation of England in the eighteenth century, E. P. Thompson believed that mob actions were characterized by "unsuspected complexities" because "behind every such form of popular direct action some legitimizing notion of right is to be found." Thompson, *The Making of the English Working Class*, 65–68; Prude, *Coming of Industrial Order: Town and Factory Life in Rural Massachusetts, 1810–1860*, 13; Escott, *After Secession*, 124; Escott, "Moral Economy," 2–3.

31. Kruman, "Dissent," 294–302; Tatum, *Disloyalty in the Confederacy*, 19–20, 111; Escott, *After Secession*, 68, 120–21; Escott, *Many Excellent People*, 36–44; *People's Press*, July 31, 1863.

32. J. C. Zimmerman to M. A. Zimmerman, November 16, 1862, and J. C. Zimmerman to A. H. Spease, May 2, 1864, James C. Zimmerman Papers, Manuscripts Department, Duke University Library; Letter from G. W. Poindexter, April 27, 1863, John F. Poindexter Papers, Manuscripts Department, Duke University Library.

33. Degler, *The Other South*, 173; Tatum, *Disloyalty*, 123, 134–35; Aumen and Scarboro, "The Heroes of America in Civil War North Carolina," 333, 345; *The War of the Rebellion: A Compilation of the Official Records of the Union and Confederate Armies*. Series IV, Volume III, 802–20.

34. J. F. Shaffner to Carrie Fries, April 29, 1862, February 1, 1863, Fries and Shaffner Family Papers, Southern Historical Collection, University of North Carolina at Chapel Hill; Carrie Fries to J. F. Shaffner, March 19, 1862, Fries and Shaffner Family Papers, Southern Historical Collection, University of North Carolina at Chapel Hill; J. C. Zimmerman to M. A. Zimmerman, November 16, 1862, James C. Zimmerman Papers, Manuscripts Department, Duke University Library.

35. J. C. Zimmerman to M. A. Zimmerman, July 30, 1863, James C. Zimmerman Papers, Manuscripts Department, Duke University Library; Escott, *Many Excellent People*, 32.

36. Wiley, *Plain People*, 29–30; *People's Press*, January 30, August 27, 1863; Escott, *After Secession*, 200; Tatum, *Disloyalty*, 120–22.

37. *People's Press*, August 27, September 24, 1863.

38. Tatum, *Disloyalty*, 129; Kruman, *Parties and Politics*, 259–64.

39. *People's Press*, August 18, 1864; John W. Fries to Rufus Patterson, August 21, 1864, Patterson Papers, NCDAH.

40. J. C. Zimmerman to A. H. Spease, March 27, 1865, James C. Zimmerman Papers, Manuscripts Department, Duke University Library; *People's Press*, May 27, 1865.

s i x *Postbellum Winston and Salem*

1. Shore, *Southern Capitalists: The Ideological Leadership of an Elite, 1832–1885*, 114–19.

2. Salem *People's Press*, April 28, 1866, February 6, 1873; Annual Message to the General Assembly of Governor Tod R. Caldwell, November 20, 1871, North Carolina Governors' Papers, North Carolina Division of Archives and History, Raleigh, North Carolina.

3. Rufus L. Patterson to Samuel F. Patterson, August 30, 1868, Samuel Finley Patterson Papers, Manuscripts Department, Duke University Library, Durham, North Carolina; *People's Press*, August 18, 1871, March 20, 1873; Winston *Union Republican*, January 6, 1876; Winston *Leader*, January 28, 1879; North Carolina, vol. 10, 463–553, R. G. Dun and Company Collection, Baker Library, Harvard University Graduate School of Business Administration, Cambridge, Massachusetts. A 20 percent sample (n = 67) was drawn from names listed in vol. 10, North Carolina, Forsyth County. The Credit Reporting Ledgers of the R. G. Dun Mercantile Agency provided important information on business from the late 1840s through the 1880s. These ledgers describe for each business capital investment, partnerships, the extent and nature of operations, credit ratings, and, in many cases, the moral character of the principals in the firm. Roger Ransom and Richard Sutch describe the Dun Collection as "the most comprehensive source of information on businesses in the South during the mid-nineteenth century." Ransom and Sutch, *One Kind of Freedom: The Economic Consequences of Emancipation*, 306–15.

4. *People's Press*, April 28, 1866; Lefler and Newsome, *North Carolina: A History of a Southern State*, 475; Gaston, *The New South Creed: A Study in Southern Mythmaking*, 7; Woodward, *Origins of the New South, 1877–1913*, 140; Roark, *Masters without Slaves: Southern Planters in the Civil War and Reconstruction*, 179–80; Billings, *Planters and the Making of a "New South"; Class, Politics, and Development in North Carolina, 1865–1900*, 61, 101; Shore, *Southern Capitalists*, 100–101; Doyle, *New Men, New Cities, New South: Atlanta, Nashville, Charleston, Mobile, 1860–1910*, xiii–xiv; Ransom and Sutch, *One Kind of Freedom*, 41–42, 53.

5. *People's Press*, February 7, 1868, March 20, July 17, 1873; Fries et al., *Forsyth: The History of a County on the March*, 179; Clewell, *History of Wachovia in North Carolina*, 259; Trelease, *The North Carolina Railroad, 1849–1871, and the Modernization of North Carolina*, 313–14.

6. Hahn, "The 'Unmaking' of the Southern Yeomanry: The Transformation of the Georgia Upcountry, 1860–1890," 180. Hahn provides an elaborate analysis of the development of market relations in the piedmont in *The Roots of Southern Populism: Yeoman Farmers and the Transformation of the Georgia Upcountry, 1850–1890*.

7. *Statistical View of the United States; Compendium of the Seventh Census. 1850; Statistics of the Population of the United States. Ninth Census. Volume 1. 1870; Statistics of the Population of the United States at the Tenth Census. 1880; Report on the Statistics of Agriculture in the United States, Eleventh Census, 1890; Report on the Population of the United States at the Eleventh Census. Part 1. 1890*. A sample of every fifth name (n = 187) was drawn from the manuscript of the 1850 Census, Agriculture schedule. Another sample of every tenth name (n = 187) was drawn from the manuscript of the 1880 Census, Agriculture. Daniel, *Breaking the Land: The Transformation of Cotton, Tobacco, and Rice Cultures since 1880*, 24; Tilley, *The Bright Tobacco Industry, 1860–1929*, 90, 94.

8. *Leader*, May 20, 1879.

9. *People's Press*, April 23, 1885, June 24, 1886, April 29, 1886; Carlton, "The Revolution from Above: The National Market and the Beginnings of Industrialization in North Carolina," 457–59; Branson, *Branson's North Carolina Business Directory*, 1872, 92–95, 1884, 300–305; Prude, *The Coming of Industrial Order: Town and Factory Life in Rural Massachusetts, 1810–1860*, 100. Data in Table 6.2 were compiled from the 1850 Census, Population Schedule manuscript microfilm, Forsyth County, North Carolina; 1850 Census, Manufacturing Schedule manuscript microfilm, Forsyth County, North Carolina.

10. Carlton, "Revolution from Above," 445–49, 461–63, 474; Cobb, "Beyond Planters and Industrialists: New Perspectives on the New South, " 53–54; idem, *Industrialization and Southern Society, 1877–1984*, 26.

11. North Carolina, vol. 10, 472, 478, 486, 490, 492, R. G. Dun and Company Collection, Baker Library, Harvard University Graduate School of Business Administration, Cambridge, Massachusetts; *Branson's North Carolina Business Directory*, 1868, 43; *Southern Business Guide, 1885–1886*, 693–706; Carlton, "Revolution from Above," 458–59; Woodward, *Origins of the New South*, 183; Ransom and Sutch, *One Kind of Freedom*, 110–15.

12. Griffin and Standard, "The Cotton Textile Industry in Antebellum North Carolina, Part II: An Era of Boom and Consolidation, 1830–1860," 160.

13. Fries et al., *Forsyth*, 195; John W. Fries, "Reminiscences of Confederate Days," Fries Papers, 1861–65, North Carolina Division of Archives and History, Raleigh, North Carolina; Daybook #15, August 25, 1869, Daybook #19, January 22, 1875, F. and H. Fries Collection, Moravian Archives, Winston-Salem, North Carolina; *People's Press*, October 20, 1871, March 4, 1880, September 1, 15, 1881, May 29, 1884, December 9, 1886, February 10, March 31, and August 25, 1887; *Union Republican*, June 17, 1886, March 31, April 28, July 28, 1887; Inquiry

from the Chief of the Bureau of Statistics, United States Treasury Department, Washington, April 17, 1886, Calvin Henderson Wiley Papers, Southern Historical Collection, University of North Carolina at Chapel Hill, Chapel Hill, North Carolina; 1870 Census, Manufacturing Schedule microfilm; *Branson's North Carolina Business Directory*, 1884, 300–305.

14. Carlton, "Revolution from Above," 461–63; Tilley, *Bright Tobacco Industry*, 11, 36, 548.

15. Fries et al., *Forsyth*, 179–80; Clewell, *History of Wachovia*, 259; Tilley, *R. J. Reynolds Tobacco Company*, 57; idem, *Bright Tobacco Industry*, 210, 260, 305, 561, 565.

16. Hardin Reynolds owned plantations of thousands of acres in Patrick and Stokes counties, North Carolina. Before the war Hardin Reynolds owned forty-nine slaves who grew tobacco as the principal crop of the plantations. Tilley, *R. J. Reynolds Tobacco Company*, 5–10; Photocopy of microfilm of Bristol (Va.) *Herald Courier* interview with R. J. Reynolds, May 23, 1915, attached to letter from Nannie May Tilley to Mrs. Nancy Reynolds, February 8, 1971, Reynolds Family Papers, Baptist Historical Collection, Wake Forest University Library, Winston-Salem, North Carolina.

17. Tilley, *Bright Tobacco Industry*, 210, 260, 305, 561; Fries et al., *Forsyth*, 180; *Union Republican*, November 4, 1886. "Chewing tobacco" included four kinds of tobacco products: "Plug" referred to a pressed rectangular pancake of Bright tobacco, usually flavored with honey or licorice; "Navy" also was a rectangular pancake but made of Burley tobacco and highly flavored; "Twist" was a rope braid of tobacco; "Fine-cut" was shredded, uncompressed leaf, much like smoking tobacco. Winston factories concentrated on the manufacture of plugs and twists. Heimann, *Tobacco and Americans*, 94, 146, 150, 174–75; *Leader*, May 6, 1879; North Carolina, vol. 10, 524, 528, R. G. Dun and Company Collection, Baker Library, Harvard University Graduate School of Business Administration.

18. Tilley, *Bright Tobacco Industry*, 496, 517, 580–82. Only eight of fifty-one North Carolina plug factories in 1882 used hydraulic or steam power. By the late 1880s mechanization was becoming more common, requiring larger outlays of capital and leading to the concentration of tobacco manufacturing in a smaller number of companies. Tilley, *R. J. Reynolds Tobacco Company*, 33, 48–49; R. J. Reynolds Tobacco Company, *A Short History of R. J. Reynolds Tobacco Company*, 1; *Leader*, May 6, 27, 1879.

19. Connorton, *Connorton's Tobacco Brand Directory of the United States*; Heimann, *Tobacco and Americans*, 135–36, 172–75; Tilley, *Bright Tobacco Industry*, 522–24; Carlton, "Revolution from Above," 461–63.

20. *Leader*, May 6, 1879; Tilley, *Bright Tobacco Industry*, 562–63; Newspaper clipping of interview with Reynolds in Nannie May Tilley to Mrs. Nancy Reynolds, February 8, 1971, Reynolds Family Papers, Baptist Historical Collection, Wake Forest University Library.

21. North Carolina, vol. 10, 472, 478, 490, 496, 528, 550, R. G. Dun and Company Collection, Baker Library, Harvard University Graduate School of Business Administration; Ashe et al., eds., *Biographical History of North Carolina from Colonial Times to the Present*, 8 vols., 139–51.

22. Tilley, *Bright Tobacco Industry*, 531, 538; John T. Moore to Clayton E. Moore, November 17, 1878, John T. Moore Papers, Manuscripts Department, Duke University Library, Durham, North Carolina; Ashe et al., eds., *Biographical History of North Carolina*, 3: 336; Hamilton Scales to John T. Moore, September 11, 1878, John T. Moore Papers, Manuscripts Department, Duke University Library, Durham, North Carolina.

23. *People's Press*, April 23, 1885; *Union Republican*, December 2, 1886.

24. *Branson's North Carolina Business Directory*, 1877–78, 113–16; *Southern Business Guide, 1883–1884*, 685–700; *Southern Business Guide, 1885–1886*, 693–706; 1850 Census, Population Schedule manuscript microfilm, Forsyth County, North Carolina; 1860 Census, Population Schedule manuscript microfilm, Forsyth County, North Carolina.

25. In 1884 Jacob Tise was listed as farmer in a business directory. 1850 Census, Population Schedule manuscript microfilm, Forsyth County, North Carolina; 1870 Census, Population Schedule manuscript microfilm, Forsyth County, North Carolina; *Branson's North Carolina Business Directory*, 1868, 43, 1872, 92–95, 1877–78, 113–14; North Carolina, vol. 10, 496, 503, 506, 514, 528, R. G. Dun and Company Collection, Baker Library, Harvard University Graduate School of Business Administration; *Southern Business Guide, 1883–1884*, 685–700, *1885–1886*, 693–706; *People's Press*, February 13, 1873.

26. *Branson's North Carolina Business Directory*, 1877–78, 113–16; 1860 Census, Manufacturing Schedule manuscript microfilm, Forsyth County, North Carolina; 1870 Census, Population Schedule manuscript microfilm, Forsyth County, North Carolina; 1870 Census, Manufacturing Schedule manuscript microfilm, Forsyth County, North Carolina; 1880 Census, Manufacturing Schedule manuscript microfilm, Forsyth County, North Carolina; *People's Press*, February 13, 1873.

27. The wealth they accumulated capitalized other entrepreneurial ventures. Many who began their adult lives as mechanics in antebellum Salem turned to agriculture after the war as another business venture. *Branson's North Carolina Business Directory* for 1872 listed nineteen "prominent" farmers in Winston and Salem. In 1884 the number had climbed to eighty-three. Among those listed as farmers in 1884, but who did not appear in 1872, were tobacco manufacturer P. H. Hanes, George F. Nissen, a wagon manufacturer, J. W. Alspaugh, a lawyer, the mercantile firm of Pfohl and Stockton, Fogle Brothers, a blind, sash, and door manufacturer, W. A. Byerly, a brickmaker, and Julius Mickey, a tinsmith. Given the dependence of the towns' tobacco factories and textile mills on tobacco, cotton, and wool, agriculture was regarded as a logical investment for businessmen, especially as tobacco prices remained relatively constant when cotton prices were spiraling downward. In the postwar economy land ownership was as much an entrepreneurial venture as textile and tobacco manufacturing and mercantile enterprises for businessmen motivated by the desire for profits. *Branson's North Carolina Business Directory* for 1884 does not list acreage, but in the 1872 directory the average acreage for those farmers listed was 235 acres. *Branson's North Carolina Business Directory*, 1872, 92–95, 1884, 300–5. Ransom and Sutch, *One Kind of Freedom*, 191–93. During the 1880s, Bright tobacco prices remained

relatively constant while the trend in cotton prices, adjusted for inflation, was downward from 1869 to 1898. Heimann, *Americans and Tobacco*, 168.

28. Carlton, "Builders of a New State," 55–56; *Union Republican*, November 11, 1886.

29. Miller, "Blacks in Winston-Salem, North Carolina 1895–1920: Community Development in an Era of Benevolent Paternalism," Ph.D. diss., Duke University, 1981, 12, 14–17, 96–100.

30. *People's Press*, January 16, 1873, December 3, 1874, October 15, 1885; *Leader*, January 21, 1879; Forsyth County. Register of Deeds, Record of Corporations, vol. 1, 1884–1903, 1–2, North Carolina Division of Archives and History, Raleigh, North Carolina.

31. *People's Press*, April 6, May 5, 7, 1885.

32. *Union Republican*, July 21, 1887; Woodward, *Origins of the New South*, 297–99.

33. Tilley, *Bright Tobacco Industry*, 567; *Laws and Resolutions of the State of North Carolina Passed by the General Assembly at Its Session of 1887*, 612–13; *People's Press*, January 2, 1890.

34. *People's Press*, February 10, 1871; *Private Laws of the State of North Carolina. Passed by the General Assembly at Its Session of 1870–71*, 19; North Carolina, vol. 10, 519, 524, R. G. Dun and Company, Baker Library, Harvard University Graduate School of Business Administration; 1860 Census, Slave Schedule manuscript microfilm, Forsyth County, North Carolina; 1860 Census, Manufacturing Schedule manuscript microfilm, Forsyth County, North Carolina; Forsyth County, Record of Corporations, vol. 1, 30–31, NCDAH.

35. Fries et al., *Forsyth*, 168–70; *Public and Private Laws of North Carolina*, 1889; *Southern Business Guide, 1885–1886*, 693–706. North Carolina, vol. 10, 463–553, R. G. Dun and Company Collection, Baker Library, Harvard University Graduate School of Business Administration; *Branson's North Carolina Business Directory, 1877–78*, 113–16; *Southern Business Guide, 1883–1884*, 685–700, *1885–1886*, 693–706; Forsyth County, Record of Corporations, vol. 1, 14–16, 46–48, 53–54, NCDAH.

36. O'Brien, "War and Social Change: An Analysis of Community Power Structure: Guilford County, North Carolina, 1848–1882," Ph.D. diss., University of North Carolina at Chapel Hill, 1975, 99–104.

37. Tilley, *R. J. Reynolds Tobacco Company*, 52–55; Ashe, *Biographical History of North Carolina*, 3: 137–40.

38. By the mid-1870s the Conservatives/Democrats had regained control of North Carolina politics. They quickly moved to rewrite the 1868 constitution, making more local offices, namely county magistrates, appointive, thus centralizing power in the governor and legislature. Therefore, the legislature depended on the local Democratic party organizations for nominations for appointed positions, giving the local organization much influence over local affairs. Lefler and Newsome, *North Carolina*, 507–11; Woodward, *Origins of the New South*, 1–2, 54; O'Brien, "War and Social Change," 114, 127; *People's Press*, January 6, April 17, 1863, January 5, March 9, 1865, January 27, 1866, July 24, 1868, May 9, 1872,

May 8, 1873, May 7, 1874, May 6, 1875, May 4, 1875, May 4, August 3, 1876, May 9, 1878, May 8, 1879, May 6, 1880, May 3, 1881, May 4, 1882, May 10, 1883, May 8, 1884, May 7, 1885, May 6, 1886, May 5, 1887; *Branson's North Carolina Business Directory*, 1877–78, 113–18, 1884, 300–305; 1850 Census, Population Schedule manuscript microfilm, Forsyth County, North Carolina; 1860 Census, Population Schedule manuscript microfilm, Forsyth County, North Carolina; 1870 Census, Population Schedule manuscript microfilm, Forsyth County, North Carolina; 1880 Census, Population Schedule manuscript microfilm, Forsyth County, North Carolina.

39. *People's Press*, March 9, 1865, April 14, 1866, May 9, 1872, May 8, 1873, May 7, 1874, May 6, 1875, May 4, 1876, May 8, 1879, May 6, 1880, May 4, 1882, May 7, 1885, May 5, 1887; *Branson's North Carolina Business Directory*, 1877–78, 113–18 , 1884, 300–305; 1860 Census, Population Schedule manuscript microfilm, Forsyth County, North Carolina; 1880 Census, Population Schedule manuscript microfilm, Forsyth County, North Carolina; Dobbins, *Descriptive Sketch of Winston-Salem, Its Advantages and Surroundings . . . compiled under the auspices of the Chamber of Commerce*, 31–44; Gutman, "Class, Status, and Community Power in Nineteenth Century American Industrial Cities: Paterson, New Jersey: A Case Study," 237, 254–56.

40. Woodward, *Origins of the New South*, 28–29, 140–41, 150–51; Wiener, *Social Origins of the New South: Alabama, 1860–1885;* idem, "Comments, 'Class Structure and Economic Development in the American South,' " 970; Woodman, "Sequel to Slavery: The New History Views the Postbellum South," 552–54; idem, "Comments, 'Class Structure and Economic Development in the American South,' " 997–1001. James Roark observed an "unalloyed capitalist ethic" which appeared in the postwar South as planters were forced to become businessmen and regard their plantations as merely investments. Roark, *Masters without Slaves: Southern Planters in the Civil War and Reconstruction*, 198; Wright, *Old South, New South: Revolutions in the Southern Economy since the Civil War*, 11, 19, 30–50; Cobb, "Beyond Planters and Industrialists," 50; Carlton, "Revolution from Above," 447, 474.

SEVEN   *Workers in an Industrial Community*

1. Shore, *Southern Capitalists*, 114–19; *People's Press*, June 11, 1869; Carlton, "The Revolution from Above: The National Market and the Beginnings of Industrialization in North Carolina," 456–57; Hahn, *The Roots of Southern Populism: Yeoman Farmers and the Transformation of the Georgia Upcountry, 1850–1890,* 189; Prude, *The Coming of Industrial Order: Town and Factory Life in Rural Massachusetts, 1810–1860*, xi–xiii, 261–62; Walkowitz, *Worker City, Company Town: Iron and Cotton-Worker Protest in Troy and Cohoes, New York, 1855–1884,* 5–8; Hirsch, *The Roots of the American Working Class: The Industrialization of Crafts in Newark, 1800–1860*, 3–4, 15–16, 29–36; Dawley, *Class and Community: The Industrial Revolution in Lynn*, especially 220–41; and Blumin, *The Emergence of the Middle Class: Social Experience in the American City, 1760–1900*, 258–90.

2. Table 7.1 illustrates the changing nature of the work force in Forsyth County. 1850 Census, Population Schedule manuscript microfilm, Forsyth County, North Carolina; 1880 Census, Population Schedule manuscript microfilm, Forsyth County, North Carolina. A 20 percent sample was created by including every fifth dwelling listed in the 1850 and 1880 censuses for Forsyth County. For 1850, n = 1865; for 1880, n = 3615. Table 7.1 is derived from those members of the samples who reported occupations other than "keeping house." It is difficult to determine precisely the skill levels of workers in various occupations. For the purposes of this study the occupation classification scheme devised by Susan Hirsch in her study of craftsmen in Newark, New Jersey, was adapted. Hirsch divided the Newark work force into nine categories: no occupation, unskilled or service, semiskilled, skilled, petty proprietors, clerical and sales, semiprofessional, proprietors and managers, professionals, and government officials. Hirsch, *Roots of the American Working Class*, 143–46. The classification of occupations used in these tables is presented in Appendix B and Appendix C.

3. The sample for Winston Township was created from the sample for Forsyth County created from the 1880 population census. The sample size is 914, of which 434 reported occupations. The categories of occupations for the Winston Township sample are the same as those for the Forsyth County sample. 1880 Census, Population Schedule manuscript microfilm, Forsyth County, North Carolina.

4. 1850 Census, Population Schedule manuscript microfilm, Forsyth County, North Carolina; 1860 Census, Population Schedule manuscript microfilm, Forsyth County, North Carolina; 1870 Census, Manufacturing Schedule manuscript microfilm, Forsyth County, North Carolina; *People's Press*, January 31, February 7, June 19, 1868; North Carolina, vol. 10, 478, 504, R. G. Dun and Company Collection, Baker Library, Harvard University Graduate School of Business Administration; Carlton, "Revolution from Above," 448–49; Hahn, *Roots of Southern Populism*, 189; Griffen and Griffen, *Natives and Newcomers: The Ordering of Opportunity in Mid-Nineteenth Century Poughkeepsie*, 140.

5. Some men who owned wagon shops identified their trades to the census taker as blacksmiths which reflected the changing activity in their shops. In these shops repairs were probably taking more of their time than actual wagon manufacturing. 1850 Census, Population Schedule manuscript microfilm, Forsyth County, North Carolina; 1880 Census, Population Schedule manuscript microfilm, Forsyth County, North Carolina; *People's Press*, February 6, 1873; *Branson's North Carolina Business Directory*, 1884, 300–305; *Southern Business Guide, 1885–1886*, 693–706; North Carolina Bureau of Labor Statistics, *First Annual Report of the North Carolina Bureau of Labor Statistics. 1887*, 66.

6. See Tables 7.3 and 7.4. 1850 Census, Population Schedule manuscript microfilm, Forsyth County, North Carolina; 1880 Census, Population Schedule manuscript microfilm, Forsyth County, North Carolina. Age grouping adapted from Hirsch, *Roots of the American Working Class*, 43. North Carolina Bureau of Labor Statistics, *Second Annual Report of the North Carolina Bureau of Labor Statistics. 1888;* McLaurin, *Knights of Labor in the South*, 31; Faler, *Mechanics and Manufacturers in the Early Industrial Revolution: Lynn, Massachusetts, 1780–1860*, 97.

7. Griffen and Griffen, *Natives and Newcomers*, 46; Kett, *Rites of Passage: Adolescence in America, 1790 to the Present*, 18, 145. Jonathan Prude finds evidence in antebellum Massachusetts of what he labels "pseudoapprenticeship," lasting only three years with small wage payments. Prude, *Coming of Industrial Order*, 70.

8. Faler, *Mechanics and Manufacturers*, 89, 96; McLaurin, *Knights*, 31; Newby, *Plain Folk in the New South: Social Change and Cultural Persistence, 1880–1915*, 70–71; Bureau of Labor Statistics, *Second Annual Report. 1888*, 3–4, 87; Forsyth County, Apprenticeship Bonds, December 10, 1878, June 27, 1880, North Carolina Division of Archives and History, Raleigh, North Carolina.

9. 1850 Census, Population Schedule manuscript microfilm, Forsyth County, North Carolina; 1880 Census, Population Schedule manuscript microfilm, Forsyth County, North Carolina; *Branson's North Carolina Business Directory*, 1877–78, 116; *Branson's North Carolina Business Directory*, 1884, 303; 1880 Census, Manufacturing Schedule manuscript microfilm, Forsyth County, North Carolina.

10. 1850 Census, Population Schedule manuscript microfilm, Forsyth County, North Carolina; 1880 Census, Population Schedule manuscript microfilm, Forsyth County, North Carolina.

11. See Tables 7.3 and 7.4; *Branson's North Carolina Business Directory*, 1884, 303.

12. 1850 Census, Population Schedule manuscript microfilm, Forsyth County, North Carolina; 1880 Census, Population Schedule manuscript microfilm, Forsyth County, North Carolina; *Branson's North Carolina Business Directory*, 1884, 304; *People's Press*, June 12, 1884.

13. 1850 Census, Population Schedule manuscript microfilm, Forsyth County, North Carolina; 1880 Census, Population Schedule manuscript microfilm, Forsyth County, North Carolina.

14. Griffen and Griffen, *Natives and Newcomers*, 150; Katz, *The People of Hamilton, Canada West: Family and Class in a Mid-Nineteenth Century City*, 72–73; Hirsch, *Roots of the American Working Class*, 43.

15. See Table 7.5; Bureau of Labor Statistics, *Second Annual Report. 1888*. Fifteen "mechanical" employers replied, including 1 tailoring establishment, 3 wagon manufactories, 3 printers, 1 buggy and carriage manufactory, 1 saw mill manufactory, 1 painting contractor, 1 builder and manufacturer of doors, sashes and blinds, 1 saw mill, 1 foundry and machine shop, 1 marble and stone works, and 1 plasterer. The saw mill, foundry, painting contractor, and plasterer operated for less than twelve months a year.

16. Bureau of Labor Statistics, *Second Annual Report. 1888*, 87–89.

17. One mechanic reported in 1888 that wood was $2.50 a cord and coal was $8 to $9 a ton. Bureau of Labor Statistics, *Second Annual Report. 1888*, 88–90; 1870 Census, Social Statistics manuscript microfilm, Forsyth County, North Carolina.

18. Bureau of Labor Statistics, *Second Annual Report. 1888*, 90; Winston *Union Republican*, April 21, May 5, 1887; Griffen and Griffen, *Natives and Newcomers*, 141; Hirsch, *Roots of the American Working Class*, 77–78; Faler, *Mechanics and Manufacturers*, 171.

19. McLaurin, *Paternalism and Protest: Southern Cotton Mill Workers and Organized Labor, 1875–1905*, 3, 12, 17, 26; Tilley, *The Bright Leaf Tobacco Industry*,

1860–1929, 515; Wiener, "Class Structure and Economic Development in the American South, 1865–1955," 978–80.

20. Hall et al., *Like a Family: The Making of a Southern Cotton Mill World*, 6–7, 13; I. A. Newby offers a vivid description of the conditions poor southerners, white and black, confronted as southern agriculture became more commercial in the 1870s and 1880s, in *Plain Folk*, 26–56. Steven Hahn provides an in-depth analysis of the commercial transformation of piedmont agriculture that produced debt and dependence through the crop lien, sharecropping, and tenancy for increasing numbers of southerners in *Roots of Southern Populism*, 137–203 especially. For an analysis of the limited choices of black southerners during these years, see Ransom and Sutch, *One Kind of Freedom: The Economic Consequences of Emancipation*, 81–105.

21. Hall et al., *Like a Family*, 13, 31–33; Newby, *Plain Folk*, 105–6, 110–11; McHugh, *The Mill Family: The Labor System in the Southern Cotton Textile Industry, 1880–1915*, 92–94.

22. 1880 Census, Population Schedule manuscript microfilm, Forsyth County, North Carolina; 1870 Census, Population Schedule manuscript microfilm, Forsyth County, North Carolina; see Table 7.6. McLaurin reports that males made up only 26.2 percent of the textile mill work force in North Carolina in 1880. McLaurin, *Paternalism*, 21, 60–61; idem, *Knights*, 28.

23. This reflects a pattern that was common for textile mill workers generally. Daniel Walkowitz also found that the textile mills in Cohoes, New York, provided a haven for widows. Walkowitz, *Worker City, Company Town*, 112; 1870 Census, Population Schedule manuscript microfilm, Forsyth County, North Carolina; 1880 Census, Population Schedule manuscript microfilm, Forsyth County, North Carolina. Massachusetts mills, after becoming established and successful, also made the transition from a work force based primarily on families with large numbers of children to a work force of adults with no families in the mill. In the South this transition is probably explained by the availability of greater numbers of young adults squeezed out of the trades and off farms as a result of the economic changes taking place during the postwar years. Prude, *Coming of Industrial Order*, 213.

24. 1870 Census, Population Schedule manuscript microfilm, Forsyth County, North Carolina; 1880 Census, Population Schedule manuscript microfilm, Forsyth County, North Carolina; Bureau of Labor Statistics, *Second Annual Report. 1888*, 154–55.

25. Newby, *Plain Folk*, 117–18. In nearby Alamance County, where mill owners responded to Bureau of Labor Statistics inquiries, the average workday in the mills was eleven and a half hours. A Guilford County mill worker reported that he worked twelve hours a day. Bureau of Labor Statistics, *First Annual Report. 1887*, 37, 142–43; McLaurin, *Knights*, 21, 28.

26. Bureau of Labor Statistics, *Second Annual Report. 1888*, 90; *People's Press*, May 22, 1879, April 5, 1883, April 1, 1886; *Union Republican*, September 13, 1887; Newby, *Plain Folk*, 120–22; Hall et al., *Like a Family*, 49–51.

27. Bureau of Labor Statistics, *First Annual Report. 1887*, 37, 142–43; idem, *Second Annual Report. 1888*, 90; McLaurin, *Paternalism*, 21, 28.

28. McLaurin, *Paternalism*, 39; idem, *Knights*, 16.

29. Tilley, *Bright Leaf Tobacco Industry*, 515; Tilley, *R. J. Reynolds Tobacco Company*, 38; McLaurin, *Knights*, 29; *People's Press*, May 4, 1882, May 22, 1884; Bureau of Labor Statistics, *First Annual Report. 1887*, 66; idem, *Second Annual Report. 1888*, 90.

30. The manufacture of twists was similar, but the filler leaves were formed into a roll of equal length to the wrapping leaf and encased in a wrapper. The roll was then doubled and twisted, literally, into a compact form. The lumper or roller was the most skilled and consequently the highest-paid worker in the tobacco factory. Tilley, *Bright Leaf Tobacco Industry*, 491–92, 516–17; idem, *R. J. Reynolds Tobacco Company*, 144–47.

31. Tilley, *Bright Leaf Tobacco Industry*, 517; *People's Press*, March 14, May 4, 1882, August 9, 19, 1878, July 1, 1886; 1880 Census, Manufacturing Schedule manuscript microfilm, Forsyth County, North Carolina. Table 7.9 summarizes data on tobacco manufacturing reported in Bureau of Labor Statistics, *First Annual Report. 1887*, 158–59; Fries et al., *Forsyth: The History of a County on the March*, 179.

32. *People's Press*, May 13, 1886; McLaurin, *Knights*, 21; 1880 Census, Manufacturing Schedule manuscript microfilm, Forsyth County, North Carolina; Miller, "Blacks in Winston-Salem, North Carolina 1895 1920: Community Development in an Era of Benevolent Paternalism," Ph.D. diss., Duke University, 1981, 81–86; Fries et al., *Forsyth*, 167.

33. See Table 7.9. Bureau of Labor Statistics, *First Annual Report. 1887*, 37, 142–43, 154; idem, *Second Annual Report. 1888*, 154–55.

34. 1880 Census, Population Schedule manuscript microfilm, Forsyth County, North Carolina. A sample consisting of every seventh tobacco worker was drawn from the 1880 census for Winston Township (n = 86). Onetime R. J. Reynolds Tobacco Company historian Nannie May Tilley reports that few records regarding employees in the Reynolds factory survive from the nineteenth century. Tilley, *R. J. Reynolds Tobacco Company*, 36–38.

35. Miller, "Blacks in Winston-Salem," 88–89.

36. Fink, *Workingmen's Democracy: The Knights of Labor and American Politics*, xii.

E I G H T   *The Industrial Community*

1. Escott, *Many Excellent People: Power and Privilege in North Carolina, 1850–1900*, 196–98. By the early 1880s Winston and Salem were commonly referred to as one city, Winston-Salem or the Twin City. However, the two towns remained separate municipalities until consolidation in 1913.

2. Janiewski, *Sisterhood Denied: Race, Gender, and Class in a New South Community*, 49; Fink, *Workingmen's Democracy: The Knights of Labor and American Politics*, xi–xiv, 39; Rabinowitz, *Race Relations in the Urban South, 1865–1890*, 3; Escott, *Many Excellent People*, xviii, 219, 240.

3. *Statistics of the Population of the United States. Ninth Census. Volume 1. 1870*, 22; *Report on the Population of the United States at the Eleventh Census. Part 1. 1890*, 473; *Branson's North Carolina Business Directory*, 1884, 300. Between 1880 and 1890 the South's urban population grew by 49 percent compared to the national average of 25 percent. Rabinowitz, "Continuity and Change: Southern Urban Development, 1860–1900," 92–122; Wieher, "The Cotton Industry and Southern Urbanization, 1880–1930," 120–25; Larsen, *The Rise of the Urban South*, 159–60; Doyle, *New Men, New Cities, New South: Atlanta, Nashville, Charleston, Mobile, 1860–1910*, 1–21.

4. *Report of the United States in 1860. Compiled from the Original Returns of the Eighth Census; Report on the Population of the United States at the Eleventh Census. Part 1. 1890*, 473. The figures on manufacturing employment were obtained from samples of the working population drawn from the 1850 and 1880 censuses of population. These percentages represent those who reported a semiskilled or skilled occupation. See chapter 7. 1850 Census, Population Schedule manuscript microfilm, Forsyth County, North Carolina; 1880 Census, Population Schedule manuscript microfilm, Forsyth County, North Carolina.

5. Salem *People's Press*, May 22, 1884; Sanborn Map Company, Insurance Map of Winston and Salem, 1885, microfilm in Forsyth County Public Library, Winston-Salem, North Carolina; 1880 Census, Population Schedule manuscript microfilm, Forsyth County, North Carolina.

6. Sanborn Map Company, Insurance Map of Winston and Salem, 1885, Forsyth County Public Library; 1880 Census, Population Schedule manuscript microfilm, Forsyth County, North Carolina.

7. North Carolina Bureau of Labor Statistics, *Second Annual Report of the North Carolina Bureau of Labor Statistics. 1888*, 88–89; Faler, *Mechanics and Manufacturers in the Early Industrial Revolution: Lynn, Massachusetts, 1780–1860*, 50; Hirsch, *Roots of the American Working Class: The Industrialization of Crafts in Newark, 1800–1860*, 134.

8. Winston *Leader*, January 28, 1879; Winston *Union Republican*, April 14, 21, 1881, February 21, 1884; *People's Press*, March 14, 21, 1878, January 25, February 15, 1883, August 7, 1884.

9. Newby, *Plain Folk in the New South: Social Change and Cultural Persistence, 1880–1915*, 70–74.

10. *People's Press*, January 4, 1876, January 11, 18, 1877, January 3, 1878, February 5, 1880, March 15, 1881, January 9, 23, 1883, January 8, 1885, March 20, 1884, June 10, 1886, January 13, 1887; *Union Republican*, January 14, 1875, January 10, February 28, 1884, November 11, 1886, January 6, June 2, 1887.

11. Bureau of Labor Statistics, *Second Annual Report. 1888*, 88–89; *Union Republican*, January 20, 1888; Dawley and Faler, "Working Class Culture and Politics in the Industrial Revolution: Sources of Loyalism and Rebellion," 62–63; Blumin, *The Emergence of the Middle Class: Social Experience in the American City, 1760–1900*, 192–95.

12. *People's Press*, February 18, 1886. The Mechanics' Union carried added significance in that it was an expression of the mechanics' recognition of the

peculiar problems workers faced. Cantor, ed., *American Working Class Culture: Explorations in American Labor and Social History*, 10; Faler, *Mechanics and Manufacturers*, 29, 142.

13. Newby, *Plain Folk*, 57–59; Hall et al., *Like a Family: The Making of a Southern Cotton Mill World*, 44; Woodward, *Origins of the New South, 1877–1913*, 223–24; McLaurin, *Paternalism and Protest: Southern Cotton Mill Workers and Organized Labor, 1875–1905*, 53; idem, *The Knights of Labor in the South*, 33.

14. *People's Press*, December 28, 1882; Prude, *The Coming of Industrial Order: Town and Factory Life in Rural Massachusetts, 1810–1860*, 111–16; Dublin, *Women at Work: The Transformation of Work and Community in Lowell, Massachusetts, 1826–1860*, 17.

15. McLaurin, *Paternalism*, 47, 57; F. and H. Fries Company, Daybook #15, February 5, 1888, Fries Mills Collection, Moravian Archives, Winston-Salem, North Carolina; *People's Press*, January 12, 1882, January 18, 1883, December 28, 1882, October 30, 1884, December 9, 1886. The F. and H. Fries Company paid the taxes of its workers and, in 1882, when smallpox struck Winston and Salem, vaccinated the operatives. Walkowitz, *Worker City, Company Town: Iron and Cotton-Worker Protest in Troy and Cohoes, New York, 1855–1884*, 185–86.

16. Hall et al., *Like a Family*, xvi, 132.

17. McLaurin, *Paternalism*, 55–57; *People's Press*, March 18, 1875, December 28, 1882; Hall et al., *Like a Family*, 222–23.

18. Rachleff, *Black Labor in Richmond, 1865–1890*, 4–5, 200–201; Litwack, *Been in the Storm So Long: The Aftermath of Slavery*, 226–28, 247, 338, 399; Ransom and Sutch, *One Kind of Freedom: The Economic Consequences of Emancipation*, 1; Janiewski, *Sisterhood Denied*, 54; Escott, *Many Excellent People*, 182.

19. Blumin, *Emergence of the Middle Class*, 193; Miller, "Blacks in Winston-Salem, North Carolina 1895–1920: Community Development in an Era of Benevolent Paternalism," Ph.D. diss., Duke University, 1981, 13–14; *People's Press*, March 7, September 12, 1878, January 1, 1891; *Union Republican*, April 8, 1875; Litwack, *Been in the Storm So Long*, 247.

20. Tilley, *R. J. Reynolds Tobacco Company*, 266–72; Miller, "Blacks in Winston-Salem," 80–81; Bureau of Labor Statistics, *First Annual Report. 1887*, 66.

21. *Leader*, March 4, 1879.

22. Tilley, *R. J. Reynolds Tobacco Company*, 38–39.

23. Faler, *Mechanics and Manufacturers*, 142; Baker, "Labor History, Social Science and the Concept of the Working Class," 101; Thompson, *Making of the English Working Class*, 9–10.

24. Tilley, *R. J. Reynolds Tobacco Company*, 247.

25. Bureau of Labor Statistics, *First Annual Report. 1887*, 4, 6; idem, *Second Annual Report. 1888*, 87–90, 154–55; idem, *Third Annual Report of the Bureau of Labor Statistics. 1889*, 248; Montgomery, *Beyond Equality: Labor and the Radical Republicans, 1862–1872*, 239. Pittsburgh, Pennsylvania, workers advocated:
Eight Hours For Work
Eight Hours For Recreation, Rest,
Eight Hours For Sleep.

26. Bureau of Labor Statistics, *Second Annual Report. 1888*, 88.

27. T. M. Richardson to Daniel G. Fowle, May 23, 1889, Daniel G. Fowle Papers, North Carolina Department of Archives and History, Raleigh, North Carolina; Bureau of Labor Statistics, *Second Annual Report. 1888*, 88; Miller, "Blacks in Winston-Salem," 63.

28. Laurie, *Artisans into Workers: Labor in Nineteenth-Century America*, 142, 148; McLaurin, *Paternalism*, 75.

29. Garlock, *Guide to the Local Assemblies of the Knights of Labor*, 356; Dobbins, *Descriptive Sketch of Winston-Salem. Its Advantages and Surroundings . . . compiled under the auspices of the Chamber of Commerce*, 18; *People's Press*, April 29, May 10, 1886, January 27, 1887; *Union Republic*, October 28, November 18, 1886, January 20, March 24, 1887.

30. Bureau of Labor Statistics, *Second Annual Report. 1888*, 88–89; Fayetteville *Messenger*, July 13, 1888. According to Leon Fink, organized labor in the late nineteenth century stressed the development of the individual, but not in competition with other individuals. Labor's philosophy ignored the individual's "right to rise," and instead promoted collective strength. Fink, *Workingmen's Democracy*, 12; Foner, *Free Labor, Free Soil, Free Men: The Ideology of the Republican Party before the Civil War*, 11–39; idem, *Politics and Ideology in the Age of the Civil War*, 105; Montgomery, *Beyond Equality*, 14.

31. Fink, *Workingmen's Democracy*, 3, 7; *Messenger*, January 13, April 20, July 13, 1888.

32. United States Senate, *Report of the Committee of the Senate upon the Relations between Labor and Capital. 5 Volumes*, 1: 3–5; *Union Republican*, October 21, 1886, January 20, 1887; *People's Press*, October 28, 1886; *Messenger*, July 13, 1888; Fink, *Workingmen's Democracy*, 3, 8–14.

33. Fink, *Workingmen's Democracy*, 26, 33; *Messenger*, July 13, August 10, 1888.

34. *People's Press*, April 22, May 6, 1886; *Union Republican*, May 5, 1887, May 3, 10, 1888.

35. Fink, *Workingmen's Democracy*, 77, 119–20, 155.

36. *People's Press*, January 20, 1887; *Union Republican*, April 21, July 7, October 13, 1887; McLaurin, "Racial Policies," 576; idem, *Paternalism*, 68, 70.

37. Fink, *Workingmen's Democracy*, 121, 130, 157–64; McLaurin, "The Racial Policies of the Knights of Labor and the Organization of Southern Black Workers," 580.

38. McLaurin, "The Racial Policies of the Knights of Labor," 580; *Messenger*, October 14, 1887, January 13, 1888; Bureau of Labor Statistics, *Second Annual Report. 1888*, 185.

39. *People's Press*, April 24, 1868, August 12, 1870, August 8, 1872, November 23, 1876, July 18, August 8, 1878, November 11, 1880; *Union Republican*, August 8, 1878, October 21, November 11, 1886; Forsyth County, Clerk of Superior Court, Record of Elections, 1878–1906, North Carolina Division of Archives and History, Raleigh, North Carolina; Shore, *Southern Capitalists: The Ideological Leadership of an Elite, 1832–1885*, 125.

40. *People's Press*, May 13, 1870, May 21, July 9, 1874, July 29, 1875; *Union Republican*, February 11, 1875; Escott, *Many Excellent People*, 172; Shore, *Southern Capitalists*, 134, 175.

41. Escott, *Many Excellent People*, 171, 181; *People's Press*, August 8, 1878, November 11, 1880, November 9, 1882, November 13, 1884, November 4, 1886; *Union Republican*, November 8, 1888; Forsyth County, Record of Elections, 1878–1906, NCDAH.

42. *Union Republican*, October 21, 1886; Winston-Salem *Weekly Sentinel*, November 11, 1886; Escott, *Many Excellent People*, 175–79; Shore, *Southern Capitalists*, 184.

43. Bureau of Labor Statistics, *Second Annual Report. 1888*, 88; *Weekly Sentinel*, November 11, 1886.

44. Escott, *Many Excellent People*, 175–79, 185–86; Shore, *Southern Capitalists*, 185–86.

45. Morgan, *American Slavery, American Freedom: The Ordeal of Colonial Virginia*, 264–70, 364–86 especially; Harris, *Plain Folk and Gentry in a Slave Society: White Liberty and Black Slavery in Augusta's Hinterlands*, 6; Rabinowitz, *Race Relations in the Urban South*, 3, 18–30, 186–87; Litwack, *Been in the Storm So Long*, 255; Newby, *Plain Folk*, 73–74; Salem *Western Sentinel*, October 18, 1888; Bureau of Labor Statistics, *Second Annual Report. 1888*, 185.

46. *Union Republican*, July 19, 1888; *Western Sentinel*, June 4, 1885; Shore, *Southern Capitalists*, 169–70, 185–86.

47. *Union Republican*, August 16, September 13, October 18, 1888.

48. *Western Sentinel*, September 27, 1888; *Union Republican*, May 10, October 18, 1888.

49. *Union Republican*, May 5, 1881; Miller, "Blacks in Winston-Salem," 20–25, 34.

50. Perman, *The Road to Redemption: Southern Politics, 1869–1879*, 277; Escott, *Many Excellent People*, 169, 194–95.

51. *People's Press*, July 10, September 18, 1890; North Carolina Bureau of Labor and Printing, *First Annual Report of the Bureau of Labor and Printing. 1901*, 388–89; Jolly, "The Labor Movement in North Carolina, 1880–1922," 365–66.

52. Tilley, *R. J. Reynolds Tobacco Company*, 152–53, 242–46, 250–51, 260–61.

53. Blumin, *The Emergence of the Middle Class*, 2–16; Bender, *Community and Social Change in America*, 118.

Conclusion

1. Bender, *Community and Social Change in America*, 6–7, 43.

2. Darrett Rutman offers a useful paradigm for explaining community change in early America as the balance in America's villages and towns shifted from homogeneity and community self-sufficiency to greater involvement in the larger economy, society, and culture that extended beyond the geographic borders of the town. But Thomas Bender warns that the old existed beside the new and older forms of community were not completely overwhelmed by the new. Rutman, "Assessing the Little Communities of Early America," 163–78; idem, "The Social Web: A Prospectus for the Study of the Early American Community,"

57–88; Bender, *Community and Social Change*, 119–20; Redfield, *The Little Community: Viewpoints for the Study of the Human Whole*, 4, 9–10.

3. Doyle, *New Men, New Cities, New South: Atlanta, Nashville, Charleston, Mobile, 1860–1910*, 7–14, 313.

4. Thomas Bender has noted that in the late nineteenth century as urban industrial society emerged in America, social experience split as "one's role as a member of a family or a circle of friends became sharply differentiated from one's role and behavior in economic relations, in dealing with the government, or in relations with any large-scale organizations." Bender, *Community and Social Change*, 108–19.

Bibliography

P R I M A R Y   S O U R C E S

Manuscript Collections

MANUSCRIPTS DEPARTMENT, DUKE UNIVERSITY LIBRARY, DURHAM, NORTH CAROLINA:

Edmund Blum Daybook
Benjamin Franklin Bynum Papers
Conrad Family Papers
John T. Moore Papers
Samuel Finley Patterson Papers
John F. Poindexter Papers
James C. Zimmerman Papers

BAKER LIBRARY, HARVARD UNIVERSITY GRADUATE SCHOOL OF BUSINESS ADMINISTRATION, CAMBRIDGE, MASSACHUSETTS:

R. G. Dun and Company Collection

MORAVIAN ARCHIVES, WINSTON-SALEM, NORTH CAROLINA:

Civil War and Reconstruction Papers
F. and H. Fries Collection
Fries Family Papers
Fries Mills Collection
John Henry Leinbach Family Papers
Salem Congregation Records
Shaffner-Fries Correspondence

NORTH CAROLINA DIVISION OF ARCHIVES AND HISTORY (NCDAH),
RALEIGH, NORTH CAROLINA:

Alexander Brevard Papers
Daniel G. Fowle Papers
Fries Papers
North Carolina General Assembly Session Records
North Carolina Governors' Papers
Patterson Papers
Thomas Marritt Pittman Papers
John Francis Shaffner Papers

OLD SALEM, INCORPORATED, WINSTON-SALEM, NORTH CAROLINA:

Map of Winston-Salem, 1876. E. A. Vogler.

SOUTHERN HISTORICAL COLLECTION, UNIVERSITY OF NORTH CAROLINA
AT CHAPEL HILL, CHAPEL HILL, NORTH CAROLINA:

Francis Fries Papers
Fries and Shaffner Family Papers
Solomon Hilary Helsabeck Papers
Jones Family Papers
Jones and Patterson Family Papers
Patterson Family Papers
Calvin Henderson Wiley Papers

BAPTIST HISTORICAL COLLECTION, WAKE FOREST UNIVERSITY
LIBRARY, WINSTON-SALEM, NORTH CAROLINA:

Reynolds Family Papers

FORSYTH COUNTY PUBLIC LIBRARY, WINSTON-SALEM, NORTH CAROLINA:

Frank Jones Collection

Books, Pamphlets, Published Manuscripts, and Speeches

Branson, Levi. *Branson's North Carolina Business Directory*. Raleigh: Levi Branson
    Office Publishing Company, 1868, 1872, 1877–78, 1884.
Colonial Records of North Carolina, 26 vols. Edited by William L. Saunders. Re-
    print. New York: AMS Press, 1966.
Confederate States of America, War Department. "Circular to the Farmers and
    Citizens of Forsyth County, North Carolina." Broadside Collection, Duke
    University Library.

Connorton, J. W. *Connorton's Tobacco Brand Directory of the United States*. Chicago: J. W. Connorton, 1887.

Deems, Charles F. "What It Has Done, and What We Must Do." Delivered before the Grand Division of the Order of the Sons of Temperance of North Carolina, October 1847.

Dobbins, D. P. *Descriptive Sketch of Winston-Salem. Its Advantages and Surroundings . . . compiled under the auspices of the Chamber of Commerce*. Winston: Sentinel Job Print, 1888.

Doub, Peter. *Address Delivered before the Grand Division of North Carolina. Sons of Temperance. At the October Session. 1852*. Raleigh: Spirit of the Age, 1853.

Martineau, Harriet. *Society in America*. New York: Saunders and Otley, 1837.

North Carolina Sons of Temperance. *Constitutions of the Order of the Sons of Temperance, 1845*. North Carolina Collection, University of North Carolina at Chapel Hill.

————. *Proceedings of the Grand Division of North Carolina. Sons of Temperance. 1851*. North Carolina Collection, University of North Carolina at Chapel Hill.

Records of the Moravians in North Carolina, 11 vols. Edited by Adelaide L. Fries, Douglas L. Rights, Minnie J. Smith, and Kenneth G. Hamilton. Raleigh: North Carolina Department of Archives and History, 1942–69.

Sanborn Map Company. Insurance Map of Winston and Salem, 1885. Microfilm, Forsyth County Public Library, Winston-Salem, North Carolina.

Southern Business Guide, 1883–1884, 1885–1886. Cincinnati: United States Central Publishing Company, 1884, 1886.

Woodmason, Charles. *The Carolina Backcountry on the Eve of the Revolution: The Journal and Other Writings of Charles Woodmason, Anglican Itinerant*. Edited by Richard J. Hooker. Chapel Hill: University of North Carolina Press, 1953.

Government Documents

Forsyth County. Apprenticeship Bonds. North Carolina Division of Archives and History.

————. Clerk of Superior Court. Record of Elections. North Carolina Division of Archives and History, Raleigh, North Carolina.

————. County Court of Pleas and Quarter Sessions. 1849–68. North Carolina Division of Archives and History, Raleigh, North Carolina. North Carolina.

————. Minutes of the Inferior Court. North Carolina Division of Archives and History, Raleigh, North Carolina.

————. Register of Deeds. Record of Corporations, vol. 1, 1884–1903. North Carolina Division of Archives and History, Raleigh, North Carolina.

North Carolina. *First Annual Report of the Bureau of Labor Statistics. 1887*. Raleigh: Josephus Daniels, 1887.

————. *Second Annual Report of the Bureau of Labor Statistics. 1888*. Raleigh: Josephus Daniels, 1888.

————. *Third Annual Report of the Bureau of Labor Statistics. 1889*. Raleigh: Josephus Daniels, 1889.

————. *First Annual Report of the Bureau of Labor and Printing. 1901*. Raleigh, 1901.

North Carolina. *Laws of the State of North Carolina. Passed by the General Assembly at the Session of 1848–49.* Raleigh, 1849.

————. *Laws of the State of North Carolina. Passed by the General Assembly at the Session of 1850–51.* Raleigh, 1851.

————. *Laws of the State of North Carolina. Passed by the General Assembly at the Session of 1852.* Raleigh, 1853.

————. *Laws and Resolutions of the State of North Carolina. Passed by the General Assembly at Its Session of 1887.* Raleigh, 1888.

————. *Private Laws of the State of North Carolina. Passed by the General Assembly at Its Session of 1854–55.* Raleigh, 1855.

————. *Private Laws of the State of North Carolina. Passed by the General Assembly at Its Session of 1870–71.* Raleigh, 1871.

————. *Public Laws of the State of North Carolina. Passed by the General Assembly at Its Session of 1856–57.* Raleigh, 1857.

Stokes County. Apprenticeship Bonds. North Carolina Division of Archives and History, Raleigh, North Carolina.

————. Inventory of Estates. North Carolina Division of Archives and History, Raleigh, North Carolina.

————. List of Taxables. North Carolina Division of Archives and History, Raleigh, North Carolina.

————. Marriage Bonds. North Carolina Division of Archives and History, Raleigh, North Carolina.

United States Census Office. Manuscript of Agriculture Schedule microfilm, 1850, 1860, and 1880.

————. Manuscripts of Manufacturing Schedule microfilm, 1850, 1860, 1870, and 1880.

————. Manuscripts of Population Schedule microfilm, 1820, 1830, 1840, 1850, 1860, 1870, and 1880.

————. Manuscript of Slave Schedule microfilm, 1850 and 1860.

————. Manuscript Schedule of Social Statistics microfilm, 1860 and 1870.

————. *Compendium of the Sixth Census. 1840.* Washington: Government Printing Office, 1841.

————. *Statistical View of the United States. Compendium of the Seventh Census, 1850.* Compiled by J. D. B. DeBow. Washington: Government Printing Office, 1854.

————. *Report of the United States in 1860, Compiled from the Original Returns of the Eighth Census.* Compiled by Joseph C. G. Kennedy. Washington: Government Printing Office, 1864.

————. *Statistics of the Population of the United States. Ninth Census. Volume 1. 1870.* Washington: Government Printing Office, 1872.

————. *Statistics of the Wealth and Industry of the United States. Compiled from the Original Returns of the Ninth Census. Volume 3.* Washington: Government Printing Office, 1872.

————. *Statistics of the Population of the United States at the Tenth Census. 1880.* Washington: Government Printing Office, 1883.

North Carolina. *Report on the Population of the United States at the Eleventh Census. Part 1. 1890.* Washington: Government Printing Office, 1893.

————. *Report on the Statistics of Agriculture in the United States. Eleventh Census. 1890.* Washington: Government Printing Office, 1895.

United States Senate. *Report of the Committee of the Senate upon the Relations between Labor and Capital. 5 Volumes.* Washington: Government Printing Office, 1885.

The War of the Rebellion: A Compilation of the Official Records of the Union and Confederate Armies. Series IV. Volume III. Washington: Government Printing Office, 1900.

Newspapers

Fayetteville *Messenger*
Journal of United Labor
Salem *People's Press*
Salem *Weekly Chronicle*
Salem *Weekly Gleaner*
Salem *Western Sentinel*
Salisbury *Carolina Watchman*
Winston *Leader*
Winston *Union Republican*
Winston-Salem *Weekly Sentinel*

SECONDARY SOURCES

Books and Articles

Africa, Philip. "Slaveholding in the Salem Community, 1771–1851." *North Carolina Historical Review* 54 (July 1977): 271–307.

Ahlstrom, Sidney E. *A Religious History of the American People.* New Haven: Yale University Press, 1972.

Appleby, Joyce. *Capitalism and a New Social Order: The Republican Vision of the 1790s.* New York: New York University Press, 1984.

Ash, Stephen V. *Middle Tennessee Society Transformed, 1860–1870: War and Peace in the Upper South.* Baton Rouge: Louisiana State University Press, 1982.

Ashe, Samuel A., Stephen B. Weeks, and Charles L. Van Noppen, eds. *Biographical History of North Carolina from Colonial Times to the Present, Eight Volumes.* Greensboro: C. L. Van Noppen, 1917.

Ashworth, John. *"Agrarians" and "Aristocrats": Party Political Ideology in the United States, 1837–1846.* Cambridge: Cambridge University Press, 1987.

Aumen, William T., and David D. Scarboro. "The Heroes of America in Civil War North Carolina." *North Carolina Historical Review* 58 (October 1981): 327–63.

Baker, Robert P. "Labor History, Social Science and the Concept of the Working Class." *Labor History* 14 (Winter 1973): 98–105.

Beatty, Bess. "Textile Labor in the North Carolina Piedmont: Mill Owner Images and Worker Response, 1830–1900." *Labor History* 25 (Fall 1984): 485–503.

Beck, John J. "Building the New South: A Revolution from Above in a Piedmont County." *Journal of Southern History* 53 (August 1987): 441–70.

Bender, Thomas. *Community and Social Change in America.* Baltimore: Johns Hopkins University Press, 1978.

Bernstein, Michael A., and Sean Wilentz. "Marketing, Commerce, and Capitalism in Rural Massachusetts." *Journal of Economic History* 44 (March 1984): 171–73.

Billings, Dwight. *Planters and the Making of a "New South": Class, Politics, and Development in North Carolina, 1865–1900.* Chapel Hill: University of North Carolina Press, 1979.

Blumin, Stuart M. *The Emergence of the Middle Class: Social Experience in the American City, 1760–1900.* Cambridge: Cambridge University Press, 1989.

Boles, John B. *The Great Revival, 1787–1805.* Lexington: University of Kentucky Press, 1972.

Bridenbaugh, Carl. *Myths and Realities: Societies of the Colonial South.* New York: Atheneum, 1974.

Calhoun, C. J. "Community: Toward a Variable Conceptualization for Comparative Research." *Social History* 5 (January 1980): 105–29.

Cantor, Milton, ed. *American Working Class Culture: Explorations in American Labor and Social History.* Westport, Conn.: Greenwood Press, 1979.

Carlton, David A. "Builders of a New State: The Town Classes and Early Industrialization of South Carolina, 1880–1907." In *From the Old South to the New: Essays on the Transitional South,* edited by Walter J. Frazier and Winfred B. Moore. Westport, Conn.: Greenwood Press, 1981.

———. *Mill and Town in South Carolina, 1880–1920.* Baton Rouge: Louisiana State University Press, 1982.

———. "The Revolution from Above: The National Market and the Beginnings of Industrialization in North Carolina." *Journal of American History* 77 (September 1990): 445–75.

Cathey, Cornelius Oliver. *Agricultural Developments in North Carolina, 1783–1860.* Chapel Hill: University of North Carolina Press, 1956.

Chambers, William Nisbet, and Walter Dean Burnham. *The American Party Systems: Stages of Political Development.* New York: Oxford University Press, 1967.

Clark, Christopher. "Household Economy, Market Exchange, and the Rise of Capitalism in the Connecticut Valley, 1800–1860." *Journal of Social History* 13 (Summer 1979): 169–89.

———. *The Roots of Rural Capitalism: Western Massachusetts, 1780–1860.* Ithaca: Cornell University Press, 1990.

Clewell, John Henry. *History of Wachovia in North Carolina.* New York: Doubleday Page, 1902.

Clinton, Catherine. *The Plantation Mistress*. New York: Pantheon Books, 1982.

Cobb, James C. "Beyond Planters and Industrialists: New Perspectives on the New South." *Journal of Southern History* 54 (February 1988): 45–68.

———. *Industrialization and Southern Society, 1877–1984*. Chicago: Dorsey Press, 1988.

Cole, Arthur C. *The Whig Party in the South*. Washington: American Historical Association, 1913.

Commons, John R., and Associates. *History of Labour in the United States*. 4 vols. New York: Macmillan, 1918–35.

Counihan, Harold J. "The North Carolina Constitutional Convention of 1835: A Study in Jacksonian Democracy." *North Carolina Historical Review* 46 (October 1969): 335–64.

Daniel, Pete. *Breaking the Land: The Transformation of Cotton, Tobacco, and Rice Cultures since 1880*. Urbana: University of Illinois Press, 1985.

Dawley, Alan. *Class and Community: The Industrial Revolution in Lynn*. Cambridge: Harvard University Press, 1979.

Dawley, Alan, and Paul Faler. "Working Class Culture and Politics in the Industrial Revolution: Sources of Loyalism and Rebellion." *Journal of Social History* 9 (Summer 1976): 466–80.

Degler, Carl. *At Odds: Women and the Family in America from the Revolution to the Present*. Oxford: Oxford University Press, 1980.

———. *The Other South: Southern Dissenters in the Nineteenth Century*. New York: Harper and Row, 1974.

Dodd, Donald B., and Wynelle S. Dodd. *Historical Statistics of the South, 1790–1970*. University: University of Alabama Press, 1973.

Doyle, Don H. *New Men, New Cities, New South: Atlanta, Nashville, Charleston, Mobile, 1860–1910*. Chapel Hill: University of North Carolina Press, 1990.

Dublin, Thomas. *Women at Work: The Transformation of Work and Community in Lowell, Massachusetts, 1826–1860*. New York: Columbia University Press, 1979.

Dulles, Foster Rhea, and Melvin Dubofsky. *Labor in America: A History*. Arlington Heights, Ill.: Harlan Davidson, 1984.

Dupre, Daniel. "Ambivalent Capitalists on the Cotton Frontier: Settlement and Development in the Tennessee Valley of Alabama." *Journal of Southern History* 56 (May 1990): 215–40.

Eaton, Clement. *The Growth of Southern Civilization, 1790–1860*. New York: Harper, 1963.

Escott, Paul D. *After Secession: Jefferson Davis and the Failure of Confederate Nationalism*. Baton Rouge: Louisiana State University Press, 1978.

———. *Many Excellent People: Power and Privilege in North Carolina, 1850–1890*. Chapel Hill: University of North Carolina Press, 1985.

———. "The Moral Economy of the Crowd in Confederate North Carolina." *Maryland Historian* 13 (Spring/Summer 1982): 1–18.

———. "Yeoman Independence and the Market: Social Status and Economic Development in Antebellum North Carolina." *North Carolina Historical Review* 66 (July 1989): 1–18.

Faler, Paul G. *Mechanics and Manufacturers in the Early Industrial Revolution: Lynn, Massachusetts, 1780–1860.* Albany: State University of New York Press, 1981.

Fink, Leon. *Workingmen's Democracy: The Knights of Labor and American Politics.* Urbana: University of Illinois Press, 1983.

Foner, Eric. *Free Labor, Free Soil, Free Men: The Ideology of the Republican Party before the Civil War.* Oxford and New York: Oxford University Press, 1973.

———. *Politics and Ideology in the Age of the Civil War.* Oxford: Oxford University Press, 1980.

———. *Tom Paine and Revolutionary America.* Oxford: Oxford University Press, 1976.

Foner, Philip. *History of the Labor Movement in the United States, Volume 1.* New York: International Publishers, 1947.

Ford, Lacy K., Jr. *Origins of Southern Radicalism: The South Carolina Upcountry, 1800–1860.* Oxford: Oxford University Press, 1988.

———. "Yeoman Farmers in the South Carolina Upcountry: Changing Production Patterns in the Late Antebellum Era." *Agricultural History* 60 (Fall 1986): 17–37.

Fox-Genovese, Elizabeth. *Within the Plantation Household: Black and White Women of the Old South.* Chapel Hill: University of North Carolina Press, 1988.

Fox-Genovese, Elizabeth, and Eugene D. Genovese. *Fruits of Merchant Capital: Slavery and Bourgeois Property in the Rise and Expansion of Capitalism.* Oxford: Oxford University Press, 1983.

Freehling, William W. *The Road to Disunion: Secessionists at Bay, 1776–1854.* Oxford: Oxford University Press, 1990.

Fries, Adelaide. *Forsyth: A County on the March.* Chapel Hill: University of North Carolina Press, 1949.

———. "One Hundred Years of Textiles in Salem." *North Carolina Historical Review* 27 (January 1950): 1–19.

———. "Salem Congregation Diacony." In *Salem Remembrancers, Seven Historians Who Presented Their Papers before the Wachovia Historical Society of Salem, North Carolina, 1898–1910,* edited by Edwin L. Stockton. Winston-Salem, North Carolina: Wachovia Historical Society, 1976.

Fries, Adelaide, Thurman L. Wright, and J. Edwin Hendricks. *Forsyth: The History of a County on the March.* Chapel Hill: University of North Carolina Press, 1976.

Garlock, Jonathan. *Guide to the Local Assemblies of the Knights of Labor.* Westport, Conn.: Greenwood Press, 1982.

Gaston, Paul M. *The New South Creed: A Study in Southern Mythmaking.* Baton Rouge: Louisiana State University Press, 1970.

Geertz, Clifford. *The Interpretation of Cultures.* New York: Basic Books, 1973.

Genovese, Eugene. *The Political Economy of Slavery: Studies in the Economy and Society of the Slave South.* New York: Vintage, 1967.

———. "Yeoman Farmers in a Slaveholders' Democracy." *Agricultural History* 49 (April 1975): 331–42.

Gollin, Gillian Lindt. *Moravians in Two Worlds: A Study of Changing Communities.* New York: Columbia University Press, 1967.

Gray, Lewis Cecil. *History of Agriculture in the Southern United States to 1860, 2 vols.* Washington: Carnegie Institute, 1933.

Greene, Jack P. "Independence, Improvement, and Authority: Toward a Framework of Understanding the Histories of the Southern Backcountry during the American Revolution." In *An Uncivil War: The Southern Backcountry during the American Revolution,* edited by Ronald Hoffman, Thad W. Tate, and Peter J. Albert. Charlottesville: University of Virginia Press, 1985.

———. *Pursuits of Happiness: The Social Development of Early Modern British Colonies and the Formation of American Culture.* Chapel Hill: University of North Carolina Press, 1988.

Griffen, Clyde, and Sally Griffen. *Natives and Newcomers: The Ordering of Opportunity in Mid-Nineteenth Century Poughkeepsie.* Cambridge: Harvard University Press, 1978.

Griffin, Richard W. "Poor White Laborers in Southern Cotton Factories, 1789–1865." *South Carolina Historical Magazine* 61 (January 1960): 2640.

Griffin, Richard W., and Diffee W. Standard. "The Cotton Textile Industry in Antebellum North Carolina, Part II: An Era of Boom and Consolidation, 1830–1860." *North Carolina Historical Review* 34 (April 1957): 131–64.

Gutman, Herbert. "Class, Status, and Community Power in Nineteenth Century American Industrial Cities: Paterson, New Jersey: A Case Study." In Herbert Gutman, *Work, Culture and Society in Industrializing America.* New York: Vintage, 1977.

Hagler, D. Harland. "The Ideal Woman in the Antebellum South: Lady or Farmwife?" *Journal of Southern History* 46 (August 1980): 405–18.

Hahn, Steven. *The Roots of Southern Populism: Yeoman Farmers and the Transformation of the Georgia Upcountry, 1850–1890.* Oxford: Oxford University Press, 1983.

———. "The 'Unmaking' of the Southern Yeomanry: The Transformation of the Georgia Upcountry, 1860–1890." In *The Countryside in the Age of Capitalist Transformation: Essays in the Social History of Rural America,* edited by Steven Hahn and Jonathan Prude. Chapel Hill: University of North Carolina Press, 1985.

Hahn, Steven, and Jonathan Prude, eds. *The Countryside in the Age of Capitalist Transformation: Essays in the Social History of Rural America.* Chapel Hill: University of North Carolina Press, 1985.

Hall, Jacquelyn Dowd, James LeLoudis, Robert Korstad, Mary Murphy, LuAnn Jones, and Christopher B. Daly. *Like a Family: The Making of a Southern Cotton Mill World.* Chapel Hill: University of North Carolina Press, 1987.

Hamilton, J. Taylor, and Kenneth G. Hamilton. *History of the Moravian Church: The Renewed Unitas Fratrum, 1722–1957.* Bethlehem, Pa.: Moravian Church in America, 1967.

Hareven, Tamara K. "Family Time and Industrial Time: Family and Work in a Planned Corporate Town, 1900–1924." In *Family and Kin in Urban Communities, 1700–1930,* edited by Tamara K. Hareven. New York: New Viewpoints, 1977.

Harris, J. William. *Plain Folk and Gentry in a Slave Society: White Liberty and Black*

Slavery in Augusta's Hinterlands. Middletown, Conn.: Wesleyan University, 1987.

Haskell, Thomas L. "Capitalism and the Humanitarian Sensibility." *American Historical Review* 90 (June 1985): 547–66.

Heimann, Robert K. *Tobacco and Americans.* New York: McGraw-Hill, 1960.

Henretta, James. "Families and Farms: Mentalité in Pre-Industrial America." *William and Mary Quarterly* 3d Series 35 (January 1978): 3–32.

Hirsch, Susan E. *Roots of the American Working Class: The Industrialization of Crafts in Newark, 1800–1860.* Philadelphia: University of Pennsylvania Press, 1978.

Holt, Michael. *The Political Crisis of the 1850s.* New York: W. W. Norton, 1978.

Isaac, Rhys, *The Transformation of Virginia, 1740–1810.* New York: W. W. Norton, 1985.

Jackson, Ronald V. *Index to the 1850 Census, North Carolina.* Bountiful, Utah, Accelerated Indexing Systems, 1975.

Janiewski, Dolores. *Sisterhood Denied: Race, Gender, and Class in a New South Community.* Philadelphia: Temple University Press, 1985.

Jeffrey, Thomas E. "County Division: A Forgotten Issue in Antebellum North Carolina Politics, Part I." *North Carolina Historical Review* 65 (July 1988): 314–54.

———. *State Parties and National Politics: North Carolina, 1815–1861.* Athens: University of Georgia Press, 1989.

Johnson, Guion Griffis. *Ante-bellum North Carolina: A Social History.* Chapel Hill: University of North Carolina Press, 1937.

Johnson, J. G. "Notes on Manufacturing in Ante-Bellum Georgia." *Georgia Historical Quarterly* 16 (September 1932): 214–31.

Johnson, Paul. *A Shopkeeper's Millennium: Society and Revivals in Rochester, New York, 1815–1837.* New York: Hill and Wang, 1978.

Jolly, Harley E. "The Labor Movement in North Carolina, 1880–1922." *North Carolina Historical Review* 30 (July 1953): 354–75.

Katz, Michael. *The People of Hamilton, Canada West: Family and Class in a Mid-Nineteenth Century City.* Cambridge: Harvard University Press, 1975.

Kennedy, Susan Eastabrook. *If All We Did Was to Weep at Home: A History of Working-Class Women in America.* Bloomington: Indiana University Press, 1979.

Kenzer, Robert C. *Kinship and Neighborhood in a Southern Community: Orange County, North Carolina, 1849–1881.* Knoxville: University of Tennessee Press, 1987.

Kessler-Harris, Alice. *Out of Work: A History of Wage-Earning Women in the United States.* Oxford: Oxford University Press, 1982.

Kett, Joseph F. *Rites of Passage: Adolescence in America, 1790 to the Present.* New York: Basic Books, 1977.

Kroeber, Alfred L. *Anthropology: Race, Language, Culture, Psychology, Prehistory.* New York: Harcourt, Brace, 1948.

Kruman, Marc W. "Dissent in the Confederacy: The North Carolina Experience." *Civil War History* 27 (December 1981): 293–313.

Kruman, Marc W. *Parties and Politics in North Carolina, 1836–1865.* Baton Rouge: Louisiana State University Press, 1983.

Kulikoff, Allan. "The Transition to Capitalism in Rural America." *William and Mary Quarterly* 3d Series 46 (January 1989): 120–44.

Lander, Ernest McPherson, Jr. *The Textile Industry in Antebellum South Carolina.* Baton Rouge: Louisiana State University Press, 1969.

Larsen, Lawrence H. *The Rise of the Urban South.* Lexington: University of Kentucky Press, 1985.

Laurie, Bruce. *Artisans into Workers: Labor in Nineteenth-Century America.* New York: Noonday Books, 1989.

Lebsock, Suzanne. *The Free Women of Petersburg: Status and Culture in a Southern Town, 1784–1860.* New York: W. W. Norton, 1984.

Lefler, Hugh T., and Albert Ray Newsome. *North Carolina: A History of a Southern State.* Chapel Hill: University of North Carolina Press, 1963.

Lefler, Hugh T., and William S. Powell. *Colonial North Carolina: A History.* New York: Charles Scribner's Sons, 1973.

Lender, Mark Edward, and James Kirby Martin. *Drinking in America: A History.* New York: Free Press, 1982.

Lerner, Eugene M. "Money, Prices, and Wages in the Confederacy." *Journal of Political Economy* 63 (February 1955): 20–40.

Lerner, Gerda. "The Lady and the Mill Girl." *American Studies* 10 (Spring 1969): 5–15.

Linden, Fabian. "Repercussions of Manufacturing in the Antebellum South." *North Carolina Historical Review* 17 (October 1940): 313–31.

Litwack, Leon F. *Been in the Storm So Long: The Aftermath of Slavery.* New York: Alfred A. Knopf, 1980.

Lockridge, Kenneth. *A New England Town, the First Hundred Years: Dedham, Massachusetts, 1636–1736.* New York: W. W. Norton, 1970.

Loveland, Anne C. *Southern Evangelicals and the Social Order, 1800–1860.* Baton Rouge: Louisiana State University Press, 1980.

McCormick, Richard. *The Second American Party System: Party Formation in the Jacksonian Era.* Chapel Hill: University of North Carolina Press, 1966.

McHugh, Catherine L. *The Mill Family: The Labor System in the Southern Cotton Textile Industry, 1880–1915.* Oxford: Oxford University Press, 1988.

McLaurin, Melton A. *Knights of Labor in the South.* Westport, Conn.: Greenwood Press, 1978.

———. *Paternalism and Protest: Southern Cotton Mill Workers and Organized Labor, 1875–1905.* Westport, Conn.: Greenwood Press, 1971.

———. "The Racial Policies of the Knights of Labor and the Organization of Southern Black Workers." *Labor History* 17 (Fall 1976): 568–85.

McLoughlin, William G. *Revivals, Awakenings and Reform: An Essay on Religion and Social Change in America, 1607–1977.* Chicago: University of Chicago Press, 1978.

McPherson, James M. *Battle Cry of Freedom: The Civil War Era.* Oxford: Oxford University Press, 1988.

McPherson, James M. *Ordeal by Fire: The Civil War and Reconstruction.* New York: Alfred A. Knopf, 1982.

Mathews, Donald G. *Religion in the Old South.* Chicago: University of Chicago Press, 1977.

———. "The Second Great Awakening as an Organizing Process, 1780–1830: An Hypothesis." *American Quarterly* 21 (Spring 1969): 23–43.

Merrens, Harry Roy. *Colonial North Carolina in the Eighteenth Century: A Study in Historical Geography.* Chapel Hill: University of North Carolina Press, 1964.

Merrill, Michael. "Cash Is Good to Eat: Self-Sufficiency and Exchange in the Rural Economy of the United States." *Radical History Review* 7 (Winter 1977): 42–71.

Miller, Randall M. "The Fabric of Control: Slavery in Antebellum Southern Textile Mills." *Business History Review* 55 (Winter 1981): 471–90.

Mitchell, Broadus. *Rise of the Cotton Mills in the South.* Baltimore: Johns Hopkins University Press, 1921.

Mitchell, Reid. *Civil War Soldiers: Their Expectations and Their Experiences.* New York: W. W. Norton, 1988.

Montgomery, David. *Beyond Equality: Labor and the Radical Republicans, 1862–1872.* Urbana: University of Illinois Press, 1981.

Morgan, Edmund M. *American Slavery, American Freedom: The Ordeal of Colonial Virginia.* New York: W. W. Norton, 1975.

Newby, I. A. *Plain Folk in the New South: Social Change and Cultural Persistence, 1880–1915.* Baton Rouge: Louisiana State University Press, 1989.

North, Douglass C. *The Economic Growth of the United States, 1790–1860.* Englewood Cliffs, N.J.: Prentice-Hall, 1966.

Norton, Clarence C. *The Democratic Party in Antebellum North Carolina, 1835–1861.* Chapel Hill: University of North Carolina Press, 1930.

Nye, Russell B. *Society and Culture in America, 1830–1860.* New York: Harper and Row, 1974.

Oakes, James. "From Republicanism to Liberalism: Ideological Change and the Crisis of the Old South." *American Quarterly* 37 (Fall 1985): 551–71.

———. *Slavery and Freedom: An Interpretation of the Old South.* New York: Vintage, 1991.

Otto, John Solomon. "Slaveholding General Farmers in a 'Cotton County.' " *Agricultural History* 55 (April 1981): 167–78.

Pegg, Herbert Dale. *The Whig Party in North Carolina.* Chapel Hill: University of North Carolina Press, 1969.

Perman, Michael. *The Road to Redemption: Southern Politics, 1869–1879.* Chapel Hill: University of North Carolina Press, 1984.

Polanyi, Karl. *The Great Transformation.* New York: Rinehart, 1944.

Potter, David M. *The Impending Crisis, 1848–1861.* New York: Harper and Row, 1976.

———. *The Social and the Sectional Conflict.* Baton Rouge: Louisiana State University Press, 1973.

Prude, Jonathan. *The Coming of Industrial Order: Town and Factory Life in Rural Massachusetts, 1810–1860.* Cambridge: Cambridge University Press, 1983.

Rabinowitz, Howard N. "Continuity and Change: Southern Urban Development, 1860–1900." In *The City in Southern History: The Growth of Urban Civilization in the South*, edited by Blaine A. Brownell and David R. Goldfield. Port Washington, N.Y., 1977.

——. *Race Relations in the Urban South, 1865–1890*. Urbana: University of Illinois Press, 1980.

Rachleff, Peter. *Black Labor in Richmond, 1865–1890*. Urbana: University of Illinois Press, 1989.

Ransom, Roger, and Richard Sutch. *One Kind of Freedom: The Economic Consequences of Emancipation*. Cambridge: Cambridge University Press, 1978.

Redfield, Robert. *The Little Community: Viewpoints for the Study of the Human Whole*. Chicago: University of Chicago Press, 1967.

Reynolds, R. J. Tobacco Company. *A Short History of R. J. Reynolds Tobacco Company*. Winston-Salem: R. J. Reynolds Tobacco Company, 1965.

Roark, James L. *Masters without Slaves: Southern Planters in the Civil War and Reconstruction*. New York: W. W. Norton, 1977.

Robinson, W. Stitt. *The Southern Colonial Frontier, 1607–1763*. Albuquerque: University of New Mexico Press, 1979.

Rorabaugh, W. J. *The Alcoholic Republic: An American Tradition*. Oxford: Oxford University Press, 1979.

Rothenberg, Winifred B. "The Market and Massachusetts Farmers, 1750–1855." *Journal of Economic History* 41 (June 1981): 283–315.

Rutman, Darrett B. "Assessing the Little Communities of Early America." *William and Mary Quarterly* 3d Series 43 (1986): 163–78.

——. "The Social Web: A Prospectus for the Study of the Early American Community." In *Insights and Parallels: Problems and Issues of American Social History*, edited by William L. O'Neill. Minneapolis: Burgess Publishing, 1973.

Ryan, Mary P. *Cradle of the Middle Class: The Family in Oneida County, New York, 1790–1865*. Cambridge: Cambridge University Press, 1985.

Schlotterbeck, John T. "The 'Social Economy' of an Upper South Community: Orange and Greene Counties, Virginia 1815–1860." In *Class, Conflict, and Consensus: Antebellum Southern Community Studies*, edited by Orville Vernon Burton and Robert C. McMath, Jr. Westport, Conn.: Greenwood Press, 1982.

Schmidt, Alvin J., ed. *The Greenwood Encyclopedia of American Institutions: Fraternal Organizations*. Westport, Conn.: Greenwood Press, 1980.

Scranton, Philip. *Proprietary Capitalism: The Textile Manufactures at Philadelphia, 1800–1885*. Cambridge: Cambridge University Press, 1983.

Sellers, Charles. *The Market Revolution: Jacksonian America, 1815–1846*. Oxford: Oxford University Press, 1991.

Sessler, John. *Communal Pietism among Early American Moravians*. Reprint edition. New York: AMS Press, 1971.

Shelton, Cynthia J. *Mills of Manayunk: Industrialization and Social Conflict in the Philadelphia Region, 1787–1837*. Baltimore: Johns Hopkins University Press, 1986.

Shore, Laurence. *Southern Capitalists: The Ideological Leadership of an Elite, 1832–1885*. Chapel Hill: University of North Carolina Press, 1986.

Siegel, Fred. *The Roots of Southern Distinctiveness: Tobacco and Society in Danville, Virginia, 1780–1865.* Chapel Hill: University of North Carolina Press, 1987.

Starobin, Robert. "The Economics of Industrial Slavery in the Old South." *Business History Review* 44 (Summer 1970): 131–74.

Surratt, Jerry L. *Gottlieb Schober of Salem: Discipleship and Ecumenical Vision in an Early Moravian Town.* Macon, Ga.: Mercer University Press, 1983.

——. "The Role of Dissent in Community Evolution among Moravians in Salem, 1722–1860." *North Carolina Historical Review* 52 (July 1975): 235–55.

Syndor, Charles. *Development of Southern Sectionalism, 1819–1848.* Baton Rouge: Louisiana State University Press, 1968.

Tatum, George Lee. *Disloyalty in the Confederacy.* Chapel Hill: University of North Carolina Press, 1934.

Taylor, George R. *The Transportation Revolution, 1815–1860.* New York: Rinehart, 1964.

Terrill, Tom E. "Eager Hands: Labor for Southern Textiles, 1850–1860." *Journal of Economic History* 36 (March 1976): 84–99.

Thompson, E. P. *The Making of the English Working Class.* New York: Vintage, 1966.

Thorp, Daniel B. *The Moravian Community in Colonial North Carolina: Pluralism on the Southern Frontier.* Knoxville: University of Tennessee Press, 1989.

Tilley, Nannie May. *The Bright Tobacco Industry, 1860–1929.* Chapel Hill: University of North Carolina Press, 1948.

——. *The R. J. Reynolds Tobacco Company.* Chapel Hill: University of North Carolina Press, 1985.

Trelease, Allen W. *The North Carolina Railroad, 1849–1871, and the Modernization of North Carolina.* Chapel Hill: University of North Carolina Press, 1991.

Tryon, Rolla Milton. *Household Manufactures in the United States, 1690–1860: A Study in Industrial History.* Chicago: University of Chicago Press, 1917.

Tyrell, Ian R. *Sobering Up: From Temperance to Prohibition in Antebellum America, 1800–1860.* Westport, Conn.: Greenwood Press, 1979.

Walkowitz, Daniel J. *Worker City, Company Town: Iron and Cotton-Worker Protest in Troy and Cohoes, New York, 1855–1884.* Urbana, Ill.: University of Illinois Press, 1981.

Wallace, Anthony F. C. *Rockdale: The Growth of an American Village in the Early Industrial Revolution.* New York: Alfred A. Knopf, 1978.

Watson, Harry L. "Conflict and Collaboration: Yeomen, Slaveholders, and Politics in the Antebellum South." *Social History* 10 (October 1985): 273–98.

——. *Jacksonian Politics and Community Conflict: The Emergence of the Second American Party System in Cumberland County, North Carolina.* Baton Rouge: Louisiana State University Press, 1981.

Weber, Max. "Class, Status, Party." In *From Max Weber: Essays in Sociology,* translated and edited by H. H. Gerth and C. Wright Mills. New York: Oxford University Press, 1946.

——. *The Protestant Ethic and the Spirit of Capitalism.* New York: Charles Scribner's Sons, 1958.

Weiman, David F. "Farmers and the Market in Antebellum America: A View from the Georgia Upcountry." *Journal of Economic History* 47 (September 1987): 627–47.

Weiss, Rona S. "The Market and Massachusetts Farmers, 1750–1850: Comment." *Journal of Economic History* 43 (June 1983): 474–78.

Wieher, Kenneth. "The Cotton Industry and Southern Urbanization, 1880–1930," *Explorations in Economic History* 14 (April 1977): 120–40.

Wiener, Jonathan M. "Class Structure and Economic Development in the American South, 1865–1955." *American Historical Review* 84 (October 1979): 970–92.

———. *Social Origins of the New South: Alabama, 1860–1885*. Baton Rouge: Louisiana State University Press, 1978.

Wilentz, Sean. "Artisan Republican Festivals and the Rise of Class Conflict in New York City, 1788–1837." In *Working-Class America: Essays on Labor, Community, and American Society*, edited by Michael H. Frisch and Daniel J. Walkowitz. Urbana: University of Illinois Press, 1983.

Wiley, Bell I. *Plain People of the Confederacy*. Baton Rouge: Louisiana State University Press, 1943.

Williams, Gail O'Brien. *The Legal Fraternity and the Making of a New South Community, 1848–1882*. Athens: University of Georgia Press, 1986.

Woodman, Harold D. "Comments, 'Class Structure and Economic Development in the American South.' " *American Historical Review* 84 (October 1979): 997–1001.

———. "Sequel to Slavery: The New History Views the Postbellum South." *Journal of Southern History* 43 (November 1977): 523–54.

Woodward, C. Vann. *Origins of the New South, 1877–1913*. Baton Rouge: Louisiana State University Press, 1974.

Wooster, Ralph. *Politicians, Planters, and Plain Folk: Courthouse and Statehouse in the Upper South, 1850–1860*. Knoxville: University of Tennessee Press, 1975.

Wright, Gavin. *Old South, New South: Revolutions in the Southern Economy since the Civil War*. New York: Basic Books, 1986.

———. *The Political Economy of the Cotton South: Households, Markets, and Wealth in the Nineteenth Century*. New York: W. W. Norton, 1978.

Wyatt-Brown, Bertram. *Southern Honor: Ethics and Behavior in the Old South*. Oxford: Oxford University Press, 1982.

Wynne, Francis Holloway, compiler. *Wake County, North Carolina Census and Tax Lists Abstracts, 1830 and 1840*. Raleigh, n.p., 1985.

Zuckerman, Michael. *Peaceable Kingdoms: New England Towns in the Eighteenth Century*. New York: Alfred A. Knopf, 1970.

Dissertations and Theses

Beck, John J. "Development in the Piedmont South: Rowan County, North Carolina, 1850–1900." Ph.D. diss., University of North Carolina, Chapel Hill, 1984.

Briggs, Martha Tune. "Millowners and Workers in an Antebellum North Carolina County." M.A. Thesis, University of North Carolina, Chapel Hill, 1975.

Butts, Donald Cleveland. "A Challenge to Planter Rule: The Controversy over

Ad Valorem Taxation of Slaves in North Carolina." Ph.D. diss., Duke University, 1978.

Cecil-Fronsman, Bill. "The Common Whites: Class and Culture in Antebellum North Carolina." Ph.D. diss., University of North Carolina, Chapel Hill, 1983.

Griffin, Richard W. "North Carolina: The Origin and Rise of the Cotton Textile Industry, 1830–1860." Ph.D. diss., Ohio State University, 1954.

Miller, Bertha Hampton. "Blacks in Winston-Salem, North Carolina 1895–1920: Community Development in an Era of Benevolent Paternalism." Ph.D. diss., Duke University, 1981.

O'Brien, Roberta Gail. "War and Social Change: An Analysis of Community Power Structure: Guilford County, North Carolina, 1848–1882." Ph.D. diss., University of North Carolina, Chapel Hill, 1975.

Stokes, Allen Heath. "Black and White Labor and the Development of the Southern Textile Industry, 1800–1920." Ph.D. diss., University of South Carolina, 1977.

Thorp, Daniel B. "Moravian Colonization of Wachovia, 1753–1772." Ph.D. diss., Johns Hopkins University, 1982.

Index

Ackerman, John, 22

Africa, 5

African Americans, 4, 148, 168, 201–2, 212, 215, 236; benevolent associations, 212; and community, 164, 212–13, 221, 235; in crafts, 47–48; culture of, 212–13; and entrepreneurship, 163–64; and Knights of Labor, 213, 218, 221–23; and paternalism, 213–14; and politics, 217, 222–31; and race relations, 222–31; and religion, 212; as slaves, 47–52; and sports, 212; in textile manufacturing, 50, 52, 87–90, 153; in tobacco manufacturing, 193–98, 212–15, 227

agriculture, 4, 7–9, 18, 24–28, 31–32, 33, 35–36, 38–39, 70–71, 142, 144, 147–49, 151, 179, 186–87, 197–98, 212, 227; and artisans, 39, 179; cash value of farms, 34; and Civil War, 132–36; farm size, 34–35, 148; farmers, 102, 106–7, 109, 111–12, 115, 132, 139, 142, 146, 164–65, 186–87, 230; labor, 35; and market, 32–35, 36, 39, 147–48, 164, 254; prices of commodities, 32–33, 36, 90, 134–35, 179, 186; output, 32–33, 147–48, 254; slaves, 35; sharecropping and tenancy, 148, 165, 179, 186, 207, 212, 227. *See also names of individual commodities*

Alamance County, N.C., 92

Alamance Volunteers, 132

Alberson, Martha, 79

Alberson, Patience, 79

Allegheny True Blues, 132

Allen, S. E., 115, 164, 166–68

Alspaugh, John W., 125, 166, 168, 280 n

Alspaugh, Samuel, 108

American Federation of Labor, 231–32

American party, 111, 123–24

Anglicans, 104

Arkansas, 128

artisans (and shopkeepers), 2–3, 7–11, 13, 18–24, 27–29, 31, 36, 39, 41–43, 81–82, 94–100, 102, 106–7, 114–16, 132, 139, 142, 146, 150, 161–62, 164–65, 169–70, 232–33, 236, 251 n, 259 n, 268 n; age distribution of, 177–83; apprentices and apprenticeship, 13, 18–22, 24, 29, 57, 82, 95–96, 98, 173, 177, 178–81, 198; challenges to congregation regulation of, 41–47, 53–57; culture of, 95–102, 205–7, 214; and employment of slaves, 47–50, 52–53, 58–59; and farming, 39, 179; and industrialization, 173–85, 198–99; journeymen, 13, 18–19, 22, 24, 29, 56–58, 81, 95–99, 177, 182, 185; and Knights of Labor, 218–19; and the market, 38–41, 176, 256 n; resistance to market, 57–58; masters, 95–97, 177; and Mechanics' Union, 206–7, 212; and merchants, 53–55; and mobility, 173–74, 178; morality of, 206; and politics, 107, 109–11, 218, 220, 223, 226, 230; and skill levels, 179, 198, 205; wages, 173, 179, 182–85, 199, 205, 219; work rou-